Gunners from the Sky

'If in the years to come, you meet a man who says
"I was at Arnhem", raise your hat and buy him a drink.'
War correspondent Alan Wood, *Daily Express*, September 1944

'The World would lose if such [a man] as you should vanish unrecorded',
adapted from *Romney's Remorse*, Alfred Lord Tennyson

for Rachael, Lyndsey, Kerry, Michael and Rebecca

Gunners from the Sky

1st Air Landing Light Regiment in Italy and at Arnhem, 1942–44

Paul and Major (retired) David Chrystal

Pen & Sword
MILITARY

First published in Great Britain in 2023 by
Pen & Sword Military
An imprint of Pen & Sword Books Limited
Yorkshire – Philadelphia

Copyright © Paul and David Chrystal 2023

ISBN 978 1 39908 808 4

The rights of Paul and David Chrystal to be identified as
Authors of this Work has been asserted by them in accordance
with the Copyright, Designs and Patents Act 1988.

A CIP catalogue record for this book is
available from the British Library

All rights reserved. No part of this book may be reproduced or
transmitted in any form or by any means, electronic or mechanical
including photocopying, recording or by any information storage and
retrieval system, without permission from the Publisher in writing.

Typeset by Mac Style
Printed in the UK by CPI Group (UK) Ltd, Croydon, CR0 4YY.

Pen & Sword Books Limited incorporates the imprints of After
the Battle, Atlas, Archaeology, Aviation, Discovery, Family History,
Fiction, History, Maritime, Military, Military Classics, Politics,
Select, Transport, True Crime, Air World, Frontline Publishing, Leo
Cooper, Remember When, Seaforth Publishing, The Praetorian Press,
Wharncliffe Local History, Wharncliffe Transport, Wharncliffe True
Crime and White Owl.

For a complete list of Pen & Sword titles please contact

PEN & SWORD BOOKS LIMITED
47 Church Street, Barnsley, South Yorkshire, S70 2AS, England
E-mail: enquiries@pen-and-sword.co.uk
Website: www.pen-and-sword.co.uk
or
PEN AND SWORD BOOKS
1950 Lawrence Rd, Havertown, PA 19083, USA
E-mail: Uspen-and-sword@casematepublishers.com
Website: www.penandswordbooks.com

Contents

About the Authors	viii
Acknowledgements	ix
Introduction	xi
Maps	xii
Glossary	xviii
Chapter 1 The History of Airborne Warfare	1
Chapter 2 The 1st Air Landing Light Regiment RA	4
Chapter 3 14283058 Gunner Eric Chrystal	9
Chapter 4 The 1st Air Landing Light Regiment's Italian Campaign	13
Chapter 5 Wounded and Recovery in Malta	42
Chapter 6 Operation MARKET GARDEN: The Plan	44
Chapter 7 The 1st Airborne Division	53
Chapter 8 The Royal Artillery at Arnhem	55
Chapter 9 The 1st Air Landing Light Regiment's Battle of Arnhem	57
Chapter 10 *A Week in Oosterbeek September 1944*, the Account of the Battle by Sergeant George Nattrass	62
Chapter 11 Day 1: Sunday, 17 September	66
Chapter 12 Day 2: Monday, 18 September	108
Chapter 13 Day 3: Tuesday, 19 September	133
Chapter 14 Day 4: Wednesday, 20 September	143

Chapter 15	Day 5: Thursday, 21 September	167
Chapter 16	Day 6: Friday, 22 September	174
Chapter 17	Day 7: Saturday, 23 September	177
Chapter 18	Day 8: Sunday, 24 September	179
Chapter 19	Day 9: Monday, 25 September	185
Chapter 20	Operation BERLIN	187
Chapter 21	The Fallout from the Failure	193
Chapter 22	Prisoner of War: Stalag XII-A Limburg, Stalag IV-B Mühlberg and Stalag IV-A Hohenstein and Zwickau	194
Chapter 23	Epilogue: Back to Boston, PTSD and Reprisals	199

Appendix I: 3rd Air Landing Light Battery, E Troop — 216
Appendix II: Other Airborne at Arnhem apart from the 1st Airborne Division — 217
Appendix III: Arnhem Order of Battle — 218
Appendix IV: Arnhem Town — 220
Appendix V: Theirs is the Glory — 222
Appendix VI: Allied Firepower at Arnhem — 224
Appendix VII: How Much is a Dutch Bridge Worth? — 225
Appendix VIII: German Forces at Arnhem — 227
Appendix IX: Some of the PoW Camps Where the Arnhem Captured Were Sent — 230
Notes — 233
Bibliography — 258
Index — 271

3 Battery Command Post and 3 Battery Flag. (*Courtesy of Gavin Frankland: relative of Gunner F.V. Brown, F Troop, 3 Battery*)

About the Authors

Paul Chrystal is the author of a number of books on conflict and military history including the best-selling *British Army of the Rhine: The BAOR 1945–1993* (2018), *Northern Ireland – The Troubles: From the Provos to the Det 1968–1998* (2018), *Women at War in the Classical World* (2016), *Roman Military Disasters* (2015), *War in Greek Mythology* (2020) and *Rome: Republic into Empire: The Civil Wars of the First Century BCE* (2019), all published by Pen & Sword. He is also the author of *A History of Britain in 100 Objects* (2022), *Wars and Battles of the Roman Republic* (2015) and *Wars and Battles of Ancient Greece* (2018). His *Bioterrorism and Biological Warfare: Disease as a Weapon of War* was published in July 2023. See his full list at www.paulchrystal.com

Major (retired) David Chrystal followed his father into the army and served for more than thirty years in the Royal Corps of Signals, rising from signaller to major, during which time he was awarded the British Empire Medal and was Mentioned in Dispatches (1980). He had postings in BAOR, Cyprus (RSM 9 Signal Regiment), southern Italy/Bosnia (attached to 4 Squadron RAF as Ground Liaison Officer) and Northern Ireland.

Acknowledgements

No book is the work of one man or woman, and this one certainly isn't. The following have been invaluable sources of information: *Regimental History of The 1st Air Landing Light Regiment* and Robert Woollacott's *Winged Gunners* (Quote Publishers, Harare, Zimbabwe, 1994)[1] which cover the history of the 1st Air Landing Light Regiment; both are long out of print. *Arnhem Bridge: Target Mike One* published by R.N. Sigmond (Renkum, NL, 17 September 2015) and authored by David Truesdale, Martijn Cornelisson and Bob Gerritson is a splendid book in many ways; Gunner Eric Chrystal is mentioned and photographed in this and in Woollacott.[2] Then there is *The Gunners at Arnhem* (1999), privately published by Captain Peter William Wilkinson MC, another Arnhem veteran. Paradata, through Ben Hill, ParaData Manager, Airborne Assault, IWM Duxford, Cambridgeshire provided a number of photos of the regiment in action, and the Pegasus Archive through Mark Hickman who provided the 1st Air Landing regimental diaries. Both have also been invaluable, as has the Alexander Turnbull Library, National Library of New Zealand, Wellington, New Zealand; Ian Baxter, Sophie ter Horst, Wybo Boersma of the Hartenstein Airborne Museum in Oosterbeek and Robert Voskuil. Roy Gledhill helped with information on the PoW camps and Colin Shearer sent me a scan of his grandfather's permit for a night out in Tunis: 14301423 Gunner Shearer. G. Shannyn Johnson, Image Reproduction Technician and Annie Lavergne at the Canadian War Museum, Ottawa helped with the fine artwork showing the regiment in Italy on page 3 of the plate section.

Thanks too to Janis McCreadie (my cousin and Eric's niece) for providing useful early history and some rare family photos; Peter Lawson and Jürgen Peters for translating those image captions that were originally in German. Some interesting propaganda here: Peter's father-in-law, Les Fuller, fought with the 3rd Battalion Parachute Regiment at Arnhem where he lost his right arm. A fellow paratrooper lost his left arm in the same battle; fortuitously their daughters got to know each other and for many years bought the two veterans one pair of gloves between them each Christmas.

Bernard Nock, curator, owner and display coordinator of the Military Wireless Museum, Kidderminster was kind enough to provide images of the 22 and 68 radio sets, as well as a copy of an unpublished manuscript written by Bombardier Leo Hall of 3 Battery, E Troop, 1st Air Landing Light Regiment written in August 1996; it reveals fascinating detail relating his experience and assessment of communications at Arnhem: https://www.qsl.net/g4bxd. John Howes was extraordinarily helpful in going to the trouble of checking Gunner Chrystal's PoW records at The National Archives, Kew. He also sent me a copy of (then Sergeant) Eric Chrystal's Mention in Dispatches in the *London Gazette*, 7 February 1958. Bob Gerritsen and Bob Hilton (ex-assistant curator at Duxford) were equally generous in providing copies of my father's correspondence with Bob Woollacott and a rare image of members of 3 Battery. Graham Francis was kind enough to send me various casualty lists, German record cards available in file WO416 at The National Archives and PoW liberation forms relating to Mühlberg. Finally, Gavin Frankland was kind enough to send me details of his relative's death when his glider crashed crossing the Dutch coast. Gunner F.V. Brown, F Troop, 3 Battery, tragically died in the crash of glider 518. Gavin is the first family member to visit the grave.

While every reasonable effort has been made to trace copyright holders of other material, the publisher welcomes any information relating to copyright that clarifies the copyright ownership of any unattributed material and will endeavour to include corrections in reprints or new editions.

Introduction

This is the story of the 1st Air Landing Light Regiment RA and its role in the Italian campaign and at the Battle of Arnhem. It is also the story of one of its soldiers: 14283058 Gunner Eric Wright Chrystal, a career soldier for almost thirty years who saw action in the Italian campaign where he was seriously wounded and in the Battle of Arnhem where he was taken prisoner of war. Later he served with the Royal Artillery in the dusty and disease-ridden Egyptian Canal Zone and in Cyprus where he was Mentioned in Dispatches for saving a comrade's life under fire. He also served in the unforgiving mountains and wadis of Aden, and with the BAOR in 24 Missile Regiment at Paderborn, equipped with nuclear-capability missiles.

It is with the Italian campaign and the Battle of Arnhem that we are concerned here: the book provides detailed context and background to both conflicts, interpolating Gunner Chrystal's early combat days with E Troop, 3 Battery, 1st Air Landing Light Regiment at Rionero, Foggia and Campobasso, southern Italy, where he was wounded and evacuated to Malta. It then goes on to trace his and the 1st Air Landing Light Regiment's pivotal (but often confused or glossed over) role at the Rhine bridge at Arnhem where he was eventually taken prisoner of war and herded off to PoW camps at Limburg, Stalag IV-B Mühlberg and Zwickau in south-east Germany.

Eric's fascinating story provides the human experience of, and the human touch to, two important chapters in modern British military history. Despite the combat experience he gained in southern Italy, when he woke up on that Sunday morning in mid-September 1944 he could have had no idea of, and could never have been prepared for, the cauldron into which he was about to glide noiselessly. For the next four to five days he would be subjected to nothing but unrelenting noise, and he and his comrades would see nothing but terrifying destruction, death and mutilation.

Maps

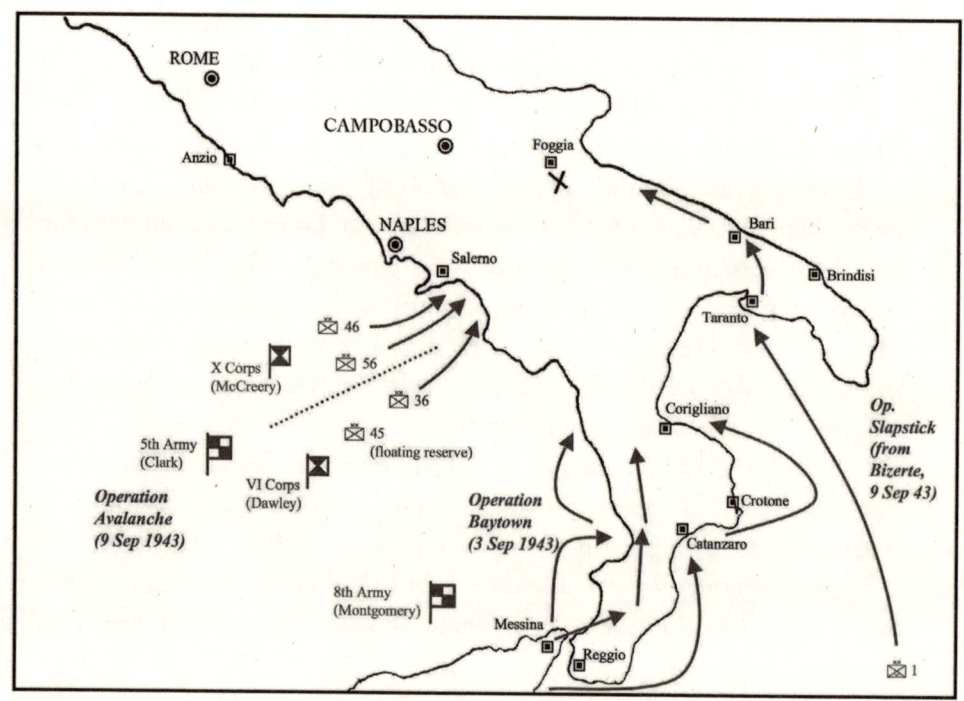

The Invasions of Italy, September 1943

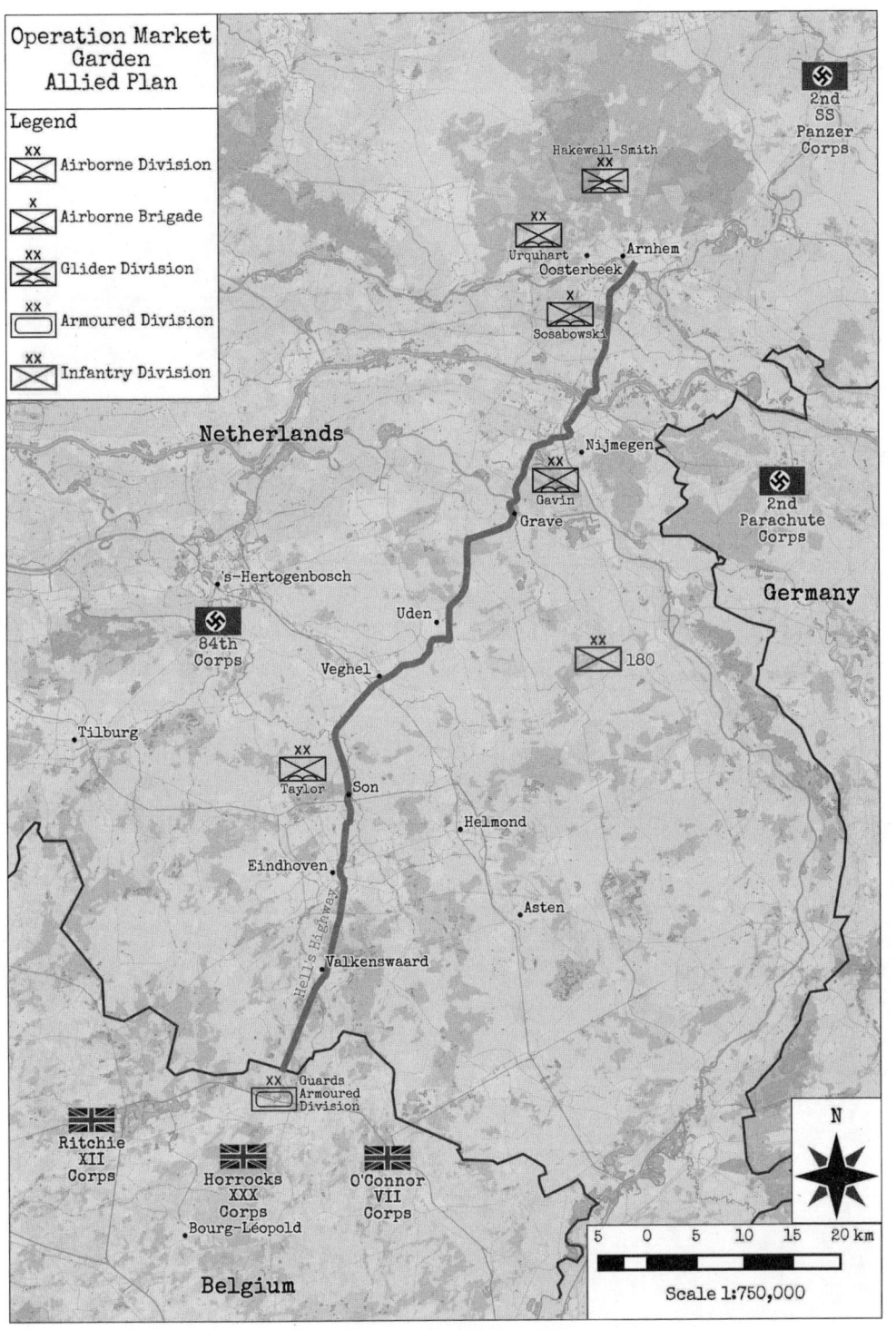

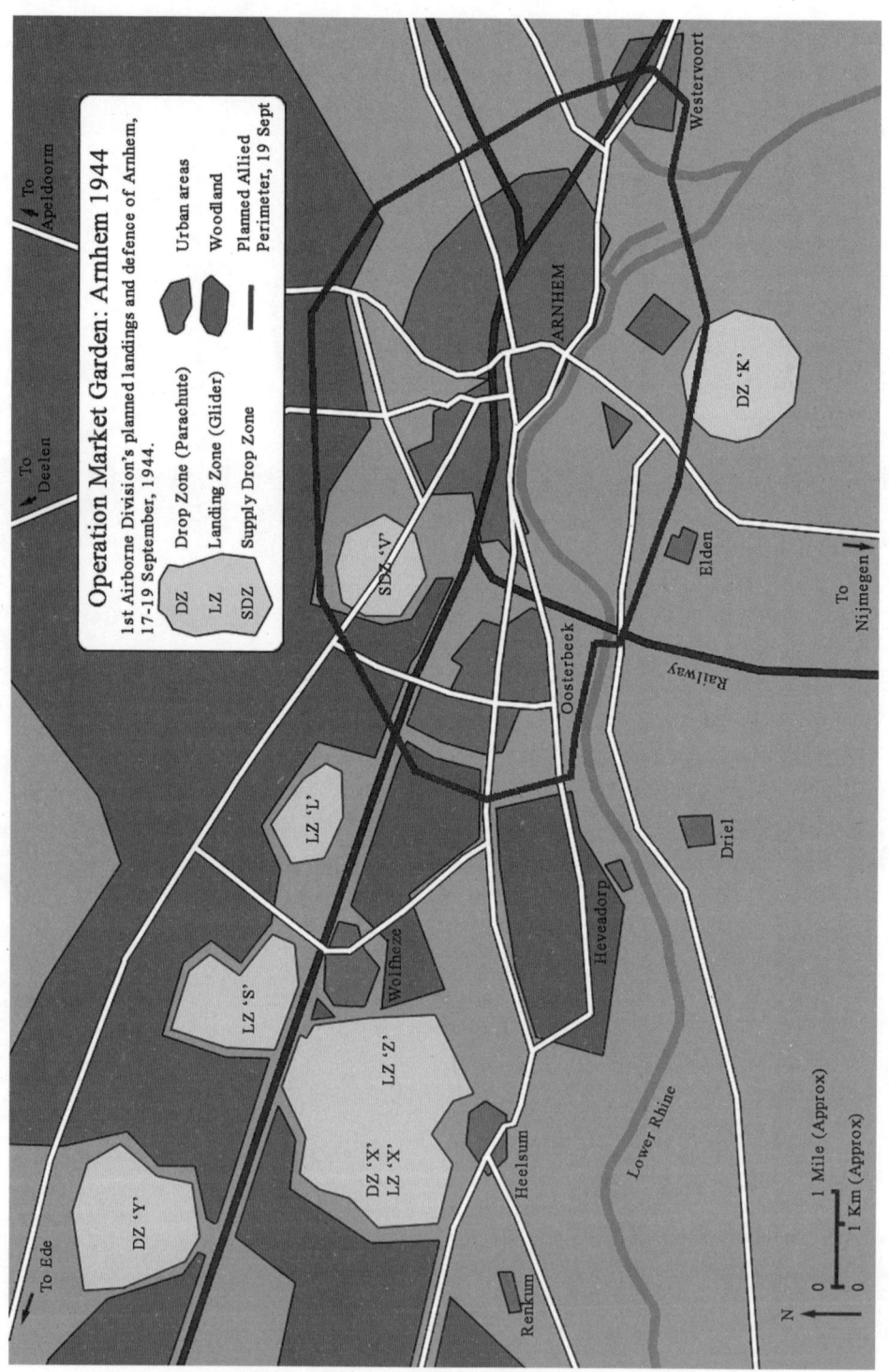

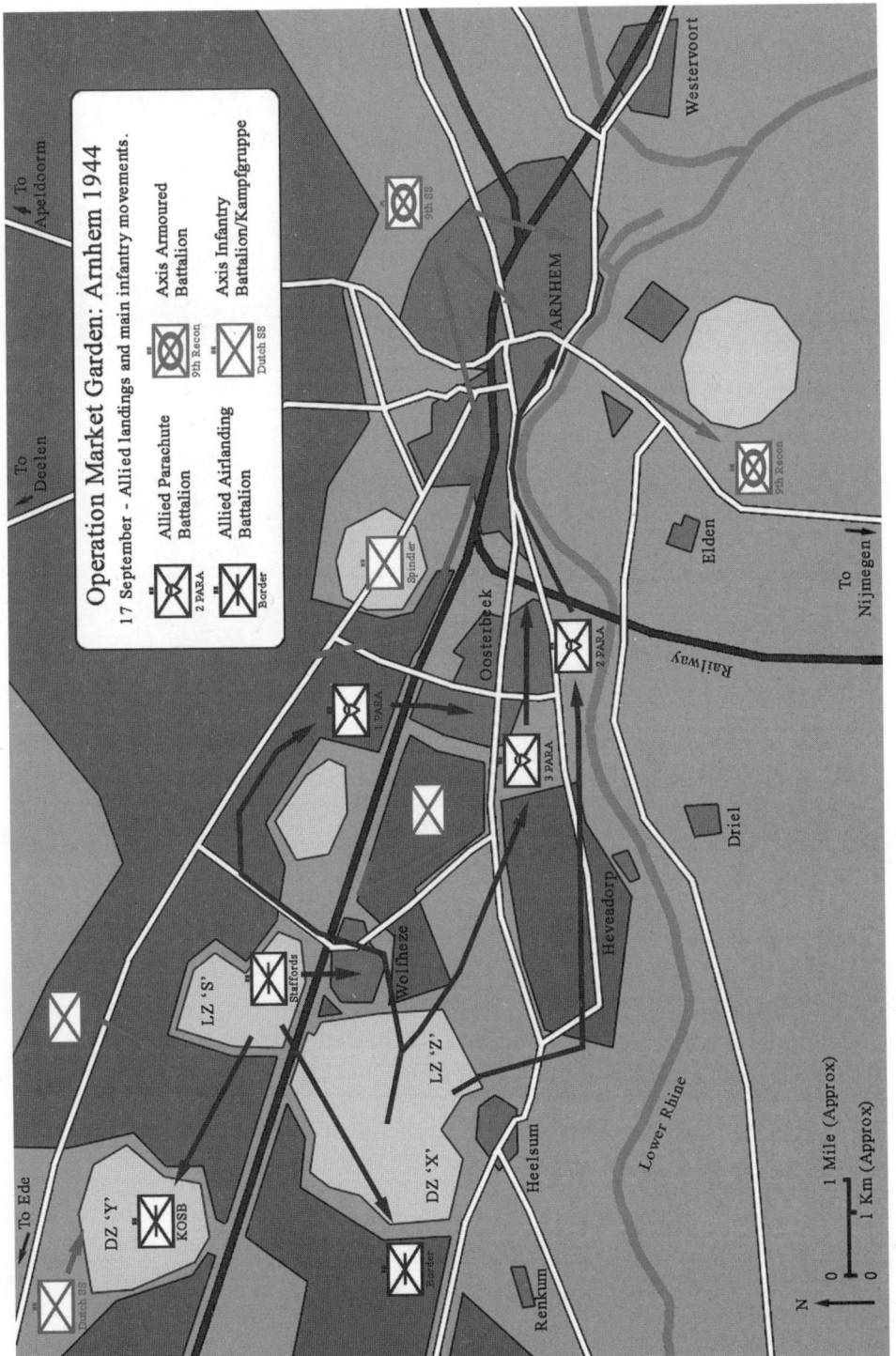

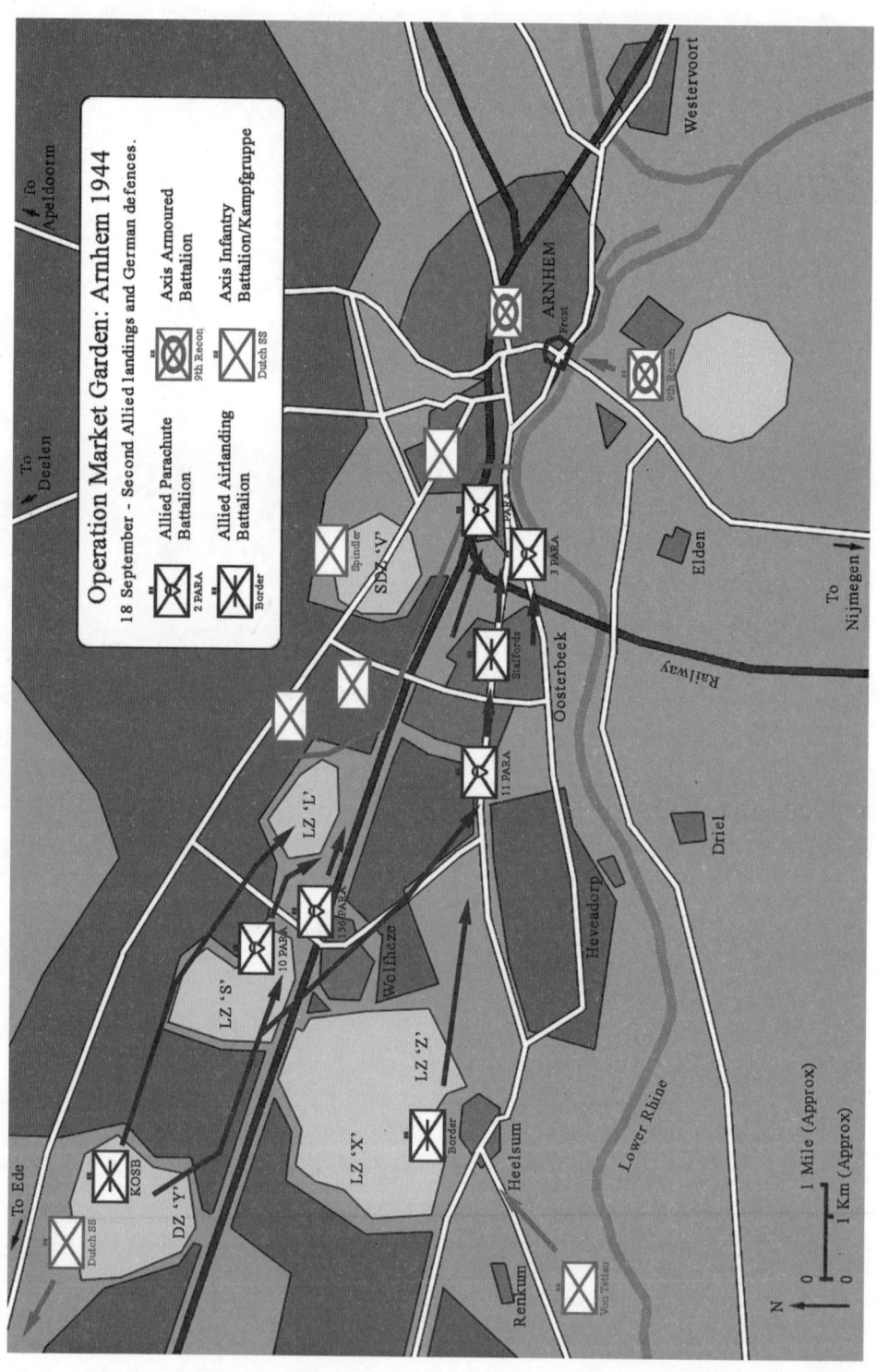

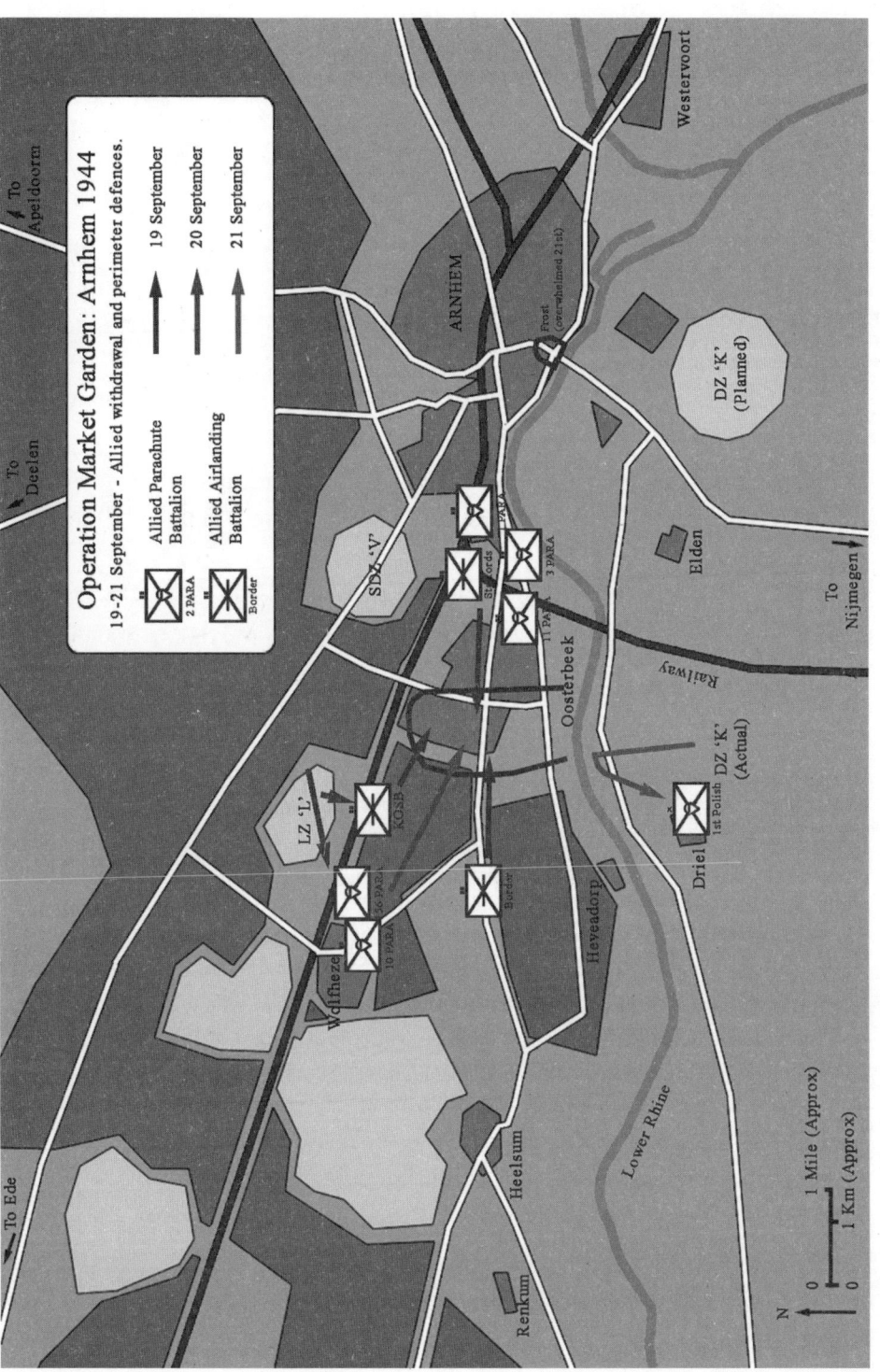

Glossary

The British Army:

Army Group: The largest military command deployed by the British army, comprising a general or field marshal with two or more armies and containing 400,000–600,000 troops.

Army: A military command controlling several subordinate corps, plus a lieutenant general with supporting forces, amounting to 100,000–200,000 troops.

Corps: A military command controlling two or more divisions, as well as other lieutenant general supporting forces, amounting to 50,000–100,000 troops.

Division: The standard 1944 British army formation, an infantry or armoured major general division containing 10,000–20,000 personnel.

Brigade: A formation that contains several battalions or regiments amounting to brigadier 3,000–6,000 personnel, which exists either independently or else forms part of a division.

Regiment: A unit typically of armoured or artillery forces amounting to 500–900 soldiers under a lieutenant colonel, equating in status and size to an infantry battalion.

Battalion: A unit usually comprising 500–900 soldiers (such as an infantry lieutenant colonel engineer or signals battalion).

Squadron: Typically a sub-unit of an armoured or recce regiment that equates in major status and size to an infantry company.

Company: A small sub-unit of a battalion. A typical infantry company could, under a major, contain around 150–180 soldiers.

Battery: Major in command of a small sub-unit, usually of artillery, that forms part of a battalion.

Unit: A small military grouping that ranges in size from a section (of ten soldiers) up to a battalion or regiment (500–900 personnel).

Formation: A large military grouping that ranges in size from a brigade up to an army group.

Other Terms:

Bailey bridge: A bridge of varying span and carrying capacity that could be speedily erected manually by unskilled labour.

BC: Battery commander.

Bdr: Bombardier.

Broad-front strategy: The Allied army groups advancing as a single entity at similar speeds.

BSM: Battery sergeant major.

coup de main: A small force seizing an objective using speed and surprise.

CP: Command post.

DS: Dressing station.

DZ: Dropping zone for parachutists.

FOO: Forward Observation Officer.

FOURA: Forward Observation Officer Unit, RA.

GPO: Gun Position Officer.

LZ: Landing zone for gliders.

Mike Target: Target engaged by a regiment of guns.

MO: Medical Officer.

Narrow-front strategy: A single army group being given the resources required to advance more quickly and further than other army groups.

OCTU: Officer Cadet Training Unit.

OP: Observation post where gunners observe and engage enemy targets.

OR: Other rank.

PIAT: Projector Infantry Anti-Tank (= bazooka).

PTSD: Post-Traumatic Stress Disorder.

RAMC: Royal Army Medical Corps.

RAP: Regimental aid post.
RE: Royal Engineers.
RHQ: Regimental Headquarters.
RMO: Regimental medical officer.
SP: Self-propelled gun, usually on caterpillar tracks.
Stonk: A heavy concentration of artillery fire.
TSM: Troop sergeant major.
Uncle Target: Divisional target.

Chapter One

The History of Airborne Warfare[1]

'Five thousand balloons, capable of raising two men each, could not cost more than five ships of the line; where is the Prince who can afford so to cover his country with troops for its defence, as that 10,000 men descending from the clouds, might not, in many places, do an infinite deal of mischief before a force could be brought together to repel them?'

Benjamin Franklin, 16 January 1784 to Monsieur Le Dr. Ingenhauss, Médecin de sa Majesté Impériale à Vienne en Autriche; written from France at a time when Franklin was serving with the American diplomatic mission.

Going to war by air rather than by land or by sea was an idea first hit upon by Benjamin Franklin who had balloons in mind as the mode of transportation, but it was the Russians in 1936 who brought that fantastic notion right up to date when parachutes formed part of the equation. General Wavell watched a demonstration of a drop by the Soviet army involving 1,500 parachute troops. Two years later they repeated the exercise with machine guns and light artillery. Frighteningly, for all the other armies watching, when they had landed these troops were ready to do battle within eight minutes. Surprise, then, was the watchword. The Germans were quick to react when General Kurt Student was tasked with commanding a new air-landing corps. By July 1939 a 1,000-strong battalion landed by parachute on a landing zone: by the time war was declared this had become the 7th *Fliegerdivision* comprising two parachute and nine glider-borne battalions. In May 1940 these troops spearheaded the blitzkrieg invasions of France, Belgium and the Netherlands. For example, parachute troops took the Belgian fortress of Ében-Émael on the Lower Meuse while 4,000 parachutists were dropped in the Netherlands supported by air-landing infantry. Winston Churchill, newly appointed as prime minister, had seen enough. On

22 June 1940 a memorandum was sent off to General Sir Hastings Ismay of the Cabinet War Secretariat saying 'We ought to have a corps of at least 5,000 parachute troops.'

This led to the prosaically-named Central Landing Establishment at Manchester's Ringway Airport 'for the development of parachute and glider techniques'. It was the men of No. 2 Commando who were selected for this, but it was not long before the unit comprised 500 trained parachutists and was rebranded the much more exciting 11th Special Air Service Battalion. The Tragino Aqueduct near Naples had the misfortune of being the first target selected to receive the attention of thirty-eight men of the 11th SAS in February 1941 in what became known as Operation COLOSSUS. After intense training in the UK the volunteers, known as X Troop, moved to an advanced operating base in Malta.[2]

Events moved rapidly for these airborne pioneers: September 1941 saw them re-designated the 1st Parachute Battalion and reinforced with the 2nd and 3rd Parachute battalions to form the 1st Parachute Brigade. Later the 4th Parachute Battalion was added. The 1st Air Landing Brigade came next from four battalions of the 31st Independent Infantry Brigade Group converted to glider-borne infantry. These two new brigades became the Airborne Division under General F.A.M. Browning with supporting arms including artillery. March 1942 saw them move to Bulford Camp. To fly the gliders the Glider Pilot Regiment was set up as part of the Army Air Corps to fly Hotspurs, and later Horsas and Hamilcars. The 1st Parachute Brigade was then joined by the 2nd Parachute Brigade made up of the existing 4th Parachute Battalion plus the 7th Battalion Cameron Highlanders and the 10th Battalion Royal Welch Fusiliers. The 50th Indian Parachute Brigade was also formed and came on board.

At a time when things were going badly, to say the least, and morale was low, the Bruneval Raid, Operation BITING, in February 1942, changed everything. The British were anxious to learn more about German radar. A raid against the radar station at Bruneval near Le Havre was proposed. The Bruneval Raid became the Parachute Regiment's first battle honour.

'C' Company 2nd Parachute Battalion under Major J.D. Frost was selected to be dropped at night by the RAF to capture and hold the Bruneval station, while Flight Sergeant C.W. Cox, an RAF technician, dismantled the radar set there. Cox, with his radar parts, was then taken to a nearby beach to be evacuated at dawn by the Royal Navy.

Despite the presence of a German naval patrol operating nearby, the raid was a complete success, capturing not only the vital radar equipment but also two German radar technicians. Apart from raising morale, it reaffirmed Churchill's belief in the role to be played by airborne forces and by radar.[3]

Airborne operations followed in Algeria and Tunisia, Sicily and southern Italy, by which time the 1st Air Landing Light Regiment had joined to provide field artillery support for the Airborne Division and the 1st Air Landing Brigade. With the creation of the 6th Airborne Division, the Airborne Division was rebadged as the 1st Airborne Division. The 6th Airborne, of course, went on to acquit itself in the Normandy landings and after, while the 1st Airborne was, most frustratingly for them, held in reserve in the east of England. Their time, however, was to come in a small town in the Netherlands, as we shall see.

Chapter Two

The 1st Air Landing Light Regiment RA

The 1st Air Landing Light Regiment was an airborne forces unit of the British army's Royal Artillery during the Second World War, raised in 1943 and attached to the 1st Airborne Division. It was the largest single artillery unit in the division. Its first taste of action came with the Allied landings in Italy at Taranto as part of Operation SLAPSTICK in the invasion of Italy. It remained in post after the withdrawal of the division to support other elements of the British Eighth Army in the Italian campaign until the end of 1943. In early 1944 the regiment returned to England and rejoined the 1st Airborne Division, training for its participation in various cancelled operations and, ultimately, in the September 1944 Operation MARKET GARDEN. During the Battle of Arnhem the three batteries of the regiment either took up position at the bridge (the OP party of 3 Battery) or formed a defensive ring around Oosterbeek; most of 3 Battery plus 1 and 2 Batteries.

In May 1945 the regiment participated in Operation DOOMSDAY – the repatriation of the German occupation army in Norway – after which the 1st Air Landing Light Regiment returned to England and was disbanded in December 1945.

How did the regiment come about? As noted, in 1940, observing the successful German airborne operations in Belgium and the Netherlands and during the Battle of France, Winston Churchill was sufficiently impressed to order the War Office to look at creating a corps of 5,000 parachute troops. This led, in September 1941, to the formation of the 1st Parachute Brigade with its three parachute infantry battalions; these were complemented with airborne support including Royal Artillery troops, among them the 458th Independent Light Battery.[1]

So in summer 1940 the War Office made the decision to form three horse-drawn light batteries, each made up of three troops. The New Year saw them reconfigured as the 1st Mountain Regiment with 451, 452, 453 and 454 Mountain Batteries, each with four guns apiece. In addition there were three mechanized independent light batteries – 455, 456 and 457 – sporting six guns. The Mountain Batteries were specialists in mountain and Arctic warfare, while the mechanized batteries were skilled in close support of beach landings. Colonel J. Wedderburn-Maxwell RA was in charge as Director of Organisation and Training of the Light Artillery. In April 1941 the three senior light batteries relocated to Scotland to join the force known as the Marine Division, then Force 10, the Expeditionary Force and then the First Army.[2] It was after service on the North-West Frontier in India that the 458th Independent Light Battery, Royal Artillery was formed on 14 February 1941 from a cadre of officers and NCOs at Ashby Folville in Leicestershire from these seven batteries and other mechanized Royal Artillery light batteries already in existence. It was commanded by Major Patrick Lloyd (ex-454 Battery) – no lover of coming second best – and equipped with antiquated First World War-vintage 3.7in mountain howitzers ('screw guns') that were designed to be broken down into eight mule loads for transport over difficult terrain.[3] These howitzers were capable of firing a 20lb shell 5,899 yards and weighed 1,610lb.[4] The original objective of this elite unit was to lend close support in amphibious assaults on beachheads; it had already acquired significant mountain experience in India on the North-West Frontier. Who could anticipate how useful this experience would turn out to be in the mountains of southern Italy in the unforgiving winter of 1943–44? Training took place in Leicester and Scotland in combined operations and in the development of pioneering methods of air-landing.

In September 1941, the fledgling British airborne forces needed an artillery capability, so the 458th was converted into an airborne unit and in October went north to Inverary for combined operations training. A number of beach landings were carried out.[5] In mid-December the battery removed to Newbury under the command of the 31st Independent Infantry Brigade which had recently joined the 1st Airborne Division as the 1st Air Landing Brigade under the command of Brigadier G.F. 'Hoppy' Hopkinson. Once assigned to the 1st Airborne Division, it assumed responsibility for providing field artillery support for the whole of the division and spent the next eleven months training for their new role, moving to Wing Barracks at Bulford Camp in January 1942.[6]

Other artillery in the division were the 1st Air Landing Anti-Tank Battery; the 283 (City of London Yeomanry) Anti-Aircraft Battery

(Rough Riders), and the 2nd (Oban) Air Landing Anti-Tank Battery. September saw the creation of a Commander Royal Artillery HQ (CRAHQ), under Lieutenant Colonel C.H.P. Crawfurd, RA.

The unit was renamed the 1st Air Landing Light Battery in June 1942, and on 6 February 1943 was expanded to full regiment status commanded by Lieutenant Colonel R.W. 'Roddy' McLeod with Major W.F.K. 'Sheriff' Thompson, second-in-command (2i/c). Thompson got his nickname while in India, and a fellow officer was nicknamed 'the Squire', names indicative of how they intended to keep the peace locally. Captain David John 'Tiny' Madden was posted in (originally from 457 Battery) to command 3 Battery until he moved on to Divisional HQ; Captain Dennis S. Munford replaced him. Lieutenant 'Tony' Harrison joined at Bulford and would later command E Troop, 3 Battery. Lieutenant T.A. Conlin arrived on 20 March and was posted to 3 Battery, as was Second Lieutenant Tony Driver who proved to be a major asset when adapting the new US howitzers using his engineering degree and experience in the oil industry. On 7 April Lieutenant Tudor Morgan Griffiths was posted into 3 Battery. Officers, signallers and OP assistants were now required to pass a parachute course to enable OP parties to drop with the parachute battalion they were there to support. A course in aircraft recognition was held on the Isle of Man with a four-week Motor Transport course in Rhyl.

The new regiment moved down-market from Wing Camp to Bulford Fields Hutted Camp.[7] Troops originating with the 458th were allocated to one of three batteries, as were those drafted in from outside the division. This elevation was facilitated by the fact that the 458th brought with it priceless experience in mountain and Arctic warfare as well as more than a passing familiarity with close support of beach landings. Warrant officers from Guards regiments were drafted in to whip the new regiment into shape.[8] Captain D.J. Madden took over 3 Battery, and it was at this point that Gunner Eric Chrystal joined the regiment.

However, this was never going to be just another ordinary regiment. Major Lloyd and Captain John Burley 'Dick' Dickinson saw to that, insisting on peak fitness, speed, strength and discipline in the soldiers under his command. All ranks, including cookhouse staff, batmen and clerks, were required to be able to march 60 miles in seventy-two hours in Field Service Marching Order (FSMO) carrying weapons. Stragglers were not shot; indeed, it was permissible to assist them as long as the unit reached their destination as a whole and could then stand to attention for inspection. Then there was that run at a minimum 6 mph...the dreaded RTU (return to original unit) awaited failure. Sport was of the essence, as was PT.[9] All officers had to be fully conversant with everything relating to gunnery: gun drill, signalling, communications and driving.

The new regiment now consisted of three batteries (1 to 3), each of two troops (A to F), with four guns allocated to each troop, making twenty-four guns in the regiment. At the same time their 3.7in howitzers were replaced by the newer and superior American 75mm pack howitzer adapted for airborne use.[10] This could be broken down into six components, originally to facilitate transportation – usually by mules – over mountainous terrain. It fired a 14.7lb shell with a much better range at almost 5.5 miles, weighing in at 1,439lb. The original issue was fitted with cart wheels, quickly replaced with pneumatic tyres on 1 April and fired for the first time by the regiment on Larkhill ranges.[11] One battery of eight guns would support each of the Airborne Division's three brigades. Other artillery units in the division were an independent anti-tank battery assigned to each parachute brigade.[12]

Logistics were an issue: mule transport was all very well, but the essence of airborne operations lay in surprising the enemy, and no mule on earth could do that. At some stage flying was necessary. Parachuting the guns in separate parts on individual 'chutes was out of the question, although the American airborne forces continued to do this. Imagine the confusion on the ground in reassembling the parts in the dark; that is assuming that all the parts, and the gunners, landed in the right and/or the same place. There was only one way for British airborne forces to transport artillery guns and their towing vehicles by air and that was by using gliders. The recently introduced Horsa and Hamilcar gliders and the American Wacos saved the day. For the 1st Air Landing Light Regiment the glider of choice was the Airspeed Horsa piloted by two men from the Glider Pilot Regiment.[13] With its 88ft wingspan and a length of 67ft, the Horsa had a maximum load capacity of 15,750lb, space for the two pilots and a maximum of twenty-eight troops or two jeeps. Variations on this payload included one jeep, an artillery gun and a half-ton trailer, or one jeep with up to two trailers.[14] The great drawback, however, was that there was room for only three artillerymen and the two pilots to be carried with the gun.[15]

Nevertheless, 12 February 1943 was a landmark day for the regiment. On that day the RAF towed two Horsa gliders loaded with a 3.7in howitzer and a 'Blitz Buggy' (jeep) from Netheravon, 4 miles north of Amesbury on Salisbury Plain. This was the first time that such a manoeuvre had been attempted; the regiment's first airborne exercise, Exercise Woolwich.[16]

The date of 3 April was another crucial day, for that was when the regiment repeated this original flight exercise, substituting the new 75mm howitzer in the Horsa for the now obsolete mountain gun. Captain David Lindsay was in charge 'using the Jeep, trailer, gun combination and a C-47 aircraft', a Dakota. The pilot obliged by including in the thirty-minute test flight a good number of banks, climbs and dives. All went well with no apparent movement of the loads.[17] Moreover, the new guns had the added benefit of fitting into a Horsa without having to be disassembled so they could, in theory, be unloaded rapidly and brought into action very soon after landing.

Chapter Three

14283058 Gunner Eric Chrystal

Eric Wright Chrystal was born on 21 December 1923 at 2 Sciennes Hill Place in central Edinburgh close to what was then the Royal (Dick) School of Veterinary Studies. After a routine education he left school and worked as a plumber's mate with Mr Pearson, plumber and ironmonger, at 182 High Street, Portobello, after moving with the family to 6 Mentone Avenue, Portobello. He returned there after release from his PoW camp in the late summer of 1945, aged 21.

His first taste of army life came when, on 17 September 1942 (a propitious date to say the least), he joined up as a private with the Territorial Army under the National Service (Armed Forces) Acts of 1939 and 1940. From 1942 all attested men were deemed to have enlisted with the General Service Corps and were sent to a Primary Training Centre to undergo initial medical checks. He would then have been tested to establish to which particular corps and trade he was best suited, and was allocated for specialist training accordingly. In the Second World War, General Service men were identified by eight-digit numbers beginning with '14'; Eric Chrystal's number was 14283058. His first posting was to the 38th Signal Training Regiment RA from November 1942 to January 1943 stationed at Redford Barracks in Edinburgh.[1] He then transferred to the Royal Artillery as a gunner and in February 1943 joined the newly-raised 1st Air Landing Light Regiment based at Bulford Fields, a hutted camp built in 1939–40 and demolished in 1978.[2] In actual fact he was posted there and was initially 'none too pleased'. However, he confessed that the red beret and the shoulder flashes brought him round and he soon became very attached to the regiment. Other recollections include the battery Chief Clerk's composition of the battery song *Anchors Away* and the disappointment of not being with the regiment in Sicily. Training for Italy would also have taken place at the School of Artillery at nearby Larkhill.

His first action was in the Italian campaign for which he sailed on 16 May 1943 from Liverpool on the MV *Staffordshire*, landing at Oran in

Algeria on 26 May when the regiment moved inland to Froha to begin live training. Thence they proceeded to M'saken near Sousse in Tunisia for more training. They were still there at the end of August, moving to Tunis and then Hammam-Lif (Arabic: حمام الأنف) on the Mediterranean about 13 miles south-east of Tunis. In September he sailed to Taranto in the heel of Italy, landing on 30 September as part of Operation SLAPSTICK. After learning that all the regiment's kitbags were at the bottom of the harbour when the supply boat was sunk, they all headed off to link with the Canadians at Campobasso. Gunner Palfreyman was killed en route by a mine. The regiment carried out a number of support operations at Foggia, Campobasso, Rionero, Orsogna and Casoli, but while firing on Campobasso Eric was badly wounded on 11 October by shrapnel in his lower back and evacuated to Malta (Casualty List No. 1287; British North African Forces M/31260 26/10). His flight from Foggia took him to Sicily and then on to Malta in a Dakota. This is how he remembered it:

> We were up at the OP directing fire onto Campobasso; Bdr Ogle I think it was, he was the OPA, and I went back a wee way to have something to eat in an old house when Gerry landed an 88mm shell on us, or very near anyway. I was the only one injured but that was it for me. Just before Christmas we were all back loaded to the regiment, or it might have been just after Hogmanay to go back home. Then it was Boston and all the training once again.

During his recuperation the regiment withdrew from the line and returned to England on 10 January 1944 where they underwent training while, with the rest of the division, they were held in reserve for the Normandy D-Day landings in June 1944. After no fewer than fifteen cancelled operations, the regiment was finally briefed on 14 September for Operation MARKET, one half of Operation MARKET GARDEN and the battle for Arnhem Bridge, three short days later.

Eric Chrystal took off in his glider with the rest of the troop on Sunday morning, 17 September. He was in 3 Battery, E Troop HQ and, on landing safely, was a member of a Forward Observation Officer party which, under Major Dennis Munford, officer commanding 3 Battery, 'was in the area of [the bridge] directing fire for three or four days'.[3] The rest of the regiment was deployed either protecting the landing zones around Oosterbeek or shelling the bridge area that was held by the ever-strengthening German forces and their armour.

Gunner Chrystal was taken prisoner of war on 25 September after four to five days of intense fighting around Arnhem Bridge.[4] (Casualty list No. 1584: 'missing, believed prisoner of war'; later confirmed in List No. 1607). After a period spent in the horrendous tented transit camp at Limburg (Stalag XII-A), he was cattle-trucked to his 'permanent' camp at Mühlberg and the satellite labour camp at Zwickau in south-east Germany near the border with Czechoslovakia (as it was then). The camp was a satellite of Flossenbürg Concentration Camp.[5] He was liberated on or around 31 July 1945 by the US army and subsequently repatriated, returning to his unit in Boston.[6]

Meanwhile, the few survivors of the regiment had returned to Boston after their miraculous escape over the River Rhine at Arnhem. The winter and spring of 1944–45 were spent in rebuilding the regiment and in training. By April it was back to full strength and in May was posted to Stavanger in Norway to oversee the repatriation of the German troops of occupation and guarding vital locations until September 1945. With peace, the 1st Airborne Division was then disbanded along with the 1st Air Landing Light Regiment RA.[7]

In 1946 Eric was at Tonfanau Camp, Gwynedd, a miserable anti-aircraft training facility where, among other things, 'he has been doing plumbing repair jobs within the camp.' His regiment was the 240th Light Anti-Aircraft Training Regiment, Royal Artillery. He was released from his army engagement on 27 July 1946 to the Army Reserve after 3 years, 292 days' service and re-engaged to the Regular Army on 3 October 1946. He then went on to serve in Egypt in the Canal Zone (February 1950–August 1952) with the 71st (Forth) Heavy Anti-Aircraft Regiment, Royal Artillery, an air defence unit formed in Scotland just before the Second World War, Cyprus (August 1956–August 1957 where he was Mentioned in Dispatches), Aden (September 1960–September 1961) and the BAOR (24 Missile Regiment RA, September 1964–February 1968). In 1952 he married Ruby Richardson, a WAAF who had been stationed in 1943 at RAF Scampton with the 617 'Dambuster' Squadron. They met at Barnard Castle while Eric was at Deerbolt Camp. They had two boys: David (b. 31 January 1953) who rose through the ranks from signalman in the Royal Signals to major – he too was Mentioned in Dispatches and was awarded the BEM – and Paul (b. 17 September 1954), whose only claim to military fame lies in the reflected glory of being born ten years to the day after the beginning of the Battle of Arnhem. Eric died on the last day of 2001 after many proud visits to the Arnhem battlefields where he and his diminishing group of comrades were welcomed most generously by Dutch residents year in and year out. No doubt, if asked, he would have said that he was very fortunate to have had those fifty-seven additional years after the battle; many others were not so lucky.

Chapter Four

The 1st Air Landing Light Regiment's Italian Campaign

The Italian campaign or, more descriptively, the liberation of Italy, was enabled in the wake of the victory in the North African campaign in May 1943. The Allied operations in and around Italy lasted from 1943 to 1945, starting with the invasion of Sicily on the night of 9/10 July 1943 and lasting until 17 August. This was followed that September by the invasion of the Italian mainland and the campaign in wider Italy, culminating in the surrender of the German armed forces in Italy in May 1945.

Sicily

The Allied invasion of Sicily, Operation HUSKY (9/10 July-17 August 1943), resulted in the Allies taking Sicily from Fascist Italy and Nazi Germany. It began with a major combined amphibious and airborne operation, followed up by a six-week land campaign. The Allies eventually expelled the Axis forces from the island, thus opening the Mediterranean sea lanes to Allied merchant ships for the first time since 1941. The downside was that the Germans were now able to transfer three divisions from Sicily and station them in southern Italy to counter the anticipated invasion by the Allies. Mussolini was deposed, leaving the door open for that Allied invasion of Italy. Hitler went so far as to cancel 'a major offensive at Kursk after only a week, in part to divert forces to Italy', resulting in a radical dilution of German strength on the Eastern Front.[1] However, the Allied strategy was even more deceptive when we add the effect of Operation MINCEMEAT to the mix.[2] The day of 25 July saw the collapse of the Italian fascist government and the rise of a new government under Marshal Badoglio. By the end of August the Allies were negotiating with Italy to secure an armistice which came into effect on 8 September, a mere twenty-four hours before the Allied invasion of the Italian mainland. Two days earlier the 1st Airborne Division received orders to take Taranto and hold the port until the arrival of reinforcements; an operation timed to coincide with the announcement of the Italian armistice and the landing of the 5th Army on the beaches of Salerno.

Ultimately, the collapse of Italy meant the demise of Italian forces in their homeland and the Balkans, resulting in a massive one-fifth of the entire German army being diverted from the Eastern Front to southern Europe, a situation that persisted until the war drew to a close.[3]

The 1st Airborne Division as a whole had not been involved in the Allied invasion of Sicily. However, the 1st Parachute and 1st Air Landing brigades participated in brigade-sized operations, LADBROKE and FUSTIAN, without any artillery support from the regiment.

As well as amphibious landings, HUSKY saw airborne troops flown in to support both the Western and Eastern Task Forces. To the east, the 1st Airborne Division, under Major General George F. Hopkinson, was tasked to seize vital bridges and high ground in support of the British Eighth Army. Elements of the US 82nd Airborne Division were held as a tactical reserve in Tunisia.[4]

It was just after midnight on 9/10 July when two American and two British airborne attacks began. The American paratroopers mainly consisted of the 505th Parachute Infantry Regiment of the US 82nd Airborne Division making their first combat drop. The British landings were preceded by Pathfinders of the 21st Independent Parachute Company; their job was to lay down markers on landing zones for the troops aiming to seize the Ponte Grande bridge over the River Anapo just south of Syracuse and hold it until the British 5th Infantry Division arrived from their landings on the Cassibile beaches 7 miles to the south.[5] Glider infantry from the 1st Airborne Division's 1st Air Landing Brigade commanded by Brigadier Philip Hicks was detailed to seize landing zones inland (Operation LADBROKE).[6] The force took off from Tunisia with a complement of 136 Waco Hadrians and 8 Airspeed Horsas. As noted, their objective was to secure the Ponte Grande bridge (which carried Highway 115 across the Anapo and its canal) before taking control of the city itself with its strategically vital docks as a prelude to the full-scale invasion of Sicily. Unfortunately, strong winds of up to 45 mph confounded the assault, blowing the troop-carrying aircraft off course and the American force was scattered widely over south-east Sicily between Gela and Syracuse.⁷ By 14 July, only about two-thirds of the 505th had managed to concentrate and half the US paratroopers failed to reach their rallying points.⁸

On 9 July, 2,075 British troops, along with seven jeeps, six anti-tank guns and ten mortars, boarded their gliders in Tunisia and took off at 18.00, bound for south-eastern Sicily. Before the landing, twelve Boeing B-17s and six Wellingtons equipped with radar-jamming devices flew back and forth along the coast in the Siracusa-Licata sector. In addition, fifty-five Wellingtons of 205th Group carried out a diversionary bombing of the port and airport at Syracuse, causing a number of civilian and military casualties including the commander of the Italian naval base, Commander Giuseppe Giannotti. Sadly appropriate in view of the Italians' reputation with marionettes, 280 puppets dressed in paratrooper uniforms were launched north of the landing area in order to baffle the Italians.

These British air-landing troops flew into what turned into an unmitigated disaster: only 12 of the 147 gliders landed on target, and 69 nose-dived into the sea, with the loss of 252 or so men rapidly drowned under the weight of their kit. The final death toll was 605 officers and men, including 88 British and 13 American glider pilots.⁹ Among those landing in the sea was Major General Hopkinson, who spent several hours clinging onto a piece of wreckage; he was eventually picked up by the landing ship HMS *Keren*. What remained of the airborne troops attacked patrols and created mayhem wherever possible. Fortunately, eighty-seven men in a platoon of the 2nd Battalion, South Staffordshire Regiment under Lieutenant Louis Withers, part of the British 1st Air Landing Brigade, landed on target, took Ponte Grande and repelled counterattacks. Unfortunately, by 11.30 a battalion of the Italian 75th Infantry Regiment under Colonel Francesco Ronco turned up with artillery.¹⁰ The British held out until about 1530 hours when, with ammunition running out and by now reduced to fifteen unwounded men, they were forced to surrender, a mere forty-five minutes before the leading elements of the British 5th Division arrived from the south.¹¹

The Italians gained control of the bridge with a view to destroying it, but were confounded by soldiers from the 1st Air Landing Brigade who had removed the explosive charges. Other troops from the brigade who had landed elsewhere in Sicily helped by destroying communications links and capturing gun batteries.

This is how Pegasus Archive sums up the mess that was Operation LADBROKE:

> In summary, the glider pilots and the British and American aircrews had effectively been given only three weeks to prepare and become accustomed to dealing with each other. During this time they had been unable to hold a single exercise that would serve as a dress rehearsal for the conditions that they would encounter during the actual invasion; the mass navigation, by night and over sea, of up to 150 aircraft, flying in formation at low altitude, and towing gliders which were to be released two miles short of the coast. They were quite unprepared for what lay ahead.
>
> https://www.pegasusarchive.org/sicily/depth_preparation.htm

Where was the 1st Air Landing Light Regiment while all this was going on? The regiment embarked at Liverpool on 16 May 1943 on the MVs *Stirling Castle* and *Staffordshire* with elements of the 1st Airborne Division destined for Oran, north-west Algeria to join the 1st Parachute Brigade. RHQ and 1 and 2 Batteries sailed on the *Stirling Castle* and 3 Battery on the *Staffordshire*.[12] The ORs (other ranks) 'were packed like sardines below decks', according to Lieutenant A.D.H. de Rivas. They all set sail at 0800 hours on 17 May. Both vessels were 1930s' ocean liners, pressed into service as troopships. The *Stirling Castle* came through the war unscathed after steaming some 505,000 war miles and carrying 128,000 personnel. Oran had been captured by the Allies from the Vichy government in late 1942 during Operation TORCH.

The 1st Air Landing Light Regiment travelled from Bulford after dark via Willesden Junction to Liverpool docks amid much (pointless as it turned out) secrecy: destination and other details were never officially revealed and airborne insignia were removed, while telltale red berets were secreted at the bottom of kit bags; the trains were direct and travelled through London with no changes. Yet all was to no avail: as the train passed through the outskirts of Liverpool, local residents revealed their location, while dockworkers correctly identified the troops as airborne, despite the absence of berets, and when the troops arrived at Oran, Lord

Haw-Haw was able to announce to anyone listening: 'British 1st Airborne Division has just landed in North Africa.'

The regiment's vehicles, 100 or so of them, drove north in convoy to Leith. The troopships were part of a convoy assembling at Govan comprising nine liners heavily defended by an aircraft carrier, a cruiser, seven destroyers and frigates.[13] They sailed at 1800 hours on 19 May. By and large it was a quiet voyage, despite concerns that the *Stirling Castle*, being the bigger troopship and close to the carrier, might attract undue attention. A raid by a high-flying Focke-Wulf Fw 200 Condor was seen off by anti-aircraft fire and carrier-launched Supermarine Seafires.[14] After enduring ten days of lectures, endless PT and routine training, the troops disembarked on 26 May, speedily unloaded and boarded capacious American army lorries ('deuce and a halfs') in which, after a night under the stars, they proceeded to Fleurus transit camp, a name that flattered to deceive because what met the troops was an open expanse of desert scrub with a stack of tinned rations piled in the middle: 'a wilderness of rock and coarse grass'.[15] The Americans provided tents, C-Rations and tools, as well as those trucks. The only problem turned out to be language as English is not always what it seems to be: 'In the artillery a British battery is an American battalion, a British troop an American battery and a British section an American platoon' (Truesdale, pp.16–17). 'Pharaoh's Revenge' (diarrhoea brought on by ingesting dirty water), the dust and the flies added to the wretched situation. Not much could be done until the guns showed up, which they did on 6 June at Oran 15 miles away.

Fleurus was also the location of the regiment's first active service fatality during the hasty night-time unloading of those guns by very tired soldiers. There were a number of accidents, one fatal. According to Tony Driver, 20-year-old Gunner Aubrey Jackson was in his 15cwt truck when the driver accidentally drove it off the road into a ditch where Jackson was pinned under the dashboard and crushed by his vehicle, dying at the scene. Court of Enquiry verdict: death by accident due to the men being exhausted and overworked.[16]

On 20 June a two-day firing demonstration and competition was held at Thiersville, 12 miles or so south of Mascara, with all three batteries firing live rounds over 1,000 friendly infantry; a first for the regiment. Another competition took place in 24–26 June at Djebel Darmouz when two regimental surveyors were injured by a smoke round that fell short and landed on the OP. Movements and safety took a lot of planning. On site, sentries from each battery were posted (a junior NCO and an 'intelligent' gunner under the RSM), equipped with a red flag and on motorcycles. An ambulance stood by at RHQ with a medical officer. All troops were warned that 1,000 friendly troops were milling around under their barrage and 'under no circumstances could loose rounds be tolerated'. Imagine the tension and the determination not to mess up (Truesdale, p.18).

Things improved generally, however, when the regiment was able to move on to the French colonial town of Mascara, 100 miles inland southeast of Oran, where they found a relatively well-appointed camp near Froha airfield. The convoy on the 6-day journey involved 42 officers, 516 ORs, 125 jeeps, 15 other vehicles, 58 trailers and 101 motorcycles. There was a rear party led by the RSM which ensured that each staging area was left scrupulously clean before inspection and a certificate was obtained from the Officer Commanding at each area.[17]

The time here was mostly spent in intensive training, notably Exercise 'SSB' ('Sweat Saves Blood') conducted with Divisional Royal Engineers north of Enfidaville; there was also a welcome four-day R&R in Tunis. Training routinely started with a parade around sunrise, followed by a swim and breakfast. Training ended at 1100 hours with lunch at midday, followed by a siesta to avoid the afternoon sun. The heat was intense and the sandstorms were ferocious, annoyingly whipped up by the slipstreams of the aircraft. An afternoon parade was followed by more training until 22.00. Inevitably the sand got everywhere and the latrines were constantly busy. The American C-Rations were 'mushy' and devoid of 'fresh meat and vegetables'. Most of the soldiers craved something to 'chew on' (Truesdale, p.19).

Six weeks later on 2 July at 0800 hours the regiment transferred with the rest of the division to M'saken near Sousse on another six-day 800-mile journey by road and by rail, destination unknown at the time. The plan was to cover 150–200 miles each day with a twenty-minute break every hour; RHQ and the three batteries took it in turns to be lead. Lance Bombardier Crook, Captain Munford's driver and a former Birmingham policeman, was the first of the regiment's malaria cases (Truesdale, p.20). Sandfly fever was also a problem. The journey took them through the notorious Kasserine Pass with the detritus of battle and burned-out

British tanks and the graves of the crews a frequent reminder of the reality of war.[18]

M'saken greeted them with most welcome olive trees and the shade and comfort these offered. Beer, however, was in desperately short supply so, according to Lieutenant Driver, former brewer Teddy Thompson was accordingly dispatched with money and a 15cwt truck complete with driver to Tunis to the brewery there 250 miles away. Several days later they returned triumphant, laden with barrels of beer (Truesdale, p.21).

So much for the road convoy. Heavy equipment and other matériel was following by train along with 106 men, 140 tons of baggage and 16 ammunition trailers for each battery. There was also one Bren gun per battery fitted on an anti-aircraft mounting along with a two-man crew. Starting at Tizi, the journey entailed unloading and swapping from narrow- to broad-gauge at Perregaux and then, down the line, back to narrow-gauge, all performed by the rail party. The train from Algiers to M'saken was subject to frequent attack by Arab robbers who targeted the regiment's invaluable mosquito nets. Lieutenant Frank 'Pepys' Moore of 3 Battery witnessed an Arab raid; an American guard shot one of them in the back and he 'fell like a rabbit'. Moore was later invaded again when getting ready for bed and had to deter the Arabs at the point of his revolver (Truesdale, pp.21, 24).

When Lieutenant Colonel C.H.P. Crawfurd, the Division's Commander Royal Artillery (DCRA), was killed in Sicily on 13 July he was replaced by Lieutenant Colonel McLeod, and the 2i/c, Major W.F.K. 'Sheriff' Thompson, was given command of the regiment.[19]

On 25 July Captain Harrison's E Troop, 3 Battery set a regimental record when they took a mere twelve minutes, five seconds to manoeuvre a gun down a track to firing. On the 27th Operation SEARAY took place, requiring the regiment, along with elements of the Air Landing Brigade and the Airborne Reconnaissance Squadron, to move to and occupy a position by night, requiring a night survey, the registration and production of a regimental fire plan and production of gun programmes. Between 27 and 31 July, the three batteries and the 2nd South Staffords supported the Air Landing Brigade in a dry exercise. Truesdale (p.24) tells of an incident that occurred in a live shoot when Lieutenant Rod Pearson was carrying out an exercise on the ridge where the OP was situated. This coincided with the regimental survey officer operating on the same ridge. Pearson gave his order to fire, but unfortunately the shell loaded was armour-piercing and not high-explosive as intended, and a shard of rock seriously injured one of the survey team in the OP. Thankfully the disparity in trajectory caused the round to fall short, mitigating the damage.

In September the regiment was expecting to get the call to advance to Salerno but, in the end, disappointingly, it was not needed; there were insufficient aircraft anyway. This was to be the first in a series of frustrating cancellations to beset the regiment in the next year or so. The few gunners who saw action on the island went into battle by parachute. The Salerno landings, south-east of Naples, were part of Operation AVALANCHE, the invasion of Italy from 9 September.[20] Henry Wellesley, 6th Duke of Wellington, who was killed in action during the fighting is buried in Salerno War Cemetery.

Small consolation as it was, the regiment did, according to Colonel Thompson, receive some extra equipment and men while in limbo: fourteen much-needed 3-tonners with drivers, four RAMC jeeps complete with three medical orderlies and drivers from 181 Air Landing Ambulance; a double issue of jeep snow chains and six Polish mine-detectors (Truesdale, pp.25, 27). The latter led to training in mine-detection and lifting (both anti-personnel and anti-tank), helped by divisional sappers who also took the time to demonstrate some elementary bridge-building.

Operation AVALANCHE

The Allies had two options for their landings on the Italian mainland: the mouth of the Volturno River north of Naples or Salerno. Salerno was preferred due to its invader-friendly landing beaches, backed up with major roads and airfields nearby that would be useful after a successful invasion. Operation BAYTOWN and Operation SLAPSTICK were launched to support the Operation AVALANCHE invasion, although SLAPSTICK actually started on the same day as AVALANCHE.[21]

The British XIII Corps under Montgomery was detailed for Operation BAYTOWN which began on 3 September 1943, six days before the Salerno landing. British and Canadian troops landed at Reggio Calabria with its objective to tie down German troops in Calabria, maybe even drawing German troops away from the Salerno sector. However, German commander-in-chief Albert Kesselring was no fool and worked out that the main Allied target was up the coast, so instead of keeping troops south to repel the British-Canadian BAYTOWN attack, Kesselring pulled the German LXXVI Panzer Corps back, leaving only one regiment and some Italian troops to deal with BAYTOWN.[22]

For the regiment, first Salerno was on and then it was off. Initially the regiment was to participate as a mechanized mountain regiment under X Corps. Training in the mountains north of Enfidaville was duly carried out, but all in vain: the 1st Air Landing Light Regiment was going to Taranto instead as part of Operation SLAPSTICK.

Operation AVALANCHE at Salerno took place on 9 September 1943, the same day as SLAPSTICK. In a bid to achieve the requisite element of surprise, it was decided that there was to be no pre-assault naval or aerial bombardment. However, the Allies were unaware that Kesselring was busy preparing for a possible invasion in the region, so there was never going to be any surprise.

The 165,000-strong Salerno invasion force, the US 5th Army under Lieutenant General Mark Clark, comprised the US VI Corps (Major General Ernest Dawley), the British X Corps (Lieutenant General Richard McCreery) and the US 82nd Airborne Division in reserve. Despite an extensive 35-mile front, only three divisions – two British and one American – made up the initial assault force, with the British landing north of the Sele River near Montecorvino and the Americans to the south of the river at Paestum. A small force of US Rangers and British Commandos was to land north-west of the British landing beaches to secure the roads leading to Naples.[23]

The Allies faced the daunting prospect of several German divisions facing them just waiting for the attack as predicted by Kesselring.

Operation SLAPSTICK

This was the code-name for the British amphibious assault on the ports of Taranto and Brindisi. Although the now-defeated Italians secretly made two port cities available to the Allies during the equally secret armistice negotiations, Eisenhower elected to land a large detachment of troops at Taranto in another attempt to draw German forces away from Salerno.[24]

The operation was cobbled together at short notice on 6 September, following a useful offer by the Italian government to allow the Allies access to Taranto.

Plans were formulated on the same day to transport the British 1st Airborne Division to Taranto from their base in North Africa, in the wake of the Italian surrender, to capture the port and establish anti-aircraft defences. The remainder of the Italian fleet still docked in the harbour was expected to have sailed away by then. The Allies relied on the assumption that the division would be up against minimal opposition and would be able to suppress any resistance with their limited naval support since air cover was not an option, Taranto being outside the range of Allied fighter aircraft based in Sicily.[25]

So the 1st Airborne Division was selected for the mission. Significantly, despite being formed two years previously in October 1941 it had yet to fight as a complete division. Their only units that had been blooded in battle were the 1st Parachute Brigade, which had fought valiantly as an independent brigade in North Africa and in Operation FUSTIAN, and the 1st Air Landing Brigade, severely depleted with only two viable battalions, which had fought in Operation LADBROKE. Neither brigade was in any condition to conduct another assault landing.[26] Of the division's other brigades, the 2nd and 4th Parachute brigades, they could offer no battle experience and, just as unhelpfully, of the two the 2nd Parachute Brigade was the only full-strength unit as the 4th Parachute Brigade could muster only two battalions, with its 3rd Battalion still operating in Palestine.[27]

Another significant problem was that at the time the division was not actually on the Italian mainland, it was still in North Africa. Normally this would not have been an issue, but an ongoing shortage of transport aircraft meant that the division could not make land in their usual, trained-for way by parachute and glider. To make matters worse, all the landing craft in the area were already allocated to the other landings: Operation AVALANCHE at Salerno (given to the US 82nd Airborne Division under Major General Matthew Ridgway) on the western coast, and Operation BAYTOWN at Calabria.[28]

The division, including the 1st Air Landing Light Regiment, had to be transported across the Mediterranean by the Royal Navy, leaving North Africa on 8 September aboard the ships of the Royal Navy's 12th Cruiser

Squadron at Bizerte. This comprised four cruisers – HMS *Aurora*, HMS *Penelope*, HMS *Dido* and HMS *Sirius* of the Royal Navy's 12th Cruiser Squadron – accompanied by the mine-layer HMS *Abdiel* and the American cruiser USS *Boise*, all under the command of Commodore W.G. Agnew.[29] Twelve 6-pounder anti-tank guns were loaded onto the decks of the *Abdiel*. Assuming a successful landing, the British 78th Infantry Division in Sicily and the 8th Indian Infantry Division in the Middle East would be sent to reinforce the airborne division under the command of V Corps.

The journey by road on 19 September for embarkation at Bizerte ended on 19 September, heavy rains having turned the ground into a quagmire contributing to 3 Battery losing twenty-eight out of its thirty motorcycles (Truesdale, pp.27–28). The 1st Airborne Division was divided into two halves. The first, comprising the divisional HQ, the 1st and 4th Parachute Brigade groups and the 9th Field Company, Royal Engineers, boarded the American LSTs (Landing Ship Tanks) at Bizerte and sailed at 1700 hours on 8 September as noted, their decks jam-packed with the division's vehicles and stores.[30] These LSTs were nothing more than huge flat-bottomed barges which exaggerated every pitch and roll, causing acute seasickness in many a soldier and major problems with the precious cargo. Concerns were raised by Admiral of the Fleet Sir Andrew Cunningham that the Italian battle fleet based at Taranto might attack the cruiser flotilla which would be hard-pushed to defend itself, overloaded as they were with troops and matériel. He therefore ordered the battleships HMS *Howe* and HMS *King George V* and their six escorting destroyers, commanded by Vice Admiral Arthur Power, to sail from their base in Malta and join the flotilla.[31] At 1830 hours on 8 September, while the convoy was at sea, General Eisenhower broadcast the details of the Italian surrender.[32]

Woollacott (p.29) describes much of the seasickness on the crossing and 1 Battery having to deal with numerous motorcycles breaking free of their ropes. No. 3 Battery had a more challenging problem: their runaways included heavy vehicles that took thirty volunteers to restrain with heavy chains. Petrol spewing out of motorcycles only exacerbated the problem.[33] At 1500 hours on 30 September, the flotilla approached the minefield protecting the entrance to Taranto. The beleaguered remnants of the Italian fleet were still causing some anxiety, particularly when, just as the Allied flotilla came into sight of Taranto, the Italian battleships *Andrea Doria* and *Duilio* and three cruisers slipped anchor and were observed leaving the harbour. The Allied flotilla went to action stations, but the Italian ships merely sailed past en route to Malta to surrender in accordance with the agreement between the Allies and the Italian government.

The destroyer HMS *Javelin* took the lead, darted through the minefield and entered the harbour, returning to the assembled flotilla two hours later having picked up a very useful Italian harbour pilot. HMS *Javelin* guided HMS *Penelope* and USS *Boise* into the harbour where they moored alongside the jetty to disembark their complement of troops, while the other ships remained outside the port deploying small boats to take their soldiers ashore. Port facilities were fully intact.

The Taranto landing met with no opposition as German troops had already been withdrawn by Kesselring two days earlier. Two days after this, it is usually reported that the British paratroopers took Brindisi, again without effective resistance, although there was some low-level German harassment. However, this is far from the truth. Warden (2015) tells us how

> the 8th Army were able to make relatively easy progress for a while up the eastern coast, capturing the Port of Brindisi, Bari, as well as airfields around Foggia, which provided a base from which US bombers were able to exploit the opportunity to bomb oil fields in Romania and various places in northern [sic] Germany. There was an interesting episode by the American Air Force who rescued 500 PoWs after landing in Yugoslavia with the assistance of the Italian Partisans.

That same day the British paratroopers, pushing westward, linked up with Canadian troops of XIII Corps. The SLAPSTICK offensive would push on to capture the airfield at Gioia del Colle in mid-September, after which it paused to consolidate the territorial gains.

Air support was obviously necessary to protect the assault. Early 9 September saw the newly-discovered landing strip at Scanzano Jonico, 30 miles south-west of Taranto, attacked by sixty-seven American B-26 Marauders from the 17th and 310th Bombardment groups. Around the same time, forty-one B-24s from the 9th Bombardment Group bombed the Foggia air facilities with some opposition; the Luftwaffe lost up to thirteen planes.³⁴

The first invasion units to hit Taranto soil had been the HQ of the 4th Parachute Brigade and the 10th Parachute Battalion, which were then mobilized to move inland to guard against a German attack.³⁵ The airborne division troops were welcomed by the Italian garrison and received the equally welcome news that the German forces had already left town. The two brigades passed through the city and set up defensive positions to the north. Major General Hopkinson established his divisional HQ in the Albergo Europa Hotel and accepted the Italian surrender from the military governor.

Their job done safely in landing the first half of the division, the 12th Cruiser Squadron set sail back to Bizerte to collect the remaining troops: the 2nd Parachute Brigade, the 1st Air Landing Brigade, the 1st Air Landing Light Regiment and the Glider Pilot Regiment.

There had been, however, significant casualties before this when, on 10 September, HMS *Abdiel*, a mine-layer sometimes deployed as a fast transport, struck a magnetic mine and sank while manoeuvring alongside the dock.

HMS *Abdiel* Goes Up

The mines had been laid only a few hours earlier by two German torpedo boats (*S-54* and *S-61*) as they retreated from the harbour. *Abdiel* was carrying troops of the 6th (Royal Welch) Parachute Battalion and 204 (Oban) Anti-Tank Battery, Royal Artillery; she headed for the berth that had been declined earlier in the day by the captain of the US cruiser USS *Boise*. Soon after midnight, two mines exploded beneath *Abdiel*, causing extensive flooding and sinking her in three minutes with great loss of life among both sailors and soldiers. The 6th (Royal Welch) Parachute Battalion took 58 killed and 120 wounded, while there were another 48 dead and 6 injured among *Abdiel*'s crew.³⁶ She was also carrying those twelve 6-pounder anti-tank guns of the 2nd (Oban) Anti-Tank Battery and the division's reserve ammunition supply. It is rumoured that the ship's degaussing equipment had been turned off to reduce noise and to allow troops a better night's sleep.³⁷ Commander F. Ashe Lincoln QC RNVR had a different take, as expounded in his book *Secret Naval Investigator*.[38] An expert in naval mine clearance, he found in the Germans' magazine in Taranto a number of large wooden wheels fitted with depth-charges with a timing clock and explosive charge in the centre. He says that one of these devices had been sunk next to the mooring buoy used by *Abdiel* when the Germans evacuated the previous night.

Notwithstanding the successful Taranto landings, the unforgiving terrain facing the Allies as they penetrated north was just as inimical as the Germans in their battling retreat. Warden (2015) again:

> With successful Allied landings completed at Taranto, units established themselves in various camps and carried out training in preparation for the fighting that lay ahead. As the Allies advanced northwards encountering increasingly difficult terrain, characterized by a succession of fast-flowing rivers and intervening ridges running at right angles to the line of advance, this prevented fast movement and provided ideal defences for the Germans.

Overnight on 9/10 September, the 4th Parachute Brigade led the advance inland and by dawn on 10 September they had reached Massafra, where they were welcomed by the locals. Next was Mottola which, unlike Massafra, was still in German hands. The Germans put up a fight against the 156th Parachute Battalion, only to withdraw soon after. This was where the division suffered its first combat casualties; the wounded were evacuated back to Taranto, where the 133rd (Parachute) Field Ambulance had established an eighty-bed main dressing station (MDS) at the Rondinella hospital. By 15 September the MDS was caring for sixty-seven wounded. In the first nine days of the operation, the brigade had 101 casualties.[39]

According to Cole (p.56), between the landings on 10 September and 5 October, 1,728 casualties were admitted to either Rondinella or the Maritima and 194 operations were carried out.

Token German resistance came courtesy of elements of the 1st Parachute Division (1 *Fallschirmjäger* Division); they continued to harass and delay the British advance with ambushes and roadblocks. It was at one of these roadblocks near Castellaneta (25 miles from Taranto) that Major General Hopkinson was hit by a burst of German machine-gun fire while monitoring the 10th Parachute Battalion's attack. He died of his wounds the following day.[40] Hopkinson was replaced as the divisional commander by Brigadier Ernest Down, previously the commander of the 2nd Parachute Brigade.

By 30 September, the 1st Airborne Division had advanced 125 miles to reach Foggia. The Foggia airfield complex was a group of military airfields located within a 25-mile radius of Foggia, a major transport hub and airfield serving the Italian army and, later, the Germans. Taking the Foggia complex gave the Allies many advantages, not least bringing their bombers within range of the Romanian oilfields as well as targets in southern Germany and central Europe. It also enabled them to drop supplies to resistance movements in the Balkans (Tito's partisans in northern Yugoslavia and the Chetniks in Mikhailovich, for example), and even Warsaw. Taking Foggia was a crucial factor in the RAF's decision to get involved in the Italian campaign.

The city fared terribly in 1943: Allied bombing resulted in 20,298 civilian victims during nine raids. The most severe were on 19 August: carpet-bombing of the entire city (9,581 victims); and 24–25 August: thousands of bombs dropped on the city (971 victims).

The Allies' objective in late 1943 was to disrupt the Germans' use of the transport network and airfields at Foggia; vital in the dispersal and deployment of German and Italian troops countering the Allied attacks on southern Italy and the invasion of Sicily in July (Operations HUSKY, AVALANCHE and SLAPSTICK). There have since been allegations of excessive force on the part of the Allies and that the raids were overzealous, causing inordinately high numbers of deaths and other casualties; about a third of the population was killed. The raids continued after the armistice signed between the Allies and Italy because German troops continued to occupy Foggia in large numbers.

The 1st Air Landing Brigade had been substantially reinforced between July and September 1943 to compensate for the casualties sustained in Sicily, and was soon sufficiently up to full strength so as to be able to accompany the 1st Airborne Division on its invasion of Italy on 9 September. Initially, the 1st Air Landing and 1st Para brigades were held in reserve, while the 2nd and 4th Para brigades advanced inland. However, on 19 September, the 1st Air Landing Brigade was ordered to advance up the line to relieve the 4th Para Brigade in its forward position;

here it remained until, soon after, the whole division, with the exception of the 1st Air Landing Light Regiment and the 2nd Parachute Brigade, sailed for England to train for Operation OVERLORD.[41]

This was to be the 1st Air Landing Regiment's baptism of fire; their first taste of combat. Their Taranto landing took place on 30 September, after which they drove the 40 miles to Gioia. A visit by Brigadier Hornby of the Eighth Army on 1 October was probably responsible for getting the regiment its first battle. The visibly impressed brigadier was particularly interested in the regiment's trailers and enquired as to how he might obtain one. Colonel Thompson replied saying that he could have one if his regiment could have a battle. By 4 October, the 1st Air Landing Light Regiment found itself attached to General Dempsey's XIII Corps and detailed to serve alongside the 1st Canadian Division on the left flank of the Eighth Army up in the mountains. Within the division they would support the Hastings and Prince Edward Regiment, the 48th Highlanders of Canada, Princess Patricia's Canadian Light Infantry and the Carleton and York Regiment (Truesdale, p.29).

No. 1 Battery was soon able to demonstrate the versatility of their guns that could go to places where the heavier 25-pounders and other guns could not; however, this came with the chilling sight of Canadian Shermans brewing up, the scene embroidered by the equally chilling row of four crosses. Five tanks and a 25-pounder with their own four crosses were destroyed by *Kampfgruppe* Heilmann which included a battalion of the 67 Panzer Grenadier Regiment and of a *Fallschirmjäger* Regiment (Truesdale, p.29). No. 1 Brigade and the regiment could clearly see the writing on the wall.

Originally the 1st Air Landing Light Regiment's role was to support the 1st Airborne Division against dogged enemy resistance, deep snow, freezing temperatures, poor visibility and sucking, sticky mud. With the division withdrawn back to England, the regiment came, as noted above, under the command of the Eighth Army in close support high up in the Apennines and in the towns and villages in the deep valleys. They went on to fire for the 1st Canadian Infantry Division at Campobasso.[42] In October they supported the British 5th Infantry Division at Rionero Sannitico (28 miles north-west of Campobasso and 9 miles north-west of Isernia) and then Isernia in November which suffered intense bombing by the Americans in thirteen separate sorties in a failed attempt to destroy the bridges of Isernia, Cardarelli and Santo Spirito which were vital for the German fighting retreat.

After Campobasso, the regiment backed up the 2nd New Zealand Division in five unsuccessful attacks on Orsogna – on the Bernhardt Line – similarly bombed.[43] Next they fired in support of the Independent 2nd Parachute Brigade and the British 78th Infantry Division from mid-December 1943 to January 1944 at Casoli (Allied bomb-free and the site of a fascist internment camp), Gessopalena and Roccascalegna. Casoli saw B Troop cut off by snowdrifts for forty-eight hours.

The 1st Canadian Infantry Division had transferred to the Mediterranean theatre in June 1943 where the division saw action in Operation HUSKY. The division came under command of the British XXX Corps, serving alongside the veteran 51st (Highland) Division, part of the British Eighth Army, commanded by Montgomery. The campaign cost the Canadians more than 2,100 casualties.

They then landed in Calabria as part of Operation BAYTOWN and battled their way up the Italian peninsula, fighting in the Moro River campaign supported by tanks of the 1st Canadian Armoured Brigade. They took part in the Battle of Ortona on the Gustav Line, fighting against the famous German *Fallschirmjäger* – crack Air Force paratroops of the 1st Parachute Division under *Generalleutnant* Richard Heidrich – over Christmas 1943. Both sides suffered heavy losses in the fight for the town, which a reporter for the *New York Times* reputedly dubbed a 'miniature Stalingrad' based on the ferocity of the street-fighting and the heavy losses on both sides; the Canadians suffered 650 casualties, mainly in the 3rd Brigade. By 27 December, what remained of Ortona after days of shelling and aerial bombardment was in Canadian hands.[44]

At Ortona the blizzards, drifting snow and freezing temperatures conspired with the terrain and the Germans to present a formidable enemy that brought progress to a virtual halt. However, Ortona was finally secured on 28 December. River Moro War Cemetery is the burial ground for 1,615 military; mostly Canadian, but it also contains other Allied service personnel. Warden (2015) adds some distressing detail regarding Sangro River War Cemetery:

> Sangro River War Cemetery has 2,617 burials, with a memorial commemorating more than 500 Indian service members who died

fighting in the sector. In addition, the cemetery contains the graves of a number of escaped prisoners of war who died whilst trying to reach the Allied lines. Sangro cemetery is the second largest cemetery in Italy after Cassino. There are 2,117 different regiments buried there, including 279 from the Royal Artillery, 352 from New Zealand, 837 from the Combined Indian Regiments and 62 from the Parachute Regiment.

After this the division spent many months kicking their heels in reserve. They eventually went on to break out of the Eighth Army's bridgehead with the second wave in the spring offensive, Operation DIADEM, the fourth Battle of Monte Cassino.

Campobasso found the Germans staging a fighting withdrawal, once again in rugged mountain terrain; 'bleak country' well suited to defence. 'Canadian soldiers.com' tells us how 'German records recorded heavy casualties, often a result of Allied artillery, and enemy commanders faced the constant dilemma of whether to continue resistance in the face of heavy supporting fires, risking further heavy losses they could not afford, or further withdrawals.'[45]

Campobasso, 'the wedding cake' of Central Italy, was the First Canadian Infantry divisional objective. G.K. Wright (1947) tells how it was

> rumoured to be the headquarters of General Kesselring, and being the main crossroads in the Daunia Mountains, its capture was of considerable urgency. With it in our hands the Allied Force in Italy would no longer have to use the roads of the Foggia plains, some fifty miles to the south.

The 1st Air Landing Light Regiment support came during this extended battle during October and November 1943, ultimately fighting for possession of the city. Such was the intensity of the shelling that many public buildings, including the City Hall and the archives deposited there, were destroyed. Thirty-eight civilians lost their lives, with an unknown number of people injured. The bombardment and subsequent occupation from 13 October by the Canadian troops made such an impression on the town that it became popularly known as 'Canada Town' or 'Maple Leaf City'.

The 1st Air Landing Light Regiment's Italian Campaign

The day of 7 October was when the Canadian 3rd Brigade took Gambatesa (12 miles south of Campobasso); the same day that the first casualties were inflicted on Air Landing Light Regiment 1 Battery. A night drive to the Fortore River led to the deaths of Gunner Stanley Briggs and Sergeant John Lees when their jeep careered into the river; despite marker stones left by the Canadians, the driver could not see that the bridge had been blown (Truesdale, p.29). Sergeant Neil Tierney tells how next day 3 Battery (whose motto was 'Bash on') bashed on and found itself 3 miles outside Gambatesa marooned in the middle of a minefield on a diversion around the blown bridge; sitting ducks for the German guns. According to Lieutenant 'Teddy' Thompson, FOO of 3 Battery, F Troop, their guns were out of range but they survived by bringing forward a battery of medium guns well to the rear.

John Widdicombe's diary reveals how 2 and 3 Batteries were positioned on a steep slope in a quagmire of slush and mud; ahead of them was Gambatesa which the Germans had vacated, but not before comprehensively mining it. The 2 Battery Command Post received near misses, while three shells fell around F Troop, killing Gunner Albert Barkham and Bombardier James Sullivan who was manning a machine-gun post at the time; Lieutenant Vergette was seriously injured. Later in the afternoon Gunner Chrystal, as noted, was also seriously injured in the lower back by shrapnel while operating his radio set in the command post; he was evacuated to hospital in Malta. A 3 Battery jeep was blown up, killing Sergeant Lees and Gunner Briggs, the OPA; Johnny Walker was injured. The Germans were shelling Gambatesa from above, and Johnny Walker tells how 'One of 2 Battery's FOO Jeeps caught it. Two fellows wounded and one killed [Sergeant Lees and Gunner Briggs, the OPA; Johnny Walker suffered a broken arm]. Also a shell dropped smack beside one of their guns behind us, killing one gunner and wounding two or three others.'[46] The batteries followed the Germans back to Jelsi, and on Saturday, 9 October the Germans started shelling a crossroads held by the Canadians about half a mile in front of 3 and 2 Batteries:

> Two or three [shells] burst unpleasantly close and shook us up considerably in the Command Post. The two shells exploded on Fox Troop position, straddling it, and another one fell right between two guns. Well, we were firing at the time and our chaps had it. Two were

wounded and Bob Vergette caught a splinter in his throat. (Gunners Hardy and Jellyman both died of their wounds a few days later)…. That afternoon we had some more and signaller Eric Chrystal was [seriously] hurt.[47]

Booby traps, like mines, were an ever-present threat. Mutilated children were not an uncommon sight, as witnessed by Lieutenant Frank Moore of 3 Battery. One such device awaited 2 Battery's Lieutenant Eustace McNaught and a sapper major during a recce in Jelsi. Returning to their jeep, they noticed a telltale wire, a sure booby trap, which the sapper started to disable. The Germans opened fire with mortars, blowing the major off his feet. Retreat was the only option given that the jeep was still live; mortar bombs pursued them all the way, the major was hit in the thigh by shrapnel and was evacuated to Malta (Truesdale, p.30).

The day of 13 October was a busy one for 3 Battery: Major Munford, Captain Harrison and Lieutenant Griffiths were deployed as FOOs for the Canadian Hastings and Prince Edward Regiment, advancing soon after midnight with their 'A' Company under Major Nichol. The objective was to take a road junction and funnel reconnaissance patrols down the Termoli road and meet up with the British 5th Division. John Buchan, 2nd Baron Tweedsmuir (the son of the novelist John Buchan, 1st Baron Tweedsmuir), CO Hastings and Prince Edward Regiment, halted his battalion at Gildone and waited until dawn broke in order to carry out a reconnaissance between Gildone and Campobasso. At 0630 hours the battalion advanced with mine-sweeping Canadian Royal Engineers, Major Munford and his men and FOOs from the 2nd Field Regiment. At 11.00 the Germans opened up. After coming under fire several times, with the loss of one dead and several injured, Lieutenant Wilkinson of the Highlanders was detailed to advance with 'B' Company of the Highlanders and take on the role of FOO for 3 Battery. He, along with Signaller G.A. Taylor and eight infantrymen, occupied a house as an OP which came under intense machine-gun fire; they exchanged grenades with German assailants and were attacked by a German Panzer which loosed an armour-piercing shell on the building. Thankfully, it had bigger fish to fry. Both Wilkinson and Taylor were injured, but managed to drive back to the battery; they were awarded the Military Cross and the Military Medal respectively (Truesdale, pp.31–33).

The 1st Air Landing Light Regiment's Italian Campaign

On 24 October 3 Battery (working with the Carlton and York Regiment of the 2nd Canadian Infantry Brigade) was relieved by 2 Battery commanded by Major James Edward Fryer 'Jef' Linton; next day they were carrying out a recce for the gun position when they were 'surprised by some enemy tanks'. However, the tanks focused their fire on a group of Canadian engineers, 3 Field Company, who were building a crossing over the Biferno. This was the first time in the war that a Bailey bridge had been constructed under enemy fire. The Canadians lost two men (Truesdale, p.33).

Truesdale (p.34) tells how 1 and 3 Batteries hitched a ride over the Biferno on Canadian Sherman tanks with the guns lashed to the engine decks: each tank carried one gun, while another four transported the ammunition, forty-eight rounds per gun. 'Sheriff' Thompson believed that this was the first time that an artillery battery had been taken into battle on the back of a tank.

Woollacott (p.43), via 'Sheriff' Thompson, tells us how the 'The Regiment, less one Battery [2 Battery] remained in Campobasso until 26th October, when they were ordered to support the 1 Canadian Infantry Brigade which was to cross the Biferno and occupy a ridge on which were the villages of Molise and Torella.' On 27 October 3 Battery, RHQ and the battery transport arrived in Molise. Major Munford, under cover of mist, set up an OP in the spire of the church.

> As the mist cleared the Germans launched a counter attack against the Canadians.... Gunner Bowles [at the base of the steeple] operated the set sending back a constant stream of messages despite ferocious German counter bombardment and flying shrapnel in and around the church tower. At a range of some 1,500 yards the enemy provided an ideal target and Munford was able to call in fire not only from both 1 and 3 batteries, but also from the guns of 2 field and a medium regiment (Truesdale, p.36).

The action as reported in post-action intelligence reports confirmed the obliteration of a German self-propelled 105mm battery and 'large amounts of transport'. Baron Tweedsmuir, CO of Hastings and Prince Edward Regiment, reported six machine-gun nests destroyed, two tanks disabled and fifty enemy troops killed. However, it came at a cost when

Lieutenant John Murray of 2 Battery was killed with a Canadian soldier, Private John Lenehan when the latter stepped on a mine, despite many of them being marked by a circle of white stones by local Italian troops (Truesdale, p.37).

No. 3 Battery's sojourn in Campobasso was short – just one day – before they vacated the town in support of the Canadians. On 27 October the regiment (less 2 Battery) was firing around Roccaspromonte with 1 Battery supporting the 48th Highlanders of Canada and 3 Battery supporting Hastings and Prince Edward's Regiment.[48] No. 3 Battery then moved 'from Campobasso to Borjano, then north through Spinetta and St Helena...and then into position near Macchiagodena from 1–3 November'.[49] The Regimental War Diary reveals that they fired at St Angelo on 1 November. It was then that news was filtering in that the 1st Airborne Division was being recalled to the UK, while the 2nd Parachute Brigade and the 1st Air Landing Light Regiment would stay until the New Year. By November two batteries – 1 and 3 – were under the 15th Brigade, British 5th Infantry Division in their advance to the Sangro River, while 2 Battery continued its support of the Canadians. That same day 3 Battery was shelled at 10.30; the cookhouse took a hit, injuring three cooks and seriously wounding Captain Hendrik Greyvenstein who was hospitalized in Cairo. Gunners Ronald Manchester (19) and Frederick O'Grady both died later from their wounds. Then 7 November saw 1 and 3 Batteries cross the River Vandra at 1800 hours with their guns in position less than four hours later, despite the reservations of the Commander Royal Engineers (CRE) of the 92 Field Regiment that the river could not be bridged in less than forty hours. On 8 November the regiment moved to south of Isernia under the command of the 15th Brigade in the 5th Division (Truesdale, pp.40–41). By 17 November RHQ and 3 Battery were in St Helena with 1 Battery and the 'A' Echelon in Spinetta.

Then 24 November saw 1 and 3 Batteries reach Capracotta (situated on a ridge at 4,000ft) after a quiet period due to atrocious weather; here they joined up with 2 Battery which had been supporting 2 Canadian Infantry Brigade since 5 November. The local response, indeed retort, to yet another German bombardment with 150mm air bursts was, as described by Sergeant Neil Tierney, the choristers of the local church, San Eusonia, in a rousing rendition of Thomas of Celano's *Dies Irae* (*The Day of Wrath*), the Amen from which eclipsed the thundering guns 'perhaps as high as the throne of God' and 'drifted down like sunbeams on the weary soldiers listening outside'. Communications were compromised when Italians started using battery land lines as clothes lines. Munford's furious threats should there be a recurrence restored relations and communications (Truesdale, p.47). After a visit to an impromptu art exhibition in Campobasso two Canadian war artists impressed Colonel Thompson: they were William Ogilvie and Charles Comfort, and they were invited to spend time with the regiment. They duly rolled up in Elena with their equipment in a 15cwt truck and were billeted above a bakery in the town. Thompson and Major Keith-Jones gave them a schedule which they completed despite the rain and captured the essence of the regiment and its work. Comfort's work is published in his 1956 *Artist at War* (Truesdale, p.43). Malaria and yellow jaundice continued to plague the regiment with numerous soldiers infected; Lieutenant Brian Devlin, the regiment's medical officer, died of yellow jaundice.

On 2 December the whole regiment descended into the plains to support 2 New Zealand Division. A German truck was taken out en route while the regiment was replaced with a battery from 78 Field Regiment.

Captain Tudor Griffiths moved with his F Troop to establish his OP in the village of Pescopennataro some two hours' march away on 26 November. Woollacott (p.65) reports a particularly unsavoury incident described in a letter from Tierney to Woollacott which took place around this time. The church at Pescopennataro, 28 miles north-west of Campobasso and about 19 miles north of Isernia, was full of wounded Italians, several of whom had their arms cut off by the Nazis; all the regiment could do was send up medical supplies the following day. This atrocity was indicative of the Germans' behaviour generally where they systematically laid waste many of the towns and villages they retreated through in a bid to destroy anything that could have been used for winter quarters by the Allies. No doubt there was a good deal of summary execution, rape and pillaging as well. Castel di Sangro,[50] Ateleta, Gamberale and St Angelo were among the places that suffered.

No. 3 Battery deployed a 'roving gun' around Pizzoferrato, successfully firing on a number of machine-gun posts and the church steeple at Quadri which the Germans had commandeered as an OP.

Warden (2015) reveals how

> What has never been reported is the raid by German bombers on the port of Bari on the evening of 2 December 1943. A small number of planes succeeded in destroying 17 Allied merchant ships and killing well over 1,000 military personnel, merchant seamen and many local civilians. The Commonwealth Cemetery in Bari contains 2,128 graves. It is reported that every available docking space was occupied, with ships anchored out beyond the jetties jutting out into the Adriatic. The dockyards had become such a beehive of activity that unloading was carried out during the night under the glare of lights. The German bombers had a perfect target – it was described as a 'cake walk'. The ships already in the harbour contained a great store of ammunition, along with trucks, bales of clothing and hundreds of canvas mail bags for the troops. Alongside them was a US Navy tanker with half a million gallons of high-octane gasoline on board. One ship, *John Harvey*, carried as part of its cargo 100 tons of mustard gas bombs. It was thought that Germany was going to use mustard gas in attacks during the campaigns in Italy; they did not!

On 7 December the Light Regiment supported the Kiwis in Operation TORSO against Orsogna, supported on the left flank by the British 2nd Independent Parachute Brigade, other artillery units and air attacks (Truesdale, p.50). They were up against the LXXVI Panzer Corps. The Light Regiment opened up at 1300 hours as planned in support of the right flank of the New Zealand 28th (Maori) Battalion. Despite the absence of the promised armour and anti-tank guns, the Light Regiment was able to help cut the Orsogna-Ortona road under the Pascucci spur. However, the enemy rallied and furious house-to-house fighting ensued; the Allied advance stalled and withdrew on 8 December. That day enemy airbursts just missed the officers' mess and RHQ; ammunition was now in short supply and limited to ten rounds per gun per day. From 19 to 25 December this was further reduced to five rounds; any more than this required the permission of the brigade commander.

On 10 December, B Troop of 1 Battery was, due to lack of space, detailed to take up positions near Sant'Eusanio where they were designated the local cemetery; unsurprisingly this did little for morale and the troops were reluctant 'to dig too deep when it came to slit trenches'. Woollacott remembers how 'It was an eerie experience with the eyes of the dead constantly keeping us under surveillance.' The situation was made worse when it was announced by Lieutenant Challoner of F Troop, 3 Battery that all the regiment's equipment had gone to the bottom of Bari harbour in that surprise air-raid.[51]

The regiment parted company with the 2nd New Zealand Division on 11 December and moved back up into the mountains at Casoli, coming under the command of the 2nd Independent Parachute Brigade.[52] On Christmas Day 1943 1 and 3 Batteries passed over to the command of the 2nd Battalion of the Royal Inniskilling Fusiliers, part of the 13th Brigade, 5th Infantry Division. Generally the winter of 1943–44 was horrendous. New Year's Eve was when the Inniskillings attacked Civitella south of Gessopalena; they were supported by an OP team led by Captain Johnny Walker of B Troop, 1 Battery and heading for one of the Inniskilling HQs on Il Monte 2,400ft above sea level. The snow came with a vengeance and motorcycles and jeeps started to disappear. The gunners' barn was badly exposed. The 78th Division lost 5 men to the unremitting deep cold, 'frozen stiff at their sentry posts', with another 113 cases of extreme exposure. The Light Regiment itself was luckier, getting away with 'a number of cases of severe exposure'.[53] The snow was 18in deep with drifts of up to 7ft in height.

The 1st Air Landing Light Regiment was withdrawn on 8 January, having handed over their newly-cleaned and polished equipment to the 132nd Field Regiment at Casacalenda and retired to the Gioia area two days later. The equipment was then handed over to the 165th Field Regiment RA at Larino. From here the regiment returned to Taranto and, after much delay, little food and the loss of yet more kit, they boarded the troopship HMS *Ranchi* on 26 January and set sail to rejoin the 1st Airborne Division in Boston, Lincolnshire.[54] It would appear that the most significant events on the journey were the frequent Freedom From Infection (FFI) checks – Captain Randall Martin recalls the regiment being infested with lice – which were a common annoyance for armies the world over throughout the history of war.

Boston, Lincolnshire

Another inconvenience was the custom check inflicted on the troops at Greenock; a much damaged port due to it being the rendezvous point for Atlantic convoys and the base for the Home Fleet.[55] Unconsumed drink, illegal weapons and other war booty all had to be jettisoned. The much-rumoured destination, Boston, was eventually established to be in Lincolnshire, thus obviating the need for an onward trip to Massachusetts. The period of 15–28 February saw the regiment enjoying disembarkation leave.

Back in Lincolnshire an intense training programme awaited the 1st Airborne Division and the regiment, which was undertaken under the supervision of I Airborne Corps commanded by Lieutenant General Browning. Particularly rewarding was the focus on communications and signals exercises; time well spent given what was to go spectacularly wrong in Arnhem. The regiment had to get used to working alongside parachute and other air-landing troops coordinating firing alongside other units, as well as perfecting the art of loading and unloading a Horsa. Salisbury Plain and nearby Hunstanton ranges were the places where many of the shoot-offs took place. Gun pit design was all-important so that the howitzer could fire in a 360° arc while providing the gunners with optimum protection from enemy mortar and small-arms fire. Viable artillery boards presented another challenge, which was eventually overcome by 'a small group of specialists trained for this vital job.' 'Airborne rafting' was revived, having been put on hold due to the often torrential nature of rivers in Italy. The aim was to build and float a raft capable of transporting a 30cwt load. One of the successes was 2 Battery's crossing of the Thames at Windsor. However, glider experience was essential: one exercise involved E Troop, 3 Battery's Gunner Len Smith, Bombardier Leo Hall, the troop lance sergeant and two other gunners whose Horsa was accidentally cast off by its Dakota tug, depositing it near Taunton some 100 miles from its landing zone. After being apprehended by the local Home Guard, they passed the rest of the evening joy-riding on Hall's motor cycle and drinking cider.

In Boston 1 and 3 Batteries were destined for the Dock Camp while 2 Battery 'were scattered around in private houses which had been requisitioned'.[56] The local area around Boston was described as 'a marvellous place for the troops, with two dance halls, four cinemas, eighty-three pubs, and the girls used to whistle at us; but, being in the Fens, the area was useless when it came to gunnery practice.'⁵⁷ However, on 1 April they moved lock, stock and barrel to the huts of Marlborough Lines in Bulford.

As we know, the division was to have no primary role in the Normandy landings, although Operation WASTAGE was a contingency plan drawn up whereby all of the 1st Airborne Division would be parachuted in to reinforce any of the five invasion beaches if delays or unexpectedly serious opposition were experienced.⁵⁸

The Light Regiment learned of the momentous events of 6 June somewhat casually at breakfast, after which they moved into the barracks just vacated by the 53rd Air Landing Light Regiment who were now busy in Normandy. This high-security barracks had the air of a PoW camp and featured wall-to-wall barbed wire.

Things were warming up: 9 June saw the individual batteries relocate to their designated airfields: RHQ and 1 Battery to Harwell, 2 Battery and the anti-tank troop to Down Ampney and 3 Battery to RAF Broadwell.⁵⁹

Aborted missions planned for the division in June and July 1944 were numerous (fifteen or so in three months), all designed to support the Allies as they pushed inland after D-Day. Some of these planned operations even got as far as troops boarding gliders; however, the rapid advance of the Allies in Normandy necessitated cancellation because airborne objectives had already been overrun:

Operation REINFORCEMENT: a parachute drop to the west of St Sauveur-le-Vicomte in Normandy to support the US 82nd Airborne Division.

Operation WILD OATS: a drop onto Carpiquet airfield, 4 miles west of Caen.

Operation BENEFICIARY: supporting US XX Corps to capture St Malo.

Operation LUCKY STRIKE: a plan to seize the bridges crossing the River Seine at Rouen.

Operation SWORD HILT: cutting off the port of Brest and destroying the Morlaix viaduct.

Operation HANDS UP: in support of the US Third Army under Patton by seizing Vannes airfield in Brittany.

In August Operation TRANSFIGURE involved the British 1st and US 101st Airborne divisions, with the 52nd (Lowland) Infantry Division and Polish 1st Parachute Brigade landing at Rambouillet-St Arnoult to plug the gap between Orléans and Paris.

Operation AXEHEAD: deployed the same force to take bridges over the Seine in support of the 21st Army Group.

Operation BOXER: using the same forces yet again to seize Boulogne and attack V1 rocket sites.[60]

Operations LINNET 1 and 2: in late August the planning for LINNET was begun with the same units. The plan was for the entire 1st Allied Airborne Army to be dropped behind the enemy and seize roads in the areas of Tournai, Lille and Courtrai in order to cut off the Germans' retreat. The second version of this plan was eventually cancelled on 5 September.

Operation INFATUATE: in early September involved 1st Airborne Corps landing in the Scheldt estuary to threaten Antwerp.[61]

See below for Operation COMET (p.48).[62]

Major Anthony Cotterell describes the tension and disappointment every time an operation was cancelled in a piece he wrote as War Staff writer while at Parachute Brigade HQ attached to the 1st Airborne Division from 8 September:

> The Bde Staff was in a state of considerable apprehension; not that the operation would take place but that it wouldn't...and they found each stand-down progressively discouraging. Chutes were drawn and withdrawn, timings were revised on account of the weather with one reveille rescheduled for 0300 and bedtime at 2000. Arnhem was delayed for 36 hours, then for a further 24 hours. On Saturday 9th September the Battery Major asked 'Do you realise we've been on 36 hours' notice for getting on for a month?.... You get no marks for mental strain.'[63]

The 1st Seaborne Echelon (1st Airborne Division)

The Regimental War Diary for 13 August 1944 reveals that 'at 7.00 Seaborne Echelon left Boston for T2 Transit Camp near London Docks.'

The 1st Air Landing Light Regiment's Italian Campaign 41

Strength was 84 officers and 2,180 ORs with 1,000 vehicles. The following day their twenty ships moved down the Thames, arriving off Normandy with little incident on 16 August. At 1830 hours on 17 August they landed on 'Mike' beach via the Mulberry Harbour. By the 18th the echelon was established in the La Mine area, where it stayed for the next fortnight. The day of 1 September saw them move off in Operation LINNET to Parnes, then across the Seine through Amiens and into Belgium, arriving at Helchteren close to the 2nd Army's bridgehead over the Meuse-Escaut Canal. Their continued progress forward eventually saw them merge into Operation MARKET GARDEN.[64]

Chapter Five

Wounded and Recovery in Malta

Malta has a proud and illustrious history of providing military hospital facilities and convalescent camps; the numerous Military Medical Units active in Malta during the Great War of 1914–19 can be found in impressive detail at https://www.maltaramc.com/articles/contents/greatwar.html

During the Great War, as in the Crimean War, Malta was regarded as a 'Nurse of the Mediterranean'. From the Gallipoli campaigns alone, 2,500 officers and 55,400 troops were treated in the Maltese hospitals, while from the 1917 Salonika campaigns even more were admitted: 2,600 officers and 64,500 other ranks. Obviously this all required a prodigious number of beds: for example, beds in the Valletta Military Hospital were increased from 26 to 340 and later to 440. The Valletta Station Hospital served as a triage base for the wounded arriving in the hospital ships before being transferred to the thirty other hospitals and camps scattered over the islands. The Valletta Hospital itself was reserved for dangerously ill cases that could not be safely moved. The principal hospitals and camps used were the commissioned naval and military hospitals: Bighi Naval Hospital, Valletta Hospital, Cottonera Hospital, Forrest Hospital, Mtarfa Hospital (commissioned in 1912) and Chambray Convalescent Depot. Other hospitals and hospital camps were set up including the Hamrun Hospital, St. Andrew's Hospital, St. George's Hospital, St. Paul's Hospital (close to St. Andrew's), St. David's Hospital and St. Patrick's Hospital, St. John's Hospital (in the Sliema Primary School), St. Ignatius Hospital (in the old Jesuit College in St. Julian's), Tigne Hospital, St. Elmo and Bavière Hospitals in Valletta, Manoel Hospital, the Blue Sisters' Hospital and the Ghajn Tuffieha Camp.

After the First World War, there was a reorganization of the military medical services on the islands. At the end of the nineteenth century, military barracks with an adjoining Military Families' Hospital had been built on Mtarfa Hill; the hospital catering only for the families of the troops housed fifty patients. The Mtarfa Hospital, commissioned in 1912, was opened on 29 June 1920, even though it had been in use for some time earlier. The Mtarfa military hospital was initially staffed by thirty members of 30 Coy, Royal Army Medical Corps (RAMC). After all other regimental hospitals had closed their doors, the Station Hospital at Mtarfa became the only army hospital in Malta: all patients in the various other military hospitals were transferred there and the military hospitals scattered around Malta were officially closed in subsequent years. During the Second World War, the Mtarfa Hospital and barracks were reorganized as 90 British General Hospital (90 BGH), and it increased its number of beds from 200 to 2,000 by taking over the whole of the infantry barracks for hospital wards and the pitching of tented wards on the football pitch. The 90 BGH reverted to 600 beds in late 1944. An underground hospital – a system of rooms and tunnels used as a shelter during the battle for Malta during the Second World War – had been excavated under the military hospital. At the end of hostilities, the 90th General Hospital was disbanded and re-formed on a peacetime footing as the David Bruce Military Hospital.

Gunner Chrystal was admitted, treated and recuperated at the 90 British General Hospital (90 BGH).

Chapter Six

Operation MARKET GARDEN: The Plan

The objectives, planning and events leading up to the Battle of Arnhem have been comprehensively and extensively examined and described over the past eighty years.[1] There seems, therefore, little need to repeat these accounts in any great detail but, since we are concerned with the role played by the 1st Air Landing Light Regiment and specifically 3 Battery in that huge, complex operation, it is necessary to offer a brief summary in order to place the actions of the regiment and batteries in context. We need to explain how and why the 1st Air Landing Light Regiment, after a period of enforced inactivity, found themselves in a hastily-planned operation hundreds of miles behind enemy lines, in some cases 7 miles from their objective, with temperamental radios and up against two German Panzer regiments lurking nearby that had, until the last minute, apparently remained invisible to and undetected by British army intelligence.[2]

In reality, Major General Urquhart, Ultra and the Dutch resistance were, of course, right. Earlier in 1944, in a bid to stem the unfolding disaster in the wider Low Countries Hitler had established the 1st *Fallschirmjäger* Army under General Kurt Student, founder of the German airborne forces made up of crack paratroopers reinforced with two divisions of aging inexperienced men and semi-invalids. These were organized into separate battalions determined by their ailments; there were even special kitchens catering for those with stomach disorders. Across the Netherlands generally there were various units comprising Luftwaffe soldiers, sailors and anti-aircraft crews all deployed to assist Student. Special trains had sped these forces into the Netherlands where they dug in along the Albert Canal to reinforce Walther Model's Army Group B.

The bad news, however, was that the II Panzer Corps was not so very far away from Arnhem. Model had ordered the regiment to rest and refit after fighting non-stop from Normandy and this they did, allowing SS *Obergruppenführer* Wilhelm Bittrich to organize the refitting and rehabilitation of the 9th SS *Hohenstaufen* and 10th SS *Frundsberg* in a remote and peaceful place not so very far from Arnhem to the northeast of the town in a densely wooded national park. *Hohenstaufen* was encamped in and around the villages of Doetinchem, Ruurlo, Zutphen, Apeldoorn and Beekbergen. Despite all the recent losses since June 1944 and the growing belief that the war was all but over for Germany, morale was high.

Major General Roy Urquhart, Chief of Intelligence British I Airborne Corps, commented: 'I simply did not believe that the Germans were going to roll over and surrender.' There was poor coordination between SHAEF, 21st Army Group and the First Allied Airborne Army, which meant that although the overall estimated strength of the German forces was reasonably accurate, Allied intelligence 'lost' the II SS Panzer Corps as it approached the Arnhem area. Most assumed that they had moved east rather than stayed around Arnhem. Reports by the Dutch resistance and last-minute aerial reconnaissance photographs indicated the presence of an armoured formation, as Urquhart commented: 'There, in the photos, I could clearly see tanks – if not on the very Arnhem landing and drop zones, then certainly close to them.' These reports were, however, dismissed all along the chain of command, the result being that 'the evaluation of intelligence on the Panzers in the Arnhem area was magnificently bungled.' (See Baxter, pp.24–25. http://www.historyofwar.org/articles/battles_arnhem.html)

In September Bletchley Park was producing Ultra intelligence reports that were sent to senior Allied commanders, but they only got to army headquarters level and did not percolate any lower (Harclerode, 2005, p.456). They revealed the movement of the 9th SS and 10th SS Panzer divisions to Nijmegen and Arnhem, creating enough concern for Eisenhower to send his chief of staff, Lieutenant General Walter Bedell Smith, to raise the issue with Montgomery on 10 September. However, Montgomery dismissed Smith's concerns and refused to alter the plans (Harclerode, 2005, p.460). For the ignoring of Ultra, see Jeffson, *Operation Market Garden: Ultra Intelligence Ignored*.

As noted above, more information regarding the location of the German Panzer divisions was revealed by aerial photographs of Arnhem taken by a photo-reconnaissance Spitfire XI from the RAF's No. 16 Squadron (Dibbs, 2000, p.119) as well as high-grade intelligence from the

Dutch resistance. Major General Roy Urquhart met with Browning to inform him of the armoured presence at Arnhem. Browning peremptorily dismissed his claims and ordered the division's senior medical officer to send Urquhart on sick leave on account of 'nervous strain and exhaustion' (Middlebrook, 1995, pp.64–66). It seems that nothing was going to derail the accelerating battle of egos raging in the highest echelons.

John C. Warren (1956, p.99) noted that MARKET was the only large airborne operation of the war in which the USAAF 'had no training program, no rehearsals, almost no exercises, and a…low level of tactical training'.

On 16 September *Generalfeldmarschall* Walther Model took up residence in the Hartenstein Hotel in Oosterbeek, east of the British drop zones. The II SS Panzer Corps did not come under Model's forces, but under Armed Forces Command Netherlands while it rested and refitted. *Obergruppenführer* Bittrich had his headquarters in Doetinchem (15 miles east of Arnhem) with his forces spread out between Arnhem and Deventer. SS *Kampfgruppe Hohenstaufen* (the remnants of the 9th *Hohenstaufen* SS Panzer Division) was due to move to Siegen (near Koblenz) to be refitted from 12 to 17 September. SS *Kampfgruppe Frundsberg* (what was left of the 10th *Frundsberg* SS Panzer Division) was then to move to Aachen. Bittrich sent *Brigadeführer* Harmel to SS Headquarters in Berlin to personally plead for reinforcements, just in case. The shortage of troops had already been noted by Rundstedt in a letter to OKW, stating that 'the danger of new reverses…can be removed only by speeding up the dispatch of the reinforcements that have repeatedly been requested.' Meanwhile, *Obersturmbannführer* Harzer got on with organizing the troops for the move east. The 17 September landings would take them completely by surprise.

Operation MARKET GARDEN took place from 17 to 27 September 1944. It was, and still is, the largest airborne battle in history; it eclipsed Operation MERCURY, the 1941 German airborne invasion of Crete, which at the time was the Second World War's only successful strategic airborne operation.[3] MARKET GARDEN also has the honour of being the Allies' only viable attempt to deploy airborne forces in a strategic role in Europe. Its protagonists were 21 Army Group under Montgomery and Army Group B under *Generalfeldmarschall* Walther Model. All in all it involved thousands of aircraft and armoured vehicles and hundreds of thousands of troops: it was the only major Allied defeat of the North-West European campaign. Its aims and scope were to carve out a 64-mile salient into German-occupied territory in the Netherlands, thus creating a bridgehead over the River Rhine that would provide an Allied invasion highway into northern Germany.[4] Two separate but complementary dovetailing operations would achieve this: first, the seizing and securing of nine bridges by combined US and British airborne forces (the MARKET element). This was to be reinforced by land forces, the Second Army, from the Dutch-Belgian border to the Zuider Zee 99 miles away, and rapidly flowing over the bridges on the Rhine and its tributaries towards Germany (GARDEN, the famous 'airborne carpet'), consolidating north of Arnhem on the Dutch-German border, poised to advance into Germany and capture the industrial heartland that was the Ruhr, the beating heart of the Reich. The principal bridges in question were, of course, at Eindhoven, Nijmegen and Arnhem with two smaller bridges at Veghel and Grave between Eindhoven and Nijmegen.[5] Success would enable the Allies to cut off the German occupying forces in the western Netherlands, disable a number of lethal V2 rocket sites and open the way for an Allied advance into the north German plain.

An over-confident Montgomery believed that it would be necessary only to hold the bridge at Arnhem for two days. Corps Commander Browning conceded ambiguously that they might hold it for four days, but added 'But I think we are going a bridge too far'; a screenwriter's dream gift three decades later.

The airborne element of the operation was to be the responsibility of the 1st Allied Airborne Army (the US Army's 82nd and 101st Airborne divisions, the British 1st Airborne and the 1st Polish Parachute Brigade), while the land operation was undertaken by XXX Corps of the British Second Army.[6] The role of the 1st Air Landing Light Regiment was clear and crucial: help to take and secure Arnhem Bridge and support the operation from the Meuse-Escaut Canal to the Rhine and the perimeter around Oosterbeek. So vital was the regiment's contribution to the success of the plan thought to be that Batteries 1 and 3 were to be in the first drop on the first day, followed by 2 Battery on the 18th. To add to the problems caused by the distance from landing zones to the objective, terrain was also an issue. The thick woodland and buildings thereabouts would not facilitate the most effective OPs and gun positions. Nevertheless, on Day

One both batteries were tasked with defending the LZs but 3 Battery could be positioned further east within range of the bridge.[7]

The combined operation succeeded in liberating the Dutch cities of Eindhoven and Nijmegen along with many other towns, and it helped eliminate some of those destructive V2 rocket-launching sites. However, it failed to secure that vital bridgehead over the Rhine and could not, therefore, deliver its hope of the war being over by Christmas that year.

How did MARKET GARDEN get to go ahead? Once the Allies finally broke out from Normandy after D-Day and the Falaise pocket was closed off, Eisenhower turned to looking for an effective strategy to pursue the supposedly devastated German armies north and eastwards across the Seine and then on to the Rhine. It is worth pointing out that by now Allied commanders were beginning to see the end of the war in their sights and were anxious to burnish their war records before it was too late and peace broke out. Egos started to displace measured and well-thought-out plans that were backed up with incisive and robust intelligence.[8]

Montgomery, above all, craved the sort of fame that only a highly ambitious, potentially war-shortening plan would deliver. Early September saw Montgomery inherit the 1st Allied Airborne Army command. Planning began on Operation COMET, described by Greenacre as 'a carbon copy of what would become "Market Garden" except that it expected 1st British Airborne Division and 1st Polish Parachute Brigade only to seize all the bridges from Grave to Arnhem.' Otway (*Airborne Forces*, p.214, note 2) adds 'D-Day was to be 10 September and take-off at 0600 hours, but at 0200 hours on 10 September, senior officers at division headquarters were awakened and told that the operation was cancelled.' The aim at this point was to impel the advance of Lieutenant General Sir Miles Dempsey's 2nd Army towards the northern Netherlands and into the north German plain. The divisional headquarters for the British 1st Airborne Division, with the 1st Air Landing Brigade and the Polish Parachute Brigade were to land at Nijmegen and the British 1st Parachute Brigade at Arnhem, while the British 4th Parachute Brigade was slated to land at Grave.[9] However, poor weather intervened and this, combined with Montgomery's growing concerns over increasing levels of potential German opposition, led him to postpone the operation and then cancel altogether on 10 September.[10] Greenacre continues:

By 1500 hours on the same day the Divisional staff had been given new instructions to begin planning 'Market Garden' to take place in less than one week's time. 'Market Garden' would closely follow the plan for Operation 'Comet' but would use the same order of battle for Operation 'Linnet'. Signals instructions issued for 'Market Garden' nearly all referred to orders issued for 'Linnet'; 'Sig[nal] arrangements are almost exactly as for Op 'Linnet'. The [orders] issued for that op[eration] will therefore hold except where amended herein. These were orders that were by now over two weeks old and had been superseded by two further operations. Extracts of the signals instructions for 'Linnet' were copied in 'Market Garden' orders including references to locations around Tournai. A lack of time for planning inevitably drove these short cuts but confusion was bound to occur as a result.

Evidently Montgomery was not going to give up. COMET was replaced by MARKET GARDEN, an even more audacious plan that entailed swerving round the Siegfried Line, allowing the Allies to launch armoured assaults over the Westphalia Plain, crossing the Rhine by way of the captured bridges: the American 101st Airborne Division ('Screaming Eagles') around Eindhoven; the American 82nd Airborne Division ('All American') around Nijmegen; and the British 1st Airborne Division with the 1st Polish Independent Parachute Brigade at Arnhem.[11] It would be a daylight jump, a controversial decision based on Allied air superiority. The operation would accelerate the advance of the British Second Army into the Netherlands, facilitating a concerted attack eastward over the Neder Rijn (Lower Rhine) into Germany. Speed was of the essence and delay could not be countenanced.

On 10 September Dempsey, the British Second Army commander, expressed to Montgomery his concerns about the plan and declared that he would prefer an advance north-eastwards between the Reichswald forest and the Ruhr to Wesel. Montgomery, with impeccable timing, replied that he had just received a signal from London that something needed to be done to neutralize the V2 launch sites around The Hague and that his plan must therefore proceed.[12]

Despite the rejection of his northern thrust plan, Eisenhower agreed to Operation MARKET GARDEN, albeit with a couple of caveats:

'limited priority' for supplies, and only as part of an advance on a broad front.[13] Eisenhower promised that aircraft and trucks would deliver 1,000 tons of supplies per day.[14] Still not satisfied, Montgomery complained about this to the Vice Chief of the Imperial General Staff (VCIGS) in London, Lieutenant General Sir Archibald Nye.[15] His complaints were in vain. As it happened, Eisenhower had for some time been under growing pressure from Washington (namely Army Chief of Staff General George C. Marshall and Commander Army Air Forces General Henry 'Hap' Arnold) to mount a major airborne operation before the war's end, and so he deployed Lieutenant General Lewis Brereton's First Allied Airborne Army, languishing in reserve in England under the control of the 21st Army Group. As the Allies' supply situation got worse and the rivalries and conflicting interests became more acerbic, an airborne solution, Operation MARKET GARDEN, started to make more and more sense to Eisenhower. Unfortunately for the Allies, German Army Group B was now under the command of *Generalfeldmarschall* Model who performed an astounding reorganization of the German forces in Northern Europe, given the time available to him.[16] This, and because they were up against generals of the calibre of Student and Bittrich, proved Allied optimism to be naïve. Moreover, as *By Air to Battle* tells us (p.95):

> There is no doubt that they [the Germans] feared an attack by airborne troops…more and more anti-aircraft guns were brought up, and reconnaissance photographs showed each day some new position where work on digging them in had begun. Agents reported that the Dutch population, including twelve-year-old children, were being pressed into service to prepare a main defence line along the Waal to the sea and a forward line following the Maas.

Model made good use of the meagre forces of Colonel General Kurt Student's First Parachute Army and General Gustav von Zangen's Fifteenth Army to defend as far as Nijmegen, while *Kampfgruppe von Tettau* and Lieutenant General Willi Bittrich's II SS Panzer Corps, well practised in defending against airborne landings, were stationed around Arnhem, as was General Christiansen, Armed Forces *Kommander* Netherlands and II Panzer Corps.

The two depleted armoured divisions that made up Bittrich's II SS Panzer Corps – the 9th SS Panzer Division and 10th SS Armoured Division – could count on fewer than 3,000 men each and were able to rely on only twelve functioning tanks between them. Model, therefore, reconfigured them all as SS *Kampfgruppe Hohenstaufen* and SS *Kampfgruppe Frundsberg* respectively. Weak as they were, they were still to prove a formidable defensive force.[17]

Operation MARKET GARDEN got off the ground just before midnight on Saturday, 16 September with 200 Lancasters and 23 Mosquitos from RAF Bomber Command wrecking four German fighter airfields in the northern Netherlands. This was followed up by 872 B-17 Flying Fortresses from the 8th Air Force on the Sunday dropping fragmentation bombs on the 117 anti-aircraft positions identified along the route designated for the transports, as well as troop positions and airfields at Eindhoven, Deelen and Ede. Support came from another fifty-four Lancasters and five Mosquitos, while another eighty-five Lancasters and fifteen Mosquitos devastated Walcheren Island. Later, German barracks at Nijmegen, Cleve, Arnhem and Ede were bombed by eighty-four Mosquitos and Boston and Mitchell medium bombers from the 2nd Tactical Air Force. Escort was provided by 147 P-51 Mustangs: seven of the paltry fifteen Focke-Wulf 190s sent up in opposition were shot down with the loss of one Mustang.[18]

Losses were light (two B-17s, two Lancasters and three Mosquitos). The Allies enjoyed significant air superiority, and to quote one German soldier, 'If you see a white plane, it's American, if you see a black plane, it's RAF. If you see no planes at all it's the Luftwaffe.' 'Losses were light': that rather depends on who you were though; 10-year-old Cor and Barta Janse lived in Wolfheze at the time and remember the bombing that was intended to soften up any German forces around Arnhem (*Arnhem 1944 Veteran's Club Newsletter*, November 1992). Eighty-two villagers and patients from what is now Wolfheze Mental Hospital died that day.

The Dutch government, in exile in London, called for a strike of all transport workers to coincide with the operation. The German reprisal was a humanitarian disaster and a tragedy for the Dutch people: the Germans ended all civilian transport throughout the country and more than 18,000 Dutch civilians died during the winter. Food supplies had been cut off.

Breakfast back in England: if you were an American you got hot cakes and syrup, fried chicken with all the trimmings and apple pie. If you were British you filled your mess tin with smoked haddock, 'quite a lot of which ended up on the floor of the aircraft', according to one sergeant. According to Buckingham, elements of the 1st Air Landing Light Regiment breakfasting at Manston with some of the 2nd Battalion South Staffords may not have enjoyed their meal when the WAAFs serving them were seen 'crying at the prospect of their customers' imminent departure for battle'.[19]

The final assessment of MARKET GARDEN

In the end, though, Montgomery believed that the operation was 90 per cent successful. Yet surely the failure to take the key objective of Arnhem Bridge had rendered the whole thing an expensive failure? However, Montgomery refused to take into account the fact that the Airborne Division, due to its losses, was unable to take any further part in the Second World War.

'My country can never again afford the luxury of another Montgomery success,' said Bernhard, Prince of the Netherlands wryly. 'In return for so much courage and sacrifice, the Allies had won a 50-mile salient – leading nowhere,' according to Dr John C. Warren.

Chapter Seven

The 1st Airborne Division

We have, of course, met the 1st Airborne Division fighting in Italy with support from the 1st Air Landing Light Regiment. By the time of its deployment at Arnhem the division comprised three brigades: two parachute and one air-landing, of which the 1st Air Landing Light Regiment was part. The 1st Parachute Brigade under Brigadier General Lathbury was made up of the 1st, 2nd and 3rd Parachute battalions which had seen action in North Africa and Sicily. Brigadier Hackett commanded the 4th Parachute Brigade which comprised the 156th, 10th and 11th Parachute battalions. All three were relatively inexperienced: by the time of Arnhem the 156th and 10th had no jumping experience, while the 11th had parachuted onto Kos but had seen no combat.

Brigadier P.H.W. Hicks led the 1st Air Landing Brigade comprising the 7th Galloway Battalion, King's Own Scottish Borderers who were going into their first and last battle; the 1st Battalion, Border Regiment, part of the BEF in 1940 and Sicily veterans; and the 2nd Battalion, South Staffordshire Regiment, veterans of India and Sicily.[1] In addition, there were the following divisional regiments that gave support in the field:

- 1st Air Landing Light Regiment, Royal Artillery
- 204th (Oban) Independent Anti-Tank Battery (later 2nd Air Landing Anti-Tank Battery) formed from pre-war Territorial Army units. The 2nd suffered heavy casualties in the HMS *Abdiel* explosion in Taranto.
- 1st Air Landing Anti-Tank Battery: TA as Oban but recruited from Barrow-in-Furness. They were equipped with new 17-pounders to penetrate increasingly thick German armour. They and their trailers fitted comfortably into Hamilcar gliders.
- 5th Air Landing Anti-Tank Battery
- 283rd Light Anti-Aircraft (LAA) Battery (later 1st (City of London) Yeomanry) Air Landing LAA Battery), left 21 February 1944
- 1st Forward (Airborne) Observation Unit, Royal Artillery.[2]

Along with the guns of the anti-tank platoons of the Air Landing Brigade, a total of fifty-two 6-pounders and sixteen 17-pounders were transported to Arnhem. For Arnhem the division was augmented by the Polish 1st Parachute Brigade.

Chapter Eight

The Royal Artillery at Arnhem

The 1st Air Landing Light Regiment was only one of the artillery regiments that went into action in the Battle of Arnhem. They were a crucial element in what was a significant artillery deployment involving a number of other units. Middlebrook (p.34) points out that 'the Royal Artillery had a large presence in the division… approximately 800 artillerymen would fly to Arnhem in about 170 gliders; many envious eyes in other units were cast on that huge glider allocation.' As noted above, in addition to the 1st Air Landing Light Regiment, the Royal Artillery, in its support of the 1st Airborne Division, made two anti-tank batteries and a Forward Observation Unit available under the command of a Royal Artillery Headquarters led by Lieutenant Colonel Robert Loder-Symonds.[1]

In field or light regiments it was usual for battery commanders and troop commanders to work very closely with the commanders of the infantry unit they were supporting by directing and observing the artillery fire. These were Forward Observation Officers (FOOs) working in Forward Observation Units and comprised gunner officers and signallers. At Arnhem the plan was for them to direct the fire of the XXX Corps guns. No. 1 Forward Observation Unit RA (FOURA) supplied those FOOs. They included attachments to the 1st Parachute Brigade, 1st Parachute Battalion, 2nd Parachute Battalion, 4th Parachute Brigade, 156th Parachute Battalion, 10th Parachute Battalion and 11th Parachute Battalion. FOURA also had FOOs attached to the air landing brigade units, including the Border Regiment, South Staffords, the King's Own Scottish Borderers and the Reconnaissance Squadron.

Destroying enemy tanks came under the remit of the 1st and 2nd Air Landing Anti-Tank batteries and the anti-tank platoons of the three air landing battalions using 6-pounders that boasted a calibre of 57mm and could penetrate up to 73mm of armour plate at just under 1,000 yards.

David Truesdale (p.63) reminds us that

> each of the Air Landing Anti-Tank Batteries had two troops of 17-pounder guns – which were the heaviest anti-tank guns in British service and the only weapon in the arsenal of the 1st Airborne Division that could penetrate the armour of the Tiger tank, using the newly introduced and very effective 'sabot' round.[2]

This was much to the surprise of the Germans.

As for the 1st Air Landing Light Regiment, this is how it was deployed. It would field three batteries (1 to 3) of two troops (A to F) each with four guns, making twenty-four in total, twenty-one of which saw action in Arnhem. Each gun was commanded by a sergeant and comprised the detachment, drivers, jeeps and trailers. The guns answered to the Gun Position Officer (GPO) assisted by the troop leader and a troop sergeant major along with signallers. The two troop GPOs reported to the Command Post Officer (CPO) who supervised and controlled the battery gun position from his command post, the battery headquarters. The CPO was responsible to the battery commander. As noted, the battery commanders and troop commanders usually stayed with the infantry commanders they were supporting.

Chapter Nine

The 1st Air Landing Light Regiment's Battle of Arnhem

The 1st Airlanding Light Regiment was one of the newest units in the [1st Airborne] division, having been formed in February 1943 with a nucleus from one of the Royal Artillery's elite batteries of 'pack gunner' or 'mule gunners' with much North-West Frontier experience.
Martin Middlebrook, Arnhem 1944, p.34.

Nos 1 and 3 batteries flew to Arnhem in eighty-seven Horsas from RAF Fairford, RAF Blakehill Farm, RAF Down Ampney, RAF Manston and RAF Keevil (about 4 miles east of Trowbridge, Wiltshire) on the first lift. The CO and Tac. HQ and elements of 1 Battery flew from Harwell near Didcot; the rest from Keevil and Manston, while 3 Battery flew from Fairford. No. 2 Battery and others flew in thirty-three Horsas from Manston on the second lift, while the rest of HQ flew from Down Ampney. All 180 of the glider pilots were under command of the regiment and converted to an infantry role, providing close protection for the guns once their pilot duties had been discharged: 'a tremendous asset during the battle'. Eventually they formed part of the perimeter in the south-east sector.

Three members of 3 Battery, E Troop – Captain Tony Harrison, Gunner Jock Morrison and Bombardier Leo Hall – were detailed to report to the 1st Para Brigade HQ near Grantham 'to be ready to jump with them to be on the spot to be ready to wireless for Battery support through our 68 set which Jock was kitbagging down with him'. Leo Hall anticipated a number of potential problems:

- Distance: the sets might be out of range
- Screening: short ground waves bouncing off buildings, trees, hills
- Interference: from other stations, unsuppressed electrical machinery, enemy jamming

- Power: the Dags (batteries) would need recharging. The facility for this was at the E Troop gun position.

Some 372 men of the 1st Air Landing Light Regiment went in: 36 died, 136 were evacuated over the river, and 200 were reported missing, mainly PoWs.

Here is the order of command of the regiment's three batteries:

1st Air Landing Light Battery: Major A. Norman-Walker (KIA 22-9-1944)
   A Troop: Captain J.H.D. Lee
   B Troop: Captain J. Walker
2nd Air Landing Light Battery: Major J. Linton
   C Troop: Captain P. Chard
   D Troop: Captain P. Taylor
3rd Air Landing Light Battery: Major D. Munford[1]
   E Troop: Captain T. Harrison
   F Troop: Captain T.M. Griffiths

Before the battle, by Tuesday 12 September most of the men had reported back from their short leave to find, to their surprise and delight (for most) that MARKET GARDEN was still actually on. So final preparations were carried out and on the Saturday most of the participating troops were briefed; not just on their unit's role but those of all other units in the division, along with an outline of the whole MARKET GARDEN plan. The message was that little opposition was anticipated. Light Regiment Gunner Dennis Bowles (HQ Group, 3 Battery) remembers being told of 'the limited opposition – the old men and the invalids from the Russian Front; Home Guard type opposition' and how they would 'probably be relieved after two days'. He adds 'Our Forward Observation party was told we were going straight to the bridge and there would be a separation from the main unit for twenty-four hours. You tend to hope that it was all true. You realise that it couldn't be as easy as that, but you hoped it was.'[2]

Corporal Bob Allen of the 3rd Battalion (3 PARA) added to the scepticism and concern: 'I remember a feeling of shock and disbelief when I heard we were to drop seven miles from the bridge. I kept my thoughts to myself.' Allen and his comrades felt they 'should drop on the polder immediately south of the town'. Nevertheless, he concluded that 'morale was sky-high. Most of us were straining at the leash to get into battle.'

Meanwhile, the transport aircraft were being meticulously prepared, while thousands of parachutes were being packed at Credenhill near Hereford. Weight distribution in the gliders was endlessly practised. At Down Ampney two load manifests show a load made up of a rifle platoon of the 7th KOSBs and a load comprising a jeep, a trailer and six men. Both manifests are stamped COMET, but overprinted MARKET. The loads were each of 3 tons with each soldier and his equipment weighing 15 stone.[3]

David Truesdale (pp.59–60) helpfully describes the meticulous process involved in loading and unloading a Horsa with light artillery. He starts by pointing out the fact that much time was spent loading and unloading because 'a fully loaded Horsa can only remain fully loaded for 24 hours before it begins to "wilt".' The procedure always had to take into account the possibility that the guns would have to go into action immediately on landing, quite likely under enemy fire:

- The 10cwt airborne trailer plus ammunition had to be loaded first; it could be manhandled by three gunners
- The jeep went in next; as it was the heaviest piece of equipment it was positioned in the centre of the Horsa, its front facing the rear ramp
- The gun came last, its muzzle facing the rear, allowing it to be wheeled out and deployed immediately if required.

What ammunition was carried? The three trailers were usually loaded with 137 rounds of ammunition per gun, comprising 125 high-explosive shells, 6 armour-piercing and 6 smoke.

BSM T.W. Kent of F Troop tells how the regiment was confined to camp on 15 September: 'They did a service and maintenance of all our equipment, then reloaded everything into the gliders.' BSM Kent describes the mounting tension and anxiety in the regiment with a vivid description of the distressing night of the 15th when F Troop TSM David 'Jock' Lawson was forever crying out in his nightmares; he was apparently going through all sorts and deaths and torture, reliving past horrors and fearful for the future. Presumably these were flashbacks from post-traumatic stress disorder (PTSD) inflicted in the Italian campaign.

However, he remained implacable and refused to go to see the Medical Officer (MO) next day, putting his nightmares down to stress from which most of his comrades were also suffering.[4] Saturday the 16th started with a briefing to assess operational readiness and 'a programme for further items that had to be taken'. Kent lists the essential items with which the troops were issued:

- Silk escape maps of Europe
- Dutch guilders and Deutschmarks (escape money)
- 48-hour ration pack and survival kit
- Six ampoules of morphine (officers and warrant officers only), with instructions on how and when they should be used. (Anyone administered morphine had to be marked with an 'M' along with time and date in order to avoid a fatal double dose.)

There then followed a parade in battle order. Kent's 'personal armoury' comprised a .38 revolver and 50 rounds, a Sten gun with 200 rounds and four Mills grenades, plus six ampoules of morphine.[5]

The afternoon saw a briefing on the operation with stereo aerial photographs (to study with 3D glasses); presumably no Panzer tanks were evident. That evening everyone wrote letters home, just in case.[6]

Tony Harrison's second-in-command in E Troop was Lieutenant Noel Farrands; Lieutenant Anthony Driver was troop leader and WOII David Lawson was TSM. Bombardier Leo Hall was in command of the troop signallers. E Troop also had Gunner Reg Butterwick, a veteran of North Africa (El Alamein) and Italy, and Gunner Eric Chrystal, signaller.[7]

The specially-formed Z Troop was set up to bolster the regiment's defence against tanks 'as the guns of the light regiment were mediocre at best when it came to the anti-tank role'. It comprised four 6-pounders and a detachment of twenty-nine men.

The plan for the regiment was that 1 and 3 Batteries would fly over to the Netherlands on Day 1, 17 September, followed by 2 Battery on the 18th. Nos 1 and 3 Batteries were expected to see action immediately close to the landing zone with 3 Battery supporting the Parachute Brigade further to the east and following their advance into Arnhem in order to bring Arnhem Bridge within their guns' range of 5.5 to 6 miles; 1 Battery would support the Air Landing Brigade. According to Truesdale (p.71), the entire regiment would eventually be relocated 'to occupy within the planned Arnhem perimeter'.[8]

Reveille on 17 September was later than usual and breakfast was a relaxed affair. On arrival at the airfield 3 Battery found that their gliders had been moved overnight and were now facing down the runway.

BSM Tom Kent went through the landing procedure with the gunners in his glider which involved the tricky manoeuvre of detaching the tail section and leaving it behind before the glider had come to a halt.[9] Women's Voluntary Service (WVS) ladies turned up with 'dainty cut boiled ham sandwiches', the first Leo Hall had seen in five years.

Enthusiastic and ardent as they were, there must have a nagging doubt lingering in the minds of many of the combatants over three cardinal operational factors: Operation MARKET was to be a daylight assault; it was to take place over three days in three lifts, and the LZs and DZs were up to 8 miles distant from the main objective. Surprise, that cornerstone of successful airborne operations, was virtually non-existent, while vulnerability, both in the sky and on land, was maximized. The anxiety went all the way to the top: General Urquhart's requests for two airlifts on Day 1 and for DZs and LZs nearer the objective were both refused. Surprise and combatant safeguarding had therefore left the room.

The following chapters give a graphic account of the Arnhem battle.

Chapter Ten

A Week in Oosterbeek September 1944, the Account of the Battle by Sergeant George Nattrass

From the Preface:

In parts the English in this vivid and moving account seems a little stilted; this is because it was initially published in Dutch and then translated back into English. It is the war diary of Sergeant George Nattrass, D Company, 7th (Galloway) King's Own Scottish Borderers. In 1983 his account was published in a Dutch monthly magazine *Documentatiegroep '40–'45* and in 1984, Nico van der Meer translated and published this account in a book called *Door de Hel van Oosterbeek 1944*. An English edition of this personal account has never been published, not by George himself or by his descendants. As the Dutch publications are not literally translations of the original war diary, and translating from English to Dutch and again reverse to English will, of course, do harm to the original text, we believe it is still worthwhile making this account available for a larger (non-Dutch) audience. The Dutch text was translated by Roland de Kwant and edited by Paul Pariso [to provide this account]. As the original text as prepared by George Nattrass is not available, it is not possible to verify if the errors in the Dutch text are the result of the first translation of the English diary (1983) to the Dutch article published by the *Documentatiegroep '40–'45* or that the original diary also include these mistakes. Notes have been added to this translation to clarify certain aspects or possible errors and clear omissions.

This is how, for one, Sergeant George Nattrass, 15th Platoon, 'D' Company, 7th Battalion King's Own Scottish Borderers, took the news of being sidelined for one of the biggest operations in

British military history, the Normandy landings, and how he fared in the days after his landing in the Netherlands. It is probably typical of many of the airborne troops' experiences and shows us just how intense and frenzied the fighting was:

> In one day the entire 1st Airborne Division was transferred to the Stonehenge and Bulford area, where, together with the 6th Airborne Division, a big exercise would be held ('Exercise Rags'). It was the end of May, and there was a rumour the Normandy invasion was about to start. The men were anxious and very curious what tasks would be assigned to the 1st Airborne Division. The almost endless practising and exercising made the soldiers get bored. They wanted to see some real action now. The 6th Airborne Division got the orders to get ready for action in France and would be involved in the coming invasion, but the 1st Division should wait and be on 'stand-by'.

Nattrass continues, at the briefing:
> Our Colonel had drawn the routes of the various Battalions in the sand-covered table and I as well updated my staff maps. At the point of rendezvous on the Ginkel Heath, the place my unit would jump, a piper would play *Blue Bonnets over the Border*.

On safely landing,

> Just as we were starting to execute the orders, a young French Lieutenant came running towards us shouting there were many Germans seen on the road Arnhem-Utrecht. We then hurried ourselves to the place we were sent to, and the first accident happened. Driver Fairlane [Lance Corporal Peter MacFarlane, 3194351, died on 18 September 1944, now buried at Oosterbeek (23.A.2)] shot himself with his own Sten gun through his head.

Later on the Monday/Tuesday night a Dutch civilian lady with a child was shot in the legs when she did not answer the password.

Directly we heard a lot of stumbling and smothered shouts behind us. After a bit the Major [Wilson] and a German soldier, who had infiltrated our lines, rolled over the ground, fighting. A moment later the Major strangled the German to death.... Suddenly all hell broke loose, enemy mortars exploded within our positions and the Germans gave us all they had. Cassidy [possibly Private Samuel Patton Cassidy, 14207764, Anti-Tank Platoon, 'C' Company. It is believed he died when a Bren gun he was trying to un-jam went off and shot him in the head. He has no known grave] and McClure were seriously wounded, while our company clerk lost half of his ear. Pearce [Sergeant R. Pearce, 3191876, Support Company] of Mortar platoon opened fire with everything he had. Vickers, Brens and other guns intensely fired at the Germans. On the command 'Attack!' we jumped out of our trenches and ran at the Germans with our bayonets on our guns and forced them back to the woods they had come from. Graham believed he alone had killed sixty Germans with his Vickers.

Things got worse: Nattrass 'lost all hope and believed this would never end...' The scene at the 'White House' (the Hotel Schoonhord) confirmed that

Just before I went to go downstairs to get Murray and his PIAT, there was an enormous explosion. We were covered with chalk and dust and fell to the first floor. I fell on my shoulder very hard, and Blackie lay on the ground, totally stunned. After five minutes we recovered a bit, and concluded we were not hurt, although blood was coming out of our ears and noses. That was due to the air pressure. We clambered back onto our feet, and wondered how Ure was, as we climbed up the heavily damaged stairs. Entering the room we saw nothing was left. Horrified, we saw the remains of Ure's body sticking to the wall, where I had previously seen a crucifix hanging. Shocked, I grabbed Ure's identity tag from the bloody mess and put it in my pocket.

Nattrass reminds us that it was not just civilians and soldiers who were caught up in this relentless carnage:

From the woods across the open grounds in front of the 'White House' heavy fire was brought on us. I saw dead cows, horses and pigs on the open ground, lying there with stomachs burst open and the air was filled with an awful smell, mingled with the smoke of burning houses.

By the Saturday night (the 23rd), Nattrass realized that the game was up. He continues his graphic account:

We got the feeling the next day, Sunday 24th, would bring the final battle and that it would be over for us by then. When it was almost dark we saw a lonely figure, bareheaded and dazed, walking between the enemy lines. It turned out to be Major Cochrane [Major Cochran was killed on 20 September 1944. It is more than likely the man Nattrass saw was Captain Steer] suffering severe shellshock, walking in circles aimlessly, pretending to be a locomotive. Despite everything we did to try and get this man into one of our trenches we couldn't and finally he got killed.

The psychological impact of seven days of relentless battling, death and mutilation was taking a heavy toll:

I looked into the desperate faces of the men around me. Their bloodstained eyes had a spooky effect. The seven days of battle had scarred all of them. Their smocks were full of blood from their own wounds, but also that of their comrades they had helped.... Intensive mortar attacks were nerve-wrecking.

Chapter Eleven

Day 1: Sunday, 17 September

The day, and the battle, started in earnest at about 1030 hours when six RAF Typhoons attacked German positions in Arnhem with rockets, including the Saksen-Weimarkazerne, the Willemskazerne (both barracks), the Royal Hotel and restaurant, the Municipal Police Station and a German storage depot. The bridge over the River Rhine and the city theatre were strafed by machine guns. The old men with their rifles guarding the bridge fled, their guard posts destroyed; there were no anti-aircraft guns. Senior officials in the regional police president's office fled for the German border due to the 'tense situation' like 'scared rabbits'. Sergeant J. van Kuijk announced: 'We are in sole charge, in fact liberated from the NSB and the Germans.' Van Kuijk's description of the ensuing battle around his police station in Eusebiusplein is in his *War at Eusebiusplein*.

In England the agonizingly long wait for take-off finally ended at 0930 hours on that early autumn English day. The tugs and gliders carrying the Light Regiment got off the ground at around 1045 hours. Due to their payload the gliders maintained a cruising speed of 120mph, somewhat slower than the 140mph achieved by the parachute troops-carrying Dakotas. Two hours later the huge airborne armada of more than 1,500 aircraft was assembled over Aldeburgh, Suffolk, and could then set off for their landing zones (LZs) and drop zones (DZs) in the Netherlands. Protection over the North Sea came courtesy of 874 fighters, while beneath them air-sea rescue patrolled the waters along the flight path.

The actual weather at take-off was at odds with the forecast – 'favourable' – on which General Brereton, Commander of the 1st Allied Army, gave his decision at 1900 hours on 16 September to green-light Operation MARKET GARDEN.

In 'A Report on Activities of the British Glider Pilot Regiment in Operation Market Garden' (W0205/873), Appendix 1 we can glean the following information:

The weather over England was far from ideal; the cloud base ranged from 500ft to 2,000 feet with 6/10 strato-cumulus. Otherwise flying conditions were fairly comfortable, but before the English coast had been crossed, of the three hundred and fifty-eight combinations that should have taken off some twenty-three had force-landed in England; one had crashed badly, crew and passengers being killed.

All but one of these (which crash-landed) returned to base and joined the second lift on the 18th. Conditions over the sea were markedly better; nevertheless, slipstream and engine failure were problems: four had to ditch, two because their cables had broken and two 'were forced to release by tug engine failure' and landed on Schouten off the Dutch coast. Over land there was flak from a barge that was silenced by fighters leaving 'only occasional bursts of small-arms fire'; slipstream remained a problem and eight gliders were lost. There was unqualified praise for the Pathfinders clearly highlighting the DZs: 'it is abundantly clear the Verey light signals assisted many combinations in their approach.' 'Pilots also report that the Smoke Candles were of value.' There were a few problems with unloading: removing the troughs from under the jeeps, for example. Nevertheless, the average unloading time was thirty minutes.

In some cases the LZ surface was 'softer than had been anticipated', resulting in two Hamilcars overturning due to earth piling up beneath the noses. One crew was killed; the other suffered injuries, although all passengers escaped with light injuries. Both 17-pounders were lost.

So, in summary, 358 gliders took off and 39 failed to arrive: 1 crashed on take-off, 24 force-landed in England, 5 were lost over the sea and 9 over the Netherlands.

Truesdale speaks of 'uncomfortable hours' spent by those 'men prone to airsickness…with their heads buried in a brown paper bag or an airborne helmet'.[1] For a few of the glider passengers, nausea was the least of their problems: Captain John Lee (A Troop, 1 Battery) and his four gunners endured a frightening aborted take-off; the pilots of Roy Staddon's glider (of the same troop) were bedevilled by patchy low cloud; Staddon watched as tow ropes broke on gliders all around him, watching 'aghast as our immediate neighbour glider turned on its side and just disintegrated'. When Staddon's glider 'got about 60 degrees out of the horizontal before the pilots got her back, only to repeat the performance, but this time they could not correct her so I ordered "cast off"'.[2] Staddon's was one of about twenty that deliberately 'cast off' from their tugs, landing in English fields or on the North Sea. 'Tom Kent watched a glider…get out of control, cast off and, after a crazy spin, hit the water' and another landing safely to be rescued by air-sea rescue launches. Tom Kent recalls 'heavy anti-aircraft fire all around us and we got the shock waves of some of the bursts…most heartening was the sight of our own fighters zooming down to deal with the gun positions from which the firing was coming…the firing stopped as quickly as it had begun.'[3] In total 874 fighters escorted the armada: 503 USAF and 371 RAF.

Here is the Regimental War Diary record:

All 1 Bty gliders, less 2, landed on LZ. Lieut. Staddon landed in England. S/Sgt Leaves landed near the town of Renkum. The latter arrived in the Bty position late in the afternoon having run into, and successfully dealt with, a little resistance en route…3 Bty landed shortly after… gliders missing. F7 force-landed in England. T.G.F. [Bombardier Robert Hempton] crashed in Holland, believed no survivors and F1 [Sergeant Leahy] came down safely in Holland near 's-Hertogenbosch.

Harold Leahy's team (chalk no. 509) was forced to abandon unloading the equipment when interrupted by the Germans. The rest of the complement was Lance Bombardier Thomas Henry Buckley, Gunner R. Jobling and Gunner Ford. Staff Sergeant W.W. Potts and Sergeant Stevenson from G Squadron were the glider pilots, towed by a 620 Squadron Stirling. 'Shortly after crossing the Scheldt Islands the tug climbed above a cloud formation… the glider pilot lost sight of the tug', causing the tow rope to slacken, 'and as it tightened the resultant jerk caused it to break' at 3,000ft, causing it to crash-land. Three circling Spitfires dissuaded a nearby flak tower from opening up. They landed about 10 miles south of 's-Hertogenbosch at a farm called Hoef Ten Halve. About 100 locals gathered round to help. Unfortunately the glider overturned during unloading and a troop of about twenty Germans appeared on the scene. Leahy and his men and the glider pilots were led to safety by two Dutchmen.[4]

Major Dennis Munford recalls how he watched a Dakota towing an 82nd Airborne Waco CG-4 come apart: 'men and equipment spilt out of it like toys from a Christmas cracker'. Other witnesses watched in horror as equipment bundles under the Dakota were set on fire by tracer which then set the C-47 alight but not before the pilot enabled the parachutists on board to jump from the blazing plane. It crash-landed on Schouwen Island, killing the crew.[5]

Bombardier Hempton and his F Troop comrades, Eric Stubbs, Henry Tustin and F.V. Brown in chalk no. 518 with their two glider pilots – Sergeant Roy Rowland and Sergeant Laurence Cook of 9 Flight, G Squadron – were either hit by flak or suffered mechanical failure and crashed behind the Reijnders Farm near the village of Nieuwe Molen near Fijnaart. They were carrying a jeep and two ammunition trailers. The sole 'survivor' was Lieutenant Frank Moore, the troop leader, who was moved at the last minute from this glider to go with Major Munford, who decided he would be more use assisting in organizing the troop. A relative of Gunner Brown's kindly sent me information relating to the tragic crash. Private Bob Elliott of the 1st Border Regiment has left us a record of the tragic events in Lieutenant Colonel John Place's glider (Middlebrook, p.88):

> The boys at the back started shouting 'Cast off! Cast off! The tail's coming off.' The lieutenant who was the glider co-pilot came back and said it was nothing, only minor damage. The two pilots smiled at each other and flew on. But, within five or ten minutes, there was a 'crack' and we were hit again, in the cockpit. The back of the glider-pilot lieutenant's head was all smashed. The blood was running around our feet – what a bloody mess! One or two of them pulled his body onto the floor and just laid him out of the way of the lieutenant colonel. Tom Watson, our platoon sergeant, was near the front and he was also hit, on the side of the face, but not too badly. He carried on, but was killed four days later.[6]

Private Johnny Peters, also of the Border Regiment, said: 'If I had been frightened before, I was petrified by now, wondering what would happen if Lieutenant Colonel Place suffered the same fate.' The Anti-Tank Battery suffered losses too: one Z Troop glider with its 6-pounder gun load was forced to ditch on Walcheren Island, while a second gun landed 20 miles short of its LZ; this was an A Troop glider carrying Sergeant Atkinson and Gunners Willshaw and Springhall (Wilkinson, p.39). Like Leahy and his comrades, they were concealed by the Dutch until the relieving forces of the Second Army arrived. Z Troop's Commander Lieutenant McNaught and his team were also given sanctuary by the Dutch when they force-landed 20 miles west of Nijmegen and awaited the arrival of elements of the 82nd US Airborne Division.

Precision planning and meticulous adherence to those plans was absolutely imperative for such a huge concentration of aircraft in a relatively small air space. Those booked for Arnhem flew a northern route, while those heading for Eindhoven followed the southern. Despite this segregation, there was one pinch-point above north London where the two routes merged, with all the attendant perils that presented.

Middlebrook (pp.88–89) documents the eight Horsas that 'came down between the landfall on the Dutch coast and their intended landing zone':

- A Horsa with a load of four artillerymen from the Light Regiment with a jeep and trailer…was seen to be hit by flak and to break into two parts; there were no survivors.
- The occupants of two gliders – a platoon of South Staffords and a gun team from the Light Regiment – which came down north of Tilburg joined up…before making contact with Allied forces more than a month later.
- Two gliders carrying 6-pounder anti-tank guns came down short of their landing zone, but the gunners somehow managed in due course to reach the scene of action with their guns.

The glider pilots had trained relentlessly to release their gliders from the tow rope about 2.5 miles from their landing zone. We can get a feel for the nerves experienced by the pilots from Staff Sergeant Trevor Francis of G Squadron who had lain awake most of the previous night going over the procedure:

> Cast loose at 3,500 feet. Sink rate at all-up weight of 1 tons – 400 feet per minute; air speed 83 mph for maximum glide. Time in the air? Go for 2,000 feet at normal glide – therefore five minutes; then the last 1,500 feet medium and full flap – say another one or two minutes.

This was followed by a gentle glide after cast-off, then a steeper dive to get through the zone of possible hostile fire, followed by a levelling-out just before landing.

Middlebrook (pp.99–100) details a typical landing via Staff Sergeant John McGough of C Squadron:

> Having picked out my particular landing site in a field bounded by woods on two sides and a farm track on the other, I made preparations for the landing. We were at a height of 2,500 feet, and I asked my tug pilot to make one or two slight alterations of course, so that when I cast off I would be in the right area to enable me to land successfully. This he did, and I pressed the red release knob; the tow rope fell away and the tug flew off, towing it behind. I was now in free flight and flew around for a very short while to plan my final approach and to ensure there was no risk of collision with other gliders. Henry, my co-pilot, must have been concerned, as he said to me, 'For goodness sake, get down; you never know what is going to happen.' I put down half then full flap and, as the glider was fully loaded, kept my air speed at about 85 mph and touched down on Dutch soil – not a shot having been fired.

Among the parachutists, first down at 1240 hours, of course, were the Pathfinders who, on exiting their twelve Stirling bombers and landing on Nazi-occupied Dutch soil, spread out their white canvas panels to mark the LZs (S and Z) and DZ X to welcome the parachutists and glider pilots following close behind. Eureka transponder beacons were set up.[7] One of their corporals dropped his Sten gun on landing: it went off and killed him. At Arnhem twenty or so of these Pathfinders were German Jews hoping to win some degree of revenge. While the Eurekas were being set up a rather ill-informed German motorcyclist rode up and asked the Pathfinders 'if they had seen any Tommies'. It was to be the last question he asked.

Pigeon Signals

Carrier pigeons saw their first Arnhem action when they were released from Company HQ to take the welcome news back to Airborne Headquarters in England of a largely unopposed landing, so far. Eighty-two homing pigeons had been dropped into the Netherlands, some with the First Airborne Division Signals, others with the 2nd Para Battalion;

the pigeons' loft was in London, which would have meant a 240-mile trip to deliver their messages which were in Slidex Code. According to the Brigade Signals War Diary, 'Just before dark [on Sunday] all Bde HQ pigeons were collected and put into a captured German vehicle. This proved to be a mistake as the vehicle broke down after 200 yds from the objective and could not be reached. All pigeons were therefore lost.' As a result only four 2nd Battalion pigeons reached the bridge area. These were carried in small cylinders by individual members of Brigade HQ, along with the rest of their kit. All four were released with messages during the battle: the first at 8.45 on Monday with a message from Major Waller, the battalion's 2i/c, which got back to London eight days later on 26 September. The message was transmitted to Airborne Forces Rear HQ. Things had moved on by then, of course, and the message that '3RD BTN EXPECT TO CAPTURE SOUTH OF BRIDGE TONIGHT' proved sadly premature.

However, David Bennett tells how the pigeons 'displayed a disturbing tendency to go on strike once released', although one pigeon from the 1st Airborne, released on 25 September, did reach VIII Corps, presumably uninvited. One pigeon was released by the 101st on D+1, reporting that the gliders had landed and giving map references of the assembly area. Of the eighty-two pigeons, fourteen returned to lofts in the London area with messages and eleven without; three returned to Airborne Rear HQ. The report concluded that 'It is really doubtful whether pigeons are worth taking on future airborne operations similar to this.'

SLIDEX is a paper-based hand-held manual cipher system used by the British army during the Second World War and during part of the Cold War for sending tactical field messages. It is based on a pre-defined matrix of letters, words and common expressions, of which the row and column IDs are used.[8]

It's probably no wonder that the pigeon service enjoyed so little success if this story from 3 Para's Stan Derbyshire is anything to go by. Seeking help to get his No. 18 wireless set onto his back, he approached another signaller who said OK, but asked him 'to hold this pigeon for me'. The canister it was in had been damaged on landing but the pigeon was OK; Derbyshire was warned to keep his hand over the damaged end to prevent escape. The inevitable followed when Derbyshire took his hand off the cylinder: the pigeon flew up into a tree, leaving its handler wailing 'What am I going to do; I've got to get it back. The last I saw of him he was shaking the seed under the tree, trying to entice the bird down' (*Arnhem 199 Veteran's Club Newsletter*, November 1995).

Pigeons were not the only birds to join the battle. Myrtle the chicken played her part too: she was the platoon mascot tucked into the tunic of Lieutenant Pat Glover who released her at 200ft and fluttered to the ground where she survived for two days. The *Sunday Express* (31 July 1994) reported that Lieutenant Glover was to repeat his jump on 17 September 1994 with a stuffed chicken, Myrtle II, down his trousers.

The Pathfinders were soon followed at 1300 hours by the gliders carrying the 1st Air Landing Brigade troops at LZ S north of the railway line; gliders carrying the vehicles of the 1st Parachute Brigade at 1320 hours of Divisional HQ, the Reconnaissance Squadron and the rest of the divisional troops. At 1350 hours, on DZ X south of the Arnhem-Amsterdam railway line, the 1st Parachute Brigade landed along with the men of the Reconnaissance Squadron.[9] Medical teams went straight into action tending glider crash casualties: sixteen brigade gliders failed to make it; eight from the 7th Battalion KOSBs. Nevertheless, mustered to the piper strains of *Blue Bonnets over the Border*, they still numbered 40 officers and 700 men.

Interestingly, as Beevor relates (p.99), one of the glider casualties had a Bren gun carrier; it was shot out of the sky with small-arms fire on the Breda-Tilburg road by a detachment made up of a platoon of Moors of the 13 SS Division *Handschar Regiment Götz Berens von Rautenfeld*. *Leutnant* Martin, the platoon commander, could not understand why the glider had written in chalk on its fuselage 'Is this journey absolutely necessary?' This was a witty reference to the British government's edict to restrict domestic travel and a rare instance of Muslims fighting with the Nazis. Whatever happened to their odious racial purity laws?

Beevor provides another uplifting anecdote: postman Jan Donderwinkel was going about his business when he arrived at the astonishing sight of LZ S where soldiers were relieving gliders of their tails to allow jeeps to be driven out. He found one soldier on the ground, his feet crushed on landing. 'Are you a postman?' the soldier asked. 'Yes,' Donderwinkel replied. 'Well then, do you have letter for me?' Donderwinkel said 'No, but do you have a cigarette for me?' and received a packet of Player's for his congeniality. The postman then helped the soldier to the casualty clearing station set up by the 131st (Parachute) Field Ambulance close to the Wolfheze asylum around which dazed patients were wandering, still in shock from when the ammunition dump nearby was hit.

Robert Woollacott tells the fascinating story of one of the Mk IV Mosquito pilots tasked with the job of photographing the airborne invasion. The log of Wing Commander Bill Meakin DFC and Bar tells us 'On September 17 1944, in a Mark IV Mosquito numbered "O" with Flying Officer L. Howard, PHOTOGRAPHED AIRBORNE GLIDER INVASION AT ARNHEM.' Mrs Meakin adds that her late husband was persuaded by photographer Howard to go low to avoid cloud at high altitude and get some low-level shots. 'O for Oscar' failed to return to base and the squadron were anxiously preparing to break the news to Mrs Meakin when a signal came through announcing that the Mosquito had landed at a forward airfield somewhere in France. His widow explains that 'they had run out of fuel' and 'were so mesmerised at the fantastic sight they were witnessing that they overlooked the little matter of fuel supply'. We have Meakin and Howard (and others like them) to thank for the breathtaking unique photographs showing the awesome panoply of those glider landings that grace so many books on Arnhem.[10]

It is true to say that for the most part the gliders of the 1st Air Landing Light Regiment landed in the right place at the right time; they could now get on with the job in hand: 1 Battery was detailed to guard and defend the LZs around Wolfheze, while 3 Battery was to support the parachute battalions in their advance on Arnhem Bridge. No. 2 Battery was arriving the following day.

Inevitably, though, there were casualties. Lieutenant Tom Barron talks of an 'ominously inauspicious' arrival when the glider he was in 'came in very fast and at a steep angle', furrowing through a ploughed field. The result: jeep and trailer broke their chains and hurtled towards Barron who was sitting behind the co-pilot strapped to the side of the glider striking his left shoulder and knocking him unconscious through the glider's nose until he came to in front of the wreckage 'with a piece of plywood still strapped to my back!' Barron had had the misfortune of being 'catapulted through the rapidly disintegrating nose of the aircraft'. Unfortunately the pilot was killed and the co-pilot's legs were both amputated by the jagged metal of the torn fuselage. He survived to live the life of a double amputee.[11]

Harry Trinder (aka 'Tommy' Trinder) of 3 Battery had a quiet flight, having crossed the coast at King's Lynn and arriving at the Dutch coast over the Scheldt estuary some forty-five minutes later: 'the scene was quite peaceful.' Tommy had the unfortunate experience of his glider overrunning the LZ and careering into a pine forest. His jeep and trailer were also catapulted forward, trapping Harry between the cockpit bulkhead and the trailer. He survived via a temporary dressing station and some houses that had been commandeered as an RAP. The MO was sorting out the cases, consigning the hopeless ones to 'a massive injection of morphine and put aside to die'. Also in the glider was Gunner Wilfred Richard Evans who suffered a shattered kneecap, broken nose and a fractured skull. Tommy was eventually taken prisoner.[12]

Glider pilot Staff Sergeant Trevor Francis of G Squadron tells the story of 3 Battery's Sergeant Lofty Marriott after 'a nightmare' landing due to his flaps failing and thus rendering the glider incapable of losing the required height. So he flew over the LZ, turned and approached into the wind, so determined was he to land the gun in the right place. Too much speed and a dangerously rapid deceleration in a ploughed field meant that the wheels snapped off, the nose disintegrated and the cockpit filled up with mud, forcing Francis and his co-pilot up against the roof of the cockpit, narrowly escaping suffocation by mud. The glider was now vertical, tail in the air, but fortunately the gun and trailer held fast in position. Marriott, a giant of a man, swung into action and got his men down to the ground, and then 'by sheer strength and energy attacked the side of the Horsa with spades and an axe until he created a hole large enough to be able to get the load out.' One gunner had been dispatched up the glider to detach the chains on the gun; when the gunner let go the gun crashed to the ground, its wheel smacking into Marriott's leg, trapping him on his back. After much bellowing and cursing, the gun was eased off the sergeant who seemed none the worse for his ordeal.[13]

The signals party of the Light Regiment's HQ was on board a 1 Battery glider which included TSM Reed and his motorcycle and a jeep carrying compo rations, the wireless and spare ammunition for the guns. At about 1340 hours it performed a 'nose-heavy landing'. Gunner George Durant, driver and wireless-operator, recalls how they landed at such a steep angle on landing that us three had to jettison the tail and drop off with it. We then had to hack enough fuselage away to extract the personnel, Jeep etc…whilst other gliders were homing in and paras literally dropping on top of us. TSM Reed had badly damaged both his ankles…so we lashed him to the Jeep and I took his motorcycle…next day we got strafed by Me 109s which at first we had thought to be Spitfires! After two or three passes, they disappeared.

'Nose down and tail high' was also the consequence of a bad landing described by Bob McLeod (1 Battery, A Troop) when their glider ploughed into a pile of potatoes. One hour's struggle later and urged on by 'spasmodic small-arms fire', the load was removed through the tail, 'foreign to the methods we had been taught,' says McLeod. The pilots were slightly injured, but apart from that the only casualty was the jeep's exhaust which had been knocked off and it now emitted a 'tremendous roar'.

Soon after 1 Battery's landing, 3 Battery arrived, missing an F Troop gun; they took up a defensive position while, according to Wilkinson (pp.44–45), 'a reconnaissance party went forward to…Wolfheze to select a gun position' but 'after about ½ mile they came under enemy machine-gun fire' and returned to the LZ. Bombardier Hall, Captain Harrison and Gunner Jock Morrison of E Troop were the last three to exit their glider with Hall suspended 6ft up in a tree for a while.[14] These three, with the addition of Gunner Chrystal, were to form the advance OP party destined for the bridge. In correspondence to Bob Hilton in July 1995 Gunner Chrystal confirms that Harrison was the OP Officer, Bombardier Ogle was the OP Ack, Gunner Morrison was the driver/Op, and he himself was the signaller.

The trio 'began our 6-mile trudge to the Bridge along with others and the bulk of the 2nd Para Bn under Lt. Col. John Frost'. Harrison's jeep finally arrived, driven by Bombardier Mick Ogle, and with kit loaded, Harrison and Ogle followed the eight jeeps and two Bren gun carriers of Frost's 2nd Parachute Battalion into Arnhem. The carriers were full of extra ammunition and other matériel such as mortars, machine guns and wireless sets. En route Harrison paused at a road junction where he picked up Hall and Morrison. Hall recalls:

At a minor junction, I saw our Jeep, the E Troop O Party transport… Ogle was at the wheel. Ogle was Harrison's Ack, his assistant in the working out of details of a shoot from an OP. There was also Gunner Chrystal, the wireless operator of the 22 set in the Jeep. 'Are you through to the guns?' I asked. Chrystal nodded [that he was]. So far, so good, I thought. 'Watch the dags,' I advised, 'we don't know when we can get them recharged.' For the same reason I didn't want to open up the 68 set humped along by Morrison, unless told to do so by Harrison. There was also the business of air security. Best to keep the 68 switched off for the present. Harrison took the Jeep ahead, with Ogle and Chrystal. For some reason he wanted Morrison and me to carry on with the 68 on foot.[15]

However, this account is disputed: Gunner Chrystal clearly states in his correspondence that 'Bdr Hall and Gnr Perkins must have been somewhere else.'

Hall and Morrison proceeded 'at a stroll' towards Arnhem with houses and gardens and small buildings to their left; Hall at the rear, Sten gun at the ready. A German bicycle patrol suddenly emerged from a side road, rifles slung. Hall's Sten, however, was at the ready and so the patrol was taken prisoner and passed on (to the 2nd Parachute Battalion?) and taken to Brigade HQ). Hall and Morrison continued with the column of troops advancing towards the bridge. At the junction of Utrechtseweg and Onderlangs where the 'Lion' and 'Tiger' routes met a loud explosion rent the air: the sound of the Germans blowing up the vital railway bridge across the Rhine at Oosterbeek, the 2nd Battalion's first objective.

Meanwhile, General Student was in his HQ in a cottage near Vught some 16 miles west of Eindhoven. He could not help but hear the constant thrumming of aircraft overhead so he went out onto his balcony and watched the aerial armada drone over, some of them at very low altitude. Student was unperturbed and resumed his paperwork. The sight of bombers heading to Berlin and other eastern cities was not unusual. Student was not alone in dismissing the mass of aircraft as routine: in Deventer SS *Rottenführer* Rudolf Trapp of the 10th SS noticed that the bombers were towing gliders. SS *Standartenführer* Lippert, commander of the SS NCO School Arnhem, realized that the hundreds of aircraft were actually landing; his binoculars told him that many of the planes had their doors open and paratroopers were jumping out. Time for action: SS *Standartenführer* Klemmeier, commander of Training Battalion 1/6 was sent with a detachment of troops to investigate the landings around Nijmegen. In the Wolfheze woods, the large unit that was Sepp Krafft's SS Training and Replacement Battalion was engaged in a training exercise very close to the DZs and would soon exchange their live exercise for the real thing. It was now apparent to all that this was an airborne invasion on a huge scale. SS *Obergruppenführer* Bittrich snapped into action, ordering the 9th and 10th SS HQs to 'stand to'. Within the hour a *Frundsberg* quick-reaction squadron was detailed to reconnoitre Arnhem and Nijmegen, and take the enemy out in the LZs at Oosterbeek. Bittrich realized that the strategically important bridge at Arnhem was in peril and his units wasted no time in securing it. Troops of the *Hohenstaufen* Division were deployed to occupy the bridge at Nijmegen and establish a bridgehead to the south (see Baxter, pp.39–40). Both bridges were quickly laced with high explosives and guarded by heavily-armed SS engineers.

What Bittrich could not know at this stage was that in one hour, according to Baxter, '331 British aircraft with 319 gliders and 1,150 US planes towing 106 gliders had begun landing men and equipment over three zones between Arnhem and Eindhoven', meaning that 20,000 parachute- and glider-borne infantry and artillery had landed behind his lines. Panic and confusion in the 9th and 10th HQs gradually turned into well-oiled command and staff procedures with efficient radio communication revealing a clear picture of the situation. From his hotel HQ Sepp Krafft had a good view of the descending gliders disgorging troops, jeeps and light artillery, and parachutes slowly descending just 100 yards away.

By mid-afternoon, the 1st Air Landing Brigade (1/Border, 7/KOSB and 2/South Staffs under Brigadier P.H.W. Hicks) were busy securing the vital dropping zones west of Arnhem and were already up against the 16th SS Panzergrenadier Depot Battalion led by *Hauptsturmführer* Sepp Krafft and scratch units from the SS NCO Training School 'Arnheim' at Wolfheze, Luftwaffe troops from Deelen in *Kampfgruppe Weber* and Dutch SS *Wachbattalion* III (the 3rd SS Guard Battalion), a 1,200-man concentration camp guard unit set up under *Höhere SS und Polizeiführer - HSSPF Nordwest*. To give an idea of the number and disparity of the defending forces, the first forty-seven prisoners taken by the British were from twenty-seven different units. Krafft's 435 men were training in the woods at Wolfheze close by the landing zones; he quickly moved his men into a defensive block.

The 1st Parachute Brigade (under Brigadier G.W. Lathbury) started to advance towards Arnhem using three routes, 'Lion' (3/Para with the brigade headquarters) which was the main Oosterbeek Highway, 'Leopard' (1/Para) to the north and 'Tiger' (2/Para) to the south. By the time the brigade had reached Oosterbeek, it was encountering increased German resistance from SS *Kampfgruppe Spindler* (part of SS *Kampfgruppe Hohenstaufen* under *Obersturmbannführer* Harzer) which gradually absorbed Krafft's force and formed a solid line by the early hours of 18 September, blocking most of the 1st Parachute Brigade from the high ground and the bridge in the town centre. The only exception to this was Lieutenant Colonel John Frost's 2 Para who, having seen the railway bridge blown in their faces, pressed on and reached the town centre where they secured the northern end of the bridge over the Nederijn (Lower Rhine) and were later joined by other elements of the 1st Parachute Brigade. When part of SS *Kampfgruppe Frundsberg* (*Brigadeführer* Harmel) tried to cross the bridge on their way to Nijmegen, they found their way blocked.

Frost's 2nd Battalion, Parachute Regiment had been tasked to reach the bridge first, after the spearhead reconnaissance patrol. Their drop was textbook perfect, with Frost's 481 men forming up and heading along 'Route Lion', supported by Royal Engineers and five 6-pounder anti-tank guns. They proceeded through Heveadorp and Oosterbeek meeting little opposition but enjoying a rapturous welcome. Captain Tony Frank remembers how 'One was [amazed by] the incredible number of orange flowers or handkerchiefs that suddenly appeared like magic. The Dutch were very much in family groups, in staid clothing, out on this fine Sunday afternoon.'

His other memory was of trying to stop them slowing down our men by pressing cakes, milk, etc. on them. It was an atmosphere of great jubilation at the start of the move, mainly in the country area near Heveadorp and Oosterbeek, but it petered out when the first hold-up and sporadic firing started. There weren't so many Dutch out then, but a few stout ones stayed on and watched the fun.

Private Sidney Elliott recalls that warm welcome: 'The Dutch population rushed out of their houses, cheered us, shook hands, gave us drinks, apples and marigolds – and some of us were lucky enough to receive the odd kiss. How could this be war? It was a question that would be answered very soon.'

As noted, Lieutenant Peter Barry and his men charged the strategically vital railway bridge, only to be confronted by the centre span of the bridge exploding in their faces: lethal projectiles that were the bridge's metal plates flew into the air right in front of Barry, bringing him and his men to an immediate halt.

> 'It was lucky that we had stopped when we did, otherwise we would have all been killed,' Barry recalled. 'No one was injured in the explosion. Then I felt something hit my left; I looked back and asked if anyone was shooting. They all said 'No.' It was a German bullet. Next I felt a searing shot through my upper right arm, and it seemed to become disconnected; it went round and round in circles; the bone had been completely severed. There were only a few shots, but whoever was firing certainly picked me out as a leader and hit me.'

Barry pulled his men off the bridge, losing one man killed by German rifle fire. Frost's plan to take the main Arnhem road bridge by sending a company over the rail bridge thus enabling them to take the road bridge simultaneously from both sides was now confounded. He now had no option but to take the road bridge at its north end and assault the south side through a *coup de main*. This obviously had serious consequences not just for Frost, but also for the other British who had already arrived at or were on their way to the road bridge.

The 2nd Battalion moved on until they reached the bridge. The battalion's 'B' Company was detained by and embroiled in a four-hour action on the lower slopes of a terrain feature called 'Den Brink', but the rest pushed on, followed by the 1st Parachute Brigade's HQ party under Major Tony Hibbert (Middlebrook, pp.148–150).

Middlebrook (pp.154–55) describes how Wilhelmina Schouten, a language teacher at a local domestic science school on the Rijnkade, was having her evening meal when she noticed British soldiers passing by her window. Her diary (translated by Adrian Groeneweg) tells us:

Someone opened the front door and within a moment the ground floor and the basement were full of soldiers...the floors and stairs were full of them, but they made very little noise. The fruit which I had brought from the Betuwe that afternoon vanished in no time, and my pupils were pleased to be able to converse with them in English. Tea was made and passed around...their next task was to occupy the bridge after a few moments' rest. Quietly and without fuss they told their stories...there were several wounded among them. One Irishman had lost two fingers along the way; he did not want to stay behind because, he said, he could still fire with one hand. Another man had been shot in the eye and the thigh. Yet another had been shot in his stomach [Corporal Maybury]; he was the worst of all.

A doctor was called who explained that the Germans had commandeered all the ambulances while Miss Schouten and a male colleague [Jan Mielekamp] nursed Corporal Maybury:

Around midnight the situation changed, but for the worse. 'I think he can still hear us,' Jan Mielekamp said. 'Do you know the Lord's Prayer in English?' And I prayed: 'Our Father, who art in heaven, etc.' He opened his eyes for a moment; he recognised something. But before I reached 'Amen', he was no longer there.

Middlebrook adds that Corporal Maybury was 'buried, rolled in a piece of cardboard, in the school garden next morning'. Later, Jan Zwolle, the doctor and Jan Mielekamp were among five men arrested by the Germans and shot for alleged looting and 'terrorism'. After the war Arthur Maybury's bereft mother visited Miss Schouten. Before the war Arthur had worked as a professional photographer and travel book author. If nothing else, this story clearly illustrates the divergent ethics in play in war: on one side compassionate care with no regard for personal safety and on the other, utter brutality in a heinous atrocity.

Around 2100 hours Sergeant van Kuijk answered the door of his police station in Eusebiusplein to find a group of British soldiers there. Cautiously they entered and asked questions about the locality; soon there were about sixty troops in the police station. Outside B Troop, 1st Air Landing Anti-Tank Battery prepared a mortar position in Eusebiusplein and positioned a 6-pounder anti-tank gun on the corner. Inside soldiers removed photographs of Göring, Himmler, Goebbels and Mussert from the walls. A bust of Hitler on Commander Feenstra's desk 'was smashed and the remnants stamped on'.

The Death of *Generalmajor* Friedrich Kussin

Friedrich Kussin was the *Feld Kommandant* of Arnhem. When the British started to land close to his adopted town, he was given the job of reporting to Berlin the latest information regarding the movements of the 1st Airborne Division. With his driver Josef Wileke and an aide, Max Koster, he sped up the Utrechtseweg in his camouflaged Citroën saloon staff car, first stopping in Stationsweg in Oosterbeek.

Seemingly not much was going on there, so he proceeded on to the Hotel Wolfheze – the headquarters of the SS Panzer Grenadier Depot and Reserve Battalion 16 – to brief its commander, SS *Hauptsturmführer* Sepp Krafft. From the hotel Kussin and Krafft were able to observe across the heath the vast panoply of the Allied invasion. According to https://ninedaysinseptember.wordpress.com

> this was 5.15pm and the sound of firing could be clearly heard coming from the surrounding woods. After an exchange of intelligence during this meeting Kussin decided to leave and return to Arnhem again along the Utrechtseweg. Krafft was against this move and advised Kussin to head back into the town along the nearby railway line instead. Kussin declined to heed this advice, which was a decision that would cost him his life.

What Kussin would not have known was that the Utrechtseweg had been designated as 'Tiger Route' and was the road into Arnhem to be taken by the 3rd Battalion of the Parachute Regiment under Lieutenant Colonel John Fitch. As the general came down the Wolfhezerweg to turn left onto Utrechtseweg he ran into the lead elements of No. 5 Platoon of the 3rd Battalion's 'B' Company led by Lieutenant Jimmy Cleminson.

Cleminson explains

> it [the car] appeared without warning, and the front men of each of my leading sections, who were just behind the junction, opened fire

with Stens and rifles and riddled its exposed flank. It was all over in a flash. I saw a body leaning out of the door but pressed on, leaving Company HQ to clear it up.

Bombardier Hall, of E Troop 3 Battery 1st Air Landing Light Regiment on his way to the bridge with Gunner Chrystal and others, writes: 'When eventually we arrived at the Bridge darkness had fallen, or almost so; one of our flame-throwers had set a magazine of ammo on fire on the Bridge; the resulting fireworks made it impossible to read the twilight sky.' Daylight and darkness have a significant effect on wireless reception.

Gunner Eric Chrystal had taken off from Down Ampney and landed in his glider without incident. This is his account of the flight over in unpublished correspondence with Bob Woollacott:

We eventually took off from Down Ampney airfield and I must say I felt quite apprehensive about where we were going and what it would be like. We had a lovely flight over; looking down we saw the rescue boats following us. I think I saw one glider go down before we came over the coast of Holland. Then we saw a lot of flak, but nothing to bother us.

He then describes his recollection of the progress towards the bridge in the OP party:

Landed about 1240 hours, very peaceful except for a little SA fire, but not near us. It was so quiet, just like our exercises. Eventually removed the tail of the glider and got the Jeep and trailer out. By the LZ some of the inmates of the asylum were watching us but scattered at the noise of more SA fire, not at us.

We drove off to the main road where we passed a German [Citroën] scout car, out of action and its occupants lying dead beside it [including Major General Kussin, Field Commandant of Arnhem]. During our journey into the town of Arnhem the people were cheering us and handing out drinks and fruit, waving flags and bunting. There were plenty of orange armbands etc. in evidence. The loud explosion we heard must have been the railway bridge going up (it may not have been, of course). [It was.] Down on the riverside road we came across a barge and took captive a couple of Germans, who we handed over to some infantry. I remember thinking at the time and saying to the others – at least we've captured something. I was [now] the proud owner of a German rifle for a wee while – I felt happier with that than the [issue] Sten gun, I can tell you.

The next few hours are a complete blank...I have vague recollections of running around in back gardens and over walls and meeting with a couple of senior officers who wished us luck. Neither can I even remember who else was in our party. It must have been the terrible noise that was going on that drove it from my mind, it was terrific.

My next memories are it was getting dark – so there is a long gap – and we were under the approaches of 'the bridge' when all hell was let loose over us. It must have been one of or maybe the first charge on the bridge itself. So we made for a building where some of 2 Para were. I remember going in and passing a room where we were told that Col. Frost was and he had been wounded in the foot, or ankle I think. That would be Sunday night...to the best of my knowledge we didn't have any equipment except for my rifle. I [had] started out with a Sten gun and my small pack. The BC's party must have been there as I was put on one of the wirelesses, but we couldn't get through. I can't remember ever getting through to the GP [gun position] and switched frequency and tried 30 Corps (I think it was 30 Corps) who were supposed to be our relief. The others went back for a new set as we couldn't get ours to work.

Between late Sunday and Wednesday morning my memories are only a series of flashes in my mind, not even interconnected. Things like we were getting shelled all the time, floor by floor, driven out of the attic by the shelling. I believe we ended up in the cellar, trying to drive out the occupants of a German tracked vehicle – with some luck; 2 Para senior NCOs and WOs were collecting men for bayonet charges on the bridge. At one time I heard the old battle cry 'Waho Mohammed' [the distinctive battle cry of the British Airborne Forces] and we thought we were getting some relief but I think it was only a few stragglers. I kept trying to raise 30 Corps, needless to say without any success. Once again I must say that I can't remember *anyone* who was there with me. I don't recall even raising the GP once we were amongst the buildings. It used to be wonderful on exercise – we always got through. There aren't many built-up areas in North Africa or the Apennines when we were in action in Italy.

Waking up from catnaps I found that my teeth were tightly clenched, presumably because of the shelling: that must be a sign of something and at no time did I feel panicky other than a bit scared, and always the terrific noise, just like being at the front of the barrel when a round is fired. It was deafening.[16]

A major at Parachute Brigade HQ reported that an attempt to cross the bridge to reach the south end was repelled by machine-gun fire and absence of cover: 'All resistance at our end [the north]…had been overcome; however, there was still a lot of firing going on in the area and one or two of the houses were on fire, so it was far from quiet.'

The regiment had lost their first gun when 1 Battery, A Troop's gun was damaged on landing. Gunner Cyril Leadbeatter, a Bren-gunner of B Troop, tells how 'at the landing zone we came straight down without banking…a bullet had got lodged in the brakes and prevented the flaps from working properly.' Imagine the horror that news was met with. The glider was then strafed by a German plane that was successfully deterred by Bren gun fire.[17]

Little else untoward happened on the landing and the immediate activity, apart from the comical incident when 'Sheriff' Thompson was on the Arnhem-Utrecht road in his jeep with driver Signalman Desmond Wiggins. Thompson adopted his usual standing position (due to a leg injury in 1941) in the front and gripping the windscreen when small-arms fire caused a lurch and the windscreen collapsed, sending the CO into a somersault which ended with him in the middle of the road, much to the mirth of the Borderers and the Germans on the sides of the road. In their haste to clear the LZ, someone had forgotten to secure the latches on the windscreen.[18]

We have seen how 1 Battery landed according to plan south-west of Wolfheze while 3 Battery had to divert to them because of enemy infantry small-arms fire from the woods and sporadic mortaring to the north-east. This is when around dusk they first encountered the terrifying screams and explosions from the 'sobbing sisters' or 'moaning minnies' as twelve shells rained down on the mental health facility nearby just north of 3 Battery's position.[19] According to Cornelius Ryan (1974), these were not the standard *Nebelwerfers*. SS Major Sepp Krafft had access to one of only four prototypes available: a multi-barrelled rocket-propelled launcher that could fire oversized mortar shells. Their shells fell close to 1 Battery's B Troop. However, 'they were much less effective than conventional shelling, as the rocket scarcely fragmented and only really did damage with a direct hit.'[20]

Lieutenant Tony Driver of 3 Battery was the FOO for the 1st Parachute Battalion which was heading for the Arnhem-Ede road, the 'Leopard' route, under fire. Captain Tudor Griffiths, commander of F Troop and his OP party joined up with the 3rd Parachute Battalion on its way from 1500 hours into Oosterbeek from DZ X. They were mobbed and hindered by jubilant Dutch men, women and children. 'C' Company, however, pressed on but were ambushed after crossing the railway line and lost seven men killed and five taken PoW. Their assailants were the SS *Panzergrenadier-Ausbildungs und Ersatz-Bataillon* 16 under SS *Obersturmbannführer* Sepp Krafft.[21]

Major Munford was also delayed, but for very different reasons. While on his way to Arnhem with driver Lance Bombardier Bill Crook and wireless-operator Gunner Dennis Bowles, Munford stopped the jeep in some woods and got out. The three were attacked by German troops on bicycles who opened fire with machine guns. The only casualty was the wireless set which required a return to Brigade HQ for a replacement after which they reached the bridge, under fire.[22]

Hitler very quickly realized the seriousness of the invasion and gave it top priority, first by allocating almost the entire front-line strength of the Luftwaffe comprising 300 fighters to *Generalfeldmarschall* Walther Model, as well as the reserves and training detachments in *Wehrkreis* VI, the German military district bordering on the Netherlands, and the re-routed 280th Assault Gun Brigade. Anyone in transit or on leave near Wesel (some 3,000 men) was dragged in too. Armed Forces Command Netherlands (*Wehrmachtbefehlshaber Niederlande*) under General Friedrich Christiansen also promised reinforcements from *Generalleutnant* Hans von Tettau. The reinforcements that had been promised to II SS Panzer Corps would also start to arrive in forty-eight hours. General Student was put in charge of operations around Eindhoven, deploying *Kampfgruppe Chill* against XII and XXX Corps, along with the 59th Infantry Division and the 107th Panzer Brigade (promised by OB West) against the 101st Airborne. Those forces from *Wehrkreis* VI under General Kurt Feldt were detailed to recapture the Groesbeek Heights from the 82nd Airborne with the help of II Parachute Corps moving up from Cologne. SS *Kampfgruppe Frundsberg* was to move across Arnhem Bridge towards Nijmegen to prevent any crossing, while SS *Kampfgruppe Hohenstaufen* held the British west of Arnhem. So all the time the Germans were rallying and strengthening their opposition on all routes leading to the bridge. *Generalfeldmarschall* Walther Model, whose HQ was in Doetinchem, moved to Oosterbeek. Model wasted no time corralling all and any available support that just happened to be in the vicinity, which included tank crews returning from leave or about to go on leave or who were just passing through. SS *Sturmbannführer* Ludwig Spindler took command of these motley units, forming them into *Kampfgruppe* Harder which elided into three companies: random dismounted tank crews, logistics personnel and conscripted sailors. Armoured support came by way of three Panther tanks.[23]

Cole (pp.111–12) tells us that by 1600 hours

181st (Air Landing) Field Ambulance were established according to plan in the area of Wolfhezen…a DS was opened up in four small houses near the railway line from Arnhem to Utrecht by half-past four in the afternoon and the first operation was performed an hour later, and by the evening some sixty casualties had been admitted and one of the surgical teams was fully functioning. Eight operations were performed during the night.

The 16th (Parachute) Field Ambulance dropped with the 1st Parachute Brigade and moved from near Heelsum 'straight through Oosterbeek and the western outskirts of Arnhem into the St Elisabeth Hospital' where casualties were waiting.

Arnhem Hospitals

Quite rightly, the role of the RAMC and the 'hospitals' in which they worked tirelessly throughout the battle have been well covered in literature. Just under 600 RAMC men were in the conflict with only 31 returning to the UK immediately after the battle, many of their colleagues remaining behind with their patients and ending up as PoWs. Such was the demand for surgical and medical treatment that twenty different locations were used, serving as dressing stations, real hospitals and everything in between:

St Elisabeth Hospital was the jewel in the medical-surgical crown, adopted by two surgical teams of 16 Para Field Ambulance who tended to between 800 and 900 casualties. On 13 October they moved with their patients to Apeldoorn.

De Tafelberg Hotel and **Schoonard Hotel**: De Tafelberg was vacated by *Feldmarschall* Model when he moved HQ, and the 181 Air Landing Field Ambulance moved in on 18 September. Sequences of *Theirs is the Glory* were filmed there.

Kaserne Wilhelm III was formerly a Military Police Training Centre and a Luftwaffe depot before three of its blocks became the Airborne Hospital, each accommodating up to 900 patients. All told, some 1,750 casualties were treated. Divisional Surgeon Colonel Graeme Warrack hid in a cupboard here before escaping on 29 October.

The Old Vicarage: the 'temporary' field station in the home of Kate ter Horst and her family. The casualties just kept coming, and she narrates her wonderful story in her *Cloud over Arnhem*.

At 1800 hours the 1st Air Landing Light Regiment got out of the blocks with a solitary shoot on the Wolfheze Hotel which was said to be hosting 150 Germans of 2 *Kompanie SS Panzer-Grenadier-Ausbildungs und Ersatz-Bataillon* 16. Glider pilot Sergeant Peter Gammon of 14 Flight F Squadron recounts how he and first pilot Staff Sergeant Ron Jones were escorting 'B' Troop FOO Lieutenant Keith Halliday and his signaller who were directing gunfire onto the hotel 'which the Germans were evacuating in great panic. Except for the unfortunate inmates of a mental home which had been bombed in the morning and who were wandering aimlessly about, all the local inhabitants had retired to their cellars.'[24]

    Meanwhile, things were moving ahead elsewhere: Dennis Munford of 3 Battery and Tony Harrison 'both ended up with Colonel Frost's 2nd

Battalion. So far as can be confirmed, a total of eleven others from the Light Regiment, OP assistants, signallers and drivers, also reached the bridge.' Brigade HQ was established in a large building overlooking the ramp leading onto the bridge 'and was joined by Major Dennis Munford [and his OP party]…and by Major Bill Arnold, 1st Anti-Tank Battery Commander, who set up his headquarters in a separate building nearer to the bridge' (Wilkinson, p.48). As we shall see, they were inevitably embroiled in the fearsome fighting in and around the bridge in the coming days. How were they deployed? Munford set up separate OPs at the bridge, posting himself 'on the roof at the south-east corner of Brigade HQ; Tony Harrison in 1 Battalion HQ building and Captain Buchanan of the FOU on the east side with Captain McKay's engineers.'[25]

Meanwhile, British reinforcements arrived: part of the 3rd Battalion, the long-delayed 'B' Company of the 2nd Battalion and more engineers. In all, Frost had a respectable force: 340 men from his 2nd Battalion, 110 men from the 1st Parachute Brigade HQ, 75 men from the 1st Parachute Squadron Royal Engineers, 45 men from the 3rd Battalion, 17 glider pilots, the advance party OP men of 3 Battery, 1st Air Landing Light Regiment RA, which included Gunner Chrystal, and even a war correspondent. There were an estimated 740 men dug into buildings around the embankment and ramp leading to the north end of the Arnhem bridge. The 1st Parachute Brigade's commander, Brigadier Gerald Lathbury, was with the 3rd Battalion's men, who were blocked from advancing to the bridge.

Tony Harrison's assistant, 3 Battery's Mike Ogle, remembers that

> we were one of the first to arrive without a shot being fired. In fact I walked along the approach to the bridge but the sound of tracks soon made me dive for cover…in the shape of a half-track with some German infantry behind we really did take cover!

They then occupied a house which made a 'wonderful' OP, but were unable to contact 3 Battery's gun position back in Oosterbeek by wireless which was still at its first position near the LZ. In fact it transpired that virtually all wireless communications failed to get through that night, cutting off Brigade, Recce and RA. Captain Harrison was tasked with restoring 'the news'.[26]

Beevor describes the frenetic action that caused Ogle to take cover, setting the scene for the unrelenting hell of the next few days.[27] Soon after nightfall Frost's 2nd Battalion had arrived at the bridge around 2000 hours while Major Digby Tatham-Warter stationed his 'A' Company men underneath. Much to the horror and terror of local residents, their neat and tidy houses were requisitioned and their innocent owners strongly advised to move away. Those neat, tidy houses were rapidly transformed into military strongholds: curtains, blinds and anything else deemed flammable was torn down, while 'baths and basins were filled with water to ensure a supply of water as the electricity was bound to go off again'. Furniture was reorganized to form barricades and firing positions, while windows were smashed to limit injuries from flying glass.

Confusion among the twenty-two vehicles of Gräbner's Reconnaissance Battalion of the 9th SS *Hohenstaufen* under *Standartenführer* Harzer saw them storm over the bridge on the way to Nijmegen on Bittrich's order instead of taking the bridge, also on the orders of Bittrich. Consequently the bridge was left in the hands of a very small German force. Denied the opportunity to storm the southern end of the bridge because the pontoon bridge 0.75 miles downstream had been disabled and the railway bridge some 2 miles further west was destroyed, Frost dispatched Lieutenant Grayson from under the bridge to advance in the face of an armoured car and 20mm flak guns. The sortie was abandoned when Grayson was wounded; he was later awarded the VC for further acts of bravery.

Frost sent a group of men under Lance Sergeant Bill Fulton to take the bridge. Fulton said later:

> I led off first, up those steps on the west side of the bridge. When I reached the top I heard voices – definitely German. I told the section to be quiet and I peeped over. There was a truck with troops in the back, facing south, only 15 yards or so away. An officer or an NCO was talking to the men in the back. I thought that the element of surprise would be gone if we burst in, so I decided to wait. It was only two or three minutes before the one doing the talking got into the cab, and the truck moved off.
>
> We started to walk along the right-hand side of the bridge. It was very dark, but you could see outlines. I caught a few of the enemy hiding in corners of what looked like small huts and passed them

back to the last man in the section and told him to take them down the steps as prisoners. You could hear firing in other parts of the town, but there was no firing on the bridge itself. Then, in the gloom, I saw a rifle starting to point at me. I swung round to the right and started firing my Tommy-gun. I know I hit him because he fired his rifle as he was falling forward and I caught the bullet in the top of my left leg. I told the section behind me to report back and say that the bridge was well-manned and would need more troops. I managed to crawl behind an iron girder, and eventually a couple of medics came for me.

Fulton spent the next two years in and out of various hospitals.

A further assault recorded by Middlebrook (p.158) around 2200 hours was equally unsuccessful when another platoon attack accompanied by an engineer armed with a flame-thrower went badly wrong: just as he was about to fire, the sapper, Ginger Wilkinson, jerked the flame-thrower upwards, missing the pillbox and engulfing two shacks behind that probably contained ammunition, fuel or dynamite – or all three – causing a huge explosion and fireball. Three passing German trucks were shot up as they tried to avoid the flames. Later that night a small convoy of German trucks trundled onto the bridge from the south. The ammunition aboard the trucks exploded, adding to the inferno and din, and the occupants of the trucks were either killed or bailed out to surrender. As it happened, the seventeen Germans turned out to be part of a unit whose day job was firing V2 rockets at southern England.

More houses overlooking the ramp were taken over by the British; jeeps and the 6-pounder were parked up. Major Lewis enjoyed some success against a motley crew of young German flak gunners equipped with dilapidated rifles, but nevertheless lost a platoon commander and a sergeant with one-third of the company taken prisoner by SS *Panzergrenadiers*. The remnants joined an engineer troop led by Captain E.M. Mackay (1st Parachute Squadron RE) in the two buildings of the Van Limburg Stirum School on the east side of the ramp.

Panzergrenadiers of *Kampfgruppe Brinkmann* or the SS Battalion *Euling* (after SS *Hauptsturmführer* Karl Heinz Euling) started lobbing grenades through the windows of one of the houses. Hand-to-hand fighting in the rooms ensued while one German poked a Spandau (an MG 42) through the window, liberally spraying the British occupants. Mackay tells how he, Mackay, 'was standing there with his .45 and just pushed it in his mouth and pulled the trigger. It blew his head off, or all that was not held on by his chin strap. I grabbed the Spandau and turned it on the Germans outside.' After the war Mackay recounted his experiences in the *Royal Engineers Journal*.

Lieutenant D.R. Simpson MC, RE, responsible for sanctioning the flame-thrower attack on the pillbox on the bridge, describes the fighting around the bridge: 'I took about 18 men into the library north of a school on the east side of the ramp and started to organise it for defence, but hardly had we done so when an attack came in.' Bitter hand-to-hand fighting followed for fifteen minutes or so with the Engineers successful, but they could not hold the library,

> so I withdrew on the school building...that night they [the Germans] fired the library and attempted to set fire [to] us by setting alight two half-tracks which that morning had crashed out of control against the western walls of the school...then at 0300 hours, the Germans blew away the south-west corner of the [school] building with an ATk projector...an hour later about 60 of them [Germans] surrounded the building...every unwounded man lined the first-floor windows, armed with Stens, Brens and grenades and I gave them the signal to fire...next morning we counted 30 enemy dead, all the result of about 30 seconds' concentrated fire (Watkins, pp.18–20).

Bombardier Leo Hall, in correspondence with Bernard Nock who runs the Military Radio Museum in Kidderminster, provides some interesting insight and useful testimony on the communications issues encountered by the 1st Air Landing Light Regiment at Arnhem Bridge. Hall was NCO i/c Troop Signals with E Troop, 3 Battery. He, along with Gunner Chrystal, was a wireless-operator at the bridge from Sunday, 17 September to Wednesday the 20th 'when organised resistance was crushed by German forces'.[28] It is important to focus on this as the communications, or alleged lack of them, was a crucial factor in the 1st Air Landing Light Regiment's actions during the battle. Moreover, as Hall maintains, much of the literature on the battle contains 'gross errors'. It is helpful to have as true an historical record as possible to clear up at least some of these inaccuracies.

Some useful introductory material:

> All forward Army units had their own Signallers, members of their Regiment, cap-badged and ranked accordingly. RA base rank is 'Gunner'; 'Signaller' was merely descriptive of a Gunner whose job lay in Signalling, not in gunning. RA Signallers were responsible for communications within and forward of their Battery.

The training of RA signallers was specific to battery needs:

- Line-laying; field telephony
- R/T (= speech) using e.g. 22 and 88 wireless sets
- W/T (=Morse) by wireless or field telephone at six words per minute
- Morse by signal lamp at four words per minute
- Procedure for passing local messages and gun control orders
- Use of RA code
- Driving and motor-cycling.

Hall adds that the RA signaller's chief task was to transmit fire orders from the Observation Post to the Gun Position Officer some 3 miles to the rear. The regiment's 75mm guns had 'a theoretical range of just over 5 miles, but were too inaccurate at that range.'

Here is how Hall defines his purpose in submitting his testimony:

> **PART 1**: To give the unpublished account of how the Artillery wireless transmissions from the Bridge became the only reliable means of communication between troops at the Bridge (2nd Para Battalion plus others) and the bulk of the remainder of the 1st Airborne Div, cut off from them, several miles to the West: the Oosterbeek area.

> **PART 2**: To correct the varying and contradictory accounts of the doings of the ten-man RA party at the Bridge, particularly on [Arnhem] D-Day and D+1, reiterated in many books, and taken from the reports of Major Dennis Munford (OC 3 Battery), leading the

RA party at the Bridge. It is important to note that the corrections I offer are of the accounts given by Major Munford in interview and from his writings some 30 to 40 years after the events, and used in published works. At no time may they be inferred as criticism of his command of 3 Battery, a command I have always respected.... A 'Mike' target is one that all 24 guns of an RA regiment are called upon to engage. 'Mike One' was the enemy area round the Southern ramp and embankment leading up to the high-level bridge that spanned both Rhine and river roads.

Hall sets the scene and gives us the *dramatis personae*:

> Task of 3 Battery, comprising E Troop (4 guns) and F Troop (4 guns) was to support with artillery fire the 1st Para Brigade in its control of the Bridge.... To this end the E Troop Observation Party ('eyes of the guns') advanced along the Southerly Lion Route 6 miles to the Bridge with 2nd Battalion (Lt Col John Frost) and some Brigade HQ and attached Paras. E Troop Parachute Observation Party: Capt. Tony Harrison, Gnr Jock Morrison (humping a 68 back-pack wireless) and the present writer (i/c Troop Signals). The three of us soon met Harrison's glider-borne Jeep, driven by Bdr Mick Ogle (Harrison's observation assistant = OP Ack) and fitted with a 22 set operated by Gnr Jock Chrystal. The 22 set was in radio contact with the guns, now in readiness near the glider Landing Zone 3+ miles back from where we met. I told Chrystal not to transmit unless ordered to, this to preserve both security and battery – the power-pack, 'Dags' for short.

Hall's anxiety over the batteries was well justified: a flat battery simply meant a breakdown in any and all communications. Greenacre explains the imperative importance of resupply and recharging facilities:

> Battery resupply and recharging was another casualty of enemy action. The No. 68 set ran off primary batteries, which needed exchanging when they ran flat. The Divisional Field Workshop held 240 spare batteries for the No. 68 set.[29] It is unlikely that all these batteries were flown in as the Workshop was only allocated four

Horsa gliders for the landings. In any case, as the battle extended beyond the predicted three to four days, battery resupply would be required. A supply of 110 batteries of all types per day was expected by air-drop during the battle.[30] Collection of these batteries would have suffered.... The Nos. 19, 22 and 76 sets all ran off secondary batteries that required recharging. Recharging was an activity that had been fraught with problems throughout the war. Originally the responsibility solely of signals electricians, the process had been decentralised to be carried out by unit driver mechanics. The advantage of more accessible recharging was countered by battery life being reduced through less expert handling. Battery charging required the movement of batteries between radio sets and charging points. This was often quite impossible to guarantee under battle conditions and....communications were liable to failure due to batteries running down.[31]

An increasingly frustrated Hall adds:

We had had the very minimum of briefing (Harrison's annoying style) but one glance at the map had shown that transmissions from the Bridge were going to suffer from screening by the buildings between the Bridge and the Oosterbeek proposed gun position, this unless we operated from a height – highly likely for an Observation Post (OP). I had been tempted to suggest a relay point [for a 68 set] on the top of a high building on the river road (a kind of 1-mile Strand leading to the Bridge).

Hall again:

Harrison went ahead in the Jeep with Ogle and Chrystal: Morrison and I continued on foot. It was...about 2000 hours when we reached the Jeep at the Bridge.... A rush of the leading 2nd Bn Paras to take the other end of the Bridge had been beaten back. Harrison was now in conference with the Battalion officers somewhere when two more pieces of bad news reached us: first that the Brigadier [Lathbury] was missing; radio contact with his Jeep was lost; second, that the E Troop 22 set in our Jeep was choked with interference making communications unworkable. There would be no artillery support unless we could communicate with the guns, scheduled to advance to an open-country position near the Old Church at Oosterbeek. The interference has been widely reported (now part of the lore) as emanating from a powerful British transmitter on a near frequency. But I recognised it, and remember it, as the sort of machine-gun crackle that unsuppressed electrical devices emit, particularly from unsuppressed vehicle engines. All Army vehicles were suppressed, as must have been all German army vehicles. An old Dutch lorry brought out by the Oranje Resistance to help us was a possibility.

'Moreover,' he adds, 'all the sets were suffering so it doesn't make sense to say that the interfering station was on our frequency when we were all netted to different failures.' 'The wrong crystals' were also blamed, and we can only speculate on how much ribbing Gunner Chrystal had to endure about this. Here is what Major John Greenacre had to say about it all in his influential and authoritative 2004 *Defence Studies* article:[32]

> Much of the popular knowledge of the Battle of Arnhem is based on Richard Attenborough's 1977 epic film *A Bridge Too Far*, based in turn on Cornelius Ryan's 1974 book of the same name. On the screen, we see meek officers of the Royal Signals not wishing to 'rock the boat' before the battle, despite being aware of the inadequacies of their radio equipment. Later, upon arrival at the drop zone, those same officers report to the divisional commander that the radios are all quite useless, having been delivered with the wrong crystals. The divisional commander himself, Major-General Robert Urquhart, instigated the commentary in 1958 with his book *Arnhem*. He describes the same moment on the drop zone when, finding his signallers were having difficulty raising communications, he received 'the first intimation of a snag that was to grow and bedevil us almost to the end.'
>
> These two accounts of the same incident illustrate the way in which facts when mixed with emotion can become misinterpreted or can be attributed with undue significance. In fact only two individual radio sets were delivered with the wrong crystals: those that were allocated to the US Air Support Signals Team from 306th Fighter Control

Squadron in order to call for air support. Vital as these two sets were, the problems incurred by being delivered with the wrong crystals were far outweighed by untrained operators who received little or no briefings and the equipment being unable to be dismounted from their vehicles. The latter failure caused the sets to be destroyed by enemy fire prior to them ever beginning to serve their purpose. As for Urquhart's account, his division had been condemned to destruction long before his signal communications began to bedevil him.

The comms 'failure' was not the only calamity; the generally unpredictable situation was exacerbated by the fact that General Urquhart had got himself isolated from his HQ, Brigadier Lathbury was, as noted, missing and the Germans had come into possession of an unabridged and unredacted version of the complete MARKET GARDEN plan. Moreover, the German opposition boasted some unexpectedly (?) strong armour, some crack troops and generals of considerable experience and tactical ability. Greenacre says of this: 'Intelligence identifying General Wilhelm Bittrich's II SS Panzer Corps in the Arnhem area had been largely ignored. These risks and others were realised in a catastrophic manner that even perfect signal communications would not have overcome.'[33]

Oddly Woollacott calls 17 September 'a good day all round' (p.119). The British did at least have some boots on the ground, very near to the north end of the bridge.

Truesdale (p.82), Buckingham (pp.125 & 161) and Beevor (p.130) assess the British strength on the bridge at this point at about 740 men, of which about 385 were infantrymen made up as follows:

- Frost's 'A' and 'B' companies with part of Major Lewis's 'C' Company of the 3rd Parachute Battalion
- The 2nd Parachute Battalion HQ
- The 1st Air Landing Anti-Tank Battery with its 6-pounders
- The 1st Air Landing Light Regiment, 3 Battery, E Troop advance party under Major Munford and Captain Harrison, including Gunner Eric Chrystal. Buckingham (p.161) says there were twelve in this group, although the Regimental War Diary quoted below and other sources name only five.
- Freddie Gough with two reconnaissance jeeps

- Elements of the 1st Parachute Squadron RE and 9th (Airborne) Company RE
- Elements of the 250 (Airborne) Light Composite Company, RASC
- GPR, REME, RAOC, Royal Signals
- No. 1 Section, 1st (Airborne) Divisional Provost CMP under Lieutenant Wilfred Morley with twenty PoWs
- HQ 1st Parachute Brigade (Major Hibbert)
- A JEDBURGH team. Typically the three-man teams comprised one native officer, a British or American officer and a radio-operator. From September 1944 to April 1945, eight JEDBURGH teams were operational in the Netherlands. The first team, code-named 'Dudley', was parachuted into the east of the Netherlands one week before Operation MARKET GARDEN. The next four teams were attached to the airborne forces that carried out MARKET GARDEN. After the failure of MARKET GARDEN, one JEDBURGH team trained (former) Resistance men in the liberated south of the Netherlands. The team at Arnhem was dropped with the 1st Para Brigade (code-name 'Claude') and comprised three men: US army officer Captain Harvey Todd, Dutch officer 2nd Lieutenant Jacobus Groenewoud and wireless-operator US Technician/Sergeant Carl Alden Scott whose wireless was lost. Groenewoud was killed on 18 September fighting in the streets a few hundred yards north of the bridge; one of his jobs had been to assess how far the Dutch telephone system could be utilized. Todd was occupied sniping from the attic that was Brigade HQ; he was awarded the US Distinguished Service Cross (the US second-highest award). Scott was taken PoW and killed on 2 November while on patrol with the US 101st Airborne Division near Wageningen.[34]
- Lieutenant Colonel Eric Townsend and 16 Parachute Field Ambulance RAMC heading for St Elisabeth Hospital.

Captain Harrison and his 3 Battery, E Troop, OP Party must have arrived at Arnhem Bridge at around 2000 hours and settled into the same building as occupied by the 2nd Parachute Battalion HQ. Defensive positions had already been set up: smashing window glass to avoid flying shards, sandbagging and the like, but there was little time before Harrison revealed they were detailed to go along the river road back towards Oosterbeek just before midnight. This is how Hall remembers the mystery tour:

Harrison reappeared; we were to go back down the River road! The five of us piled in the Jeep and into the blackness of the night.... We ran over a dead body as we went. Harrison didn't tell us the reason for the patrol/journey, and we didn't ask him. I assumed he was looking for…the missing Brigadier [Lathbury] who had been last seen going down that way.... At this junction we stopped and switched off the engine. Harrison appeared puzzled, undecided. The opposite bank of the Rhine was quiet. Back at the Bridge the magazine was still giving off minor explosions. Over the main road, to the west was the light of activity: small arms and a good deal of tracer.

Hall recalls that Morrison was driving with Harrison in the passenger seat; Hall stood behind Morrison with Gunners Chrystal and Ogle in the back. The Regimental War Diary WO166/14933 entry for 23.30, 17/09/44 and Buckingham (p.130) have a different configuration: Harrison was driven by Bombardier Michael Ogle and accompanied by Gunners Jock Chrystal and Jock Morrison, and all returned safely to the perimeter.

Gunner Chrystal, however, is quite clear in his correspondence with Bob Hilton: 'Captain Harrison took everyone back to the GP in Oosterbeek. Everyone that is except me and my set, and that was me until the Wed/Thursday.'

By this time Harrison had revealed that Brigadier Lathbury was missing. Apart from small-arms fire and tracer in the distance the journey was peaceful; indeed, the main event was provided by that dead German, as Hall tells us:

> suddenly I saw a figure lying across our path. Morrison bumped the Jeep over it. We stopped, Harrison alert: 'What was that?' he asked. 'A German, Sir,' I said. 'Is he dead?' 'He is now,' I replied. No one fancied examining a bloody mess of flesh for signs of life, so we drove on.[35]

Hall remembers that

> the E Troop party (self, Morrison, Chrystal and Ogle) waited for some sort of orders.... Harrison did not discuss the wireless difficulties or

even mention them. After taking us back a couple of miles down the river front to where the 3rd Para Btn's route converged with ours, he paused, then turned us all back to the Bridge and went to report.

This is recorded in the Regimental War Diary: WO166/14933 entry for 05.00, 18/09/44 and in Buckingham (p.130). Harrison duly left his report on the capture of the north end of the bridge with Urquhart's HQ 'which was spending the night in four abandoned Horsas on LZ Z along with a group of war correspondents'. In so doing he triggered the main part of 3 Battery's move on to Oosterbeek the next day. The return journey was even more uneventful with no signs of Germans or of airborne troops.

Some contend that two jeeps actually left the bridge that night. When Major Munford learned that his signallers could not make contact with their battery either with the 22 set or with the 68 set, he checked with Majors Gough and Hibbert and found that none of their sets could make contact with the divisional area either. Quite simply, without communications there was no chance of support from the battery of 75mm guns which would move forward to Oosterbeek in the morning. Munford apparently decided that he and one of his officers, Captain Harrison, would go back to the divisional area to check the sets on their jeeps and collect fresh batteries. According to Martin Middlebrook (pp.161–62):

> This the two Jeeps did, being driven at top speed along the Utrechtseweg and surprising the Germans who were not expecting any approach from the direction of the bridge. Reaching their destination, Munford left a report on the situation at the bridge – the first news to reach Divisional HQ – had the two sets renetted and their batteries checked, and then set out back to the bridge. Munford's Jeep made it, but the second Jeep was hit, and Captain Harrison was shot in the stomach and seriously wounded. Dennis Munford's skilful Jeep driver who made this round journey of about 14 miles in the dark through German-occupied areas was Lance-Bombardier Bill Crook. Ironically, while the two officers had been away, Bombardier J.L. Hall, one of the artillery signallers who had been left behind at the bridge, had moved to a different building and, experimenting with different aerial positions, had made contact with his battery on a 68 set.

Beevor (pp.130–31 with no references) writes how they 'retuned their No. 22 sets there, collected more batteries, and reported on the situation at the bridge and drove back once more through German lines. Only Munford's jeep got through. The other officer [Harrison] received a serious stomach wound and was captured.'

This, of course, conflicts with the independent testimonies of both Bombardier Hall and Gunner Eric Chrystal, neither of whom mentions a second jeep with Major Munford on board, neither mentions getting to HQ and Hall tells us that he was actually on the mission, in the jeep and not 'left behind at the bridge'. Like Chrystal, he does not mention the injury to and capture of Captain Harrison or his jeep being shot up,[36] nor is there mention of Munford's journey in either, or Harrison's injury, in the unit War Diary as might be expected. Confusion in battle, of course, often leads to similar confusion in the recounting. Buckingham (p.117) mentions the following:

> Captain Anthony Harrison from the 3rd Air Landing Light Battery RA [1st Air Landing Light Regiment, 3 Battery, E Troop]. Harrison and the Forward Observation (FO) party from his E Troop had accompanied the 2nd Parachute Battalion to the Arnhem bridge and had been despatched back to the landing area by the Battery Commander, Major Dennis Munford, to report the seizure of the bridge to Division HQ and bring the Battery forward in support.

Nevertheless, the obituary posted in the *Arnhem 1944 Veterans' Club Newsletter* relates how 'Early in the battle he [Harrison] was hit in the stomach by a bullet and lost consciousness after being given morphine. When he regained consciousness the following day, he walked out of the dressing station and returned to his gun position which was under fierce attack.'

Neither does the *Daily Telegraph* obituary (7 September 1995) mention a jeep journey, but rather suggests otherwise and that Harrison was wounded at his gun post in a private house:

> The Germans, however, were now attacking briskly, and Harrison was wounded by a bullet in the stomach.... 'I laid back and undid my shirt and I must say there was a nasty little hole with blood

coming out. Before I had time to protest, a medical orderly rushed up and gave me a large shot of morphine.' When Harrison recovered consciousness at the dressing station the next day mortar bombs were falling all around, so he decided to discharge himself and went back to his gun position in an empty house. This too was being heavily mortared and the bombardment continued all day. Casualties mounted steadily. The shells of advancing Tiger tanks went through all eight walls of the house, making large holes in each.

Greenacre puts it well when he asserts 'Many causes and contributing factors [of the failure of the operation] have been identified and many of the facts have become obscured by myth and hearsay during the intervening years. The issues surrounding the contribution of signals communications during the battle have not escaped that obscuration.'[37]

Here is Hall's recollection of what happened next, including the awful realization that he could not secure radio contact with the regiment's guns back at the LZ:

We headed back and unloaded the 22 set from the Jeep into the 2nd Battalion HQ, overlooking the embankment of the high-rise ramp leading up to the main span of the Bridge. Back came Harrison to tell us that we were joining the OC's party in Brigade HQ next door.... So we lugged the 22 set, the 68 set and all our gear into the high Attic of Brigade HQ [in Eusebiusbinnensingel west of the bridge ramp].... I rigged up our E troop 22 set at the top of the Attic steps under a skylight; the rod aerial I poked through the skylight as high as I could, worried that I might be risking trouble if the Germans spotted it at daylight. I switched on the set: still the crackle of interference making communications impossible. In order to check, I think, that the 22 wasn't faulty ('Dis'), I rigged up the 68 Back-Pack set that Morrison had humped the 6 miles-plus from our Dropping Zone. The aerial reached almost to the apex of the pitched timber-lined roof. Switching on, I found interference still evident, but much less so than that on the 22. I called up Control (the Battery Command Post) on my 22 set, asking '...report my signals, over'. Through the 68 set came the clear reply, 'OK, over.' So that was it, cracked: transmit on the reasonably powerful 22 with outdoor aerial and receive on the less powerful 68 with indoor aerial.

Back beyond Oosterbeek, 1 Battery and the rest of 3 Battery had been getting ready for the night south-west of Wolfheze at the edge of a wood where, Tom Kent recalls, gun pits and slit trenches were dug, passwords issued, night sentries posted and smoking banned. Unnecessary talking and movement were also restricted. The slightest sound, even snapping twigs, set everyone on edge. A padre with the division caused a scare and escaped death when he approached the gun emplacement and did not respond to the password; he certainly had God on his side that night, confessing that he had forgotten the reply to the password.

It was by now about 0100 hours on Monday, 18 September.[38] Hall catnapped during the night, occasionally calling up Control to be sure he still had contact. For whatever reason, quite extraordinarily he omitted to send a message down to Munford and Harrison that they were through to the battery. However, Munford let it be known 'that Harrison was going to make his way back to the Battery and that [he] Munford was coming up to the Attic to register the area at first light'.[39] This he did: in order to be within range of the bridge, 3 Battery had moved its guns onto the area around Oosterbeek Old Church at around 05.00, and Munford fired off six rounds to register the south end of the bridge as Target Mike One; that is a whole regiment twenty-four-gun shoot.[40]

Bennett (2007, p.42) describes the communications breakthrough and its huge consequences:

> On the morning of D+1, the artillery link opened between Divisional HQ Royal Artillery and the 3rd Air Landing Light Battery HQ at the Arnhem road bridge. Not only did Frost get artillery support but the link enabled Division to open communications with 2nd Battalion for the first time since it left the Drop Zone on [Arnhem] D-Day.

Captain John Lee of the 1st Air Landing A Troop had been able to get round the communications disaster when, with Gunners Wally Bowtell and Percy Aldred with Bombardier George Stubley, he travelled with the Border Regiment B Company to Renkum on a mission to block the

Utrecht-Oosterbeek-Arnhem road. Lee and Major Tom Armstrong, B Company Commander had a prime position on the roof of a brickworks whose manager was happy to lend his fully-functioning land line to Lee.[41] Greenacre points out that the Dutch telephone system could have provided an effective alternative, if temporary, means of communication; a fact that was acknowledged when, before the battle orders were issued, prohibiting any destruction of communications infrastructure. While the Germans astutely made good use of the local telephone system throughout the battle, the British were much more cautious, believing that pro-German Dutch staff might intercept their communications and use them against them. Granted, the Netherlands 'contained a higher proportion of Nazi sympathisers, always willing to betray resisters, than any other occupied country'. In reality the Dutch Resistance 'had reliable men and women placed in the local telephone exchange'.[42] To give one example, when Captain Rutherford, one of the battalion MOs, was trying to arrange the evacuation of thirty-five wounded paratroopers, he picked up the phone and spoke to the St Elisabeth Hospital on the civil line. The doctor had, to put it simply, spoken from a British position to a point in German-occupied territory. The Dutch Resistance, confident in the security, had pointed out to at least one senior British officer 'the great advantage the airborne forces could derive from the private telephone system of the Gelderland Provincial Electricity Board (PGEM)', but was told that the 'paratroopers' own field transmitters would do'. In effect, the Resistance had three telephone lines at their disposal. In addition to the PGEM there was an entirely separate network, also belonging to the PGEM, to which every transformer substation in Gelderland was connected, which in turn was linked to similar networks in all the provinces in the Netherlands, including Nijmegen. In addition, 'it was possible to access the public telephone system by dialling a secret number' (Bauer, p.127). As stated, the Germans took full advantage of this telecommunications bonanza: the commander of the *Hohenstaufen* Division said 'it was an advantage for our command that an excellent telephone system existed in Holland and in particular in Arnhem. This made it possible to dispense almost entirely with radio communications during the battle, especially as our signals section possessed very few transmitters that were of any use.'

There were undoubtedly persistent problems with the radio equipment, for which Browning blamed his signals section, but there were certainly other means of communications available, such as the GHQ Liaison Regiment that was in contact with London through its special radios, as was a BBC news team with a VHS set. The 1st Airborne had direct contact with 2/Para and with the Corps rear headquarters at Moor Park, Hertfordshire that was also in intermittent contact with Browning. The Dutch Resistance were sending coded messages to the 82nd Airborne, warning them that the 1st Airborne was in trouble on a telephone system that reached as far south as Son and the 101st Airborne. According to http://www.historyofwar.org/articles/battles_arnhem.html 'The failure was not primarily one of communications but one of staff work and experience. British I Airborne Corps asked Moor Park for copies of the signals and contact was established the next day, but for the first two vital days of the operation, Browning was never in complete control.'

Greenacre illuminates the communications issue when he points out that the Royal Artillery

> established its own signal training regiments throughout the war. This resulted in a level of signals communication capability at Arnhem that 'the divisional gunners demonstrated, as gunners had done before, displaying an expertise that seemed to be denied to other operators' [e.g. the Royal Engineers]. The imperative behind the requirement for the highest levels of skill in signals communication for the RA is clear. Infantry battalions and armoured regiments could still operate to some extent even in the event of a complete communications failure. For the artillery a break in communications between guns and observers would render those guns useless without target information to prosecute. The communication links studied for the purposes of this article were all manned by Royal Signals or RA personnel, all of whom were trained to high levels. Training, therefore, is unlikely to have been a factor in those early communication failures.

By the end of the day the 2nd Battalion, Parachute Regiment was isolated around the northern end of the road bridge in central Arnhem. The progress of the 1st and 3rd Battalions had been decisively checked on their way into Arnhem by unexpected opposition. Over the next twenty-four hours attempts to reach the bridge were made in a number of spasmodic attacks, each along the same route. All were repulsed, resulting in the 1st, 3rd and 11th Battalions, Parachute Regiment and the 2nd Battalion, South Staffordshire Regiment being practically destroyed as fighting units. Greenacre concludes that 'the lack of coordination was the crux and the failure of communications between Divisional HQ and the bridge was a significant factor within it.'

Generally, the technical inadequacies of the radio sets together with unfavourable environmental factors have been blamed. Urquhart wrote: 'We were soon to learn that our radio sets were inadequate for the purpose, and their effectiveness was to be further limited by the sandy, heavily-wooded terrain.'[43] The official report agrees, stating that on the divisional command net, 'it is found that the range of the [No. 22] set is not always sufficient, and the receiver owing to its lack of sensitivity frequently made communications most difficult.'[44] Greenacre asks: 'How did an elite fighting formation such as the 1st British Airborne Division, at the cutting edge of military development, come to be so poorly equipped in such a key area?'

In an effort to explain why communications were so temperamental or non-existent, Greenacre cites the experience of the 1st Air Landing Light Regiment: 'If the area had presented unique challenges to communication then it might be expected that all links would be affected by it. This, however, is not the case. All [eventually] of Light Regiment RA's links appeared to function, although many of these were over relatively short distances.' He reminds us that the HQ RA net was working and the Divisional HQ link to the bridge was reliable after 0820 hours on D+3.

Of particular note is the link maintained by 3 Battery of the Light Regiment RA. This link was maintained from D+1 until the evening of D+3 between the Officer Commanding 3 Battery, Major Dennis Munford on the bridge and the battery command post near Oosterbeek Lower Church. The battery's gun lines were in support of the 1st Parachute Brigade; hence Munford was attached to the Brigade HQ on the bridge.

Greenacre asks the question that historians, military specialists and veterans have been asking since 17 September 1944:

> E Troop 3 Battery's and the Divisional HQ link to HQ 1st Parachute Brigade were almost exactly the same in terms of length and both used the same equipment at either end of the link.... What then

caused one of them to not function for the first sixty hours of the battle while the other was perfectly operational 'apart, that is, from a few minor hiccups and interruptions on the way'?[45]

Greenacre concedes that the 3 Battery link had a more direct and unobstructed path over the flood plain of the Neder Rijn, while the Divisional HQ link followed a path over urban areas. However, the frequencies in use were very low and 'at the lower end of HF terrain shows no appreciable additional loss [of a signal]'.[46] In short we must conclude (with Greenacre) that

> there appears to be no technical reason for the discrepancy. If 3 Battery was able to maintain their link there should have been no reason technically why Divisional HQ should not also have had communications with the bridge. Communication from Hartenstein to the bridge was not only possible, but should have been easy.[47]

Chapter Twelve

Day 2: Monday, 18 September

Jo Van Velzen, 20 years old and living with her parents close to the battleground, describes how the national flags the Dutch had jubilantly hung out on Monday 18 September were soon withdrawn when German troops started moving into her street, rapidly converting it into a muster area for troops preparing to repulse the British:

> Some of them came into our house. I noticed their ages seemed to vary from sixteen to sixty. They came right into the house and cellars. There was no unusual behaviour [euphemism for sexual violence?] and they were there until Friday morning. On Thursday we saw them being sent off to attack the British positions, shitting themselves with fear.

When Jo and Elly were permitted to go to the dairy, 'There were terrible sights of the heavy fighting. British soldiers dead and dying, blood dripping from their mouths and ears – not being looked after. The German dead were covered by blankets…I think we were lucky not to be shot for walking across the battlefield.'

Such was Jo's conclusion after being asked for their papers which they did not have, only their cans of milk as evidence of their innocence which probably saved their lives and persuaded the Germans that they had not been harbouring British soldiers.

As noted, the Germans were beginning to systematically and methodically deconstruct the British defences, deploying a brace of Tiger tanks that managed to nudge their way through the wreckage of Gräbner's wrecked vehicles still strewn across the Arnhem Bridge. 'Two 88mm Flak guns were set up on either side of the southern approach to the bridge, delivering point-blank fire.' Flak guns were obviously anti-aircraft guns, the abbreviation for the German *Flugabwehrkanone*.

The Battle of Eusebiusplein

Eusebiusplein and the area around it was the scene of some of the most intense and bloody fighting over the next few days. An Airborne pillar on the grass next to Eusebiusbuitensingel, close to the northern ramp of what is now named the John Frostbrug, commemorates the defence of the Van Limburg Stirum School by a group of Royal Engineers.

In September 1944 three properties stood on the site, running from the pillar down to the present-day Airborneplein (Airborne Square). The houses fronted onto Eusebiusbuitensingel. Closest to the Airborneplein was the villa of Countess Cornelia van Limburg Stirum, Eusebiusbuitensingel 67. Next to this was the villa which from 1897 to 1938 was the 'Red School' (Eusebiusbuitensingel 68) that housed the school of the Association for the Establishment and Maintenance of Schools with the Bible for Primary Education. After that it was the office of the Municipal Tram Company until 17 September 1944. A path ran from the back garden of No. 68 up to the northern bridge ramp ('Bleckmann's little path'). The Van Limburg Stirum School stood at the corner of Marktstraat and Eusebiusbuitensingel. The Airborne pillar stands more or less on the site of the school.

The 1st Parachute Squadron, Royal Engineers was commanded by Major Douglas Murray, with orders to render harmless any demolition charges found under the railway bridge at Oosterbeek and the ship bridge and road bridge in Arnhem. Captain Eric Mackay of 'A' Troop wrote:

> The enemy was now interposed between my small troop and the force at the bridge. They were in a plaza which lay directly in our path. My first attempt to cross this 'trap' failed, but we succeeded in driving them into a side street. They now set up two machine guns in a couple of ground floor windows from where they could cover the entire square. But it was essential that we reached the bridge, so I gathered my troop, with handcarts, at the edge of the square. When everything was ready we crossed the 40 metres of open terrain at a jog-trot. It was a gamble, but it paid off and there were no more casualties. We pressed on and arrived at the bridge a few minutes later. Shortly after arriving we went over on to the attack, supported by our R.E. with flame-throwers. A bloody fight ensued with heavy losses on both sides.[1]

On arrival, the 1st Parachute Squadron was deployed to various positions around the bridge to reinforce the perimeter and to fulfil their role as sappers if and when required. Major Douglas Murray probably remained in and around Frost's battalion HQ in Eusebiusbinnensingel, while Lieutenant Donald Hindley and his ten men from the 1st Parachute Squadron HQ took up positions at the corner of Eusebiusbuitensingel and Westervoortsedijk.

Captain Mackay moved into the 'Red School' with his 'A' Troop. Earlier, Lieutenant Dennis Simpson and half of 'B' Troop had occupied the Van Limburg Stirum School. Around midnight Simpson's group was reinforced with the arrival of Major Peter Lewis and fourteen officers and men of 'C' Company, 3rd Parachute Battalion. Shortly after reaching the British perimeter Lewis's company was attacked and suffered heavy losses. Besides his own group in the school only 8 Platoon was left, and that had occupied positions in the Camiz dairy factory in Westervoortsedijk and the Jos Pé picture postcard business at the corner of Badhuisstraat and Nieuwe Kade.

At 24.15 'C' Company's 7 and 9 Platoons were attacked. Simultaneously, 'A' Troop, in the building to the north of the Van Limburg Stirum School, came under heavy machine-gun fire. Mackay:

> The enemy crept up to us through the shrubbery before we realized what was happening. They threw hand grenades through the windows of the ground and first floors. Almost at once they established a foothold in the souterrain, but a violent man-to-man fight with fists, boots, rifle butts and bayonets drove them out again. But our position had suddenly worsened. The Germans now brought up a machine gun and by pushing it through a window opening could cover everyone in the room. Luckily I was standing close to the window and shot the gunner: I then turned the machine gun on the enemy outside. Now hand grenades rained in through all the windows and a hellish racket began. It was obvious that if we stayed here much longer we would all be killed or wounded: half of the group was wounded.[2]

Several sappers were wounded in the fighting around the 'Red School'. At about 0045 hours, Captain Mackay decided to abandon his position and withdraw to the nearby Van Limburg Stirum School. He and five men cleared the garden of Germans using hand grenades and with semi-automatic Sten gunfire. The wounded were brought out and the whole group joined the remaining half of 'B' Troop.

Captain Mackay again:

First of all I took a quick look around the school. It consisted of a basement, two storeys and an attic. I decided to continue the fight from the first floor, defend only the ground floor, and use the attic as a lookout post. I had fifty men (including seven wounded and one lieutenant), six Bren guns, plenty of ammunition, hand grenades and some explosive materials; no anti-tank guns, very little food and just the water in our canteens; no medicines except morphine, and some emergency dressings.[3]

There were two more German assaults during the night, both of which were repulsed. At first light, German machine-gunners opened fire from the 'Red School', shooting at the north side of the Van Limburg Stirum School.

Soon after 0900 hours on the 18th a German reconnaissance unit, SS *Panzer-Aufklärungs Abteilung* 9 from SS Panzer-Division *Hohenstaufen*, led by *Hauptsturmführer* Viktor Eberhard Gräbner, drove across the bridge from the south.

Later that day Colonel Frost decided to commit his reserve: 6 Platoon from his 'B' Company under Lieutenant James Flavell which retook Rijnkade 119 as well as the Public Works building, but this had to be abandoned a few hours later when the Germans set it on fire with phosphorus shells.[4] The German *Kampfgruppe* Knaust brought up heavy mortars and began bombarding the roof of the Van Limburg Stirum School. The 'Red School' was deliberately set on fire by them and burning debris fell on the wooden roof of the adjacent building. This caught fire at around midnight, but the fire was eventually put out. Infantry attacks were repulsed.

The Germans mistakenly believed that the British had been eliminated and a large group of about sixty soldiers went out onto the grass strip by the Van Limburg Stirum School to have a smoke. Major Lewis and Captain Mackay ordered their men, on a given signal, to open fire and throw grenades. The result of this sudden hail of bullets and grenades was devastating. Some forty or so Germans lay dead or dying on the ground. Only a few escaped. Lieutenant Wright wrote later that a laughing Major Lewis went from room to room, shouting that he had never had such a good time.[5]

Sergeant van Kuijk describes the action around Eusebiusplein on the 18th:

> Tommies occupy the corner houses in Oude Hofstraat…the building [the police station] begins to receive many direct hits from German artillery and machine guns. In one of the front rooms we find an unexploded [12cm] shell…in the evening the building of the Queen's Commissioner on the Markt is set on fire which eventually sets fire to other adjacent buildings. Houses in Eusebiusbinnensingel are also ablaze…. Tommies come in and out…a few names I remember are Private Harry Wood [corporal in 'B' Company, 2nd Parachute Battalion] and Captain Killian [actually Captain J.E. Killick, commander of the 89th Parachute Field Security], a real battler who fights without a helmet and goes through hell and high water for his men.

Significantly van Kuijk writes how he and his staff were 'concentrating mainly on the passing on of messages by telephone to other police stations, and the observations of German troops in our surroundings. Since we ourselves are armed only with FN pistols we are given the rifles of wounded soldiers.' Van Kuijk adds that they were in contact with the Resistance fighting forces 'and we have regular communication with the men at the municipal police station who keep us up to date with events in other parts of the town.'

On Tuesday the 19th the Germans deployed tanks and began shelling the south wall of the school. The corner house at the other side of Marktstraat, defended by Lieutenant McDermont's platoon of the 2nd Parachute Battalion, was also attacked. This group was forced to withdraw. A counter-attack led by McDermont failed and he was badly wounded in the attempt. Two days later he died of his wounds in the Municipal

Hospital. The only other house still in British hands on the east side of the bridge was the building occupied by Captain Briggs and Lieutenant Hindley.

The Benzedrine tablets dispensed by Captain Mackay did not have the desired effect. Many soldiers began to hallucinate and others began to suffer from double vision.

During Wednesday afternoon the British in the Van Limburg Stirum School heard the sound of heavy 'A' Company of the 2nd Parachute Battalion was driven back to the west side of the bridge: Lieutenant John Grayburn was killed during this withdrawal. After the battle he was awarded a posthumous Victoria Cross, and was posthumously promoted to captain.[6] A Tiger tank began a systematic shelling of the building and one shell after the other drilled through the walls. Fire broke out in three places, probably caused by the German use of phosphorous shells.[7] The water supply had been cut off so the fires could not be extinguished.

Captain Wilfred Robinson was one of the few officers not wounded during this shelling. He recalls:

When I relieved Lieutenant Wright in the observation post in the school attic I could see a German gun in the road just to the north and east of the bridge. It fired at the school. Suddenly I saw an explosion near the gun and I thought it had been hit by one of our own shells. It dawned on me later that of course we had no supporting guns of that calibre with us. The explosion I saw was the gun being fired, and virtually simultaneously a shell struck the attic roof, just to the right of my observation point. The roof had caught fire. I thought at the time that it was a phosphorous shell, but I'm not sure that the Germans were using them. I left the attic immediately. This shell had wounded Major Lewis and Lieutenant Wright who were having a sleep on the first floor. By the time I reached the first floor where Major Lewis and Lieutenant Wright had been I heard that he, Lewis, had given the order to evacuate the building. I was last to leave the school because there were many wounded on stretchers and I had to make sure that they were all brought out. When I came outside I realized that the Germans had us pinned down from a position north of the school. There was nothing we could do. The increasing losses forced Major Lewis to surrender. As I was not wounded I felt it was my duty to try to escape, but I also felt guilty at leaving the wounded. I asked Major Lewis if I could leave and he yelled to one and all that everyone who was capable of doing so must attempt to escape. We crossed the road to the east side of the school and hid among the shrubs in a garden. I hoped that when it became darker we could possibly join Lieutenant Colonel Frost's force to the west of the school on the north side of the bridge. I can't remember how many of us were in the garden. I would say between five and nine men. I recall that Captain Mackay of the 1st Parachute Squadron RE was one of the group. I peeked around the corner of the fence on the east side of the garden we had entered and saw that the street was full of German soldiers who seemed to be taking a break and were unaware of our presence. But they must have seen us crossing the road because they began searching the garden. We were well hidden in the shrubs in our camouflaged uniforms, but sadly enough a young German trod on someone's arm or leg, and he gave a shout. Suddenly several Germans stormed into the garden and I thought they were going to shoot us. They took us prisoner and next day we were taken by lorry to a PoW transit camp in Emmerich, Germany.

At some point Brinkmann ordered an ill-fated assault on Frost's stronghold. The troop-filled lorries were met with a fusillade of fire from Frost's men, and anyone who leaped from the blazing trucks was promptly cut down by Bren gun fire. A similar fate awaited a group of SS soldiers hiding in an ambulance; an armoured assault was likewise destroyed by two British 6-pounder anti-tank guns (Baxter, p.71).

The Undoing of *Hauptsturmführer* Viktor Eberhard Gräbner

Enter *Hauptsturmführer* Viktor Gräbner.
    Things changed dramatically in the mid-morning of Monday, 18 September. Between Arnhem and Nijmegen the 9th SS Panzer Division's Reconnaissance Battalion was skulking somewhere on the road between Arnhem and Nijmegen. The 9th was a tough outfit equipped with twenty-two armoured cars, half-tracks – some of which sported anti-tank guns – and armoured personnel carriers. A proud Viktor Gräbner had received the Knight's Cross of the Iron Cross the day before for bravery in

Normandy. That Monday he had led his Reconnaissance Battalion over the bridge before the British got there, on a sweep down to the main road to Nijmegen. Nothing doing there, so he turned back to return over the bridge to reach his divisional command post in Arnhem.

Gräbner was a skilful, experienced former Wehrmacht officer who had transferred to the Waffen SS and was described as 'an impressive soldier, the right man for the job.' Both popular with and esteemed by his men, he was always up for the fight and was unafraid to make himself highly visible when necessary in action.

Gräbner's particular asset to the German military lay in his predilection for blitzkrieg speed and shock, enthusiastically deploying the firepower of his assault guns and armoured cars, some of which boasted mounted 75mm guns; all had machine guns. Gräbner's was the highest concentration of armoured vehicles in the 9th SS Panzer Division.

At 0900 hours the SS men settled into their vehicles, wearing their 'Waffenrock' mottled camouflage uniforms. Gräbner, at the front as usual and peacocking in a captured British Humber armoured car, jabbed the air twice and the column was off, roaring 'like a Grand Prix start', in the words of Robert Kershaw (*It Never Snows in September*). The battalion rumbled and clattered northwards up the two-lane road to the bridge with armoured cars leading the way, followed by the half-tracks. Behind them came sandbagged trucks loaded with more infantry.

So speedy was the advance that some of the leading elements crossed the bridge and sped down the ramp into the town, but not everything was going as Gräbner would have liked. The British, in the upper storeys of their buildings overlooking the bridge, held their fire in the midst of German tracer. Two armoured cars rolled over, then three more, and then the British opened up with everything they had, blazing away with Bren and Vickers machine guns, anti-tank guns and PIAT anti-tank weapons. C Troop's Sergeant Cyril Robson, wielding a 6-pounder, remembers how 'An armoured car hit a British mine in the road and its wheel exploded skyward, flying into the air in slow motion, halting the vehicle' (Middlebrook, p.292). British troops lobbed grenades into the open-air half-tracks; nearly every German vehicle was hit by PIATs or anti-tank guns. 'Robson fired solid-shot shells at the parapet at the side of the bridge until he cut a V-shaped section away and was then able to fire into the sides of German vehicles passing the gap.' Robson's gun probably did more damage than any other weapon.

The carnage was total: German troops were cut to pieces, while 'some vehicles toppled over or slewed off the embankment of the lower ramp'. Major Freddie Gough blazed away with his jeep's Vickers machine guns. Maybe one of his shots killed *Hauptsturmführer* Gräbner, his opposite number. Gräbner was shot in the chest and his body was never found. *Hauptsturmbannführer* Karl-Heinz Recke took over command.[8] Two German half-tracks came to a halt on 'Bleckmann's little path' at Eusebiusbuitensingel 68. The occupants were riddled with British bullets and none survived.[9]

The only British officer who was not firing was Frost himself, who watched the battle and said later, somewhat pompously, 'A commander ought not to be firing a weapon in the middle of an action. His best weapon is a pair of binoculars' (Middlebrook, pp.293–94). You can see his point, but a pair of binoculars never killed your enemy, especially when he needed to be killed.

Captain Mackay remembers:

Suddenly I heard a rumble from just under the window. When I looked outside I saw one of them [half-tracks] immediately below me. It was only a metre and a half away from me and I looked the driver straight in the face. I don't know who was more surprised. The vehicle must have come down the narrow path between the ramp and the school. He reacted quicker than me because, with a dirty great grin, he loosed off three shots at me. The only shot to hit me splintered the field glasses that were hanging around my neck. The lads quickly arrived at my side and within seconds he and his men were no more.[10]

Corporal Geoff Cockayne also described the action:

I had a German Schmeisser and had a lot of fun with it. I shot at any Gerry that moved. Several of their vehicles – six or seven – started burning. We didn't stay in the room we were in but came out to fire, keeping moving, taking cover and firing from different positions. The Germans had got out of their troop carriers – what was left of them – and it became a proper infantry action. I shot off nearly all my ammunition. To start with, I had been letting rip, but then I became more careful; I knew there would be no more. I wasn't firing at any German in particular, just firing at where I knew they were.

German vehicles crashed into each other, German soldiers evacuated and were cut down. Some even jumped over the balustrade into the river to avoid the certain death that awaited them on the bridge, which was now comprehensively blocked.

As we have noted, all the while Major Dennis Munford was calling down 'Mike One' fire from 1 and 3 Batteries, 1st Air Landing Light Regiment over in Oosterbeek.

Vehicles ground to a halt when driver and co-driver were immobilized or killed while Gräbner's attack began to disintegrate. SS Corporal Mauga, crouching in his half-track, witnessed the reverse, saying that 'Suddenly all hell broke loose ahead of us. All around my vehicle there were explosions and noise and I was right in the middle of this chaos.'

As noon approached, the Germans began to withdraw on foot, abandoning the twelve wrecked vehicles of their assault convoy. The British lost nineteen men and the Germans something in the region of seventy. Gräbner's defeat impacted hugely on the morale and tactics of the 9th SS Panzer Division; Commander Walther Harzer decided he would now shift his focus to the north side of the bridge to dig the British out. The wreckage on the bridge presented a major obstacle. SS *Sturmbannführer* Brinkmann's 10th *Kampfgruppe* under the command of the 9th SS were detailed, with the 25-year-old SS *Sturmbannführer* Knaust's *Panzergrenadier* Training and Replacement *Bocholt* to clear the northern ramp of all that detritus. In the meantime SS *Standartenführer* Heinz Harmel was none too pleased that the bridge was closed to him and he had to take a long and tedious detour over the Rhine ferry crossing in order to reach his objective of Nijmegen. Meanwhile, house-to-house and hand-to-hand fighting broke out as British paratroopers tried in vain to reach Frost, and the situation was exacerbated as terrified civilians broke cover and fled their houses only to be cut down in murderous crossfire.

Despite the success over Gräbner, the British were soon being assailed by two *Kampfgruppen*, Brinkman and Knaust, and from three directions (Baxter, p.93). Tiger tanks and 8.8cm flak guns were deployed against

Frost and his men; the eighteen buildings they had occupied were now reduced to ten.

Unfavourable weather started to play a part in operations. The air support planned for the operation was drastically curtailed, thanks in part to the weather but also to Browning's astonishing failure to arrange RAF and USAAF liaison officers for British I Airborne Corps and Brereton's insistence that aircraft in Belgium remain grounded while his were in the air. In Germany and the northern Netherlands, the weather cleared just in time to allow the Luftwaffe's full effort to begin. MARKET GARDEN was the only battle in the campaign for North-West Europe to be fought with Allied air inferiority, much of it self-inflicted (http://www.historyofwar.org/articles/battles_arnhem.html).

As noted, first light on Monday, 18 September had dawned around 0715 hours (according to Bombardier Hall), with Munford climbing to the attic and registering the 'Mike' targets around the bridge now that he was in contact with the 3 Battery Command Post at Wolfheze. F Troop, 3 Battery had moved to a position near the church at 0700 hours and were in position by 0830 hours with no enemy in sight. Their shelling added considerably to the ongoing mayhem and slaughter at the bridge, notably among the occupants of the armoured vehicles as they bailed out, joined by a number of equally doomed motorcyclists. Civilians in Oosterbeek, meanwhile, were bringing sandwiches, milk and the like for the British. No. 2 Battery was on its way from England in the second lift so only six guns were available for the time being as 1 Battery was setting up defences at the LZs and DZs where the 4th Parachute Brigade and other units of the division were due to land. Munford describes the reluctance on the part of his fellow officers, fearful of a repeat of the 'drop-shorts' endured by the paratroopers in North Africa (not by the Light Regiment): 'But I persisted and was allowed to register on the approach road at the south end of the bridge – only about six rounds – but we got E and F troops ranged on to it and recorded it.'

In Oosterbeek 'Sheriff' Thompson declared that it should be recorded as 'Mike One'.[11] Captain John Lee, B Company, Border Regiment, wiped out a group of German infantry near Renkum and later directed 1 Battery's first shoot.

No. 3 Battery had, as we have seen, at 0500 hours hurriedly relocated from its night position at Wolfheze to the area around the Old Church in

Lower Oosterbeek, thus bringing their guns within range of the bridge. They were protected during their move by a force of forty glider pilots under Major Croot. The three guns of F Troop were allocated a position just to the east of the church, under Lieutenants Tom Conlin and Frank Moore. Noel Farrands of E Troop started up his guns along a track running west of the church (Wilkinson, p.55). The Battery Command Post was established by Lieutenant Peter (Sam) Wilkinson in an attic along Kerkpad between the two gun positions.

On the previous evening 3 Battery's Lieutenant Frank ('Pepys') Moore was busy making a meal, the first since arriving in the Netherlands. The field phone rang: it was Battery Captain David Lindsay to say that 'Sheriff' Thompson 'felt we were very isolated and exposed and he wanted to bring us back to the main divisional area'. Lindsay begged to differ, feeling that the battery was in the best possible position and urged Moore to be in no rush getting back to Thompson as it would soon be dark anyway and too late to move. Moore was more than pleased to be able to get on with his meal.[12] He adds that he later drove up to RHQ to find 'Sheriff' who was amazed he'd got through given that a platoon had been virtually wiped out on the route earlier in an ambush: '3 Battery never moved. Had we done so the whole Division could easily have been surrounded and the eventual escape route would never have existed.'

That move to the Old Church took 3 Battery along a route 'barely cleared of enemy', and TSM Tom Kent recalls how 'We commenced to dig in, deep slit trenches and gun pits to give us access to fire on a 360-degree arc. We even built a toilet in the bottom of a slit trench on that first day.'

E and F Troops' positions were separated by an apple orchard, the trees of which were heavy with fruit. The fruit was picked and the trees felled in order to afford a clear field of fire and to facilitate movement, with the added advantage that it ensured the perimeter would not be cut off from the river.[13]

By 0900 hours the guns were all in place, they could see the bridge and the Command Post was in contact with Major Munford at Parachute Brigade HQ at the bridge. The CRA agreed that the guns of the 1st Anti-Tank Battery should reinforce 1 and 3 Batteries so two 17-pounders from D and P Troops were brought up (Wilkinson, p.55).

It was at about this time that Kate ter Horst, her house and her family entered the battle. Medical officer Captain Randall Martin had dropped on the 17th and immediately started attending to glider casualties and the wounded on the LZs. Martin asked Kate ter Horst if her house, the Old Vicarage, near to the church, might be used as a Regimental Aid Post (RAP), assuring her that he did not anticipate any significant inconvenience since only the lightly wounded would be treated there with the more seriously injured dealt with elsewhere, namely the hospital in the Hotel De Tafelberg three minutes away. As Truesdale says (p.86): 'Eventually the ter Horst house would become hospital, mortuary and burial ground.' A detailed and moving account of the family's magnificent efforts in tending for the wounded, providing a mortuary and a graveyard in their garden, can be found in Kate's *Cloud over Arnhem*. One of the casualties there, now General Sir Frank King GCB, MBE, described her in the foreword to the book as 'shining like a beacon of sanity, comfort and hope'. That about says it all.

Woollacott tells us that Major Munford ordered Tony Harrison and Mike Ogle to speed back from the bridge to the main body of the regiment and 'ensure that wireless communication between 3 Battery and the OP was made effective immediately'. This was described by 'Sheriff' Thompson:

> Early on the 18th 3 Light Battery made a rapid advance through country only partly cleared of enemy to a position by Lower Oosterbeek Church which had been reconnoitred by Captain C.A. Harrison on the way back from 2 Parachute Battalion at Arnhem Bridge. By this time the Germans had already cut off the bridge party from the remainder of the Division and Captain Harrison had to drive at speed through their lines.[14]

Ogle confirms it was only he and Harrison who made the dash: 'Tony and I went by Jeep to the Battery position to try to get the communication going again', while Thompson adds: 'From their new position 3 Light Battery was able to establish wireless communication with the troops at the bridge and this was to be the only link we had until the remnants of the bridge party, after a splendid resistance, were ordered to surrender early on Thursday 21st.'

Day 2: Monday, 18 September

The 3 Battery War Diary states the guns were firing from around 1000 hours, but other evidence tells that 3 Battery E Troop began firing at targets on Arnhem Bridge at 0900 hours. The guns and the OP were now working well in concert and were now 'able to provide invaluable artillery support, with the whole Regiment gradually also becoming available. In fact so much ammunition was expended during the next few days that a critical shortage was created for the latter stages of the battle' (Woollacott, p.120).

With 1 Battery remaining in its original position until 18.30 that evening and 3 Battery firmly established down by the church, the steam laundry and the Ulo school, their 'eyes and ears' in the shape of the OP teams continued to play their part in some of the grim battles that were taking place.

For 3 Battery F Troop, who opened up thirty minutes earlier, Bombardier Ron Green tells us how:

> Stand down is given and once more we get everything ready, check ammunition, check charges, check firing lines. Towards Arnhem we can hear the battle warming up and smoke is rising above the town and I can see the railway bridge is broken. At last we are given a target and with that the tension goes out of me. The Germans are giving some back and they do have some heavy stuff.

Generally, a shortage of gun tractors meant that each gun had to be laboriously manhandled and also had to be sited in a vulnerable position.

Back at the bridge things were hotting up. Overnight, Lieutenant John Grayburn had led his Paras 'in two determined attacks across the bridge to try and capture the southern end only to be beaten back each time by the Germans'. No. 3 Battery OP, Chrystal and the others, was delighted to record 'had a first good look at the bridge in daylight and saw a mass of wrecked German vehicles. These were the remnants of the desperate attempts by truckloads of German infantry to force a way across [which] had ended in a bloody and fiery mess' (Woollacott, p.121). No. 3 Battery OP tells us 'wireless set went dis [faulty] but borrowed one from Recce. Called for fire on various concentrations of Germans which was very effective.'

Then at 9.30 menacing German armoured vehicles were spotted again heading north from the south end about 15–20 yards apart. Any hopes that this was XXX Corps riding to the rescue were quickly disabused. The reality was that these were the personnel carriers, half-tracks and armoured cars of the SS *Aufklärungs-Abteilung* 9 (reconnaissance battalion of the *Hohenstaufen*) commanded by SS *Hauptsturmführer* Viktor Gräbner, the very same unit that had been observed the previous day at 1800 hours heading south towards Nijmegen. We have, of course, already described the Grabner attack, but these alternative perspectives are illuminating. The vehicles were state-of-the-art Puma eight-wheeled armoured cars, open half-tracks and Opel Blitz trucks protected only by sandbags, which he stationed on the southern ramp, confounding British attempts to secure both ends of the bridge. Dennis Munford recalls the engagement:

> I received permission to open fire, and when the German column moved off, all I had to do was call 'Target – Mike One', and the boys at the battery did the rest. There was no need for further correction. The Germans had to drive through it. I ordered a cease-fire when they left the Mike One area and came on to the bridge. I didn't want to damage the bridge.

One way or another 3 Battery played a significant part in the assault on Grabner's force in the attempted crossing of the bridge. The OP party joined the fusillade of fire raining down and the rest of the Battery opened up from Oosterbeek. Unfortunately the first five Pumas got through with only one sustaining minor damage. They had swerved round the anti-tank mines. By the time they reached the north end, however, they all came under intense fire – anti-tank guns, Vickers machine guns, rifles, Brens and Stens – from the soldiers in the buildings around the north ramp, including the 3 Battery OP party: Hall, Chrystal, Morrison and Munford. To amplify the attack the 3 Battery anti-tank guns and 75mm shells in Oosterbeek joined in having received their range from the OP party and seven German vehicles were hit. Gräbner's force suffered heavy casualties and failed.[15] As noted, Gräbner was killed. Morale among the British soldiers fighting around the bridge rocketed.

This is how Major Ernest Watkins, War Staff writer describes the German attack: he reports that 'at first light, on Monday, the situation still looked pretty good. We held the bridge and denied it to the enemy':

The first lot were a column of armed cars and half-tracks that came over the bridge from the south. We had laid some mines in the carriageway. The first vehicle missed them all; the second went over one with its track. It didn't wreck the vehicle but threw the solitary soldier in the back into the air and he landed rather heavily in the roadway. The next second he ceased to exist. Almost every MG that could see him, I should think, opened up on him and he was literally disintegrated. The rest of the column was then disposed of. It was a shambles. Still some Germans, even ration trucks, tried to use the bridge. They did not get through.

Lieutenant Simpson tells how the armoured roofs of some of the half-tracks had been blown off by the 6-pounders while crossing the bridge so 'their occupants fell easy prey to the Sappers firing from the [school] windows and from those of nearby houses…Corporal Simpson and Sapper Emery…stood up and fired straight into the half-tracks with Bren and Sten guns. The range was about 20 yards.'[16] Five out of the six half-tracks were knocked out and ablaze, blocking the north end of the bridge completely. The sixth passed under the windows of the school, its crew killed. Beevor vividly describes the mayhem and carnage:

> Vehicles crashed into each other. A half-track backed into one behind and they became locked. The open half-tracks proved to be death-traps. Their ambushers were able to fire down and lob grenades into both the driver and panzer-grenadier compartments. One tried to escape down the side bank of the ramp and smashed into the school building. Another crashed through a barrier and fell to the riverside road which ran under the bridge. Some of those trapped on the bridge jumped from the parapet into the Neder Rijn. Gräbner himself is said to have been killed when he climbed out of his captured Humber armoured car to try to sort out the chaos. The smell of roasted flesh permeated the air for hours afterwards, mixed with the stench of the oily-black smoke from the blazing vehicles. Gräbner's body was never identified among all the other carbonized bodies.

Up in the roof Lieutenant Todd was 'shouting down targets to the 6-pounder anti-tank crew below' and claims to have picked off six 'as they tried to cross the roadblock along the bannister of the bridge'. He paid the price when a sniper's bullet came through the window, glanced off his helmet and showered his face and eyes with glass and splinters. The paratrooper who replaced him was wearing his red beret – something of a beacon – which a sniper spotted, fired and killed him. A lesson was to be learned there.

Mike Dauncy recalls how he witnessed a group of gunners in the downstairs school gathered round a fire over which a tin bath was boiling away full of chickens being cooked.[17]

Private James Sims of the 2nd Parachute Battalion's Mortar Platoon attests to the thick mist over the river when he followed Lieutenant Woods, his Platoon Commander, using a roll of signal wire, their mission being to set up an OP in the warehouse occupied by the Machine-Gun Platoon.

Later that evening a tank attack was repulsed with the loss of one tank while four houses held by 2nd Battalion paratroopers were torched and evacuated. 'At some point the strains of "Waho Mohammed" rent the air – the battle cry of British Airborne units.' Casualties were increasing all the while with doors ripped from houses acting as makeshift stretchers to be carried to the St Elisabeth Hospital. The dead were stacked in a yard behind Brigade HQ. British 3in mortars continued to bomb German vehicles at the south end of the bridge with some success. Knaust's *Kampfgruppe* including a panzer unit from Bielefeld were grouped to the east of the bridge ramp in a dairy on the Westervoortsedijk and attacked Digby Tatham-Warter's A Company, seized two buildings and took over the area under the bridge. Knaust lost four company commanders in the skirmishes.

Throughout Arnhem generally there was now intense fighting raging around the St Elisabeth Hospital and the two barracks, the Willemskazerne and the Saksen-Weimar-Kazerne and the large Wehrmacht depot were still on fire. The tower of the Grote Kerk, St Eusebius, was under fire from a German 75mm anti-tank gun trying to dislodge British snipers thought to be up there.

At one point in the morning Wilkinson (p.59) tells how 1 Battery 1st Air Landing Light Regiment 'was machine-gunned by about twenty enemy fighter aircraft but no damage was caused'.

Meanwhile, in Berlin, Hitler was ranting over the Luftwaffe's limp contribution to the battle so far, and Gräbner won no friends over his aborted journey to Nijmegen and for littering the approaches to the bridge with his own wrecked vehicles. Accordingly, Lieutenant General Willi Bittrich (II SS Panzer Corps) ordered Gräbner to transfer his reconnaissance battalion to the 9th *Hohenstaufen*. Bittrich considered Gräbner's conduct 'utterly inexplicable' and, on inspecting the battleground personally in an armoured vehicle, 'ordered them [the artillery] to fire, starting right under the gables and shooting metre by metre until the house collapsed' in order to eliminate the British snipers.[18] Beevor (p.147) goes on to tell that this would have been a single 150mm gun which was shelling 'the buildings on the west side of the wide Eusebiusbinnensingel' with virtual impunity until, that is, a stray shot from a mortar or a howitzer killed the crew and rendered the gun useless, thus saving John Frost the trouble of an attacking raid against the gun. Horst Weber, a young *panzergrenadier*, later remarked: 'It was the best and the most effective artillery fire I have ever seen. They shot metre by metre starting from the top. Buildings would finally collapse like dolls' houses.' To make matters worse, 40mm flak guns started turning up south of the river which proceeded to wreck the roofs of the buildings where the Vickers machine guns were positioned. The building exploded in flames and the crew was forced to relocate. As we have seen, Major Munford, acting as FOO of the Light Regiment's 3 Battery, continued to direct fire onto the southern approaches of the bridge, ever careful not to damage the bridge itself, crucial as it was to XXX Corps' advance.

The 3 Battery firing from Oosterbeek obviously soon attracted German artillery retaliation in the form of mortar bombings. F Troop Command Post was quickly moved inside the vestibule of the church and sandbagged; drivers took shelter further in under the spire. So far the Germans had caused little damage other than the sonorous tinkling chimes of some dislodged organ pipes. At 1000 hours Captain Harrison and Lieutenant Driver requested 'fire to be put down on enemy mortar positions on the southern side of the river'.

Bombardier Hall's attic 22-set link was still the only viable wireless link to his comrades manning the guns in Oosterbeek. He recalls that at about midday the officers present in the attic instructed him to transmit a message requesting air support to bomb and strafe a square [Eusebiusplein] which included the southern end of the bridge. Hall received confirmation from the 3 Battery CPO operator that the call had passed through to the CRA at Divisional HQ. He records that 'he felt highly chuffed that we, the Royal Artillery Signals, had got the important Brigade-Divisional request through. But the support never came.'[19]

Later in the day, 3 Battery assisted in stemming a tank attack at the junction opposite the St Elisabeth Hospital along with mortars and Vickers guns which destroyed two flak guns on the riverbank (Buckingham, p.205).

The SS attacked again with truck-borne infantry and Private James Sims, a 19-year-old mortar crewman, saw the Germans bail out of their shot-up vehicles:

> One terribly wounded German soldier, shot through both legs, pulled himself hand over hand toward his own lines. We watched his slow and painful progress with horrified fascination, as he was the only creature moving among a carpet of the dead. He pulled himself across the road, and over the pavement, then he dragged his shattered body inch by inch up a grass-covered incline leading to the bridge road. Once he had cleared a slight parapet at the top of the incline he would be back in his own lines. He must have been in terrible pain but he conquered the incline through sheer willpower. With a superhuman effort he heaved himself up to clear the final obstacle. A rifle barked out next to me and I watched in disbelief as the wounded German fell back, shot through the head. To me it was little short of murder, but to my companion, a Welshman, one of our best snipers, the German was a legitimate target. When I protested he looked at me as though I was simple.

Then there was the instance when the Germans sent in an ambulance with SS troopers hidden inside. Tumbling out and firing their submachine guns from the hip, their charge was annihilated near Frost's headquarters. 'I suppose they'll send a hearse next,' a British paratrooper drily commented. So far the attacks were piecemeal and uncoordinated, but that would change.

No. 2 Battery, 1st Air landing Light Regiment and the Second Lift[20]

In Manston, Kent the second lift was delayed due to bad weather, and with it 2 Battery. Truesdale (p.88) tells how the only entertainment during a boring morning was the take-off of a Gloster Meteor of 616 Squadron, the first British jet fighter to see action. The second lift finally got off the ground at midday, comprising 4,000 or so aircraft including more than 1,000 gliders. The accompanying fighter screen held the German fighters at bay, although many had returned to their bases to refuel after an equally uneventful morning over the LZs and DZs. Flak was heavier than on the first lift: Gunner Herbert Drinkwater, a Regimental HQ clerk, remembers following the 'lines of tracer arching up towards' and banished the thought of what he couldn't see from his mind. One burst of machine-gun fire did penetrate his glider but caused no serious damage. Flak did, however, make its mark when Bob Christie recalls how

> the three of us at the rear of the glider heard a series of sudden tearing noises further forward under the Jeep and 10cwt truck. Our immediate thoughts were that the lashings were working loose…if that happened the glider would go out of control. I crawled up the floor between the wheels in their metal troughs and the skin and frame members of the Horsa…sudden shafts of sunlight appeared through jagged holes. It was flak. Relieved, we returned to our seats and, as one, removed our P-type steel helmets and sat on them to protect our vital assets![21]

What started out as an uneventful flight over for Bombardier Ken Borley turned into a horror show when flak hit their glider and 'over to the right an aircraft was on fire and chaps were jumping, no falling for I could see no 'chutes opening'.[22]

An early 'casualty' was Captain Bob Elliott, 2i/c of the 2nd Anti-Tank Battery whose glider was forced to cast off and make a forced landing even before they reached the coast. They nevertheless got back to their airfield and successfully reached Arnhem in the third lift with the Polish Parachute Brigade. Much more serious was the fate of the two gliders that ditched in the North Sea. A Hamilcar carrying Lieutenant R.L. McLaren, commander of F Troop of the Anti-Tank Battery with one of his 17-pounder guns, disintegrated when it smashed into the water. The gun broke loose, trapping McLaren who drowned along with Sergeant Crawford; the others survived and were rescued.

Where did all those gliders land? No. 2 Battery came down on LZ X; gliders carrying the rest of 1 Battery, the FOURA and an F Troop gun landed on LZ Z. Captain Colin Kennedy and his men did not arrive and they missed the battle. When Signalman Eric Weeks landed he soon realized that he could not contact control amid small-arms fire: they joined a group from 4 Parachute Brigade heading towards Arnhem only to sustain heavy fire. The same happened when they drove up the railway embankment, so they had to give up trying to make contact. They then joined what was left of the 156th Parachute Battalion and were given perimeter defence duties. As they advanced towards Oosterbeek air bursts showered them with shrapnel:

> I was hit in the base of the spine and lost the use of my legs. Eventually I was taken prisoner and brought to a collection of other wounded. Here a little Hitler Youth wanted to toss a grenade into our midst, but received a belt round the head from one of their sergeants. I eventually got the use of my legs back, but the small piece of shrapnel was too close to my spine and had to remain there.[23]

Gunner Bird describes what sounds like a textbook landing:

> We felt the airspeed drop as the tow was jettisoned and we were in the 45-degree to avoid stalling and then bump, bump, we had landed. I unstrapped the axe, jumped out and hacked through the four bolts that fixed the tail section to the main landing…within a few seconds the jeep and trailer were out…and on our way towards a gap in the hedge surrounding the landing zone.

Bird watched a Hamilcar during a 'bad landing' when a Bren carrier 'had obviously snapped its moorings and smashed through the cockpit.… An elderly gentleman dressed in some form of local costume appeared in the hedgerow and said to me 'You are English, aren't you, I can tell by your smell.' Bird was another who witnessed the bullet-riddled body of General Kussin and his shot-up Citroën; a sobering sight that had now been there some twenty-four hours. Flowers and fruit flowed from the delighted Dutch inhabitants.[24]

Colonel Thompson had reviewed the regiment's dispositions and around 1630 hours moved 1 and 2 Batteries further east and within range of the bridge. Mills recalls that forty to fifty rounds were fired at targets around the bridge. No. 1 Battery relocated to a field just north of Utrechtseweg. Gunner Eric Mills was driving his jeep away from the LZ when he was ambushed; his trailer full of ammunition exploded in flames. Ron Davies in the jeep behind stopped (contrary to orders), picked up Mills and hurtled towards the 2 Battery position where they dug in in a cabbage field on Oranjeweg next to 1 Battery who had taken over the area vacated by 3 Battery.

Z Troop had a fraught time of it. Lieutenant McNaught's glider landed some 20 miles to the west of Nijmegen and was sheltered with his men by local Dutch people until they were able to link up with elements of the 82nd US Airborne Division whence they made their way to 1 Airborne Corps HQ. Chalk No. 1007 of No. 10 Flight, G Squadron crash-landed near Oude-Tonge on the island of Overflakkee: they had almost collided with a Dakota tug crossing the Dutch coast. Slipstream had forced their Stirling tug towards the Dakota: the Stirling's nose went down, the glider's nose went up and the tow rope snapped. The pilot successfully landed the glider, hoping to unload with Germans racing towards the scene. Unfortunately the nose was over a dyke and the tail was 15ft in the air so unloading was off, apart from a Bren gun and ammunition; the gunners removed the firing pin and torched the glider to prevent it falling into enemy hands. Gunner Brett tells us '[I] saw three ladies and a young boy came out of a cottage nearby. The boy said in English 'Are you going to fight?' to which I replied 'Yes, if we get attacked.' The pilots and Brett's sergeant agreed that unloading the anti-tank gun and jeep 'didn't seem possible. So a decision was made to blow it up completely.' A Dutch gentleman appeared and gave an estimate of the German army's strength in the area, but they were already in sight:

> They then approached us and we surrendered. I think my worst moment was when they set up a machine gun in front of us. We thought this would be the end, but thank God it didn't happen. Two large cars appeared to take us off, and escorted by a German guard they took us to their barracks.[25]

Around 1500 hours Captain Chard and his C Troop OP party landed without loss with the 4th Parachute Brigade. Lance Bombardier Reddy suffered a bad ankle sprain, while Chard was unable to get through to battery by wireless, but then Chard's No. 18 set spluttered into life and he got through to Major Linton, the Battery Commander, telling him the location of the 4th Parachute Brigade and that he was on his way to meet him to pick up his jeep and his proper wireless set.

Machine-gun fire greeted Lieutenant Roy Staddon's glider on landing: 'I could see sparks flying all over the jeep and trailer.' He was wounded in the shoulder, while Gunner James Hall and Lance Bombardier Thomas Morgan were killed. One of the glider pilots dressed Staddon's wound under cover of the Horsa while the other unloaded the Bren and returned fire. 'He must have gone in the front and out the back door faster than a ferret down a rabbit hole.' Gunner Farnish was wounded as well. 'He'd caught it in the arse region' and both the injured men reached an aid post for some much-needed morphine.[26] This was the Staddon glider complement's second attempt to reach Arnhem; Staddon was eventually taken prisoner.

Other casualties included Lance Sergeant Norman Spendlove of D Troop that failed to take off. A B Squadron Horsa chalk no. 878 piloted by Staff Sergeant Ron Watkinson and Sergeant Arthur Jones was carrying C Troop's B submachine gun, jeep and trailer. They were hit by flak over Middelburg and landed near a farm at Fijnaart. The nose wheel broke off and smashed through the cockpit window, fortunately with no injuries. However, the flak had done considerable damage, buckling the vehicle troughs. Assisted by enthusiastic Dutch people, they unloaded the jeep, gun and trailer only to find that the towing hitches had been damaged. They were then attacked by a strong force of Germans, but despite return fire from the glider pilots they were hopelessly outnumbered. So they smashed the dial sight and consigned the breech block to a ditch. However, Sergeant Jones incurred a serious injury and Gunner Spence was shot in the face, the bullet passing through both cheeks and miraculously missing any bone or teeth.[27] The Germans overran the position and took the injured to a nearby farmhouse. The others were marched off to Dordrecht from where they were sent to PoW camps, and this marked the regiment's third gun loss.

Two gliders of the Light Regiment had bad experiences with flak. Lance Bombardier Parkes of C Troop had the unfortunate experience of watching Sergeant Clarke's stricken glider go down. Parkes spent the rest of his flight perched on the bonnet of the jeep to avoid the flimsy floor as the flak intensified. Clarke and his comrades were taken prisoner, as was Bombardier Spendlove with his glider-load of ammunition.[28] Parkes recalls how no one seems to have been alerted at the briefings to the important fact that the Dutch and Germans drove on the right side of the road. Much swerving ensued generally, but Percy Parkes solved the problem by driving down the centre of the road.

F Troop of the Anti-Tank Battery also suffered when the tug pulling their Hamilcar carrying Sergeant McDonald and his gun crew was hit by flak; they ended up in a field where they were shot up by a German machine-gun crew. Nevertheless, they returned fire with their Bren and, with the help of two Dutch Resistance fighters, unloaded their gun and trailer and finally reached Division HQ. The Resistance fighters offered to take the injured Gunner Martin to hospital.[29]

At 1535 hours the seven guns of 2 Battery were firing around Wolfheze, not all that successfully in some cases as reported by Gunner Ron Gibbs of D Troop when the first salvo hit the tops of trees some 80 yards distant. 'I could add that some of our gun team never made it at all so we were two gunners, Gunner Rodgers, myself, Sergeant Fletcher on the gun with only one trailer of ammunition, which wasn't much.' No. 1 Battery remained in place until 1830 hours, but there was increasing frustration over the 'lack of targets'. Major Linton sent Captain Percy Buck Taylor, commander of D Troop, to the 11th Parachute Battalion as FOO. Meanwhile, 3 Battery's E Troop Captain Harrison and Lieutenant Driver were with the 1st Parachute Brigade. The 1st Parachute Battalion's CO Colonel Dobie requested they bring fire down on a German anti-aircraft gun emplacement on the far side of the river. Driver recalls they were lying behind a low stone wall: 'Tony [Harrison] told me to order some airburst saying he had a sniper's rifle with him and would knock the Jerries off when they were forced out of their trenches.' The airburst had the desired effect, but a German sniper returned the compliment with a shot that ricocheted off the wall and hit Harrison 'who had to be evacuated. Luckily it was only a surface wound and he went back to the gun position.'[30]

Buckingham describes how LZ X was attacked by *Standartenführer* Hans Lippert's SS *Unterführerschule Arnheim* that had encroached on the LZ through woods on the western edge, shooting up at least three Horsas before they landed. Among the passengers were troops from the 1st Air Landing Light Regiment, two of whom were killed.[31]

As the day wore on the priority became support for the Air Landing Brigade who had fulfilled their task of supporting the LZs and DZs. No. 1 Battery then moved east, north of the main road into Arnhem and south-west of 2 Battery around Koude Herberg.[32] Concerns continued that night over the vulnerable position of 3 Battery at the church and so they were reinforced with a detachment of glider pilots and a troop of 6-pounder anti-tank guns.[33]

Chapter Thirteen

Day 3: Tuesday, 19 September

'a day of constant pounding...'
Major Dennis Munford

Various war diaries characterize the night of Monday the 18th/Tuesday the 19th as 'noisy'. Gunner Eric Chrystal's testimony alone would endorse that: '...it must have been the terrific noise... and always the terrific noise.' Woollacott (p.127) describes it as noisy and 'a night of movement and high drama'. When 'Dicky' Bird abandoned his jeep 'somewhere near the bridge that carried the railway over the bridge and proceeded on foot, the sounds of battle had increased in intensity to reach an ear-splitting cacophony that would last for the next seven days.'[1]

The deteriorating weather was blamed for the fact that the airborne troops in the Netherlands failed to get any close support compared to the support given by the Luftwaffe to their troops who flew 125 sorties. The weather certainly did put paid to the scheduled drops by two battalions of the 325th Glider Infantry (82nd Airborne) and the 1st Polish Parachute Brigade, but no one told the 2nd Tactical Air Force in Belgium about this so they continued to fly support according to the original plan.

At about 07.15 Major General Urquhart's day started with his arrival back at Divisional HQ in the Hartenstein Hotel; he had been rescued by the South Staffords when they reached the house in which he was hiding. Lieutenant Clapham, the Anti-Tank A Troop Commander, drove him back at high speed under fire. Obviously Urquhart would have asked for a situation report and the situation was not good:

- Divisional resupply was in a mess
- XXX Corps had not yet reached Nijmegen
- Hackett's 4th Parachute Brigade was suffering heavy casualties in their bid to take the high ground near Johannahoeve

- The South Staffords and 11th Parachute Battalion were being contained near the St Elisabeth Hospital and the monastery, the Gemeente Museum, Arnhem by infantry and self-propelled guns
- By the end of the day at 1800 hours the two companies of the South Staffords would be down to 40 men, while the 1st Parachute Battalion could muster only 100 men. The precise whereabouts of the 1st and 3rd Parachute Battalions on the lower road along the Rhine was unclear; what was clear was that they 'had been cut to pieces by the combined fire from mortars, machine guns and anti-aircraft guns firing from south of the river'. Colonel Fitch had ordered the 3rd Battalion back to the Rhine Pavilion, a large restaurant on the river. Every officer and man for himself. In the retreat Colonel Fitch was caught in a shell blast and killed.

The only good news was that Colonel Frost and his valiant band of brothers still held the north end of the bridge, thanks to the accuracy of the gunners back in Oosterbeek and the risks taken by the OP teams at the bridge to overcome dangerous and difficult, if not impossible, observation. Enemy shelling could be heard in Arnhem and north-east of 3 Battery's position. F Troop moved into the porch of the church 'to have better command of guns' and started digging and covering slit trenches, firing on enemy tanks which were now much closer.[2]

Before all that 'at a candle-lit council of war in a ruined house' close to the Rhine Pavilion Lieutenant Colonel Dobie of the 1st Parachute Battalion was taking the initiative. A report that the Germans had retaken the northern end of the bridge was found to be fake news and that night's attack was on again. 'The idea was to attack in the dark and fight through to the bridge before first light' despite the German machine guns, flak guns and artillery they would face.[3]

However, the day started badly for the regiment: Captain Tudor Griffiths, 1st Air Landing Light Regiment, 3 Battery, F Troop, had been with Fitch with his OP party who were now either dead or wounded. Griffith himself, already once a casualty, was taken prisoner when his position was overrun by five armoured vehicles, assault guns and a force of twenty SS infantry. The survivors were taken in ambulances to Queen Wilhelmina's summer palace, Het Loo, at Apeldoorn.

The only comfort the men at the bridge in the E Troop OP team (Munford, Hall, Chrystal and Morrison) had was that the shelling they were directing to the guns in Oosterbeek 'was causing a degree of discomfort to the enemy attacking their positions'. Munford recalls how

> I remember the 19th as a day of constant pounding. The Germans shot at you with everything including the guns of heavy tanks which were cruising the streets. I think they were loading high explosive and phosphorous because they were causing so many fires. We collected chunks of masonry and some sandbags we found in the building and built a sangar around the signallers and the set in the corner of the building. Visibility was excellent, as by now we had lost most of the roof and the whole town seemed to be on fire.[4]

More German armour and artillery was arriving by the hour, including the 208th Assault Brigade from Denmark and Flak Brigade von Swoboda. Things, however, were only to get much worse when the Germans brought up a 105mm field gun. Munford remembers

> It looked like a 105mm and, when the Germans trundled it into position on Tuesday, I was looking straight down the muzzle at about 200 yards. The gun was sitting on the crossroads north of the bridge with the crew sheltering behind a substantial shield. My immediate request to engage it as a 'close' target was not granted as our own chaps were too near but, in consequence of the demolitions following the first few rounds, Tony Hibbert [Brigade Major, 1st Parachute Brigade] told me to go ahead. I requested all help to spot the first round which would be smoke as the area was densely built up. Sam Wilkinson [at 3 Battery Command Post] must have been surprised to learn from the order that an enemy field gun was in our position since I gave him my own map reference. True to form, 3 Battery gave me a wonderful first round. I reported 'shot' and everyone saw it 200 yards over and we soon put paid to the gun after that.

However, Private Cecil Newell of A Company, 2nd Parachute Battalion has a slightly different version of events relating to the silencing of the 105mm gun. He claims that it was engaged by the battalion mortars and by himself with a Bren gun; maybe it was a lethal combination of 3in and 75mm ordnance that dealt the death blow?[5] No. 3 Battery's E Troop Leo Hall who was with Munford, Morrison and Chrystal overlooking the bridge remembers it differently again:

> Then there was the business of the gun…. Immediate calls for our guns to respond were unsuccessful; for once, when support was critical to our positions I couldn't get through. I was particularly relieved when our mortars opened up and neutralised it with a direct hit. Failures like that weigh heavily on a Signaller.[6]

Perhaps this is the place to quote the citation Major Munford received for the Dutch Bronze Lion awarded for his conduct throughout the battle, for not only does it describe Major Munford's bravery and conduct, in so doing it also sheds light on the valour demonstrated by all the other soldiers fighting around him:

> Major Munford established an Observation Post in the attic of a large building on the North-West end of Arnhem bridge. He remained on duty at this Observation Post for three days without being relieved, from 2300 hrs 17th September until the building was burnt down at 2000 hrs 20th September. During all this time the attic was under continuous fire from weapons of all calibre, receiving three direct hits from 15cm shells, and several 81mm mortar bombs. The attic was also under observation and fire from snipers by whom Major Munford was wounded in the face on the first day. Ignoring his wounds and showing complete disregard for personal safety he maintained the Observation Post in the attic during the whole engagement, thus enabling accurate and effective fire to be brought to bear on the enemy at all times. He continued to give fire orders until the end though the building was burning fiercely and the attic was under the heaviest fire. Eventually his wireless set received a direct hit, killing the operator. He was then ordered to evacuate the building.

Then after the battle:

After organised resistance had ceased on the bridge he took command of a small party and attempted to lead them through the enemy lines, but was surrounded and taken prisoner. Whilst being evacuated he jumped off a lorry on the move, and succeeded in escaping, but was re-captured again.

Throughout the engagement Major Munford was an example and an encouragement to all ranks in his courage and devotion to duty. His skill, perseverance, and determination alone were responsible for the maintenance of communications with his Regiment. By exposing himself in an exceedingly open and hazardous position for three days he enabled the fire support to be brought down at all times, which was so decisive in holding our force on Arnhem bridge.[7]

Hall gives us more on the activity in the 3 Battery OP and on the general situation:

On the Tuesday, the third day, D+2, Munford wanted a relay to be run from the 22 to the floor below. Chrystal and the Battery team worked that end, sometimes relieving me as I stayed in the Attic monitoring the behaviour and safety of the set with the remote control point below. Some damage had been caused to the North-East corner of the Attic by shelling, and Bowles and Chubb had suffered from fairly minor bullet wounds. Bdr Ogle, I discovered recently, had driven Harrison back to Oosterbeek at first light on D+1. Morrison had joined a suicide dash across the Bridge in an armoured carrier flown in, presumably, by Hamilcar glider. Such a vehicle offers protection only from small-arms fire. The last I saw of Morrison was as he crouched behind cover, wearing body armour, rifle in hand. I was relieved when the venture was cancelled, Morrison staying, I guess, with the Paras. To his great credit, truculent bugger though he could be, Morrison had accepted the near suicide detail without a murmur.

Here are Hall's observations on the wider situation:

It would be on that Tuesday when security on the air counted for little. Another 22 set in the Attic (possibly that of Munford's group) had been searching the frequencies when contact was made with an advancing XXX Corps Tank. The Brigade Major spoke to the tank commander, ignoring all security: 'This is the First Airborne Division at the Bridge at Arnhem. When can we expect you?' (or something similar). The hesitant reply gave a time for their attack, but none of us believed it. Munford, having to go down from the Attic on one occasion had given me permission to call for a round on Mike One if requested by a Para Officer. I was sorely tempted to do so anyway, just for the hell of it! Not many Bombardiers get the chance to fire a regiment of field guns! This account does not include much of the goings-on; we all knew the position was serious, that we must hang on, waiting for the relieving XXX Corps troops advancing from Nijmegen and that we could expect no help from the rest of our Division being slowly strangled around Oosterbeek. But looking through the bashed-out windows of Brigade HQ, giving south, east and west views I saw to the west the nearby church of St Eusebius completely on fire. We were in the centre of a circle of blazing buildings. Our turn must soon come. The relieving XXX Corps of the 2nd Army had better put a move on – there was never any doubt that we should be relieved soon.[8]

Hall adds that 'morale, never low, surged at hearing a distant "Waho Mohammed"…and a V peeped out from a jeep horn'.

In nearby Eusebiusplein Sergeant van Kuijk tells us how 'the Tommies still don't give an inch, and the battle flows back and forth.' The Germans were now 30 or 40 metres from his building. No one was convinced by the two Germans who approached dressed as British parachutists. For their troubles they were shot dead by snipers; the Germans were also making use of large Alsatian dogs. Telecommunications continued to allow van Kuijk and his colleagues to maintain contact with the Resistance and to establish a connection with the parachutists in Oosterbeek and Nijmegen. More British arrived, making the number in the building seventy or eighty; the telephone stopped working and there was no water after 1600 hours. Germans were crawling across the square and their tanks were firing at the building from Rijnkade. By evening houses all around were in flames, opposite and at the corner of Kadestraat. Germans were using flame-throwers, and the situation was now hopeless so van Kuijk and the soldiers all left the building and crossed over to Hofstraat to join some other British soldiers. At 21.00 the force exited the square via the back garden over a wall and gathered in a building supply firm's premises, but they were turned back by a senior officer. A British soldier with a gash in his cheek approached wielding a white flag; he was sent by the Germans to offer surrender, but nothing doing. A number of British were later killed when trying to leave the square again. Trenches were dug and a cold, sleepless night ensued.

Over in Oosterbeek the day started badly for the 1st Air Landing Light Regiment with heavy mortaring from 0700 hours and a direct hit on 3 Battery's HQ by a 150mm *Nebelwerfer* delivered at 1100 hours, fortunately with no casualties (Buckingham, p.289). No. 2 Battery continued to work within the 4th Parachute Brigade while 1 Battery was kept busy, moving their guns to alternative firing positions in the wake of the Germans' repelling of the 4th Parachute Brigade with tanks and self-propelled anti-aircraft guns. Colonel Thompson ordered the two batteries to deploy close to 3 Battery near Oosterbeek church under enemy mortar fire. At 1640 hours there was a re-supply flight that had not received signals regarding the division's change of position and despite the frantic use of smoke, yellow triangles and even white handkerchiefs, most of the containers fell to grateful Germans. While the 10th Parachute Battalion was retreating across LZ L pursued by the enemy, the anti-tank element of the Polish Brigade was struggling to unload their gliders. Absolute chaos ensued as a lethal mix of Polish language and grey instead of maroon berets created the perfect storm in which both sides fired on the Poles who returned fire, causing several incidents of friendly-fire casualties.[9]

Communications through the 68 sets gave up so Major Jeff Linton, Captain Peter Chard and Lieutenant Halliday headed for Divisional HQ from where Linton and Halliday returned to 2 Battery by separate routes. Colonel Thompson directed 2 Battery C Troop to its position opposite the church between the Concert Hall and the Van Dolderen Laundry. Mr and Mrs Dolderen and their daughter Toni invited Bombardier Bob Christie to their home for a cup of tea: 'We all sat on the front porch, sipping tea and eating some sweets.' Christie assured them they were there for the long run and 'while we talked about peace from down the road some two or three hundred yards away and around a bend there was the rattle of machine-gun fire and the sharp crack of rifle bullets'.[10] The Old Rectory of the ter Horst family was already the aid station for the

Light Regiment and was to develop into the 'hospital' for the south-east sector of the perimeter.

Gunner Bird, 2 Battery D Troop, describes how he and his comrades found themselves near the entrance to the St Elisabeth Hospital when a doctor emerged and told them that unless they left in two minutes the Germans would carry out their threat to shell the hospital. They retreated, only to find themselves face to face with a German self-propelled gun (StuG) which opened fire with its machine guns. Bird saw 'men falling like nine-pins'. The battery gun was beaten to the draw and the StuG fired first with its HE shell putting the detachment out of action and 'sending Bird flying to the ground'.[11]

The 3 Battery War Diary tells us how ranges for the battery's support of those defending the north end of the bridge were 'decreasing all the time as the distance between targets and friendly troops came closer'.[12]

Driver:

> It was pretty hellish. I can still picture…the body of a Battalion's officer slumped against a wall, with the two smoke grenades in his front pouches alight giving an eerie green and red light. We had machine guns firing at us and German tanks ahead of us. Desperate stuff.

Dobie and Driver and his signallers then advanced on a house occupied by Germans. Driver made for the stairs but was confronted by a stick grenade hurled at him; his 'fancy' body armour saved him but he had no option but to surrender. All this was going on while the Dutch family who owned the house was sitting downstairs. The rest of the OP team made their way back to Oosterbeek where they met Captain Caird, FOURA attached to the 1st Parachute Battalion; Caird took over the team that comprised Lance Bombardiers Morris and Ingram and Gunner Maclachlan. Driver was later shipped off to Oflag 79: 'what an inglorious way to finish'.[13]

Lance Sergeant Thain, 3 Battery F Troop had come in, at the second attempt, on the second lift; however, they crash-landed and spent four hours unloading the damaged glider.

That afternoon the CRA decided that Light Regiment 1 and 2 Batteries should move nearer to 3 Battery at the church to form a regimental position and reduce their increasing vulnerability. Wilkinson says (p.81) 'By dusk

Children standing on top of the ruins of the demolished village of Gessopalena, Italy. (*Courtesy of Alexander Turnbull Library, Wellington, New Zealand. /records/22368065. Taken by George Kaye on 16 December 1943*)

Panzergrenadiers march towards the battlefront in late 1943 during operations near Gaeta.

Panzergrenadiers supporting a Tiger tank during its drive towards Nettuno, prior to the Battle of Anzio. (*Courtesy of Ian Baxter, author of* The Waffen-SS at Arnhem)

LXXVI Panzer Corps in late 1943. Littoria, Italy. (*Courtesy of Ian Baxter, author of* The Waffen-SS at Arnhem)

No. 3 Battery four-day R&R in Tunis. L-R: Gunner W.B. Reidie (signaller), Bombardier M.C. Ogle, Gunner J.E. Whittlesey (driver) and Gunner E. Chrystal (signaller).

A GPO (Gun Position Officer) of the 1st Air Landing Light Artillery Regiment, serving with the 5th Division, gives the order to take post at a 75mm howitzer battery during the advance on Isernia, 3 November 1943.

1st Air Landing Light Regiment supporting a Canadian attack on Campobasso, October 1943. (*Courtesy of the Canadian War Museum, Ottawa*)

Operation MARKET GARDEN begins.

Horsa and Hamilcar gliders of the 1st Air Landing Brigade litter landing zone 'Z' west of Wolfheze, 17 September.

A No. 68 set, courtesy of Bernard Nock, curator, owner and display coordinator of the Military Wireless Museum, Kidderminster.

A No. 22 set mounted in an airborne jeep. (*Bennett 2007, p.44. Laurier Centre for Military Strategic and Disarmament Studies (LCMSDS) Photo Collection*)

Soldiers of the 101st Airborne examine what is left of one of the gliders that 'cracked up'. (*Source http://www.army.mil/-images/2007/09/16/7187/ Author: US Army Signal Corps /US Army Military History Institute/Photo Courtesy of US Army*)

From a collection of seventy-five British official photographs relating to the 1st Airborne Division at Arnhem, Operation MARKET GARDEN, September 1944. (*2005-12-38-69 National Army Museum, out of copyright*)

17 September. The CO has landed at LZ 'Z' with Tac. HQ 1st Air Landing Light Regiment. L-R: Signalman Des Wiggins in the jeep; Lieutenant Colonel W.F.K. 'Sheriff' Thompson. At the trailer stand, L-R: Sergeant K. Brown (1 Flt A Squadron, Glider Pilot Regiment); Signalman D.A. Gault, Thompson's driver; glider pilot Norman Hardie (OC 1Flt A Squadron, Glider Pilot Regiment). Note the crashed gliders behind.

The bullet-riddled body of *Generalmajor* Friedrich Kussin, the *Feldkommandant* of Arnhem and his shot-up Citroën. Also killed were his driver Josef Wileke and an aide, Max Koster.

Men of the 2nd Battalion, South Staffordshire Regiment, of the 1st Air Landing Brigade advance towards Arnhem towing a 6-pounder anti-tank gun with them on 18 September. (*Photograph by Sergeant D.M. Smith, Army Film and Photographic Unit, World War Two, North-West Europe, 1944*)

Most of the 1st Airborne Division's landing zones were 7 miles from the bridge at Arnhem and only one battalion managed to reach the objective, while the rest of the division was squeezed into a pocket around Oosterbeek to the west. (*From a collection of seventy-five British official photographs relating to the 1st Airborne Division at Arnhem, Operation MARKET GARDEN, September 1944. 2005-12-38-1. NAM, out of copyright*)

The bridge too far.

Disconsolate captured German soldiers of the 9th SS Reconnaissance Battalion at the Arnhem Bridge on 18 September 1944 shortly before being handed over to the Military Police, Arnhem. (*Photograph by Sergeant D.M. Smith, Army Film and Photographic Unit, World War Two, North-West Europe, 1944*)

The Airborne troops at Arnhem found themselves confronted by elements of the 9th and 10th SS Panzer Divisions that were refitting in the area. Allied Intelligence had failed to confirm their presence prior to the launch of Operation MARKET GARDEN. The three guards in the background are glider pilots who fought as infantry after landing their gliders. (*From a collection of seventy-five British official photographs relating to the 1st Airborne Division at Arnhem. 2005-12-38-64 NAM, out of copyright*)

British paratroopers of 2 Para surrendering. One of their captors was SS *Rottenführer* Rudolf Trapp who helped escort them along the Rijnkade. (*Courtesy of Ian Baxter*)

A well-camouflaged *Sturmgeschütz* in Onderlangs, 19 September. (*Courtesy of Ian Baxter*)

Unknown Airborne troops – one, presumably a casualty, sporting non-regulation trousers – in Eusebiusplein.

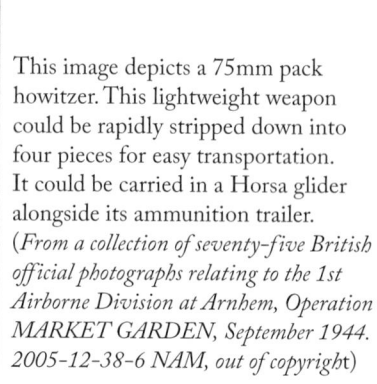

This image depicts a 75mm pack howitzer. This lightweight weapon could be rapidly stripped down into four pieces for easy transportation. It could be carried in a Horsa glider alongside its ammunition trailer. (*From a collection of seventy-five British official photographs relating to the 1st Airborne Division at Arnhem, Operation MARKET GARDEN, September 1944. 2005-12-38-6 NAM, out of copyright*)

British airborne soldiers unwrap a Parapack dropped on a resupply flight. Thick fog in England and low clouds over the battle zone at Arnhem hampered both resupply and the air-lifting of reinforcements. (*From a collection of seventy-five British official photographs relating to the 1st Airborne Division at Arnhem, Operation MARKET GARDEN. 2005-12-38-53 NAM, out of copyright*)

A young SS machine-gunner. The way in which he is wearing the ammunition belt around his neck suggests that he was inexperienced. Veteran machine-gunners always wore their belts with the bullets pointing outwards so as to avoid them digging into the body. Note his M1924 grenade stick and 6x30 Zeiss binoculars. (*Courtesy of Ian Baxter*)

A German officer making notes before entering the fighting in Arnhem. He appears to be armed with a Beretta submachine gun, while the soldier behind him has a *Panzerfaust* anti-tank rocket.

A Tiger knocked out on Weverstraat.

The 1st Air Landing Light Regiment in action.

A German *Sturmhaubitze* 42 at Arnhem. (*This image was provided to Wikimedia Commons by the German Federal Archive* (*Deutsches Bundesarchiv*) *as part of a co-operation project*)

Scherl Picture Service West, September 1944: failure of the Anglo-American encirclement plan at Arnhem. German army grenadiers advance through a complex network of ditches. (*This image was provided to Wikimedia Commons by the German Federal Archive* (Deutsches Bundesarchiv) *as part of a co-operation project*)

German *truppen* on their bikes heading for Arnhem: SS *Rottenführer* Trapp's company of about fifty *Frundsberger* 1st SS that cycled from Deventer to Arnhem.

A *Sturmhaubitze* (self-propelled gun) supported by infantry moves into Euhenweg, Oosterbeek. The shell cases littering the road would suggest that it has just fired off a number of rounds. The photograph was taken on 25 September by *Leutnant* Seuffert, a *Kriegsberichte* in the Luftwaffe Propaganda *Kompanie*.

A group of British soldiers pause in front of a war grave, having removed their caps in a solemn and contemplative moment. The grave is unmarked, but there are six berets present and multiple floral tributes indicating that it is likely the grave of six men, probably of the 1st Airborne Brigade. Although obscured by trees, the building in the background looks very similar to the Hartenstein Hotel.

The wonderful life-saver Kate ter Horst. Kate was initially reluctant to feature in the 1946 film *Theirs is the Glory*, which was shot in Arnhem and Oosterbeek. However, she finally relented, and this is the scene in which she read out Psalm 91 to the wounded soldiers filling her house. (*This shot was taken in the basement of the Pietersburg Airborne Museum, Oosterbeek, courtesy of Sophie ter Horst. Thanks to Robert Voskuil and Wybo Boersma*)

Civilian patients being evacuated from the St Elisabeth Hospital in Utrechtseweg.

030: No. 1 Gun (a 75mm howitzer) of 'D' Troop, 2nd Battery, 1st Air Landing Light Regiment, 1st Airborne Division in the Oosterbeek perimeter in the sloping field north of the Rozenpad footpath, 21 September 1944. The large building in the background is in the Bildersweg. The crew, from L-R: Gunners R. Miller and H.G. Davey; Lance Bombardier K.W. Alsop and Gun Commander Lance Sergeant E. Prentice. (*Smith, Dennis M. (Sergeant), No. 5 Army Film and Photo Section, Army Film and Photographic Unit. From a collection of seventy-five British official photographs relating to the 1st Airborne Division at Arnhem, Operation MARKET GARDEN, September 1944. NAM, out of copyright*)

A 6-pounder anti-tank gun in action against a German self-propelled gun west of Oosterbeek, 20 September 1944. (*Photograph by Sergeant D.M. Smith, Army Film and Photographic Unit, World War Two, North-West Europe, 1944. From a collection of seventy-five British official photographs relating to the 1st Airborne Division at Arnhem, Operation MARKET GARDEN, September 1944. 2005-12-38-20 NAM, out of copyright*)

Airborne soldiers armed with Sten guns defend the Oosterbeek pocket. The soldier on the left is a signaller wearing headphones connected to the jeep above him. (*From a collection of seventy-five British official photographs relating to the 1st Airborne Division at Arnhem, Operation MARKET GARDEN, September 1944. 2005-12-38-49 NAM, out of copyright*)

Members of the 1st Airborne Division take cover in a shell hole at Arnhem, 17 September 1944. (*Photograph by Sergeant D.M. Smith, Army Film and Photographic Unit, World War Two, North-West Europe, 1944. From a collection of seventy-five British official photographs relating to the 1st Airborne Division at Arnhem during Operation MARKET GARDEN, September 1944. 2005-12-38-72 NAM, out of copyright*)

British dead along Amsterdamseweg 6km outside Arnhem, originally published in Arnhem in September 1944 in the German propaganda magazine *Signal*, ostensibly showing things 'as they really were'... Dr P.R.A van Iddekinge. The reporter, according to despatch rider SS Corporal Alfred Ziegler, was subsequently killed in Oosterbeek. He asserts that 'they were killed by us lying in ambush in the woods. We were told first of all to let the British through, and then we opened up and cut the first lot down. There must have been 30 to 40 prisoners. They were so beaten and submissive that it only needed one ma to march them off to the rear.'

One of the moving and dignified annual flower-laying ceremonies in Oosterbeek War Cemetery in the 1990s. (*Photographed by former Gunner Eric Chrystal. Author's collection*)

Bill Cotterill's first letter home since becoming a PoW in September 1944. All such letters from Stalag XII-A written by other prisoners at this time are almost identically phrased.

Surrendered British paratroops being interrogated. (*Courtesy of Ian Baxter*)

British prisoners at Arnhem Bridge, unshaven after four days of fighting.

Three German guards waiting at the gate to Stalag XII-A Limburg.

Left—Signaller Eric Chrystal, R.A., 6 Mentone Avenue, Portobello, missing, believed prisoner of war. Right—Pte. Patrick J. Donlevy, Royal Scots, 83 Lochend Gardens, Restalrig, Edinburgh, died of wounds.

Gunner Eric Chrystal finally reported missing as a PoW.

MISSING—BELIEVED PRISONER
Signaller Eric Chrystal, Airborne R.A., is reported missing, believed to be a prisoner of war. He is a native of Edinburgh, and in civil life was an apprentice with Mr Pearson, plumber and ironmonger, 182 High Street, Portobello. He is 20 years of age, and the younger son of Mr and Mrs J. J. Chrystal, 6 Mentone Avenue, Portobello. His brother James is serving in the N.F.S.

14283058
WO2 Eric Chrystal
Airborne/ Royal Artillery

Gunner Eric Chrystal with his medals.

the guns moved down to their new positions and the regiment was soon ready for action as a complete unit.' Indeed, during the night 'a number of regimental targets were engaged in support of the troops at the bridge and of 7th KOSB to the north and the Border Regiment to the west.' The position was further strengthened by the arrival of fifty South Staffords.[14]

Things generally were getting increasingly critical and desperate. The crew of a Stirling bomber shot down in the second lift was detailed to help with the unfamiliar task of trench-digging around 1 Battery, while a steady stream of demoralized and disorganized soldiers, mainly South Staffords and the 11th Parachute Battalion, turned into a torrent that was largely leaderless and without orders as they passed 3 Battery's positions. Colonel Thompson, though, was not having any of this, and he confronted the men between Acacialaan and Oosterbeek-Laag railway stations with a jeep roadblock opposite the church. Morale was at rock bottom, but Thompson 'replenished them with ammunition, food and cigarettes from a dump I [Thompson] had formed at the church'. This was the famous 'Thompson's Force'.[15] Everything was witnessed by TSM Tom Kent, 3 Battery F Troop: '…wearing his red beret, Sten gun in hand and ordering the Paras to stop and start digging right in front of our guns. I hate to think what would have happened had they chosen to ignore him, such was the man and his mood at the time.'

Thompson then proceeded to organize the area into a defensive position with the South Staffords' two Vickers machine guns and three 6-pounders along with a Bren carrier. In the meantime the German mortars and artillery continued to rain their shells down on the battery gun positions. Gunner Aubrey Pitt was killed by a salvo of shells that hit him as he and Gunner Durant parked their jeep briefly outside the church to get a radio fix. Durant survived. A mortar bomb hit Signalman Bloomfield's jeep in which he was manning a wireless near the Concert Hall that was being used as RHQ. Bloomfield was hurried to the RAP but died later. Fire calls continued to be answered immediately, despite the unrelenting bombardment.[16] According to Truesdale (p.100), 3 Battery's Command Post was home to 'a very large and somnolent black and white rabbit' named Joe by the gunners. Apparently he could hear the approach of mortar bombs and shells, at which he would scramble to the back of his hutch to take cover. Joe even survived a bomb blast that shattered a jar of ammonia and covered his hutch.

The 3 Battery War Diary, despite the frenetic activity described above and the well documented testimonies, bizarrely described Tuesday as 'quiet'.[17] 'Relatively quiet' it may have been in view of what was to come, but the Germans were reinforcing quietly in the background all the time. *Schwere Panzerabteilung* 506 was on its way from Paderborn, the home of heavy German tank training, with its fourteen Tiger tanks commanded by *Hauptmann* Hans Hummel. The unit had been recently re-equipped with a full complement of forty-five Tiger Ausf.B tanks (Tiger IIs). It was entrained from Paderborn to Bocholt, but the line was blocked after Bocholt so the Panzers took to the roads where, embarrassingly, mechanical breakdown did for all but three of the Tigers. These three, however, soon made their mark, being deployed with *Kampfgruppe Brinkmann* at the bridge where at 2000 hours they shelled the surrounding British positions causing widespread damage and numerous casualties. One of the three was hit by a sapper of the 9th Field Company and Captain Frank of the 2nd Parachute Battalion with a 6-pounder anti-tank gun, causing the two remaining Tigers to withdraw.[18]

Valiant efforts to resupply were going wrong. When supplies were dropped at around 1530 hours the pilots were met with 'considerable ack-ack' which brought some planes down including a C-47 about 800 yards from the F Troop position, but the crew walked away.

Chapter Fourteen

Day 4: Wednesday, 20 September

'The Red Devils still fought back and battled for every room and every house, for every piece of ground or garden no matter how small it was — like cornered tigers.'

SS Battalion Commander

'Never have I felt so humiliated.'

Gunner Eric Chrystal on
being taken prisoner of war

Sergeant van Kuijk tells us how by 0600 hours the fighting was raging again around the Eusebiuskerk. The British force was being machine-gunned from all sides and shot at from the Rijnkade and the Markt; it retreated to the State Water Board Building by the north ramp. There were sixty-six German prisoners in the cellar and forty or so civilians — men, women and children — evacuated from their burning houses. There were also a number of wounded British soldiers. The British commanders were still optimistic that they could break out, but they were being slowly encircled and the longed-for reinforcements never arrived. By 1800 hours German fire was relentless and within the hour three German tanks drove into the courtyard and began firing. The German superiority in equipment and their constant replenishment of troops began to tell. A final attempt to break out by the beleaguered British failed. Surrender was the only option, and the order was given for Sergeant van Kuijk and his colleagues to ditch their police uniforms and weapons and join the civilians in the cellar to avoid summary execution.

The Germans were soon swarming over the building, disarming the British soldiers; sporadic fire continued and a bomb went off in the entrance, killing many. After a night in a house in the Johan de Witlaan up the ramp van Kuijk and the others were released with the other civilians, but were advised to go into hiding as the Germans were looking for them. They were eventually taken in by the Resistance.

Following the imminent failure to relieve John Frost's force at the Arnhem road bridge, a defensive perimeter had started to coalesce in Oosterbeek centred on the Divisional Headquarters at the Hartenstein Hotel. According to https://ninedaysinseptember.wordpress.com 'this perimeter, a thumb-shaped area with its base on the Northern Bank of the Lower Rhine was created in the hope of giving XXX Corps, pushing up from the South, a bridgehead to mount a crossing of the river.'

The defence of the lower eastern flank of the perimeter was formed by an ad hoc force comprising elements of the 1st, 3rd and 11th Battalions of the Parachute Regiment, the 2nd Battalion, South Staffordshire Regiment, glider pilots and the guns of the 1st Air Landing Light Regiment. It was initially called the 'Thompson Force' after the CO of the Light Regiment, Colonel W.F.K. 'Sheriff' Thompson and, after he was wounded, 'Lonsdale Force' after Major Dickie Lonsdale from the 11th Battalion.

Foul weather in England set the tone for the day over in Arnhem, as well as delaying the third lift and the long-awaited arrival of the Polish Brigade on Dutch soil. Some necessary repositioning was taking place around the 1st Air Landing Light Regiment gun positions at the Old Church in Oosterbeek: the South Staffords moved up to a site northeast of the church in and around the Van Hofwegen laundry. The glider pilots were detailed to operate on their left flank with Major Lonsdale in overall command.[1] The air was filled with the cacophonous din created by enemy armour patrolling the Batoswijk area: the self-propelled guns firing on houses around the forward gun positions and controlling the Ploegseweg-Benedendorpsweg junction. Two German tanks and two self-propelled guns, with infantry, met with the South Staffords' 6-pounders at the Benedendorpsweg-Acacialaan junction: Lance Sergeant John Daniel Baskeyfield opened up at 100 yards range knocking out the leading vehicle, while a second shot destroyed one of the tank's tracks. Fire from the 11th Parachute Battalion engaged the German soldiers. Tragically, one of the self-propelled guns scored a direct hit on one of the 6-pounders, wounding Baskeyfield in the leg and killing the rest of the crew. The crew on the next gun was also killed so the lance sergeant, having refused treatment, moved over onto that gun and knocked out another self-propelled gun, but the Germans returned fire and killed Baskeyfield. He was awarded the Victoria Cross for his valour.

The onslaught continued at Oosterbeek. A shell exploded next to Gunner Hall's trench, burying him alive, but he was dug out and resuscitated by Sergeant Sinclair and Gunner Jannicki from 1 Battery A Troop. Then a mortar bomb came through the roof of the school command post, killing a sapper and wounding five others. Lance Bombardier Tarr 'was dragged from the wreckage suffering from shell shock'.[2] The church at Oosterbeek was taking a hammering and the organ was blown off the wall.

Captain John Lee had the misfortune to witness yet another supply drop going nowhere, a harrowing spectacle shared by Gunner 'Dicky' Bird of 2 Battery D Troop: 'With horror we saw at least one Dakota come crashing down in flames and from another a dispatcher falling headlong to his death.' Lee and his OP party had deployed north-east from the Hartenstein 'in case any support was required for an impending supply drop'. Lee went some way and then half-hid the jeep and continued on foot carrying the 68 set, eventually occupying the top floor of a building overlooking the railway and open fields. Apart from the distressing sight of watching the errant supply drop, little was being achieved so the party returned to the jeep and Border HQ. Despite this non-event, the Light Regiment War Diary recorded that 'Captain Lee reported a most successful shoot with the Border Regiment.' More self-inflicted fake news.[3]

Captain Johnny Walker, 1 Battery B Troop, found himself 2i/c of the remnants of D Company KOSBs which had suffered a close-range attack from a German self-propelled gun on their base in the White House (Hotel Dreyeroord). The Light Regiment War Diary reports that Walker 'fired several M targets as morale shoots' when what really happened, according to Lee, was 'In order to dislodge us from the White House a tank appeared and fired shells at a range of about 150 yards.' Walker was 'on the lavatory at the time and had to make an undignified and hasty exit'.[4]

Meanwhile 1 and 3 Batteries were loosing off a number of Mike targets in the vicinity of the bridge on both sides of the Rhine. The enemy counter-bombardment on Oosterbeek was increasingly intense, and casualties continued to pile up. Fatalities included Gunner George Gray (1 Battery); Gunners Davidson and Lynch of 3 Battery were injured when a mortar bomb exploded in a tree above the E Troop Command Post trench. BSM Jock Lawson, he of the pre-battle nightmares, was killed, while Gunner

Nichol was wounded at the regimental aid post. No. 3 Battery Command Post took a shell that torched Sergeant Newton's motorcycle.[5]

Lance Sergeant Alfred Rouiller of 2 Battery answered the call for volunteers to man B Troop's last surviving gun. Back home he had been acting mess sergeant at Regimental HQ and had nagged RSM Siely to include him in the flight roster. As Rouiller and three others edged towards the gun, he saw 'a small group of men in a line…shaking uncontrollably… suffering from shellshock.' He recognized some of them and started to feel scared himself: '…if this sort of thing could happen to tough, battle-hardened men, it could happen to him.'[6]

If this was bad, then, as we have seen, things at the bridge were much worse. Middlebrook (p.308) reminds us of the confusion and fog of battle at this point: 'The reports of action at the Arnhem bridge steadily became more confused. The exact sequence of events cannot be guaranteed, though all the incidents described here did happen on this day and, combined, they form a true reflection of what were to be the final hours of resistance.'

Around the ramp it was perilous in the extreme to make any movement in and around the British positions. The Germans allowed safe passage for stretcher-bearers, but beyond that there was precious little chance of venturing into the open. The Germans were now firing from the east and the north and then from the west when they blew a hole in the high prison wall which had until then sheltered the British from assault from that direction. The name of the game was now fighting on until the building they were in was destroyed. German shells from over the river continued to rain down; tanks were, in the words of Middlebrook, cruising into the perimeter at will in 'what was becoming a hopeless situation'. Moreover, the Germans had realized that it was more effective to destroy 'these stout Dutch buildings by fire than by blowing them slowly to pieces and were using more phosphorus shells to cause fires'. Relief would have to come from the south in the form of the 82nd US Airborne Division, but they had still to capture the bridge at Nijmegen.

Lance Bombardier Arthur Perkins, 3 Battery HQ, was up in the loft with Major Munford, Chrystal, Hall and others: 'The Germans now heavily outnumbered us in every way and decided to destroy systematically all the buildings we now occupied.' PIAT ammunition was all gone and the anti-tank guns were out of commission. The survivors depended on shells from the Light Regiment in Oosterbeek called down by Munford.

His final message back to 3 Battery was, according to the 1st Air Landing Light Regiment's War Diary: 'We have been blown off the top storey. We are quite OK. We have killed 300 or 400 Germans for the loss of 30. The bridge is blocked with German half-tracks, armoured cars etc. We need small-arms ammunition.'[7]

Things reached a nadir when at about 1330 hours John Frost was wounded in both legs by a mortar bomb; the brigade major announced that the building was to be evacuated and the wounded were to be carried from the basement. A prowling tank then scored a hit on the corner of the building, sending the sangar, 22 set and most of the men flying helter-skelter down the stairwell. The set was rendered out of action and Bombardier Hall was badly injured. Major Hibbert appointed Major Freddie Gough of the Reconnaissance Squadron 'to command the brigade'. Frost later said 'that was the very worst time, the most miserable time of my life', observing as he did his 'battalion gradually carved to bits' around him. Frost again:

> We were always hoping, right to the bitter end, that the ground forces would arrive. As long as we were still in place around the bridge, preventing the Germans from bringing up anti-tank guns to engage the 30 Corps tanks, we were doing our job. But it was only isolated groups by then, with no proper control over the area.

The situation grew even worse when the Royal Engineers and 3rd Battalion paratroopers who had been holding the Van Limburg Stirum School on the east side of the ramp with their one and only Bren gun and small arms were overwhelmed. Was it a tank on the ramp or artillery further away that dealt the lethal blow? No matter; the top storey, where most of the thirty unwounded defenders were, was blown away and the building was ablaze.

Sapper George Needham was in the school, one of the first buildings to be hit by the tank:

> Suddenly there was a terrific explosion underneath this flight of stairs. It was the first time the building had been hit by such a big shell. There was a tank on the ramp firing at point-blank range. We had been used to small-arms fire and mortaring, but it was absolutely stunning when this explosion took place.

Then there was the house occupied by a party of twelve Royal Army Ordnance Corps and Royal Signals men. Private Kevin Heaney of the RAOC describes the shelling:

> A shell came whooshing through the open bedroom window and hit the back of the house. The back wall became a pile of rubble, and the floor fell in. One of the signallers, resting on a bed in the back bedroom, came down with the floor and was trapped. He could not move, as his back was broken. Sergeant Mick Walker, one of our men, climbed down to give him a morphine injection. My pack was in the back bedroom and I was disappointed when this was lost; I had not touched the rations inside. We then took shelter in a cellar and started hoping for the best. There was a noise at the top of the stairs, and someone started to wave a white handkerchief, but Mick Walker knocked this out of his hand. It was probably only more rubble falling down.

Heaney adds:

> The atmosphere and tension became unbearable. We were expecting to be attacked but uncertain from which direction this was going to come. The mood varied between hope and despair, and the lack of news from the rest of the division or of progress by 30 Corps was bad for morale.

What happened next is confused and mired in controversy. Middlebrook (pp.312–13) describes the sequence of events as follows:

> The building [the Van Limburg Stirum School] had to be evacuated. Captain Mackay appointed a party of sappers to remain at their positions to cover the evacuation. The wounded were brought up from the basement with the eight most seriously wounded on doors and mattresses whence they were lifted over a low wall exposed to German fire.
>
> One unconscious Royal Engineer clutching a photograph of his wife and children was hit again by machine-gun fire...and one of the 3rd Battalion men was hit in the face and killed by a mortar bomb

burst; a third man was hit in the head and killed as he climbed over the wall.

All the while the school was being hit, with two men killed and one badly crushed. Major Lewis called out from his mattress: 'Time to put up the white flag.' Some of the uninjured made an unsuccessful attempt to escape capture: every man for himself? The decision to leave the injured was not universally popular among the Engineers, particularly the senior NCOs: 'Some of us felt that was the time an officer should have stayed with his men.' In the event, when a sapper was sent up the embankment with a white towel tied to his rifle he was shot in both legs by machine-gun fire, dying of his wounds five months later. Middlebrook (p.314) provides no reference for this, or for his coda stating that 'accounts say that the German who fired that last burst was shot by one of his own officers for firing on the white flag.' More confusion follows when Middlebrook then asserts that 'this German officer inspected the sapper who was so badly wounded and unconscious, declared that there was no hope, and shot him in the head with a pistol.' The brave sapper who died twice?

Sergeant George Lawson recalled:

I heard the shout: 'Every man for himself.' A group of us made a dash for it. We had to go through a mortar barrage first; that's where young Waterston got hit. He was leaning against this wall. I thought I should go back for him, but he was turning blue, and I carried on. Several of the others were hit, too; I was hit in the face by shrapnel. I now slung my rifle away because the bloody thing was useless; it wasn't working properly. I took the bolt out and threw it away. A group of us then tried to cross the open road, but four or five of us were mown down by machine-gun fire. I turned back and took refuge in one of the burnt-out buildings – how long for, I don't know, but I was forced to get up because my gas cape and my smock were burning from the hot stone.

Middlebrook (p.315) records how Heaney and six men were trapped in a hallway with the Germans 50 yards away. 'How about packing it in?' Heaney asked his colleagues, including a wounded man:

'One chap said, "I'm easy"; I don't think he was ready to surrender, though. I put my hand inside my jacket, tore off my vest, gave it to the man nearest the opening, and he waved what was, in effect, the white flag,' Heaney said. 'The Germans shouted for the British to come out. When they did, the Germans opened up with machine-gun fire, hitting the first four Britons. I assumed the Germans who fired were themselves under fire from our men. That was my charitable interpretation as to why they fired, because they were very chivalrous generally.'

He and the wounded men got back into the house and sat in the rubble, listening uneasily to mortar fire. 'We were there for about two hours. I had my prayer book open and was saying the *Prayers for the Dying*. Later on, the Germans came in, rescuing the trapped men and taking them prisoner, and this great big German came and took the two of us also.'

This is how Major T. Hibbert remembers the final countdown:

As the last of our buildings were destroyed or set alight, attempts to re-occupy burned-out ruins failed as the ashes were too hot. John Frost, Doug Crawley, Father Egan, Pat Barnett and Digby Tatham-Warter were wounded and Freddie Gough took over command. By dusk Brigade HQ was being heavily shelled, the fires were out of control and the medical situation was getting pretty dire. In the basement of Brigade HQ we had by now nearly 300 wounded, many of them very seriously; they were packed like sardines and lying in the dark. They were now in danger of being burned alive as we had no water to tackle the fires eating into the house. We asked the Germans for a two-hour truce and assistance to get the wounded out of the cellar who included a number of Germans. The Germans agreed, but during the cease-fire they infiltrated the perimeter. The area round the bridge was ablaze and we no longer dominated it. We were down to around 100 unwounded and walking wounded, with about five rounds of ammunition per head. I formed the survivors into patrols of ten men and an officer, with orders to escape to the perimeter.

The German Perspective at the Bridge

It is interesting, and instructive, to gain some idea of how the Germans saw the end of this heroic though costly action by the British forces at the bridge. The following is based on an account by https://warfarehistorynetwork.com/2016/11/30/arnhem-bridge-why-it-was-britains-alamo-in-wwii

The defence was now squeezed into an area one-fifth of its original position, holding ten of their original eighteen buildings. The British troops were exhausted, with no food and little water, and most were kept going on Benzedrine tablets. Two German battle groups, backed by rocket artillery and Tiger tanks, were applying relentless and remorseless pressure on the British.

As noted, the Germans systematically and methodically deconstructed the British defences, deploying a brace of Tiger tanks that managed to nudge their way through the wreckage of Gräbner's wrecked vehicles still strewn across the Arnhem Bridge. 'Two 88mm flak guns were set up on either side of the southern approach to the bridge, delivering point-blank fire.' SS Section Commander Alfred Ringsdorf of the 10th SS Panzer Division's 21st *Panzergrenadier* Regiment is on record proclaiming that the only way the British were going to get out was to be carried out 'feet first'. He was also the author of these fine words:

> This was a harder battle than any I had fought in Russia. It was constant, close-range, hand-to-hand fighting. The English were everywhere. The streets for the most part were narrow, sometimes not more than 15 feet wide, and we fired at each other from only yards away. We fought to gain inches, cleaning out one room after the other. It was absolute hell!

These days, the British armed forces' terms for concentrated urban warfare are OBUA (Operations in Built-Up Areas), FIBUA (Fighting In Built-Up Areas), or sometimes (colloquially) FISH (Fighting In Someone's House), or FISH and CHIPS (Fighting In Someone's House and Causing Havoc In People's Streets).

SS Grenadier Private Horst Weber recalled the heavy artillery barrage: 'Starting from the rooftops, buildings collapsed like dolls' houses. I did not see how anyone could live through the inferno. I felt truly sorry for the British.' Another SS officer, *Rottenführer* Rudolf Trapp from *Panzergrenadier* Regiment 21, watched artillery firing point-blank down the Eusebiusplein: 'An artillery piece was trundled into our street from the Battalion Knaust behind us. This was two or three days after the battle started. It was the biggest gun I've ever seen, and was manhandled up along the side of the Rhine.' The big problem with the gun was getting it into action while under fire. Trapp continued: 'I covered it by shooting up the British positions along the street with long protracted bursts from my machine gun.' The Knaust gun crew was with the first Wehrmacht troops to enter the Arnhem battle. It opened fire on Major Crawley's position, reducing a strongpoint to rubble with seven or eight shots. After the barrage, Trapp's men stormed the position and found the occupants all dead, lying in slit trenches and prepared positions.

Battle Group Knaust was commanded by Colonel Hans Peter Knaust, a one-legged Eastern Front veteran; his powerful group fielded Panther and Tiger tanks. Two of them clanked into action near Weber, who saw them hurling shells into each house at close range. Weber recalled a corner building

> where the roof fell in, the top two storeys began to crumble and then, like the skin peeling off a skeleton, the whole front wall fell into the street revealing each floor on which the British were scrambling like mad. Dust and debris soon made it impossible to see anything more. The din was awful, but even so, above it all, we could hear the wounded screaming.

Knaust's tanks were the tipping-point in the battle. Frost's men, immobilized by the superior weight of infantry around them, were being systematically pummelled into submission by the heavy guns. One of Knaust's men, Lance Corporal Karl-Heinz Kracht, was a loader on a Mark III tank. His killing machine rumbled past the wreckage of Gräbner's vehicles:

> Personally, I felt quite a bit of apprehension as our vehicles moved into Arnhem. I still had to overcome the shock at the destruction and the corpses lying by the roadside. Maybe we were to be the next victim of the British anti-tank guns? This feeling was amplified when the company lost its first tanks.

Kracht and his tanks supported SS infantry winkling out British paratroopers. By now the exhausted Britons were beginning to surrender:

> As far as we were concerned, this shooting lasted for two days until nothing more stirred on the bridge. Panzergrenadiers, also suffering most of the casualties, had to do the dirty work again. Even so we lost another tank. All around the bridgehead was a nightmare of buildings reduced to rubble, shot-up vehicles and guns, and corpses – of friend and foe alike.

Collecting the wounded was becoming a problem for the Germans. The 19-year-old SS machine-gunner Rudolf Trapp (3 *Kompanie SS Panzergrenadier*) was assigned to the gruesome task:

> We were told to get some wounded or dead SS men out of the enemy field of fire. To achieve this we got an armoured half-track. Putting down covering fire with two machine guns on it, we would race down the street, open the rear door, pull our mates in, and fire away as we sped back to cover. All the time we would hope there would not be a stoppage on the machine gun because the British fired very accurately. In one case they shot a man in the heart straight through his military record book.

Trapp was ordered to take his half-track to crawl through the rubble and link with troops coming in from the east. The route they would have to take was dominated by a British anti-tank gun. Trapp recalled:

> Bernd Schultze-Bernd was our driver, a farmer's son from Sendenhorst in Münsterland. He was one of the three old company veterans. There were tears in his eyes. He told our company commander that this was not going to work. But an order is an order. To be on the safe side, the two of us stuffed the pockets of our smocks with hand grenades and ammunition for the .008 pistols. We raced past the crossroads and got hit on the left, near Bernd's driver's seat. The vehicle came to a halt. Bernd was dead, a direct hit from the shell.

Trapp and his surviving comrades bailed out of their half-track and took refuge in a ruined cellar. As the British closed in on them, they grenaded their way out and made their way to the riverbank. There they shed their uniforms and swam through the murky water between moored boats, under rifle fire, until they reached their own men. In more ways than one, this was a chilling foretaste of what awaited the surviving British troops in a few days' time. Trapp and his crew had their wounds dressed, were issued uniforms from their dead comrades and rejoined the fighting.

After the battle, Munford described the absolute mayhem and utter carnage at the bridge:

> The set was smashed and Bdr Hall badly hurt. Crook, Lowe (OPA [Observation Post Assistant]) and I dug ourselves out of the rubble and carried Hall down to the Regimental Aid Post, difficult because the stairwell was filled with debris. The cellars were crowded with wounded; we left Hall with the MOs and returned to salvage our gear. The 68 set was still functioning but we were unable to contact Captain Buchanan, the FOU [Forward Observation Unit] east of the road by the river. Later, as a PoW, I heard that a bomb or a shell through the roof of the OP had killed them all but, as far as I know, 'Buck' was never found.
>
> Battalion HQ next door was now burned out and Brigade HQ burning; as everyone else had left the building, we clambered down to the ground floor.... Freddie Gough...told us to cease firing as the Germans had agreed to allow us to remove our wounded to collection points where we should find their medical orderlies. We all helped with this task, not forgetting our own Bdr Hall, until the indefatigable Freddie ordered us to rendezvous, if possible, in a school on the crossroads as the truce was broken and 'the bastards are infiltrating our positions'. Tanks were once again prowling the streets and infantry closing in from all directions so we had to leave by vaulting boundary walls behind houses on the main street leading north. We had seen many soldiers killed in the last few days and I did not think I would be so moved as I was when we came upon Dutch civilians lying dead in their own homes and gardens.
>
> https://www.pegasusarchive.org/arnhem/dennis_munford.htm

Bombardier Hall gives a different situation report: significant among the day's events was, he recalls, Wednesday, D+3, 'for some reason, a weakening of signals between our 22 and Oosterbeek. Perhaps some of my poked-out aerial had been shot off – it didn't occur to me to look: I was receiving them, with a little difficulty, but my transmissions went unnoticed.' After the war he learned, recently, of that move by the 3 Battery Command Post 'from its own attic position near the Old Church at Oosterbeek into a cellar – could this account for the failure of communications from my 22 from that time?' Anyway, Hall decided to try Morse with its longer range. Crucially he recalls: 'There is a buff card containing the "RA Code" which reduces any gun-control order to a two-letter group; Signallers were permitted to remember only the code for "fire", which was "WA".'

Hall explains the circuitous route by which signals, now 'fading from the Oosterbeek end', were sent and received. It is often assumed that the link between Thompson and Munford was a direct connection that allowed the two men to speak directly to each other, but it was not so. Hall reveals that the 22 set used by Munford and operated by him was on the 3 Battery net and the 22 set used by Thompson was on the regimental net. Messages were passed from the bridge to the 3 Battery Command Post Officer Lieutenant Wilkinson, and from him to the Acting Adjutant Lieutenant Humphries at Regimental HQ near the Old Church.[8]

Hall came down from the attic and went to the back of the two (brigade and battalion) buildings where about ten jeeps were parked. He searched the glove compartments of two jeeps – Munford's and Harrison's – for copies of the RA Code, but was unable to find them, only to be told later that no one ordered them to be brought. He returned to the attic, switched to MCW (a Morse note) and tapped out the call sign. No response. 'The air was filled with mild interference of other faint R/T and W/T. I realised my fears, that my Morse was just another element of interference in the headphones of the Net.'

Hall returned to the attic with little to do 'except take in the continuous sound of battle. No gun orders were being attempted; the two sides locked too close for Artillery support. Late afternoon Munford suddenly appeared: "Come on!" he said, "We're evacuating the building." I got up. "What about the set?" I asked. "Fuck the set!"' Hall remembers how he turned back anyway to switch it off to save the battery, ever confident that he would need it again when relieved by the advancing XXX Corps.

On the floor below the battery OP team stood waiting for them at the top of the steps leading down to the first floor: 'The din of the battle was almost deafening to me now that I was without a headset for the first time in hours.'

> The noise of battle occupied every second; outside a German Tiger tank roamed up and down the road outside, unchallenged, firing at will at any likely resistance. Suddenly, everything happening within a second, a shell-burst fragment caught my hip, flinging me into the down-well of the stairs. My right leg and buttock were paralysed, useless; warm blood trickled down the lower sensitive parts. Munford and two others [Crooke and Lowe] carried me down into the cellar for a dressing and eventual placing alongside the other wounded.[9]

The explosion had hit the south-east corner of the building just as Hall was taking a cigarette. After a difficult descent down the rubble-strewn stairway, Munford handed him into the care of Captain J.W. Logan of the 16th Parachute Field Ambulance, MO to the 2nd Parachute Battalion. Truesdale (p.109) records a rather unsavoury episode that cannot have made Hall feel any better. While an orderly was cutting away Hall's battledress trousers, a wounded paratrooper stumbled in clutching his stomach. Logan took one look and ordered 'Morphine!' However, it was too late: the paratrooper vomited blood and parts of his stomach straight into Hall's face.[10]

Hall also remembers an altercation that took place that day in the room below the attic in Brigade HQ, recorded in Truesdale but not in Hall's *Signals from Arnhem Bridge*.[11] When he went below to tell 'the Signaller' that it was time for his stint as Hall felt he'd been in the attic long enough without a break, the signaller refused to go. 'I'm not going up there,' he said, while all the other signallers were watching at the foot of the stairs while the battle noise was increasing. Hall responded with 'It's your turn.' He was quite firm in his resolve and again refused. I said, 'it's your turn, I'm ordering you to go.' But he wouldn't budge! 'I don't care,' he said, quite evenly, 'you can shoot me if you want but I'm not going up there.'

Charitably, Hall maintains anonymity and ascribes the insubordination to the fact that the signalman in question had, like a number of the other signalmen, 'been shelled in an Italian OP, his back was still heavily scarred where falling masonry had put him in hospital there.... I was glad that Munford wasn't a witness. "Don't be silly," I said and went back up the steps to monitor the set.'

The point that Hall makes by relating this incident is presumably not just that discipline is paramount in battle, but also he wanted to highlight the devastating and long-lasting effect that combat can have on a soldier. The unnamed signalman was undoubtedly at fault for refusing an order, but he was also a victim of what we now call PTSD and, as we know, if these conditions are not treated, they may never go away and often recur in subsequent conflict.

Meanwhile 3 Battery Gunners Crook, Chubb and Bowles had the misfortune to endure a salvo of machine-gun fire through the roof of the building they occupied in Oosterbeek, with the latter two injured in the arm.[12]

For Hall and the others at the bridge the game was surely up, much as the valiant defenders may have wanted to continue the fight.

Hall continues, illustrating how enemies can be compassionate, particularly to the battle-injured:

> Eventually I heard calls above for the walking wounded and, I think, for an English-speaking German prisoner. Then there was a silence; we knew that the Germans were coming in the building. A medical orderly, tending one of our wounded, kept calling '*Kamerad*' until a wounded officer told him to shut up. They came in, the Waffen SS, to help us out. They laid me on the embankment [with some compassion] opposite our HQ, now ablaze and suffering the same fate that all the surrounding buildings had had. I was glad of the blaze; it was dusk, a chilly evening. A young SS [infantryman] came to me, gave me a lighted cigarette and a swig of cold ersatz coffee from his water bottle. They put me with others without serious wounds in a half-track and lurched us through the dark ghostly streets to St Elisabeth Hospital. Next day I was transferred to St Joseph's Lazaret in Enschede, a small town on the German border. Here I realised that the supreme faith I had of XXX Corps relieving us was misplaced.... I had kept my balance when both officers and men at the Bridge had lost theirs – but then, I was concentrating on the earphones; the din of battle (its most unnerving feature) was attenuated; and

I had the false safety of the attic. I viewed my future as a Kriegie philosophically; I wasn't angry at the outcome: it had been a gamble anyway and, in a sense, for me, but not for others, certainly not for the Dutch for whom I grieved and felt my shame, an adventure.... In my dealings with my German captors in the battle area I must emphasise that they behaved most honourably to me. A comrade-in-arms; I was, so to speak, one of them. I do not wish to deny atrocities – and there were undoubtedly some – but what I have just said about the German front-line soldier had to be said.

Hall adds how two days later he was 'caught in suspicious circumstances with two Dutch "visitors" and an officer arranging a getaway. I found myself within hours in another hospital tucked away in the security ward filled with SS wounded.' When the German equivalent of NAAFI came round, 'there was an immediate whip-round to pay for mine', even though he had been with them for less than a day.[13]

Before he was blown 15ft down the stairs, Hall noticed that Gunners Ogle and Chrystal were missing; it later transpired that Ogle had left the building.[14]

Gunner Chrystal takes over the story of the retreat from the burning building:

Early Wednesday morning, it was still dark, we were told we were leaving and we were led to a small church. There was quite lot of us there – I hadn't realised we were so many. We were addressed by a senior officer, a major I think he was. After a pep talk we were told we would be leaving the church in parties of six and eight I think, it was under an officer or senior NCO or WO. The party I was in came under an officer who said he was an IO [Intelligence Officer] but I had never seen him before. It could have been anyone for all I knew. We set off scrambling about in the ruins, dodging the Schmeissers and other small-arms fire until we lost two of our number. Immediately after that this officer said it was useless to try and get any further and he surrendered us. As our captors said to us, 'for you the war is over'. I was struck by the absence of any animosity – but it didn't help my feelings. After that it was a case of being searched, waiting for daylight, being taken to Zutphen, interrogated.

During this apart from giving my name, rank and number I didn't have to tell him a thing: he knew the battery and regiment. It was then that they relieved us of our airborne smocks – I didn't think much to that. The only good thing was that my parents heard that I was a PoW in a broadcast by Lord Haw-Haw.

Gunner Chrystal ends his account by asserting that 'never have I felt so humiliated'.[15]

Gunner Alan Coogan remembers the capitulation too and how they were told 'every man for himself' as the situation had become impossible: 'There was no food and no ammunition and the basement of the house was full of wounded soldiers, including Colonel Frost.' Coogan and those with him were told to make for the river and try to cross to Nijmegen. He and Roderick Morrison escaped from the house and spent the night in a garden shed 200 yards or so from the HQ at about 2300 hours. Next morning some Germans kicked in the door and took them prisoner. Coogan remembers seeing his jeep which had been commandeered by a German soldier, bewailing the sad fact that it had been loaded with chocolate, tea, sugar and coffee, all of which he would discover to be in short supply in the PoW camp that awaited him.[16]

By Air to Battle gives the bigger picture of the final stand at the bridge:[17]

Ammunition was running short, and the key house commanding the north end of the bridge had been burnt down. The Germans posted in houses further back nearer the town, though making no attempt to infiltrate, kept the whole area of the defence under more or less continuous small-arms and automatic fire. The number of wounded had now reached serious proportions. They were lying in the cellars of a house, attended by two Royal Army Medical Corps doctors, Captains J. Logan, D.S.O., and D. Wright, M.C., who did particularly fine work in dreadful conditions and remained with them to the end. The order to surrender the wounded was given by Colonel Frost after the house had been set on fire. Wednesday, 20 September, brought no relief. By then the force had been burnt out of its original positions on or near the bridge and was fighting in the ruins close to and beneath it. Presently German tanks were able to move across the bridge from north to south, for the 6-pounders, sighted to cover it, were under small-arms fire and could not be manned. Aircraft also played a part in the German attacks, and a Messerschmitt 109, diving on the position, hit the steeple of a nearby church and crashed. Nevertheless, the defence was still maintained and hopes were still high, for news had been received that the 2nd Army would attack the south end of the bridge that afternoon at five p.m.

By Air to Battle goes on to inform us that the last stand was made, first in a warehouse and then underneath the bridge itself with about 110 men and 5 or 6 officers still able to fight. Luckily a German tank and armoured car were unable to target the British position under the bridge due to the trajectory.

Lieutenant Grayburn, whose valour earned him a Victoria Cross which he did not live to receive, led a series of counter-attacks in one of which Germans laying charges to blow the bridge were killed and the charges torn out. Every time a patrol went out it suffered casualties, and with each hour the situation became more and more hopeless. There was no more ammunition, there had been no food for a long time and hardly a man was not wounded. The very ground on which the defenders stood or crouched was constantly seared by flames from the burning houses about it, and no man could remain there and live. So in the end the gallant remnants were dispersed or captured.

Royal Engineer Lieutenant Donald Hindley recalls, with some of his 'A' Company men, being part of Grayburn's heroic sortie working so close to all the explosives that 'could be fired at any moment'. Grayburn was wounded again, but returned to the fray 'one arm in a sling and with bandaged head'. Hindley and the others were fully expecting the Germans to restore the fuses so made a 'second, heavier attack…to remove the charges themselves', but the enemy had brought up a tank to cover the work. 'We were quickly mowed down. Lieutenant Grayburn was killed – riddled with machine-gun fire. I escaped with flesh wounds in my shoulder and face.'[18]

The inevitable conclusion was that the 1st Airborne Division's objective of taking the bridge at Arnhem had not been and was not going to be achieved. A bridge too far, indeed.

For TSM Tom Kent over in Oosterbeek, much of that night was spent trying to retrieve some of the supplies that had fallen outside the perimeter.

Crawling like worms, he and a glider pilot, Staff Sergeant Trevor Francis, foraged in the hazardous territory that is no man's land, ever vulnerable both to enemy firing or 'friendly fire'. Sadly, much of what they found they already had in plenty: the petrol was useless 'as they had no vehicles to run' and they had small-arms ammunition aplenty. The discovery of a forty-eight-hour ration pack lifted morale no end when Kent was able to hand out a cigarette and two sweets to each of his comrades.[19]

Gunner John Myles of 1 Battery B Troop was not so lucky when he was sent with a message to RHQ, communications being non-existent. The area was being shelled as he passed a trench with two soldiers and Myles addressed them, only to find that they were both dead. When he got back he went straight to his own trench only to find an arm sticking out: Myles pulled at it and it came away in his hand. They had run out of ammunition for their guns so dug trenches all round the gun positions for defence; two men in the next trench were killed by a shell.

The carnage continued unabated. Captain C.A. Harrison recounts how one of E Troop's guns commanded by Sergeant John Wyatt with Gunners Dawson and Boland was firing at a target 1,500 yards distant, range and distance called by Lieutenant Farrand, Gun Position Officer. Staff Sergeant Trevor Francis (mentioned above) had been asked by 3 Battery Command Post to go out with four men including Sergeant David Thompson and search a field for an ammunition canister they believed to be somewhere there. Francis was unexpectedly called back to the Command Post, telling the others to wait for him. When he went to rejoin the group, Thompson went forward just as Sergeant Wyatt's gun opened fire, hitting Thompson in the chest and blowing him to bits. Jack Briggs had a different view of it: 'A glider pilot wandering aimlessly about our gun position walked in front of No. 1 gun just as the limber gunner pulled the lanyard. It was a very dark night and I am sure the crew hadn't seen him.' Result: glider pilot struck in the chest at about 6ft range with a 75mm shell, killing him instantly. However, there was, says Briggs, more: 'shrapnel rebounded onto the gun crew, killing three of them.'

Francis received a right-hand injury from shrapnel. Gunner Jack Briggs searched Thompson's body for his papers and removed his ID disc. Captain Harrison ordered the body to be buried immediately so that the shocking sight would not depress morale even further. Padre Pare attached to the unit read the full burial service while under continued shelling; Sergeant Wyatt died after taking a shrapnel wound in the groin and Gunners Lynch, Dawson and Boland were all injured.[20] Francis and his men eventually continued the search but found nothing.

One of the most accurate ways of determining a true and vivid picture of a conflict as it unrolls is to see it through the eyes of the medical staff looking after the casualties in the various casualty stations and hospitals. Lieutenant Howard Cole provides an admirable description of events in his *On Wings of Healing*. What follows paraphrases his observations from around 19 to 21 September in and around Oosterbeek.[21]

The morning of 19 September saw casualties 'coming into the Hotel Schoonhord (the MDS) at such a rate that it became impossible to accommodate them'. This necessitated the occupation of more buildings, including a large house opposite and a school 100 yards away where Captain Doyle and the Reserve Section of the 181st (Air Landing) Field Ambulance 'were running a secondary DS for the lightly wounded, which by eleven o'clock totalled some 300'. The commanders of all the sections on detachment were called in and bolstered by Corporal Cooling with the glider-borne element of the 16th (Parachute) Field Ambulance. Despite constant small-arms fire, the medics worked to full capacity. The 'burly figure' of General Urquhart on a visit with Colonel Warrack raised morale no end. Around the same time Lieutenant Colonel Alford, Captain Mawson, RMO of the 11th Battalion, Parachute Regiment with forty or so all ranks of the 133rd (Parachute) Field Ambulance with two surgical teams entered Oosterbeek and were absorbed into the existing medical teams 'which then comprised the complete 181st (Air Landing) Field Ambulance; part of the 133rd…and the Reserve Section.' Apart from the surgical teams still operating in the St Elisabeth Hospital, the whole of the 16th were now prisoners of war. Over the next two days casualties continued to stream in: 'Dutch nurses, despite the conditions, had all volunteered to stay, and as the number of casualties grew it would have been almost impossible to have carried on without their help.' Water supply and lighting had failed, making it very difficult for the civilian caterers that included a number of German nuns. Emergency lighting was available in the operating theatres, but the X-ray equipment was rendered out of service.

On 20 September around 1000 hours saw German troops take over the DS under heavy mortar fire. They took prisoner the walking wounded and the remnants of the 133rd (Parachute) Field Ambulance, leaving only Alford, two surgeons, the dental officer and about ten other ranks to tend to the more seriously wounded: 'Their operating theatre, the surgery of a Dutch dentist, was deliberately wrecked by a small party of German infantrymen.' So as to avoid capture Colonel Warrack ripped off his tabs and badges of rank and masqueraded as an orderly. Lieutenant Colonel Marrable, the SMO, insisted of the senior German officer that he keep all his staff as he had 400 or more wounded to look after, including some Germans. The German agreed, but pointed out that all of the British were now prisoners of war.

Outside about 20 yards away a minor skirmish was occurring between a German SP field gun and a 6-pounder British anti-tank gun; the SP was able to 'put four shots through [the DS] – although it was clearly marked with the Red Cross'. Luckily there were only two wounded inside at the time and these were carried out between salvoes, although one of the padres (the Reverend B.J. Benson) and the Orderly Room sergeant of the 181st were both wounded. Later a German officer 'clumped into the DS, went straight to the German wounded demanding if they were receiving proper treatment. He was evidently assured that the treatment was the same for all, for he saluted meticulously and stalked out.' Drugs aside, there is very little that can compete with excruciating pain: pain takes over everything, all emotions and psychological processes, as this example shows. A 25-year-old Nazi was brought in suffering from a shattered knee, but stubbornly refused treatment or pain relief. Four hours later he finally broke down begging for morphine, so even the most fanatical Nazi supporters have their breaking-point.

The afternoon saw the shelling die down to some extent. In the Hotel Schoonhord Lieutenant Colonel Marrable was continuing with his amputations, but his saws were being used by his surgical teams over in the Hotel Taffelberg. No problem: Marrable, when faced with a young soldier whose leg had been shattered, simply made use of an escape file produced by the DADMS (Deputy Assistant Director of Medical Services) to saw through the tibia, 'which was cleaned and sterilised and worked very satisfactorily.' The surgical teams in the Taffelberg were assisted by Dr Giesbert, a Dutch doctor, and a Mr Bauman, a local electrician who 'rearranged the lights so that an efficient operating theatre could be established'.

The Light Regiment's RAP (Regimental Aid Post) led by Captain Randall Martin RAMC had been moved under unrelenting enemy fire when conditions 'became untenable…nearly 100 casualties were held there at the time and they were evacuated under almost impossible conditions' to the Schoonhord, the more seriously wounded by jeep. In the school, the small DS with its 100 or so lightly wounded men was being repeatedly hit by small-arms crossfire and mortars. Captain Doyle and five men were killed, while others were re-wounded. By the evening what became known as the 'Hospital Area' was looking after 'well over 1,000 patients' while surgery in the Taffelberg DS was abandoned when a ceiling of one makeshift operating theatre 'had come crashing down, littering doctors and patients with plaster; the windows of the other "theatre" had been blown in. The second ceiling collapsed soon after 1700 hours.' News was received that the RAP of the 2nd Battalion Parachute Regiment was still performing near the bridge under RMO Captain J.W. Logan.

On 21 September the German ADMS (Assistant Director of Medical Services) arrived to warn of the impending arrival of several hundred more wounded.

German traffic from one end of the bridge was restored with the collapse of the British defence and coincided with the capture of the Nijmegen bridge thanks in great part to the US 504th Parachute Infantry Regiment. By 1830 hours Sergeant Peter Robinson of the Grenadier Guards was leading his column of Sherman tanks over the bridge despite the threat of a watery grave had the Germans blown the bridge, but of course the road from Nijmegen to Arnhem was now strongly defended so the Guards made little progress to help their comrades in Arnhem for whom the promised breakthrough never came.

At the bridge in Arnhem the Brigade HQ building and one other were all that was left; HQ survived because it was set back and protected by the prison wall and other buildings, now gutted due to the incessant shelling of the last few days, but HQ was now on fire so the wounded had to be evacuated into the last remaining building not consumed by flames. A truce was required so German prisoners were dispatched with white flags; in the shell-free two hours that ensued, unwounded men at the HQ were sent north into Arnhem town to rendezvous at a convent school just outside the perimeter. With virtually no ammunition, around 0200 hours on the Thursday, Major Hibbert split the survivors at the convent into groups of ten men and one officer to slip through enemy lines and make for the divisional perimeter at Oosterbeek. Sadly all were captured.

The 2nd Battalion soldiers were still in their slit trenches near the bridge and impolitely declined a German officer's request that they surrender. Being called 'silly bastards to carry on fighting…why don't you give up?' simply evinced a chorus of 'Piss off!'[22]

The 280 or so casualties, including Dutch civilians and Germans, all made it out and eventually reached the St Elisabeth Hospital. Medical staff that stayed with them were taken prisoner.

Lieutenant 'Tom' Ainslie, Commanding Officer, 133rd Parachute Field Ambulance, provided a fitting and typical epilogue: he recalled his party being trapped in a house, with Germans outside calling on them to surrender:

Some of my group had already been hit, so I yelled back in German, 'Don't shoot. There are wounded here.' And we walked across the street into captivity. The first person in authority we saw was an NCO. He was slightly cross-eyed, his tunic was open, and he was wearing a blue-and-white striped civilian shirt underneath. He said, 'Good evening. That was a lovely battle, a really lovely battle. Have a cigar. We are human too.' So, after doing what we could for the wounded, we all sat down, smoking foot-long cigars, and had a matey chat about the events of the past few days.

As Middlebrook importantly points out, 'There is general agreement that those Germans of the 10th SS Panzer Division who had been fighting at the bridge behaved correctly and with much consideration for their opponents in the immediate aftermath of the fighting, belying the reputation for savagery and cruelty usually accorded to the SS.'[23] This view was endorsed by John Frost when he said 'The SS men were very polite.'

An unsuccessful attempt by the KOSBs with two Bren gun carriers to reach the bridge marked the end of resistance at about 0500 hours on Thursday.

All that was left now was to defend the bridgehead on the northern bank of the Rhine on the western side of Oosterbeek and hope that XXX Corps might still get through from the south and assist in a safe river crossing from the north. The three batteries of the 1st Air Landing Regiment RA were still very much part of that battle. The objective now was to construct a defensive perimeter and hold it against the 9th Panzer Division and other forces whose objective was to force the British yet further from the bridge and eliminate the bridgehead.

The only troops on the two main routes in from Arnhem made a motley and insubstantial line of defence: they were the gunners of the 1st Air Landing Light Regiment, some glider pilots who were dug in near the church, the RAMC manning the nearby dressing stations on the Utrechtseweg and some Reconnaissance Squadron patrols.[24] The survivors streaming back from Arnhem would now form the core of the defence in and around Oosterbeek.[25]

Chapter Fifteen

Day 5: Thursday, 21 September

News of the end of resistance at the bridge would initially have plunged those still fighting tenaciously to hold the perimeter around Oosterbeek into profound despair, deflating morale. However, it seems that this was a passing phase and the embattled British were all the more determined to give at least as good as they were getting for the next five days. The gunners of the 1st Air Landing Light Regiment were no exception, dismayed as they must have been to hear that so many of their comrades were dead or injured or taken prisoner of war: eighty-one Airborne were killed fighting for the bridge, thirty-one of whom have no known grave. Woollacott (p.143) asserts that 'at the base of this perimeter were the twenty-three 75mm guns of the 1st Air Landing Light Regiment. The Regiment had now become the sheet anchor on which the whole defence would rely.' Buckingham says 'twenty-one guns remained in action' (p.374).

The Poles finally got off the ground in England, but some 41 out of 114 Dakotas had to turn back or land – almost the entire 1st Battalion – due to the weather and more than 100 Luftwaffe fighters were in the air to greet those who continued as they approached the landing zone. A number broke through the fighter screen and claimed several more Dakotas; however, Major General S. Sosabowski landed with more than 750 men, but with no heavy equipment which had been lost in the gliders two days previously. *Obersturmbannführer* Harzer rapidly organized some 2,500 men as a blocking force (*Sperrverband Harzer*) between the Poles and Arnhem Bridge. There was another resupply drop, but only some 41 tons of supplies got through to the British.

For their part the Germans had undergone something of a shake-up in their command structure, giving overall command to General Bittrich and his II SS Panzer Corps who in turn delegated to *Obersturmbannführer* Harzer, commander of the 9th Panzer SS Division. As Midddlebrook points out (p.341), 'the Germans now decided that the time was ripe for an all-out attack at Oosterbeek...to commence at 0800 hours.' The German forces, however, were of such variable quality with a command system that lacked efficiency, 'particularly in the west where Von Tettau's HQ had all the characteristics of "an old gentlemen's club".' Effective coordination was never a factor at this stage. The stinging remark was made by a Colonel Fullriede who commanded several battalions of the Hermann Göring Division; the same Fullriede who, a few weeks after the battle, set fire to the Dutch village of Putten as a reprisal for Resistance activity and dispatched the entire male population to concentration camps.

Thursday the 21st was a significant and crucial day on the communications front. After many problems there was a significant breakthrough while General Urquhart, the CRA and Colonel Thompson were doing the rounds of the 1st Air Landing Light Regiment gun positions. Thompson's account (Wilkinson, pp.97–98) tells us how the CRA took the headset and microphone offered to him by Captain McMillen (1 FOU) and, having identified himself as 'Sunray' (code for commander), announced that he had made contact with 64 Medium Regiment: 'The tense atmosphere in the command post relaxed in a sense of elation...we were now linked by wireless to the Corps Artillery through 64 Medium Regiment and from now on they gave the Division continuous support.' Fire orders apart, 'much vital General Staff signal traffic' began to pass over [this RA net] on what was 'the only link between the Division and XXX Corps.'

So the soldiers fighting on the Oosterbeek perimeter were themselves supported by the guns of the 64th Medium Regiment RA who had crossed from Belgium into the Netherlands at 1630 hours the previous day, reaching Eindhoven at dusk. They fought through the congestion through the night south of Nijmegen where they pulled into a position at 0900 hours on Thursday morning. The regiment was a London Territorial unit with two 4.5in batteries and one of 5.5in guns. By 1035 hours 211 Battery was able to contact the FOO in Oosterbeek reporting that they were ready to fire their eight 4.5in guns on one of the three targets they had been allocated, strengthened at 1600 hours by a battery of 155mm 'Long Tom' howitzers. No. 212 Battery was ready by 1300 hours with their eight 5.5in howitzers. Once they were all up and firing, 'uncanny accuracy' was the verdict, even though the range was 15km; they were assisted by the 1st Air Landing's FOOs. According to Paul Johnson of their air support party they 'were able to adjust the fire of some of the XXX Corps 150mm guns…[and] managed to knock out two assault guns and damage a third, thus saving the south-east flank from a dangerous attack.'[1]

Kampfgruppe Knaust reinforced with Panther tanks and self-propelled guns was enjoying its renewed ability to cross the road bridge with impunity. Meanwhile, the tanks of the Irish Guards were on their way from Nijmegen to Arnhem while the Irish Guards launched a left flanking attack; both were stopped in their tracks by the armour of *Kampfgruppe* Knaust 2 miles outside Elst.[2]

Truesdale reveals that a report from the CRA stated 'that 137 rounds per [1st Air Landing Light Regiment] gun were carried into battle (125 HE, 6 AP, 6 smoke) and approximately 50 rounds per gun were received in resupply' until 22 September when resupply came to an end. By then about fifty rounds per gun were left. This was largely expended on 'repelling assaults on their own areas and for occasionally thickening up the most important and urgent targets engaged by XXX Corps'. Many of the regiment now became skilful 'tank hunters' and really quite good at dealing with troublesome snipers. Defence of the perimeter, however, was obviously the main focus of attention. German mortar shells continued to rain down, liberally showering shrapnel, and trenches were dug ever deeper in the sandy soil, counteracted by the increasing danger of those trenches collapsing.[3]

Lance Bombardier Whiteley was, by common consent, 'severely shell-shocked' by the persistent firing of a 75mm self-propelled gun into his B Troop position, pumping shells into the house. Soon after, amazingly, he volunteered for a sortie against the German-held gasworks. Woollacott (p.150) sums it up when he says 'the spirit he shows at that moment could only be admired.' Lieutenant Tom Conlin, GPO F Troop disposed of an enemy mortar team setting up on Benedendorpsweg through Sergeant McBain's F3 gun, 'engaging by open sights'. Later German troops were spotted 'upstairs in the houses overlooking our gun position…we pumped smoke shells from two guns directly through the windows'. No. 3 Battery's TSM Kent saw it too: 'We resorted to a trick proved in Italy earlier and fired direct over open sight at the windows of the house using phosphorous smoke shells. The whole row of houses was ablaze in seconds and the snipers must have got a very warm reception.'[4]

Wilkinson (p.106) usefully gives us the deployment around the F Troop command post at the porch of the church: on the far side the 17-pounder of the 1st Anti-Tank Battery of Sergeant Thomas; in the churchyard Sergeant Gullane of the 2nd Battery; Sergeant Hughes' 17-pounder which was brought up from the western part of the perimeter, manhandled over a wall to a site in an orchard below the 3 Battery command post to command the approaches from Arnhem. Unfortunately they received a direct hit, but not before they took out some armoured cars and shelled enemy positions on the embankment.

The steadily diminishing range of targets (causing problems of crest clearance) was hampering F Troop, as witnessed by TSM Kent:

> The Troop Command Post was situated just outside the door of the church itself and our vehicles were deployed along the front of the church and along a lane by the side of the church. On our left front… was a 6-pounder anti-tank gun and just ahead and to one side of that a 17-pounder anti-tank gun manned by members of the Anti-Tank Battery to give us cover against tanks…it was completely open land ahead until one came to a railway embankment some 700 yards away.… The other Batteries in the Regiment were in action to our left and further away from the river.

At 10.00 that morning Lieutenant Colonel Thompson, Brigadier Hackett (commanding the eastern half of the perimeter) and Major D.J. 'Tiny' Madden (former commander of 3 Battery) were crossing in front of the ter Horst house after leaving the 3 Battery command post when they were met by a salvo of mortar bombs exploding on the lawn. Fragments from the bombs wounded all three, Madden fatally when he went to assist Thompson. Command of the regiment and the glider pilots passed from Thompson to Major de Gex, 2i/c of the Light Regiment, while the Thompson Force was taken over by Major Lonsdale.[5] Still the mortar bombings continued, as did precision sniper fire: Lieutenant Keith Halliday of B Troop was wounded in his OP, as were Lance Bombardier Whiteley and Staff Sergeant Leeves. A supply drop at 1245 hours managed to get containers into the 3 Battery position, only for the eagerly expectant gunners to find that they contained petrol – not needed – and 75mm ammunition incompatible with their guns.

Antony Beevor, however, tells a less disappointing tale when he records that 'the Light Regiment Royal Artillery had been down to less than thirty rounds per gun, and its effectiveness was saved by that day's delivery of nearly 700 rounds of 75mm shells for the howitzers.'[6] This came after the distressing testimony of a Lance Bombardier Jones:

> My eye caught one of the burning Dakotas. For the briefest second two figures appeared at the doorway. One had a chute and the other didn't and they were jumping on the one chute. As they came out of the doorway they parted. The one floated down in his chute; the other fell to earth like a stone. I can still picture him falling, his arms akimbo, diving head first towards the ground.

The rest of the day was taken up with small sorties against the enemy manning the gasworks, and by tank hunts led by Major Cain of the South Staffordshires and his PIAT in one of which Lieutenant Ian Meikle was killed in his anti-tank OP. Cain had, according to *By Air to Battle* (p.118), in one confrontation with an SP fired off some fifty bombs before he was badly injured when his last, the sixth PIAT bomb blew up in the muzzle, injuring him in the face. It knocked him unconscious, gave him two black eyes and ruptured both his eardrums; when he came round he had basic first-aid, stuffed torn field dressings in his ears and returned to his command. Cain was awarded the VC for his persistent brave actions.[7] Before that he narrowly escaped injury when a chimney pot crashed down from a house 'and nearly brained Major Cain'. The only casualty was a rifleman with him 'who ran screaming to the rear not to be seen by Cain again' (Middlebrook, p.344).

The PIAT was also the weapon of choice for Captain Peter Chard outside the Koude Herberg restaurant to the west of the Hartenstein on the Utrechtseweg. Chard targeted a tank, one of seventeen of *Panzer Kompanie* 224 commanded by *Oberleutnant* May in a converted French Renault, its 75mm howitzer replaced with a flame-thrower. The accompanying infantry was disposed of while Chard stalked the tank with his PIAT. His bomb misfired so he resorted to lobbing a grenade into the turret, only to be met by a sheet of flame. His supporting team ran forward to roll him in sand as Chard implored someone to come forward and finish him off, but to no avail: the Germans recovered Captain Chard and took him to the St

Liduina Hospital in Apeldoorn where he died of his wounds almost three weeks later. One of the official photographers had photographed Chard in all his agony but, unsurprisingly, the shocking image never made it to the final collection.[8]

Gunner Harry Stockton, 2 Battery, was saved from spending the rest of the war in a PoW camp by shelling courtesy of the Medium Regiment which was exploding on enemy positions only 50 yards from their positions. The shells deterred a troop of Germans in the woods nearby and in buildings overlooking their position as well as two tanks only 300 yards away; they had already landed a mortar shell in the 2 Battery gun pit. The hero of the hour, however, was Sergeant Newland who, after one of the tanks had been dealt with by a PIAT, hooked his gun onto a jeep and made for the second, under heavy fire from its guns. His manoeuvre enabled him to fix on the tank, shielded as it was in its pit, and he scored a direct hit with his first shot, following this up with two more rounds to set it ablaze. For his initiative and single-handed bravery Newland was awarded the DCM.[9]

Casualties continued to mount for the gunners, with a particular shortage of subalterns in 1 Battery B Troop due to casualties. Indeed, the guns of 1 Battery were divided up between 2 and 3 Batteries under Major James Linton of 2 Battery and Captains John Lee and Raymond Stevens of 1 Battery and No. 1 Forward Observation Unit respectively. In the afternoon 2 Battery had to deal with a menacing German armoured vehicle: a tank-hunting party of glider pilots led by Major Robert Croot from G Squadron.[10]

Nor did this stop BSM Richard Barrett, however, who, under constant fire and with no officer available, set about reorganizing the gun positions and repelling successive enemy assaults. Barrett was awarded the Military Medal.[11] Gunner Mills (2 Battery, D Troop) recalls how he and others were moved across to support 1 Battery and found themselves up against a machine-gunning tank at the elementary school in Weverstraat, 75 to 100 yards away. That man Cain again, ably assisted by Sergeant Daly, fired their 75mm gun over open sights and registered a direct hit on its tracks. The crew bailed out and was met with small-arms fire. Unfortunately their victim was immediately replaced by another, but another 75mm shell destroyed it when the first tank was hit and exploded in flames, putting the second tank out of action.[12] It transpires that one or other of the incapacitated tanks was one of the new King Tigers, the largest and best armoured in the German army. Daly was awarded the Distinguished Conduct Medal. In a bid to deter an attack on B Troop by a tank and an SP gun, Lieutenant Halliday climbed to the top of a nearby building to direct fire onto the German armour. Sadly, the tank turned its guns on him with deadly effect.[13]

By now the RAP in the ter Horst house was filled to overflowing. Alf Rouiller of Battery HQ could hear 'the noise of men screaming, babbling, begging for water and crying out the names of family…he was horrified to see the large number of bodies lying in the garden, they were literally piled one on top of the other.'

Nebelwerfers were whooshing away around the gasworks, while generally food was running low at the British gun positions. Bombardier Jack Briggs of 3 Battery E Troop recalls how 'a very brave Dutch woman [presumably Kate ter Horst] came on to the gun position with a cauldron of mashed potato. It was heaven on earth as far as food was concerned.'

The cellar of a house opposite the Old Church became the RHQ since the original, the Concert Hall, had no cellar, and a 'chilly, sullen night' was had by all.

Chapter Sixteen

Day 6: Friday, 22 September

Der Hexenkessel – The Witch's Cauldron, inferno

Kate ter Horst began her diary for the day with a ringing endorsement of the professionalism and maturity of the wounded British soldiers who had filled her house (p.45):

> I am struck more and more how all these young men – most of them no more than 20 or 25 – not just in their voices and gestures but also in their whole bearing, show a self-control, sense of responsibility and discipline which makes one think of fathers of 40 or over rather than young lads straight from the school benches. Most of them are stalwart fellows, particularly the Scots.

The sixth day of the battle saw the advance of XXX Corps brought to a halt in the village of Elst, while the 129th Infantry Brigade crossed the Waal but could proceed no further towards Elst. Meanwhile the German forces just kept getting stronger, and not just because of the redeployment of troops and armour from the bridge. After crossing the Arnhem Bridge *Kampfgruppe* Knaust was reinforced with a number of *Sturmgeschütze* (assault guns), along with more anti-aircraft guns to deal with resupplies. Eight Panther tanks and Tiger 1s were from *Schwere Panzer-Kompanie Hummel*, all of which positioned themselves around Elst, but five of the Tigers were lost, either in the muddy ditches at the side of the road or through the opposition from the British 43rd (Wessex) Division. King Tiger tanks of the 506th Heavy Tank Battalion were trained in, fifteen of which went to the 9th SS Panzer Division which was further reinforced by a *Panzergrenadier* battalion. Another thirty were sent to the 10th SS Panzer Division further south to deal with the advance of XXX Division from Nijmegen. A rested elite unit of what was the NCOs' school of the Herman Göring Division was hurried in and took no time in taking high ground overlooking the river at Westerbouwing from B Company, Border Regiment. This was a bit of a Pyrrhic victory for the Germans who lost half their men, but it was compensated for by the capture of the ferry crossing, although the ferry boat had been sunk.[1]

Meanwhile, at Oosterbeek all was going as well as it could be, with a CRA message at 1845 hours the evening before to the 64th Medium Regiment saying 'Support Excellent. Having Magnificent Results'. On this day alone they assailed thirty-one targets as well as supporting the 43rd (Wessex) Division holed up in Elst.

A sense of reality regarding the overall situation was now itself becoming a reality. Urquhart had briefed Lieutenant Charles Mackenzie (GSO1) and Eddie Myers CRE to stress to Browning and Horrocks that unless the 1st Airborne was effectively relieved that day 'it would be too late, but within the Headquarters intransigence seemed to rule.'[2]

In true Gothic style, the Germans had nicknamed the perimeter *Der Hexenkessel* (the witch's cauldron), a reflection of its ferocity and the fear it evoked. The onslaught of mortar rounds continued unabated from dawn to dusk, the former becoming known as the 'early morning hate' or, in the words of the morale-booster Canadian BBC reporter Stanley Maxted, *Jerries Hymn of Hate*. Shell craters were so numerous and contiguous that they became a major hazard, especially in the dark. Doors and supply containers were used as trench roofs for the slit trenches.[3] Ammunition, food and water were desperately short. Gunner Thomas Sime of 1 Battery B Troop was killed by a mortar bomb and hastily buried; so hastily that his grave was lost and to this day he languishes in an unknown grave. Another casualty was 1 Battery Commander Major A.F. Norman-Walker from an enemy shell while he was at Air Landing Brigade HQ. He was replaced by Captain B.A.B. Taylor of 2 Battery.

It was on the Friday that the church tower in the Old Church at Oosterbeek became a place of even greater strategic importance. A diary describes it as 'beginning to look like a pin cushion'. Lieutenant Widdicombe and Gunner Neale of 3 Battery set up an OP in the tower, and Lance Bombardier Bogan and Lieutenant Pepys Moore went up the spire to observe targets for the Second Army guns. Bogan tells how the Germans positioned a tank close by and blew him and his signaller out of the tower but both survived.[4]

Gun wheels were now punctured, making the guns extremely difficult to manoeuvre, while an ammunition trailer near the church took a hit and sent 'bullets etc flying about in all directions'. Supply parachutes continued to drift towards enemy positions. Woollacott (p.167) lists the daily toll suffered by the pilots and crew of the resupply planes:

19th: 3 aircraft shot down; 97 damaged
20th: 9 aircraft shot down; 62 damaged
21st: 7 aircraft shot down; ?? damaged
23rd: 6 aircraft shot down; 63 damaged

F Troop engaged German infantry digging in at the destroyed railway bridge. A mortar shell struck Gunner Bingham and he died later; a Stirling crashed on the riverbank and was burned out.

Chapter Seventeen

Day 7: Saturday, 23 September

Saturday the 23rd carried on as the 22nd had finished with shelling, mortaring and the infernal cacophony continuing throughout the day. According to Geoffrey Powell in his *The Devil's Birthday*:

> 'Saturday was to prove to be the hardest day to bear. The weight of metal poured into the area by the German mortars and guns seemed to be heavier than ever, and there were few anti-tank weapons of any type left to halt the German armour.' He paints a desolate and dystopian picture of 'everywhere men now crouched in their slit trenches, their ears straining above the noise of the shelling for the German tanks clanking towards them unrelentingly, the sound echoing ever nearer through the woods and the narrow suburban streets.'

In the wreckage of her house, the Old Vicarage, Kate ter Horst observes 'how the soldiers appear dazed and rigid in their horror at this fight. They were in Dunkirk, El Alamein and Italy. They are veterans, these boys, and in pride they say "We'll never give in, we cannot surrender. That does not exist for the First British Airborne Division."'[1] She too cannot fail to remark on the terrific noise: 'The padre brings in a shell-shocked officer called "Lion" [just blown off a school roof in Weverstraat], who needs a respite from the hellish noise. At every new explosion he grips his head, the noise being almost unbearable for him…from time to time he can't get his mental bearings.' A little later she records how 'the devilish noise swells into a living orgy. The atmosphere is one of ever-impending doom' (p.58).

Fearful noise and noise-induced fear merged as the dreaded sounds of approaching tanks filled the air around the Old Vicarage and a terrified Kate ter Horst describes it:

A new sound grinds through the night; heavy chains seem to rattle over the road. We clearly hear it drawing nearer. Then it stops and a strange groaning sound follows, as if a giant dragon were blowing out its breath. This is followed by heavy drum fire, and then silence. Upstairs the men pant in deadly fear. They know the noise…this approaching disaster will be the end – irrevocably…cries of horror and wild agony break from their dry throats. Tanks! Tanks! Listen! They are shooting into every house along the road.

Enemy tanks continued to emerge, not least in the area occupied by 2 Battery, but most were repulsed. One of the heroes of these tank battles was Major Croot of the Glider Pilot Regiment, as recorded by both 1 Battery and 2 Battery War Diaries. F Troop took on a squadron of enemy tanks and infantry at a range of 1,200 yards and won, although Sergeant Thain was later wounded by mortar fire and Gunner George Lakin was killed. Bombardier Ron Green watched as an airburst hit Sergeant Newman's F3 gun pit: 'We were unable to get to them in daylight as snipers had us covered…as darkness fell we made our way to the gun and discovered the entire detachment had been hit…the injured were taken to the RAP' with Green apologizing for 'standing on a man near the door. I later discovered he was dead.'[2]

Chapter Eighteen

Day 8: Sunday, 24 September

The unflappable and courageous Hendrika van der Vlist wrote in her diary from the Schoonoord Hotel:

> Sunday, September 24. This is the day of the Lord. War rages outside. The building is shaking. That is why the doctors cannot operate or fix casts. We cannot wash the wounded because nobody can venture out to find water under these conditions. The army chaplain scribbles in his notebook. I ask him what time the service will be held.

Padre G.A. Pare finished his notes. He and Hendrika then made the rounds of all the rooms in the hotel. The shelling seemed 'particularly noisy', he recalls, 'and I could hardly hear my own voice above the battle outside.' Yet, 'Looking into the faces of men stretched out all over the floor,' Pare 'felt inspired to fight the noise outside with God's peace inside.' Quoting from St Matthew, Pare said 'Take no thought for the morrow. What ye shall eat or what ye shall drink, or wherewithal ye shall be clothed.' Then he, like the men in the artillery positions, began to sing. As he began *Abide With Me*, men just listened. Then they began to hum and sing softly themselves. Against the thunderous barrage outside the Schoonoord, hundreds of wounded and dying men took up the words: 'When other helpers fail and comforts flee; Help of the helpless, O abide with me.'[1]

It will not have gone unnoticed that the accounts of the last few days are somewhat slimmer than those of the early days of the Battle of Arnhem. Truesdale (p.128):

> As with most books dealing with the British in the Arnhem-Oosterbeek battle the first week is usually well described, while those final days are somewhat vague. The role of the Light Regiment is no different; tiredness and time dull the memory, but some excellent diaries and accounts remain as sources.

Truesdale goes on to point out how 'by now most men had learnt to live with the near constant noise of shelling, mortaring and small-arms fire. This noise was such that attempts to gather cohesive thoughts was difficult, never mind any attempts at talking.' We have read how Gunner Chrystal described it: 'It must have been the terrible noise that was going on that drove it from my mind, it was terrific… and always, the terrific noise.'

Bob Christie recalls

> the incessant noise of battle. I haven't words to describe the noise. It got worse and worse. It was difficult to think clearly, never mind carry out calculations in the troop command post. There were constants: mortaring, small-arms fire, shelling, the thump of our guns firing. Other components emerged from time to time: the clatter of tank tracks on cobbles, the roar of diesel engines, the explosions of burning vehicles and ammunition, sobs and shrieks, it went on and on.[2]

Christie adds that his recollections of exactly what happened and when became scrambled after about 1000 hours on Wednesday, 20 September when C Troop was hit by a sudden and prolonged barrage of rockets, mortars and shells: 'The pace and pressure of events rose to a crescendo which was sustained almost without pause throughout the remaining days…even only weeks after the battle it was impossible to sort out memories into any proper sequence.'

Percy Parkes recalls how during the cease-fire negotiated with the Germans to evacuate casualties 'The firing suddenly diminished and then stopped altogether. The overwhelming noise had become normal and I found this so unreal that for a moment or two I thought I was dead! When it all started again I felt relieved – almost!'[3]

No. 2 Battery Command Post was out of food, having consumed their allotted two twenty-four-hour rations packs each and one box of Compo rations by 22 September and foraging produced next to nothing other than some 'preserving jars of boiled unsweetened crab-apple pulp. Ghastly and with violent effect.' The Dutch were just as hungry. Sleep, such as it was, was fitful and fatigue began to take over, with the smallest task requiring the largest effort.[4] The psychological impact of the noise, tiredness, death and destruction was incalculable. The only respite was during supply drops when German guns were focused on the British aircraft and there was an opportunity for those not frantically waving yellow identification panels to bring up ammunition, maintain defences, re-lay telephone lines damaged by shrapnel and machine-gun fire and tidy up gun pits.[5]

Gunner Cook was manning a 6-pounder gun when he was 'startled by a large cluster of tiny lights dropping towards him'. They turned out to be fragments of burning paper coming from an ammunition dump that had been set ablaze by a direct hit from a mortar. Sergeant Davis was awarded the Dutch Bronze Cross for organizing a party to fight the fire amid exploding ammunition. F Troop 3 Battery's guns were reduced to two when one took a direct hit.

Shrapnel damage to telephone wires was a serious and recurring problem: the one between Regimental HQ and 3 Battery was particularly susceptible to sniper fire and enemy armoured vehicles prowling within 100 yards of 3 Battery's position. Sergeant Derrick Newton, 3 Battery Signal Sergeant 'made persistent forays out to repair the line', thus permitting communications essential for artillery support as required. Newton was awarded the Military Medal.[6]

It was not unusual for wounded soldiers to be wounded over again as they lay in the RAPs, dressing stations or in the ter Horst house. Gunner Ron Gibbs of 2 Battery tells how Sergeant Fletcher repositioned his gun to deal with a lurking tank; he sat on the gun trail waiting for a chance to shoot but was wounded by a sniper. He was loaded onto a jeep by Captain 'Buck' Taylor and they set off for the RAP under small-arms fire. Fletcher was hit at least twice during the journey and died of his wounds. Captain Taylor himself, an inveterate morale-booster 'who stomped around the battlefield with a black ebony walking stick, with a silver knob on it, was himself wounded. He declined assistance…but was killed when he tried to get back unaided.' Such was D Troop's Lance Bombardier Jim Jones' account. Harry Lingard, signaller and dispatch rider, adds some detail:

> Out with Captain Taylor in the jeep. We came under heavy mortar fire and crashed into a tree stump completely wrecking the vehicle. We retreated to nearby woods and dug in with other troops, and it was here that Captain Taylor received fatal shrapnel injuries to the right side of his chest and hand. I was hit in the higher part of my upper leg. It happened when Captain Taylor got out of the trench

looking at his map. A medical orderly put a field dressing to stop the bleeding, but it was useless. I was taken to the nearby church.[7]

After Harry was taken to a makeshift hospital in the church, he was captured and taken to Stalag XI-B in Fallingbostel in Lower Saxony, north-western Germany. He escaped.

In the ter Horst house the casualties continued to pile up. This episode, best related in Ryan's *A Bridge Too Far* (p.493), captures the bravery and the defiant stubbornness of the patients and staff there:

> Corporal Daniel Morgans, hit in the head and right knee as he was holding a position near the Oosterbeek church, was carried to the ter Horst house just as a German tank came up the road. As an orderly was explaining to Morgans that 'they were practically out of dressings and had no anaesthetics or food and only a little water', the tank sent a shell crashing against the house. In an upstairs room, Private Walther Boldock, with bullet wounds in the side and back, stared in horror as the tank 'ground and wheeled. I could hear the gibberish chatter of machine guns and then a shell tore through the wall above my back. Plaster and debris began falling everywhere and many of the wounded were killed.' Downstairs Bombardier E.C. Bolden, a medical orderly, was in a white-hot rage. Grabbing a Red Cross flag, he rushed out of the house and straight for the tank. Corporal Morgans heard him clearly. 'What the hell are you doing?' Bolden screamed at the German tank commander. 'This house is clearly marked with a Red Cross flag. Get the hell away from here!' As the anxious wounded listened, they heard the sound of the tank backing off. Bolden returned to the house, 'almost as angry', Morgans remembers, 'as when he left. We asked him what happened.' Bolden replied tersely: 'The German apologised but he also got the hell out.'

Terrifying and terrific noise and shell shock were ever-present in the Hotel Schoonoord hospital. Ryan relates this episode, redolent with pathos and tragedy:

> In the Schoonoord the critical cases and the walking wounded were gone, but shell-shocked men still lingered in the big hotel. As

Chaplain Pare walked through a half-deserted room, he heard a thin shaking voice somewhere in the echoing building singing *Just a Song at Twilight*. Climbing to an upstairs room, Pare knelt beside a badly shocked young trooper. 'Padre,' the boy said, 'will you tuck me in? I get so frightened with all the noise.' Pare had no blanket, but he pretended to cover the trooper. 'That feels fine, Padre. I feel very well now. Will you do me one more favour?' Pare nodded. 'Say the Lord's Prayer with me.' Pare did. He soothed back the young man's hair. 'Now close your eyes,' Pare told him. 'Sleep well. God bless you.' The trooper smiled. 'Good night, Padre. God bless you.' Two hours later a medic came for Pare. 'You know that lad you said the prayers with?' Pare asked, 'What's wrong?' The medic shook his head. 'He died just now. He said to tell you he couldn't stand the noise outside.'[8]

When 2 Battery HQ Gunner Baisden was delivering a message to 1 Battery he was machine-gunned by a tank. The Command Post there was a trench covered with corrugated tin, parachutes and earth. The CP received a direct hit from mortars; Lance Sergeant Alf Rouiller and a comrade ran over to the rescue of those inside, but the tin roof was too hot to move. Voices were heard inside and Rouiller shouted 'Hold on, we're coming, only a few minutes.' When the metal was finally pulled away, Lieutenant Leitch, the CPO, was dead. A muffled voice made the lance sergeant begin digging again. Suddenly a pair of eyes emerged through the soil…as they dragged him free it was noticed that the man still held a piece of paper in his hand. He turned to Rouiller and said 'I'm going to get the bastards who did this.' Gunner Mills and Lance Bombardier Noons, both D Troop 2 Battery, buried Lieutenant Leitch and Gunners Baisden and Oliver Adams. On his way back to the gun position Mills saw three South Staffords sitting in a trench: all three were dead.[9]

A mortar bomb exploded in a slit trench near the door of the church and it killed Lance Bombardier Harry Pearson. Lance Bombardier Rose, next to him, was unharmed as Pearson had taken the full force of the blast. All the while the 2 Battery position was under threat of an attack that might well cut the perimeter in two. Morale, nevertheless, was still high with no sign of despondency. Things got better still when Lance Bombardier Jim Jones, a flautist, followed Lieutenant Woods around the gun positions playing *British Grenadiers* and *Scotland the Brave* with the soldiers adding percussion accompaniment on their helmets.[10]

Gunner Ron Gibbs of D Troop was 'scared stiff and pretty helpless with no means of defence against the tanks which were infiltrating the position' when he and two others dived into a slit trench only to be pinned down.

The day saw the 64th Medium Regiment continuing to fire on orders from Oosterbeek, bolstered by another battery from the 7th Medium Regiment. There was even morale-boosting 'highly successful' air support when rocket-firing Typhoons did damage in the north-west sector of the perimeter.

However, Wilkinson (p.137) tells us how a large number of German infantry were penetrating the woods just to the north of 2 Battery, severing their communications. These were followed by tanks, against which 'no additional tank defence weapons were available'; all the men could do was stay entrenched and use their guns over open sights. The tanks, however, demolished the Battery Command Post; C Troop engaged them but was inevitably overrun. Lieutenant Woods was killed along with the majority of the battery either killed, wounded or captured. Twenty survivors withdrew and continued to engage the enemy with small-arms fire under the command of BSM Goodman. Lieutenant Donaldson and Lance Bombardier Dickson were particularly courageous: under fire they crossed open ground to reach a Polish 6-pounder, most of whose crew had been killed and, with two Polish survivors, fired hits on a Tiger II tank until it responded with its machine gun. Still under fire they then moved to one of C Troop's guns, unsuccessfully loosing off its four remaining shots at the tank. Donaldson gathered three rounds of armour-piercing ammunition from another abandoned gun, but could only fire two before the gun jammed. Undeterred, Dickson went back to the wagon lines and brought back a PIAT with which Donaldson engaged the tank, wrecking its tracks. This was the only Tiger II the Germans lost in the Oosterbeek fighting. Donaldson was awarded the DSO, while Dickson received the MM.[11]

The guns of 1 Battery were also reduced to an anti-tank role. While Sergeant Daly at B Troop position managed to destroy one tank, the men of A Troop were all captured when tanks emerged from Weverstraat and overran the position.

Chapter Nineteen

Day 9: Monday, 25 September

A misty dawn greeted the beleaguered gunners in Oosterbeek which, when it had cleared, revealed a hive of German activity. Lieutenant Widdicombe describes how the day got off to a good start:

> We waited until we saw sections of infantry coming down an approach outside our line of view, deploying westward into the woods. Then we brought down the mediums and opened up with a Bren along the road over which the enemy had crossed. The shells sorted them out and they had to come back across the road covered by the machine gun. For half an hour afterwards we had good practice.[1]

However, the good luck soon ran out when two self-propelled guns hove into sight and proceeded to blast holes into the houses as they approached. The tower of the church took a direct hit, causing the tower to fall in. RHQ later, at about 0730 hours, sent a message ordering the church to be used as an aid post and that the tower was no longer to be used as an OP. The tower had been under bombardment for a week or so and was a kind of talisman for the battery. Lance Bombardier Percy Parkes was one of the many who felt that as long as the tower stood then 'we could hold out…it was like we were destined to follow it…there was almost continuous mortaring and shelling and the noise of it overwhelmed me. It got so the noise was normal and the silence, which should have been normal, was unreal.'

The direst of situations by now was that the enemy was so close that there was no need for OPs as they were in plain sight. Lieutenant Peter Wilkinson, GPO 3 Battery, wrote: 'The guns of E and F Troops were firing directly at tanks and infantry advancing along the roads and through houses towards our positions…the doggedness and courage of the gunners…ensured that the remainder of the Division to the north were not cut off from the river.'[2]

One of the gun commanders, Sergeant McCleod, wrote to his A Troop GPO, Lieutenant Barron, after the war:

> On the last day, Monday for us…Jerry broke through with tanks and when I looked out of my trench there was a tank about 30 yards away which had blown my gun to pieces, also Bob Gibson's and Donald Sinclair's. We were shocked as no order had been given for 'tank alert' or 'take post' and because of the terrible din of firing and mortaring we did not distinguish the tank noises. In no time…the whole troop was overrun. It was a sad day for us.

Sergeant McCleod's totally unwarranted shame and humiliation at the surrender is palpable in his final words: 'It was a sad day for us Tom for I'm sure that you are aware that A Troop conducted itself in an excellent manner until then. I'd love to have had at least one go at the tanks that eventually knocked out my gun.'[3]

The Germans had now overrun A and D Troops and most of C Troop, so the unfortunate reality was that now only 3 Battery south of the Benedendorpsweg stood between the enemy and the river.

When Lieutenant Woods crawled over from the school cellar to Lance Bombardier Jim Jones (D Troop, 2 Battery) and two signallers – Bert Duxbury and Les Newham in the Command Post dugout – to tell them to stay where they were as there was nowhere else to go anyway, he had no idea that this would be the last thing he ever did. Machine-gun fire cut him down as he made his way back. All three were later captured. Lance Bombardier Jones recalls how 'some of the troops who captured us could speak English and were anxious to see the end of the war.' The bitter irony was that Operation MARKET GARDEN was designed to hasten the end of that same war.

Chapter Twenty

Operation BERLIN

'It [the River Rhine] was very wide, in full flood and the current looked to be about 9 knots. It wasn't a very promising sight.'
Lance Bombardier Percy Parkes

Monday, 25 September was notable for one other event: it was the day when Operation MARKET GARDEN elided into Operation BERLIN. Operation BERLIN was the evacuation of the surviving troops of the 1st Airborne Division. *By Air to Battle* (p.134) elegantly sums up their achievement and the ultimate achievement of those killed, left behind wounded, and taken prisoner:

> With no weapon larger than a seventy-five mm. gun, and for the most part only with Brens, gammon bombs and PIATs, which can be carried and handled by one man unaided, they attacked Tiger tanks weighing fifty-six tons, and self-propelled guns with a range of seven miles. Of these they destroyed or put out of action some sixty. The number of the enemy they killed or wounded is not exactly known, but it is not less than 7,000. With no reinforcements save the wounded, who, if their legs would still bear them, staggered back to the firing line, they fought on. With an enemy growing ever stronger, pressing against them on all sides but one – and that a wide, swiftly flowing river – they fought on. Without sleep, presently without food or water, at the end almost without ammunition, they fought on. When no hope of victory remained, when all prospect of survival had vanished, when death alone could give them ease, they fought on. In attack most daring, in defence most cunning, in endurance most steadfast, they performed a feat of arms which will be remembered and recounted as long as the virtues of courage and resolution have power to move the hearts of men.

Obviously, everything that could be done was done to conceal the evacuation from the Germans. Boots were muffled, usually with torn-up blankets, white tape showed the way after dark and each man in the column kept in touch with the man in front by grasping the tail of his smock. German prisoners remained just that until the very last minute courtesy of the Military Police.[1] Any equipment that was not being taken was rendered unserviceable. Because they were where they were, the surviving men of the 1st Air Landing Light Regiment were among the last to leave. To cover the retreat a sustained bombardment was provided by the 43rd (Wessex) Division and XXX Corps artillery while British and Canadian engineers crossed the Nederrijn to start ferrying the survivors of the 1st Airborne back across the river. About twenty gunners in 2 Battery held the Germans at bay until ordered back to the wagon lines; very bad timing since this coincided with XXX Corps' barrage and 2 Battery was caught in the middle of it.[2] E Troop, 3 Battery War Diary is unusually descriptive and graphic at this point:

> News of evacuation received. Mortars, tanks, our own guns opening up from across the river and the ever-present stench of the dead combined to make the last few hours an age of horror and uncertainty. We consumed the remaining rations. After dark the breech blocks were removed from the guns.

Percy Parkes found out about the evacuation plan when he was actually part of it and came across 'a long line of people...by this time it was almost dawn. There were still three or four hundred people on the bank... but all the boats had been sunk.'[3]

> I was tired and I was wounded and I didn't think I could make it. I could see men jumping in fully dressed and being swept downstream. Others made it across only to be shot scrambling out of the water. Finally we watched one chap paddle across on a plank, still carrying his pack. I thought he was pretty heroic and I decided if he could do it, I could.

Parkes stripped down to his underwear, disposed of all his possessions including his much-prized gold Hamilton pocket watch, and then he and Evans attempted to swim the river, angling their strokes against the current:

> The water was surprisingly warm, but as soon as I got in my underpants slipped down and I kicked them off. I swam as hard as I could and I eventually got across and hid on the bank under some bushes until I got my breath back. Then I made a dash for the winter dyke over open ground where I had seen the others shot. I was going great until I fell into a 15 foot ditch full of nettles, but the stings didn't register until later.[4]

Elsewhere he describes the quandary in which many of the evacuees must have found themselves:

> The following morning we found that the majority of the Division had been evacuated across the river during the night, and as fast as we could we made for it ourselves. Unfortunately the river here was up to a quarter of a mile wide, with a dangerous current of eight knots, and there was a quarter-mile of open country to cross. When we got to the banks it was unfortunately a case of those of us who could not swim staying behind whilst the rest stripped and jumped in. It took me a long time to make up my mind to risk swimming in the condition I was in, but the Germans made up my mind for me and in I got.[5]

Sergeant Mashiter of Z Troop received a severe chest wound that morning but, despite this, he amazingly swam the Rhine before collapsing on the far bank, finally rejoining the regiment on recovery. Sergeant Hardie of 3 Battery E Troop tells us how to scupper a gun: 'We prepared to move out that night, shoved a shell up the breech, and one down the "spout", removed our dial sights and the breech block from the gun and dropped them in the deep part of a stream.'[6]

Hardie and his comrades made it to the river where they joined the orderly single-file queue waiting for boats or opting to swim. Even then the largely silent soldiers shuffling forward to the boats could not escape 'the perpetual din of the artillery barrage' assaulting their senses. Once on the south bank they were taken by truck to Nijmegen where rows of beds and a meal awaited them. Having been so long without a substantial meal, those men who wolfed it down were sick. For example, Glider Pilot Staff Sergeant Trevor Francis had survived the last nine days on one forty-eight-hour ration pack, the water in his water bottle and some unripe pears scrumped from an orchard. From Nijmegen they were all transported in RASC trucks to outside Louvain in Belgium, then Brussels and finally on 30 September by plane to an airfield in Lincolnshire. There a reception meal awaited them in a hangar.

Dawn broke and the mist cleared, but 'several hundred men were still waiting to cross and were now exposed to the full force of the enemy fire. In an effort to relieve the situation, the field artillery on the south bank fired smokescreens but casualties became heavier.'[7]

TSM Tom Kent, F Troop tells the story of his arduous journey to Nijmegen, including taking the hand of one of the bombardiers whose 'nerves were shattered by his experience' and how

> the air raid siren sounded in the town and this really did frighten me. I was really terrified by this for the first and only time since leaving England. I had gotten out of a hell hole and this really threatened my liberty. I was exceptionally low, both mentally and physically. Whilst it lasted for some thirty minutes or so it really was agony and a great relief when the all-clear sounded…it was well into the following day when I awoke from a dreadful nightmare that left me feeling a physical wreck, then perhaps that really was the state I was in.[8]

Kent soon discovered that only one-third of his troop had succeeded in crossing the river. Jack Briggs tells us how Colonel Loder-Symonds, the CRA no less, was very nearly shot when Charlie Anderson opened up on him with his Sten gun and missed as one of 'three shadowy figures' emerged from the trees.[9]

Some of the Light Regiment gunners must have felt let down when they were taken prisoner: Gunner George Edwin Durant, for example, who was part of a motley party of eighteen men who were ordered to 'hold three slit trenches at all costs and stay there alive or dead until further orders'. The reason was that 'there had been a breakthrough and relief forces were coming over the Rhine.' There was a relentless barrage that eventually faded out, but dawn broke only to find the men totally surrounded by German troops.[10]

So, in the end, the 1st Air Landing Light Regiment sent 374 men over to Arnhem of whom 36 were killed in action and 136 escaped across the Rhine while 202 were listed as missing, most of whom became prisoners of war. Tom Barron provides some detail: 'Only ten ORs and myself got back in A Troop and out of ten officers in 1 Battery only Johnny Walker and I returned and we both came out with the infantry. 2 Battery survivors totalled only three officers and twenty-five ORs.'

The wider picture reveals that

> of the 10,000 or so officers and men who had flown in or landed on the north bank of the Lower Rhine…approximately 2,300 were ferried or swam across the river that night…a remarkable achievement and a tribute to last-minute improvisation and the covering fire provided by the artillery.[11]

The Germans had occupied the pocket by 1400 hours the next day and taken prisoner those troops who could not be moved.

The battle may well have been over, but soldiers from the regiment continued to die: on 9 October Captain Peter Chard died of wounds in Apeldoorn hospital, on 31 October Sergeant Stanley Hardy died in Stalag XI-B, and 8 December saw Lance Bombardier Tatton also die in hospital at Apeldoorn.

Of the wider operation, http://www.historyofwar.org/articles/battles_arnhem.html provides the detail:

- First Allied Airborne Army had carried out 4,852 troop-carrying aircraft sorties, of which 1,293 had delivered paratroopers, 2,277 had landed gliders and 1,282 resupply.
- 164 aircraft and 132 gliders had been lost with USAAF IX Troop Carrier Command suffering 454 casualties, RAF 38 and 46 Group another 294 casualties.
- 39,620 troops had joined the battle by air: 21,074 by parachute and 18,546 by glider along with 4,595 tons of stores. Only 7.4 per cent of stores intended for the 1st Airborne had reached it.

- Another 6,172 aircraft sorties were flown in support of MARKET GARDEN for the loss of 125 aircraft against 160 enemy aircraft destroyed.
- 10,300 troops of the 1st Airborne Division and the Polish 1st Independent Parachute Brigade had landed at Arnhem, some 2,587 escaping (1,741 from the 1st Airborne, 422 from the Glider Pilot Regiment, 160 Poles and 75 from the Dorset Regiment) in Operation BERLIN and some 240 later with the help of the Dutch resistance. The Germans claimed to have taken 6,450 men prisoner.
- The Poles took 378 casualties, with the 101st Airborne suffering 2,110 and the 82nd Airborne suffering 1,432. The British ground forces suffered some 5,354 casualties, while the German casualties, like their unit strengths, are almost impossible to calculate accurately, but are likely to range somewhere between 4,000 and 8,000. Some 3,300 casualties have been admitted – conservatively – by Model.
- Five Victoria Crosses were awarded, and two posthumous Medals of Honor.

Chapter Twenty-One

The Fallout from the Failure

Had it succeeded

the new salient would have cut off the German forces left in the western Netherlands, but with the Allies now concentrating on an advance to the Rhine, with the ultimate objective of crossing it in the spring, the main attacks were by the First Canadian Army to clear the Scheldt estuary and open Antwerp to cargo ships. It cost 21st Army Group over 30,000 casualties but was completed by 28 November. The additional frontage meant that Montgomery needed to retain the 82nd and 101st Airborne Divisions in the line until the 13th and 27th November respectively and both divisions suffered high casualties as a result. In response to the Dutch strike timed to coincide with Market Garden, the Germans stopped all civilian transport in the country and over 18,000 Dutch civilians died during the winter.[1]

As noted, Montgomery, from somewhere inside a world of his very own, estimated that the operation was 90 per cent successful, but surely the failure to take the final objective – that of Arnhem Bridge – had rendered the whole operation pointless? It is worth repeating those quotations from two people perhaps better equipped to assess the relative success or failure of the operation, free from the hyperbole and spin of ego and one-upmanship: 'My country can never again afford the luxury of another Montgomery success' (Bernhard, Prince of the Netherlands), and 'In return for so much courage and sacrifice, the Allies had won a 50-mile salient – leading nowhere' (Dr John C. Warren).

Chapter Twenty-Two

Prisoner of War: Stalag XII-A Limburg, Stalag IV-B Mühlberg and Stalag IV-A Hohenstein and Zwickau

Limburg (Stalag XII-A)

Gunner Eric Chrystal, along with many of his comrades-in-arms, was ignominiously taken prisoner of war and carted off to a transit camp at Limburg (XII-A). His PoW number was 075100.[1] In correspondence with the Arnhem Veterans' Club he records with some irony how he 'enjoyed' the hospitality at Limburg. Frank Newhouse of the AVC added 'what a rotten place that was – remember the tents?'[2] According to Geoffrey Megargee in his *United States Holocaust Memorial Museum Encyclopedia of Camps and Ghettoes* (2022):

> Stalag XIIA had numerous special tasks and special functions…from October 1944 on, British and US PoWs who were part of the enemy paratroops, anti-aircraft artillery troops, and air-landing troops from the west were placed in the central camp in Limburg before being sent on to Dulag West in Wetzlar, another transit camp, mainly for aircrew.[3]

Pegasus Archive gives us some detail regarding Stalag XII-A, its function and its raison d'être,[4] ascribing its 'rottenness' with next to nothing in the way of facilities largely to the fact that 'Stalag XII-A's primary function was to act as a transit camp which processed newly captured Prisoners of War before distributing them amongst the other, better organized Stalags in Germany. Typically a new prisoner would arrive, be interrogated, documented, and moved on within a few weeks.' Its transitory nature also meant that new arrivals did not receive 'the luxuries of the frequently life-saving Red Cross Parcel'.

Four capacious marquees formed the temporary accommodation for the British and Americans, totally devoid of furniture and with so little space that everyone had to sleep back to back on the floor, which in some cases was cobbled stone with, if they were extremely lucky, a loose scattering of straw for bedding.

There were more or less starvation rations, no entertainment and no lighting, so as soon as it got dark men slept until dawn because there was no point in staying awake. Disease, especially diarrhoea, was ever present with almost no medical facilities, and the stone toilets serving several thousand men gave off an ineffably foul stench.

On arrival the basic ground rules of stalag law were spelled out, one of which was particularly memorable: the warning that prisoners would be shot if they placed as much as a finger upon the barbed-wire fence surrounding the camp. One high point was that for many newly-captured troops Stalag XII-A gave them their first chance to write a postcard home to their family, and although it would take weeks to arrive it was often the case that this would be the first news that their loved ones would receive telling them that their PoW who had been posted as missing in action was alive. One of the more memorable sights at Stalag XII-A was that of more than 15,000 discarded American helmets. After the liberation, these were fashioned into a huge pyramid outside the gates; an iconic image frequently captured on film ever since.[5]

When it was time to leave Stalag XII-A behind for a more permanent camp, most were sent by rail from Limburg station on a mystery journey that could last anything from a couple of days to a week, extended by the constant threat of strikes by British and American fighters: 'There were several instances of planes strafing a train which, against the rules of the Geneva Convention, the Germans failed to paint markings on it to indicate that it carried PoWs, and as a result some men were killed or wounded.'

The cattle trucks that the prisoners travelled in were even worse than the conditions at Limburg. Typically fifty or so men were sardined into each wagon, with standing room only for most. There was precious little food or water, although occasionally men were issued with a large sandwich before departure which they had to make last for a week; others were given a foul cheese en route. Nevertheless, some German guards were open to trading their own rations for what remained of the prisoners' kit. One toilet per wagon, usually in the form of a deep tin or milk churn, was the norm. Diarrhoea was a constant companion.

As with many thousands of others, Gunner Eric Chrystal obviously took a dim view of the hospitality he received courtesy of the Limburg staff. As with many others, he then endured the inhuman, fetid conditions of his journey to his 'permanent' camp: destination Stalag IV-B Mühlberg, 28 September 1944.

It was not uncommon for PoWs to be shunted from one camp to another – often on foot – according to the vagaries of war: overcrowding, bombing, movements of the front line or labour force requirements were the usual reasons.

Stalag IV-B, Mühlberg

Mühlberg was one of Nazi Germany's biggest PoW camps, host to around 30,000 prisoners from 40 countries between 1939 and 1945 and covering 74 acres. When the Soviets liberated the camp in April 1945, there were about 30,000 PoWs crammed into the facilities, 7,250 of whom were British. About 3,000 prisoners died, mainly from tuberculosis and typhus, and were buried in the cemetery in neighbouring Neuburxdorf, Bad Liebenwerda. Today a memorial and a museum commemorate them.

The Soviet 'liberators' detained the British and American prisoners in the camp for over a month. This was probably the only PoW camp in the world housing both men and women, and in which eleven babies were born and assigned PoW registration numbers. In August 1945 the Soviet secret police NKVD opened one of its special camps under the name 'Speziallager Nr. 1 Mühlberg' using the shacks of Stalag IV-B. More than 22,800 persons were imprisoned and more than 6,700 of them died before the camp was closed in 1948. Kurt Vonnegut was a PoW here in 1945. He was moved from Mühlberg on 14 November to Stalag IV-A on a hard labour detail. This is listed as Hohenstein (also listed as Stalag I-B), but it is actually Flossenbürg, of which Zwickau was a sub-camp.

Zwickau Sub-Camp, 15 November 1944–15 April 1945

Zwickau was a sub-camp of the notorious Flossenbürg concentration camp. In the second half of 1944, forty-five new camps were created to ramp up production of Messerschmitt Bf 109 fighter planes and other armaments for Germany's war effort; this compared to the three camps established in the previous six months. In total around 100 sub-camps were established, concentrated mainly around armaments industries in southern Germany and western Czechoslovakia. Flossenbürg's sub-camp system was one of the three most important to the Nazi Germany economy, along with Dachau and Mauthausen. By April 1945, 80 per cent of the prisoners were at the sub-camps. More than 1,000 men arrived in Zwickau on several inaugural transports at the end of August 1944. Along with 437 Poles (of whom 30 were Jewish) and 306 Russians, there were 85 Italians, more than 70 French, 65 Hungarians (among them 59 Jews), 55 Czechs and 30 Germans, along with prisoners from 9 other countries. On 29 March 1945, the SS hanged thirteen Allied prisoners of war including one US soldier who had been captured behind German lines on the Normandy coast in the previous summer.

The website tells us that the Zwickau prisoners were required to work on the production of army vehicles, airplanes and torpedoes for the Horch-Werke Zwickau (a division of Auto Union, later Audi) in the 'Hochbau' factory. The prisoners were quartered in a barracks compound on the factory grounds. At one point the factory management complained to the SS about the 'dismal state of the prisoners, which was a source of epidemics threatening the civilian workers'. In February and March, more than 350 sickly prisoners were transferred back to Flossenbürg concentration camp where most of them died. Before its liberation by the United States army in April 1945, between 89,964 and 100,000 prisoners had passed through Flossenbürg and its sub-camps, of whom just over 16,000 were female, between 1938 and 1945 including 3,515 Jews. Around 30,000 died from malnutrition, overwork, executions or during the death marches. Between 13,000 and 15,000 prisoners died at the main camp and more than 10,000 at the satellite camps. When members of the 358th and 359th US Infantry Regiments (90th US Infantry Division) liberated Flossenbürg on 23 April 1945, just over 1,500 prisoners remained in the camp. An estimated three-quarters of the deaths occurred in the nine months before liberation. As many as 200 of them died after liberation. Some of those responsible for these deaths, including administrators, guards and others, were tried and convicted in the Flossenbürg trial. The last camp elder, Anton Uhl, was beaten to death by prisoners after the liberation.

The Zwickau camp was evacuated on 14 April 1945. The prisoners were initially force-marched in the direction of Flossenbürg; however, due to the changing front-line situation, they were then force-marched towards the Leitmeritz sub-camp.

In the 1950s factories were built on the Zwickau camp grounds, on which a commemorative plaque was mounted, memorializing the sub-camp. On 11 September 1948, a 'Memorial to the Victims of Fascism' was unveiled at the swan pond in Zwickau Municipal Park. It was here that the urns of 320 prisoners from Zwickau and Mülsen St. Micheln had been formally interred on 12 August 1945. In the 1960s the old commemorative site was demolished and the new memorial and museum opened in 2007 in what had been the laundry room. A second exhibition opened in 2010 in the prisoner kitchen. A list of the names of more than 21,000 prisoners who died at the camp is available on the museum's website.[6]

Chapter Twenty-Three

Epilogue: Back to Boston, PTSD and Reprisals

Over the years since 1944 the consequences, fallout and ramifications of the Battle of Arnhem have been many and numerous for a good number of the veterans and civilians involved: pride, self-worth, homes and families, physical health and mental health have themselves all been long-term casualties for some. Given this, it seems hugely disingenuous just to leave the story of Arnhem as if a neat and tidy conclusion ended it all when the now notorious river was crossed and the survivors began their journeys back to Boston. It didn't end there; not by any means. This chapter, therefore, looks at the extensive post-battle consequences; consequences that are of no less importance and significance than the battle itself. Any description of any battle is only half complete if it ends abruptly with victory or defeat, with waving white flags or triumphant regimental colours. Arnhem is no different: this chapter is just as essential as any of the others preceding it as its inclusion allows the book to give us as complete a 3D, full-screen picture of the Battle of Arnhem as possible.

Boston

So, in the summer of 1945, 14283058 Gunner Eric Chrystal, like thousands of other Arnhem veterans, returned home to resume 'normal' life. In Eric's case it was to Portobello just outside Edinburgh to continue a career in the British army that lasted until 1969. It took him to conflicts in Egypt, Cyprus and Aden, and to the threat of conflict in Cold War West Germany.

Before Eric and other PoWs got home, the survivors who made it across the Rhine had returned to Boston in the autumn of 1944. Decimated as it was, the regiment had to pick itself up, count the cost and move on. The personal effects of the dead or missing were solemnly put into safe custody. Later, an equally solemn roll call took place with many an unanswered name and a show of hands where a survivor might add information relating to an absentee. Silence can sometimes speak louder than words. Forms, including MI9 PoW forms, were completed, rail warrants were issued, pay was collected and leave was taken. Those few who remained behind in Boston began the harrowing task of writing to the anxious next of kin. On Tuesday, 3 October 1944 a memorial service was held in Boston's St Botolph's Church to honour the dead before a diminished congregation and that was it: job done, move on. Par for the course in those days.

There is still uncertainty surrounding the total casualties incurred by the 1st Air Landing Light Regiment. Oosterbeek church roll of honour lists forty-two dead, but we know that that probably falls short. Woollacott adds that 3 Battery returned the largest number of survivors, even though the regiment's team at the bridge was entirely 3 Battery Forward Observation Officer (OP) party, none of whom survived or got back in 1944. A Troop returned only one officer with two officers out of ten surviving from 1 Battery; 2 Battery survivors totalled three officers and twenty-five other ranks. Wilkinson gives us figures for Royal Artillery personnel (p.147):

> Numbers flying in to Arnhem: 372 1st Air Landing Light Regiment; 359 1st & 2nd Anti-Tank Batteries; 73 of the 1st FOU making a total of 804. Of these 92 died (11.44%), 464 (57.71%) were taken PoW or were missing; 248 (30.84%) were evacuated over the Nederrijn.

Post-Traumatic Stress Disorder (PTSD)

However, can the serviceman who has seen a period of intense combat ever return to 'normal' life? The impact of disability through lost limbs and other physical trauma is life-changing and lifelong; it impacts not just the veteran but also the veteran's family, changing their lives forever. Then there is the psychological trauma: it may look as though the transition back to normality has been made with no ill effects, but no one can know what is really going on in the mind and memory of many a returning soldier, sailor or airman. All former combatants feel some degree of fear when in action, especially in a cauldron (*hexenkessel*) like Arnhem. Often in the field it resolves into aggressive, adrenaline-fuelled reaction – flight or fight – but extended periods of fear and anxiety can later turn into long-term PTSD: post-traumatic stress disorder or combat stress reaction.[1]

No one without first-hand experience of sitting cramped in a glider with a 75mm howitzer and a few worrying mates for company, the wind incessantly howling, the tug insistently droning and the flak exploding can ever know what it is like to feel so vulnerable, protected only by a fragile layer of what might as well be balsa wood, to go into stomach-churning freefall as the earth rushes unforgivingly up at you, to then deplane and put your howitzer back together again (in four minutes flat), perhaps under enemy fire. None of us who have not been there have the slightest clue what it is like then to spend the next five, six or seven days under relentless explosive fire from close-quarter mortars, long-distance heavy artillery and prowling Panzers and Tiger tanks – to say nothing of machine-gun and opportunistic sniper rifle fire – with your comrades all around you scared witless, being blasted to bits and killed.

Most combatants will not admit to feeling frightened, but some did. Private Johnny Peters said 'If I had been frightened before, I was petrified by now.' We have seen how Padre Pare knelt beside that badly shocked young trooper: 'Padre,' the boy said, 'will you tuck me in? I get so frightened with all the noise.' Two hours later a medic came for Pare. 'You know that lad you said the prayers with?' Pare asked, 'What's wrong?' The medic shook his head. 'He died just now. He said to tell you he couldn't stand the noise outside.' We have seen how BSM Tom Kent, F Troop tells how he took the hand of one of the bombardiers whose 'nerves were shattered by his experience' and how

> the air raid siren sounded in the town and this really did frighten me. I was really terrified by this for the first and only time since leaving England. I had gotten out of a hell hole and this really threatened my liberty. I was exceptionally low, both mentally and physically. Whilst it lasted for some thirty minutes or so it really was agony and a great relief when the all-clear sounded…it was well into the following day when I awoke from a dreadful nightmare that left me feeling a physical wreck, then perhaps that really was the state I was in.

Before the battle BSM Kent had described more fear with the mounting tension and anxiety in the regiment on 15 September when 'F Troop

TSM David "Jock" Lawson was forever crying out in his nightmares, he was apparently going through all sorts of deaths and torture', reliving past horrors and fearful for the future. As noted above, presumably these were flashbacks from PTSD inflicted in the previous year's Italian campaign. Lawson remained implacable and refused to go to see the Medical Officer (MO) next day, putting his nightmares down to stress.

We have seen how Gunner Chrystal, having reached the north end of the bridge on the evening of 17 September, describes how he felt that night: 'Waking up from catnaps I found that my teeth were tightly clenched, that must be a sign of something, and at no time did I feel other than *a bit* scared, and always, the terrific noise.'

It is worth repeating how, usually a non-combatant, Lance Sergeant Alfred Rouiller of Light Regiment 2 Battery answered the call for volunteers to man B Troop's last surviving gun. As Rouiller and three others edged towards the gun, he saw 'a small group of men in a line… shaking uncontrollably…suffering from shellshock.' He recognized some of them and started to feel scared himself: 'if this sort of thing could happen to tough, battle-hardened men, it could happen to him.'

With disarming innocence, Marie-Anne, the 15-year-old author of a fascinating diary *The Tommies are Coming!* tells us 'We are still being shelled' and how Len [one of the British occupants of her requisitioned house] 'keeps diving in the cellar when he hears them come. Apparently he is rather afraid of them', while 'Gerald stays upstairs in the sitting room. He only comes down when their burst is near.' Shortly afterwards we hear how

> some soldiers come down the stairs carrying a man. They say that he is wounded and they put him down on the floor on a blanket…then Len and Gerald come down too…they have examined the wounded man and say that he is not wounded. Apparently a shell has exploded very near to him and he is now very frightened, 'shocked' the English call it. He seems somewhat calmer now. They have given him some eau de cologne and now he seems asleep.

Gunner Ron Gibbs of D Troop was 'scared stiff and pretty helpless with no means of defence against the tanks which were infiltrating the position' when he and two others dived into a slit trench only to be pinned down.

Epilogue: Back to Boston, PTSD and Reprisals

It is worth repeating how later in the battle we learned from Bombardier Hall the altercation in the room below the attic in Brigade HQ. When he went down to tell 'the Signaller' that it was time for his stint as Hall felt he'd been in the attic long enough without a break, the signaller refused to go. 'I'm not going up there,' he said, while all the other signallers were watching agog at the foot of the stairs while the battle noise was increasing.

Charitably, Hall maintains anonymity and ascribes the insubordination to the fact that the signaller in question had 'been shelled in an Italian OP, his back was still heavily scarred where falling masonry had put him in hospital there'. 'Don't be silly,' I said, and went back up the steps to monitor the set.

As we said, the point that Hall makes by relating this incident is presumably not just that discipline is paramount in battle, but also he wanted to highlight the devastating and long-lasting effect combat can have on a soldier. The unnamed signalman was undoubtedly at fault for refusing an order, but he was also a victim of what we now call PTSD and, as we know, if you don't treat such conditions, they may never go away and can often recur in times of stress or in subsequent conflict. Hall adds later in his *Signals from Arnhem Bridge*: 'The few months that followed included, for many of us, a so-called Death March, which wrought damage, both physical and mental, on our pitiful state.' Readjusting was 'a struggle which is now only evident in retrospect.' Hall recalls that even at the annual reunions in Arnhem 'there was little exchange of battle information. Our experiences were locked within, neither forgotten nor modified – contaminated if you like – by other accounts.'

No one who has just read as far as this final chapter can have failed to notice the frequent references within the many testimonies to unabated and deafening noise, to fear, to stress and to demoralization, to hopelessness. Some of this is, of course, counteracted by a heroic reaction, a commensurate adamantine will to get through it all, to retain hope and to valiantly win through. One 19-year-old glider pilot recalls how he realized that 'fear and courage are strange emotions. Before I was hit I felt it very important not to show fear. One had to behave well in front of comrades. Being wounded brought you to the conclusion that you could have been one of the corpses.' Be that as it may, for those who did eventually 'get through it all' there was for many a residual psychological scar, a haunting memory, a non-negotiable denial perhaps of what actually happened in those mid-September days in 1944. Today, as we have already noted, we ascribe this to combat stress reaction or post-traumatic stress disorder.

However, it's not just the soldiers who blank it out; it seems that the writers of the numerous books written on Arnhem do so as well. Very seldom is the fear and psychological impact of the combat experience explored to any viable extent and rarely do we hear of the incessant ear-splitting noise the soldiers had to endure, so anxious are the authors and publishers to assail us with the recorded official statistics and facts, and rarely do the authors pause to assess the psychological toll, so avid are some (and their editors, no doubt) to parade before us the death tolls, the mutilation and the sensational.[2] In reality, the psychological, the PTSD, just worms its way silently and surreptitiously in the background that goes on to constitute the combatant's mind and memory. Many of the accounts of the Battle of Arnhem give PTSD short shrift. For those written soon after 1944 it may be excusable as psychiatric knowledge of the long-term effects of combat was in its infancy, but there is no excuse for more recent publications: post-conflict fear and the struggle to cope should be a soundtrack to the narrative describing the battle since it was always there in the real world, persistent and insistent, but it rarely features; the soldiers heard the noise and felt the fear and so should we. It is as important a facet of the battle as descriptions of heroic action, death and destruction.

Relentless noise can be a trigger for and a symptom of PTSD. As we have seen, Gunner Chrystal says so: 'The next few hours are a complete blank.... Neither can I even remember who else was in our party. It must have been the terrible noise that was going on that drove it from my mind, it was terrific…and always the terrific noise.'[3] Robert Woollacott says so; SS Corporal Mauga says so too; Dicky Bird recalls how 'The sounds of battle had increased in intensity to reach an ear-splitting cacophony that would last for the next seven days'; Bombardier Hall had little to do 'except take in the continuous sound of battle…the din of the battle was almost deafening to me now.... The noise of battle occupied every second…the battle noise was increasing'; he also recalls the 'unimaginable noise' at the bridge. Marie-Anne, the diarist of *The Tommies are Coming!* referred to above, tells us in the entry for Monday, 25 September how Frank the gunner of the mortar gun outside our house…must go up from time to time. The rest of the time he stays down in the cellar with us to fire his gun. He says the noise of the gun has given him severe headache…. I give him an aspirin and tell him to lie down.

It was not just the men in the Oosterbeek gun positions or at the bridge who suffered: those suffering in the 'hospitals' had also to endure the endless cacophony. Kate ter Horst questions 'Isn't it enough to be wounded once? Wounded and disfigured and shaken with fever, tortured with pain and thirst they lie in this hellish noise…the noise makes one crazy' (*Cloud over Arnhem*, pp.48–49).

Referring to that old army adage 'stay alert, stay alive', Larry Decuers, former curator at The National WWII Museum and veteran of the US Army's 101st Airborne Division, asks the question 'How long can a soldier remain in a constant state of alertness before damage is caused to their mental state? How long before this damage becomes permanent?'[4] Decuers continues:

> During World War II, it is estimated that only one million men (or roughly one out of every 16 service members) saw what could be considered sustained combat. This group, however, accounts for the majority of the war's casualties. Even when enemy bullets and shrapnel failed to kill or physically wound, they inflicted casualties nonetheless. More than half a million service members suffered some sort of psychiatric collapse due to combat. Alarmingly, 40 per cent of medical discharges during the war were for psychiatric conditions. The vast majority of those can be attributed to combat stress.
>
> More than 500 elite Marines returning from Guadalcanal in 1945 were treated for symptoms such as tremors, sensitivity to loud noises and periods of amnesia.

Because PTSD was not recognized as an official disorder until 1980, it is almost impossible to estimate its prevalence during the Second World War. A rough estimate found through hospitalization records suggests that approximately 43 per 1,000 soldiers were hospitalized due to battle traumas, but this estimate can only be based upon those relatively few who actually sought help.[5] Another rate, from the 1950s, suggests that about 10 per cent of Second World War soldiers have had PTSD at some point.[6]

Research from the Centre for Military Health Research at King's College, London, reveals that there is now a consensus that a close relationship exists between the incidence of death and injury on the battlefield and the number of psychiatric casualties, though it may be mediated by the nature of the fighting, the morale of the troops and the quality of leadership. Given the intensity of the fighting in and around Arnhem compressed into those traumatic nine days, it seems reasonable to assume that there would have been a high number of corresponding psychiatric casualties.

A report by the BBC's Stephen Mulvey, published on 8 June 2019 and titled *The Long Echo of WW2 Trauma*, showed how in a study of people receiving war pensions for psychiatric illness between 1940 and 1980, a team of researchers found that the ten most common symptoms were anxiety, depression, sleep problems, headache, irritability/anger, tremor/shaking, difficulty completing tasks, poor concentration, repeated fears and avoidance of social contact.[7]

Mulvey adds that 'Some of these symptoms could contribute to the "shared emotional cauldron" as detected by Robert Rosenheck in traumatised veterans' families, which led some children to share their father's pain.'

Professor Siobhan O'Neill of Ulster University adds that

> 'the most obvious way for a parent's trauma to affect a child would be by hindering the development of a strong and secure attachment between parent and child in the early years of the child's life. It's pretty well accepted that an impact on the attachment between parent and child will impact on mental health,' she says. 'A traumatised parent can have difficulty forming a secure attachment with the child.'

One of the most prevalent symptoms of PTSD is 'avoidance': not wanting to talk about the traumatic experience.[8] We've all been there: we see this time and time again with the children and grandchildren of veterans drawing a blank when they ask about the war, or when they themselves rekindle an interest in the war years, frustrated as they are by reticence and a reluctance by the veteran to expatiate on their awful experience. Sadly, with the passing of nearly all Arnhem veterans, that self-imposed silence, that amnesia, is now permanent, so it is doubly incumbent on us to report and describe past, present and future conflict and combat honestly, but based on the actual facts and not on sensationalism and embroidered facts. Likewise we need to systematically address these issues with veterans of the Falklands War, Northern Ireland, Bosnia, Iraq and Afghanistan and the Ukraine, whenever they emerge.

One assumes that diagnosis and treatment of PTSD is increasing and improving all the time and that combatants in twenty-first-century conflicts will be better served and equipped to deal with combat stress reaction, both in terms of preparedness and in dealing with it when it insidiously strikes.[9] Military medicine and psychiatry have moved on since 1944, but only painfully slowly. Gunner Eric Chrystal, like everyone else, received no post-combat counselling because it was barely understood and simply not done, and the outward show of alpha-masculinity within a regiment, company, battery or platoon was all-important. More alarmingly, though, is the fact that veterans of the much more recent 'Troubles', military and civilian, are still largely left to fend for themselves – and that was just twenty-five years ago – as are Falklands War veterans.[10] 'The overall rate of probable PTSD among current and ex-serving military personnel was 6 per cent in 2014–16, compared with 4 per cent in 2004–06. The rise in the condition was mainly seen in military veterans who deployed to Iraq and Afghanistan, the researchers said.'

The findings are from the third phase of a major cohort study by King's College London, which has been running since 2003 and is led by Dr Sharon Stevelink from the Institute of Psychiatry, Psychology & Neuroscience (IoPPN) and funded by the Ministry of Defence. The rate of PTSD among the civilian population is about 4 per cent. The findings are based on questionnaire responses from 8,093 current and former members of the armed forces. Of the 8,093 participants included in the third phase of the study, 62 per cent had deployed to Iraq or Afghanistan. The findings have been published in the *British Journal of Psychiatry*.[11] 'The study supports the current focus on providing and improving mental health services for both serving personnel and veterans. During 2014–16, the rate of probable PTSD among ex-regular veterans was 7.4 per cent, compared with 4.8 per cent among those currently serving as regular personnel, the study found.'

Former military personnel who deployed to Iraq and Afghanistan were more likely to report the symptoms of PTSD. For veterans who deployed, the rate was 9.4 per cent compared with 5 per cent among those who did not participate in the two conflicts, the research found. Ex-serving military personnel deployed in a combat role were found to have higher rates of PTSD at 17.1 per cent, compared with 5.7 per cent of those who had been in a support role such as medical, logistics, signals and aircrew.

Today PTSD patients can select from various medications, including selective serotonin re-uptake inhibitors (SSRIs) such as fluoxetine. Other therapies include various forms of group therapy, traditional therapy and eye movement desensitization and reprocessing (EMDR).

To better understand what some Arnhem veterans may have endured post-war, it is instructive to look at one Second World War book (and subsequent film) that deals head-on with PTSD: that book is Eric Lomax's *The Railway Man*, which focuses on the long-term impact of the extreme torture and cruelty endured by Lomax while slaving away on the Siam-Burma Railway. Flashbacks and memories haunt Lomax, defining his life as he tries to readjust: obsessive behaviour relating to all things railway, a difficult relationship with his new devoted wife, a refusal to engage in real life, debt and nightmares all conspire to climax in a violent attack. Lomax eventually agrees to face his demons only after his wartime comrade has alerted him to the terrible truth that his torturer, Nagase, a young translator, is still alive and making a living out of Burma railway tours, and Lomax's friend hangs himself – on a signal gantry – as a consequence of his own struggle with undiagnosed PTSD. So Lomax trains back to Burma and confronts Nagase, his tormentor (past and present), intending to kill him in revenge. Bridges are a common theme for us. In his review of the film of Lomax's book, Michael Fass points out how in David Lean's *The Bridge on the River Kwai* (Spiegel & Lean, 1957) about the building of the Thai-Burma Railway how Major Clipton's (James Donald's) concluding words are 'Madness, madness!'[12] Some fifty years later director Jonathan Teplitzky picks up the theme of madness in his adaptation of the *The Railway Man*.

As Fass concludes:

These intense scenes of confrontation between Lomax and his ex-tormentor feature many of the therapeutic aspects of a contemporary therapy for PTSD known as prolonged exposure therapy (PE). In this popular PTSD therapy, the client/patient re-experiences the event or events through recalling or revisiting the location of the trauma and then engaging himself or herself with the emotions that rise to the surface. Through this accidental, self-administered form of PE, Lomax not only confronts the physical location of his trauma but also confronts the source of his trauma. Ultimately deciding not to kill his tormentor, Lomax is able to forgive Nagase and thereby experience a profound catharsis that puts him on the pathway of healing and reconciliation. This remarkable telling of a real life story goes one step further, and as the film ends, the viewer learns that Lomax and Nagase become friends and work together to bring their respective countries to meaningful reconciliation.

The victims speak with pathos of 'doing time', 'sometime the hating has to stop', 'I'm still at war', a 'code of silence' and, most tellingly: 'We don't live, we're miming in the choir, we can't love, sleep; we're an army of ghosts.'

Who knows how many Italian Campaign or Arnhem veterans of the 1st Air Landing Light Regiment – and the tens of thousands of other units on all sides which saw combat – suffered like Lomax, and a thousand others? Who knows how many have availed themselves of the therapies gradually becoming available? Rhetorical questions both; the only certainty is that those veterans of subsequent conflicts need to be encouraged to access what help is out there now.

Aldershot Military Museum is running two projects taking place at the museum focusing on improving mental health and wellbeing: Vehicle Conservation and the Resilience Garden.

Combat Stress
Combat Stress is one of the principle UK charities 'offering therapeutic and clinical community and residential treatment to former members of the British Armed Forces who are suffering from a range of mental health conditions; including post traumatic stress disorder'. See https://combatstress.org.uk/
See also https://www.riflemantours.co.uk/shell-shock-and-ptsd/

Shell Shock was also prevalent in the Second World War. One famous person to suffer from this was the comedian and poet Spike Milligan. He was affected while serving and his treatment, in his own words, was to be sedated and effectively put to sleep for 7–10 days.

Many soldiers who serve their country today have and do suffer with this condition, only today we know it as Post Traumatic Stress Disorder and a number of soldiers who returned from the Gulf Wars of the 90s and the policing of Afghanistan suffer from it. It has finished their careers as soldiers and in many cases destroyed their family units and a number of soldiers who have left the army have become homeless and destitute due to this crippling illness.

Lest we forget.

Reprisals, Revenge and Retribution

Back in the Netherlands, in mid-September 1944 the people of Arnhem were quite simply in the wrong place at the wrong time: all they did wrong was to be at home in Arnhem when that massed army of British airborne troops landed in and near their quiet town from 17 September. They did not ask for the British and Poles to descend on them, but they nevertheless delighted in the prospect of liberation from their oppressive Nazi occupiers and went out of their way to accommodate and assist the Allies in their efforts to win back their bridge for them. As was often their wont, these Germans exacted reprisals on the good people of Arnhem with a vengeance. Their zeal and characteristic efficiency knew no bounds.

Even before the surviving soldiers of the 1st Airborne Division reached the southern bank of the Lower Rhine on the night of 26/27 September, the German military had issued an order on 23 September that Arnhem's citizens be immediately expelled from their home town. Apart from the forced expulsion of 150,000 residents, what happened next is described by Reinier Salverda as 'the brutal realities of forced evacuation, of the subsequent large-scale plunder and of the destruction of Arnhem between September 1944 and Liberation in April 1945.'[13] The residents of Arnhem, like many before and many after, had been reduced to homeless and dispossessed refugees in their own country. Many of those Dutch people would have carried the memory of that hellish week in September in their dejected minds for the rest of their lives, just like the soldiers

Epilogue: Back to Boston, PTSD and Reprisals

on both sides. The soldiers, though, had some moderating factors, albeit slight: their previous combat experience and training, but the Dutch had the benefit of neither. The first they knew about MARKET GARDEN was columns of British troops walking past their windows, requisitioning their gradually deconstructed homes, setting up ad hoc hospitals, firing and shelling incessantly; or maybe their first warning of trouble to come was the German tanks and heavy artillery returning that fire, also filling up makeshift hospitals with the injured and dying.

As noted, on Saturday, 23 September the German military command ordered the immediate evacuation of the population of Arnhem. Salverda (pp.107–108) tells us

> according to *Höhere SS und Polizeiführer* Hans Albin Rauter, the highest German police and security authority in occupied Holland,[14] this order came right from the top, i.e. from *Generalfeldmarschall* Walter Model, as Rauter stated after the war during his trial as a war criminal – at a time when Model was already dead.

However, the reality is 'that the order was issued by SS *Obersturmführer* Helmut Peter of the *Feldgendarmerie* of the 9th SS-Panzer Division Hohenstaufen. Debate continues about who issued that order, whether they had the authority to do so, and the fact that this may well have been a war crime. The Red Cross authorities were given three days to complete the evacuation, after which there would be systematic carpet-bombing of the entire city: '*mit Bombenteppichen muss gerechnet werden*'. Salverda continues: 'Given what had happened in May 1940 to Rotterdam and more recently in Stalingrad and Warsaw, such a message, coming from the German SS *Feldkommando*, could not be taken lightly.' Dr van der Does and the Red Cross got on with it.

So in the next chaotic three days 150,000 people were on the move. Not only young, old, women and children, the ill and the wounded but, more dangerously, all those who in the last four years were forced to go into hiding underground: Jews, students, policemen and Roma, as well as a large number of escaped British soldiers. Not only all these but also the Dutch civilians who had helped them now risked summary execution by the Germans.

Lifelong belongings, many with irreplaceable sentimental as well as commercial value, were piled high on handcarts or similar humble and humiliating modes of transportation. The evacuation became a graphic symbol of the horrors of tyranny and war, and of the tenuous hold on life to which the Dutch were clinging. It is there in the disarmingly honest and innocent account by 15-year-old Marie-Anne in her diary *The Tommies are Coming!* (p.35):

> We stayed in our house till the end of October…then we were driven from our house by the Germans. During the winter of 1944–1945 we found shelter in an old hen coop at Harskamp on the Veluwe. We often went hungry and had to eat boiled nettles as there was nothing else to be had. We were liberated in the spring of 1945. After some time we were allowed to return to Oosterbeek. Our house was in ruins and so we went to live in the shed. Many of our English friends had been in the meantime buried in our garden. I felt very sad.

It is there too in Kate ter Horst, the Angel of Arnhem's, account of the role she and her family played when their house, the Old Vicarage, was converted into a functioning field hospital, saving the lives of many (*Cloud over Arnhem*, p.14):

> [Kate] was ordered brusquely to leave her home and the village. Loading a pitifully small collection of personal belongings onto a handcart, with the baby in a box and the next youngest aloft as a guardian, with three other small children helping to push and pull, she set off wearily to the north, hoping to find a new refuge and fresh friends.

People were fleeing anywhere and everywhere, seeking refuge in places such as the zoo and the Open Air Museum, both just north of the city. Many also gravitated to neighbouring villages and cities, expecting to return home after a short while but ended up staying away until well after liberation. Others still were forced much further afield with some as far away as Friesland. Amid the chaos that ensued, the city was subjected to widespread looting by organized 'plunder crews' and destruction.

The only positive news, as noted by Salverda, was that a few well-organized people managed to rescue considerable food stocks, which they distributed in places where large groups of evacuees had congregated. Others, at great personal risk, succeeded in rescuing many priceless art treasures from the grasping Germans.

Obviously it was not just Arnhem that suffered from these depredations by those modern-day Vandals and Huns: the whole of the Netherlands was brutally relieved of infrastructure and cultural heritage; in short its very civilization. Salverda enumerates it (pp.109–110): 'Bridges, railways, church bells, bicycles, radios, industrial installations, railroads, harbours and shipyards, hospitals, universities and research facilities, sluices and dykes – everything was stolen or else destroyed. In 1945 the Dutch claim on Germany for war damages and reparations amounted to 3.6 billion guilders in total.'

However, Arnhem, by common agreement, suffered worst due to the help the people gave the Allies; in fact the claim for Arnhem alone has been estimated at 40 million guilders, or more than 10 per cent of the national war claim of 3.6 billion:

> These crews and their Dutch helpers proceeded to plunder and destroy Arnhem on a truly colossal scale, affecting all sectors of society and economy: factories, shops, banks, offices, laboratories, machines, stocks and supplies, raw materials, farms and livestock; but also Dutch culture – paintings, libraries, antiques, museums and special collections; as well as all private property, houses, furniture, clothing, valuables, pianos, beds, books, paintings and other household goods. Everything of value was taken and carried off, and the rest was destroyed, thrown out into the streets, put to fire, or left covered in excrement. The loot, systematically collected by a wide range of German organisations, was registered in the Beutesammelstelle, the loot-gathering station at the Burgemeestersplein, before being shipped off to Germany in many wagonloads per day.

Gerard Aalders (2004) tells how

> In the Netherlands, 8.5 million citizens suffered losses estimated at 3.6 billion guilders. Approximately one-third of these losses

were borne by Jews, who comprised only 1.6 per cent of the total population. In today's terms, the German occupiers stripped the Jewish population of assets worth $7 billion.

The summer of 1945 saw the dispossessed of Arnhem drift back to a city they hardly recognized: 'a city of ghosts, of rats and ruins, weeds and silence.' They were, nevertheless, determined to get on with the gigantic task of cleaning up, clearing up and repairing, but wholesale destruction was not the only toll the citizens of Arnhem had to pay. While 3,000 Allied soldiers had died in the battle along with 188 civilians including 40 or so summarily executed by the Germans, around 2,000 more citizens died during the evacuation due to starvation, more executions, razzias and other atrocities.[15]

One visitor in July 1945, from Rotterdam, was Cornelis Doelman who wrote that Arnhem was a 'dead town in need of everything'. A report he quoted from the municipal social services department stated that

> the people of Arnhem did not have anything left: no beds, chairs, windowpanes, pans, cutlery, coffeepots, curtains, pencils, telephones, absolutely nothing. So Doelman's message to the rest of the Netherlands was: come over and help Arnhem! And that is what happened: the city of Amsterdam, together with the Red Cross, straightaway adopted Arnhem, and all through the summer, the services, the citizens, engineers, nurses, carpenters, cleaners, mechanics, etc. of Amsterdam came over in large numbers and helped the people of Arnhem on their way.

Aid packages even came in from Switzerland, the Philippines and Brazil.

The aftermath of the battle, however, continued to resonate well after the British withdrawal: courageous Dutch men and women, underground and overground alike, insisted on and persisted in helping 300 or so British soldiers to evade capture to get back to England to fight again. Safe refuges and safe passage, food and water, medical care and travel plans were selflessly provided at tremendous personal risk, but there was worse: in 1947 the eldest son of the ter Horst family innocently jumped from a tree onto a land mine and was killed.[16] Tragedy followed tragedy when in 1992 Kate and her husband, both in their 80s by then, were knocked down by a car outside their home: Kate was killed and Jan badly injured.[17]

Memorials abound in the area[18] and the war cemetery remains a beautiful haven of peace and serenity. Every year a dwindling number of veterans return to the battlegrounds, while the Dutch insist on coming out in droves to show their respect and gratitude, with their children laying flowers, and some veterans still performing parachute drops. Gunner Eric Chrystal proudly returned to Arnhem many times before his death in 2001.

It is, however, relatively recently that Germans have been welcome at these ceremonies.[19] Significantly there are still some 140 Allied soldiers missing in action, unaccounted for and graveless, languishing somewhere under the fields, woods and streets of Arnhem and Oosterbeek and all points in between.

In September 1944 the Netherlands was effectively a divided country with the Dutch in the south enjoying the fruits of liberation while their cousins in the north were still under the cosh. They did, however, remain defiant and organized a national railway strike in which 30,000 Dutch railwaymen stopped work during the operation in an attempt to disrupt German manoeuvres. The ruthless Germans retaliated by banning the transportation of all goods by barge on the numerous rivers and canals on which the nation then depended to a large extent. Food in the west began to run out, presaging the atrocious 'Hunger Winter' (the Dutch famine of 1944–45) that killed 18,000 men, women and children.[20] Other reprisals included men of fighting age being sent into forced labour. Arnhem became the symbol of enduring Anglo-Dutch solidarity in the fight against Nazi Germany, according to Kamphuis.

Appendix I

3rd Air Landing Light Battery, E Troop

Commander: Major Dennis Munford
Battery Captain: Captain D. Lindsay
Command Post Officer: Lieutenant Peter Wilkinson
Assistant Command Post Officer: Lieutenant J.W. Widdicombe
Battery Sergeant Major: BSM A. Garnett

E Troop
Commander: Captain Tony Harrison (Forward Observation Officer, 2nd Battalion)
Troop Leader: Lieutenant A.V. Driver (Forward Observation Officer, 1st Battalion)
Gun Position Officer: Lieutenant N.F. Farrands
Troop Sergeant Major: TSM D. Lawson
E1 GUN Gun Commander: Sergeant Horace F. Marriott
E2 GUN Gun Commander: Sergeant J.E. Coates
E3 GUN Gun Commander: Sergeant J.H. Wyatt
E4 GUN Gun Commander: Sergeant D.C. Hardie

Appendix II

Other Airborne at Arnhem apart from the 1st Airborne Division

1st Air Landing Brigade
1 Airborne Corps
First Allied Airborne Army
US 101st Airborne Division
US 82nd Airborne Division

Appendix III

Arnhem Order of Battle

First Allied Airborne Army commanded by Lieutenant General Lewis H. Brereton, USAAF

British I Airborne Corps Lieutenant General Frederick Browning; also deputy commander of the 1st Airborne Army

Organization of I Airborne Corps during Operation MARKET GARDEN

British Airborne Units

1st Airborne Division, Major General Roy Urquhart

1st Parachute Brigade, Brigadier Gerald Lathbury

1st Parachute Battalion, Lieutenant Colonel David T. Dobie

2nd Parachute Battalion, Lieutenant Colonel John Frost

3rd Parachute Battalion, Lieutenant Colonel John A.C. Fitch

4th Parachute Brigade, Brigadier John W. Hackett

10th Parachute Battalion, Lieutenant Colonel Kenneth B.I. Smyth

11th Parachute Battalion, Lieutenant Colonel George H. Lea

156th Parachute Battalion, Lieutenant Colonel Sir Richard de Bacquencourt Des Voeux

1st Air Landing Brigade, Brigadier Philip Hicks

1st Battalion Border Regiment, Lieutenant Colonel Thomas Haddon

2nd Battalion South Staffordshire Regiment, Lieutenant Colonel W. Derek H. McCardie

7th Battalion King's Own Scottish Borderers, Lieutenant Colonel Robert Payton-Reid

1st Airborne Reconnaissance Squadron, Major Charles Frederick Gough

21st Independent Parachute Company (Pathfinders), Major Bernard Wilson

1st Airborne Divisional Signals, Lieutenant Colonel Thomas G.V. Stephenson

1st (Airborne) Divisional Provost Company, Corps of Military Police, Captain William B. Gray
89th (Parachute) Field Security Section, Intelligence Corps, Captain John Killick
Royal Artillery, Lieutenant Colonel R.G. Loder-Symonds

1st Air Landing Light Regiment, Lieutenant Colonel William F.K. Thompson
1st Air Landing Anti-Tank Battery, Major William F. Arnold
2nd Air Landing Anti-Tank Battery, Major A.F. Haynes
1st Forward (Airborne) Observation Unit, Major Denys R. Wight-Boycott
Royal Engineers, Lieutenant Colonel E.C.W. Myers
1st Parachute Field Squadron, Major Douglas C. Murray, then Captain Eric Mackay
4th Parachute Field Squadron, Major Aeneas Perkins
9th Airborne Field Company, Major John C. Winchester
261st (Airborne) Field Park Company, Lieutenant William H. Skinner
Royal Army Service Corps, Lieutenant Colonel M. St John Packe
250th (Airborne) Light Composite Company, Major D.G. Clarke
Royal Army Ordnance Corps, Lieutenant Colonel G.A. Mobbs
1st (Airborne) Divisional Field Park, Major Cecil Cyril Chidgey
Royal Electrical and Mechanical Engineers
1st (Airborne) Divisional Workshops, Major Jack Carrick
Royal Army Medical Corps, Colonel Graeme M. Warrack
16th (Parachute) Field Ambulance, Royal Army Medical Corps, Lieutenant Colonel E. Townsend
133rd (Parachute) Field Ambulance, Royal Army Medical Corps, Lieutenant Colonel W.C. Alford
163rd Field Ambulance, Lieutenant Colonel Martin E.M. Herford
181st (Air Landing) Field Ambulance, Royal Army Medical Corps, Lieutenant Colonel Arthur T. Marrable
Glider Pilot Regiment, Lieutenant Colonel George Chatterton
No. 1 Wing, Lieutenant Colonel Iain Murray
No. 2 Wing, Lieutenant Colonel John Place
Sztandar 1 SBS, Polish 1st Independent Parachute Brigade, Brigadier General Stanisław Sosabowski (arrived 21 September)

Appendix IV

Arnhem Town

'Arnhem is a quiet Dutch town.' So wrote Major Ernest Watkins in his *Arnhem: 1. The Landing and the Bridge* first published by the Army Bureau of Current Affairs 1944 (p.7). It is situated on the 'northern bank of the river Rhine, there about 150 yards wide, with a fast-flowing current'. Population about 94,000, 'it lies on the flat lands alongside the river, but immediately to the north the land rises sharply to a maximum of 250 feet.' Arnhem lies a few kilometres from the border with Germany.

'In the 1930s Arnhem was a proud and pleasant city, green, modern and full of enterprise, home to large industrial companies…and with a new bridge built across the Rhine in 1935' (Salverda, p.107). In May 1940 the Germans brought with them their fascist New Order and *Führerprinzip*: a 'fundamental attack on Dutch civil society, on its traditional principles of liberty, justice and equality, and its ancient freedoms of religion and association', Salverda adds. The summer of 1944 saw Arnhem rudderless: no mayor, alderman or city council. Only the Red Cross remained, under Dr Van der Does.

'On 16 September [1944] it was a quiet and peaceful town…with no presentiment of the events of the following week.' The main road from Utrecht approaches from the west, the Ede road slightly north approaches from the south-east, and the railway runs parallel to this. When the railway enters Arnhem there is a junction with a branch line from the south; this runs along an embankment and crosses the Rhine on a high steel bridge.

The road bridge, the main objective, takes the road from the south into the centre. In September 1944 both ends were protected by strongpoints with an 80mm gun at the south end enjoying a field of fire straight down the bridge to the north end. At the north end, a ramp brought the bridge road down into the town, terminating in a 'small oblong open space' around which were houses and other buildings. Two arches took the bridge road over two side roads that ran at right angles to the bridge road.

Reinier Salverda tells us that 'Before the war Arnhem was a provincial town of comfort and leisure. [It was] severely jolted by the onslaught of May 1940...followed by evacuation and the almost total destruction of the city. When liberation came in April 1945, there were only ruins in Arnhem; it was a dead city with almost no people' (*Beyond a Bridge Too Far*, p.104).

The local newspaper, *Arnhem Dagblad*, reminds us all how 'With Liberation Day, thoughts mainly go back to May 1945, when the capitulation of the German army in the Netherlands was signed on May 4 at the field headquarters of Montgomery on the Lüneberger Heide.'

In Arnhem, however, there were no cheering people on the street or young people touring the streets on the tanks and jeeps of British, Canadian or American soldiers. The evacuated Arnhemmers were mainly concerned with returning to their shelters in the Veluwe and from Friesland. They found a comprehensively looted and destroyed city. For many, the joy at the end of the war gave way to horror at the look of their homes and household effects.

Arnhem Dagblad, 5-5-1945.

Horlings, A., *Arnhem Ghost Town: Eyewitness accounts of the Battle and Evacuation*.

Vredenberg, J., *Reconstruction: Urban planning and architecture in Arnhem 1945–1965*, Utrecht, 2004, Matrix Publishers.

The good news is that the following twenty-five years or so of rebuilding and renewal 'have ensured the rebirth of Arnhem, rising phoenix-like from its ashes as a new and modern model garden city of the post-war era.'

Appendix V

Theirs is the Glory

Theirs Is the Glory (also known as *Men of Arnhem*) is a 1946 British war film about the British 1st Airborne Division's involvement in the Battle of Arnhem. It was the first film to be made about the battle, and the highest-grossing UK war film for almost a decade. The later film, *A Bridge Too Far*, depicts the operation as a whole and includes the British, Polish and American Airborne forces, while *Theirs Is the Glory* focuses solely on the British forces and their fight at Oosterbeek and Arnhem.

The film was directed by Brian Desmond Hurst, himself a veteran of the First World War, having survived Gallipoli where he had served with the Royal Irish Rifles. The script was written mainly by Louis Golding but honed by Hurst's protégé Terence Young (who went on to direct *They Were Not Divided* and the early Bond films). Using the original locations of the battle, the film features veterans who were actual participants in the battle. Young had been in the Irish Guards with the Guards Armoured Division with XXX Corps during the battle, hence the authenticity of the eventual storyline. Although no credits appear before or after the film, more than 200 veterans appeared as actors and they also collaborated on the script.

The film's narrator tells us that the soldiers are 'just ordinary men',

> but when you next watch the film, look closely at the faces of the men and especially at their eyes in the many close shots that Brian Desmond Hurst arranged. When you look into the eyes you will start to gain a little bit of the experience that those ordinary men went through.

Paradata adds (https://www.paradata.org.uk/article/theirs-glory-1946):

> Among the persons appearing in the movie were Lt Hugh Ashmore, Maj C.F.H. 'Freddie' Gough, Maj Richard 'Dickie' Lonsdale, Mrs

Kate ter Horst, Pte Tommy Scullion of County Antrim, Pte Peter Holt from Middlesex, Pte David Parker from Scotland, Cpl Pearce from Wales, Pte George 'Titch' Preston from Grimsby, Pte Frank 'Butch' Dixon (proven lethal with a PIAT), Sgt John Daley of Waterford, and war correspondents Stanley Maxted and Alan Wood. In addition, the total cast included other paratroopers, gunners, sappers, RAMC, RASC, reconnaissance squadron and glider pilots – all veterans of the battle. Each member was paid £3.0s.0d per day by the Rank Organisation.

The movie had simultaneous premieres in Ottawa, Arnhem and the Gaumont Theatre in the Haymarket London on the second anniversary of the start of the battle, 17 September 1946. A remastered high definition version was shown in the Astra Cinema on the Imperial War Museum Duxford site on 10 September 2014 to commemorate the 70th anniversary of the battle, organised by Gil Boyd and Jon Baker of The Parachute Regiment and Airborne Forces Museum with the assistance of Allan Esler Smith, the nephew of Brian Desmond Hurst. Attendees at the screening included three Arnhem veterans and the Colonel Commandant of The Parachute Regiment.

A detailed article on the making of the film is contained in *After the Battle Magazine*, Issue Number 58.

http://www.battle-of-arnhem.com/these-british-units-fought-during-the-battle-of-arnhem

Appendix VI

Allied Firepower at Arnhem

The British Airborne Division consisted of 12,416 officers and men. They were armed with the following:

2,942 pistols and revolvers
7,171 rifles
6,504 Sten guns
966 Bren guns
46 Vickers machine guns
474 2in mortars
56 3in mortars
5 4.2in mortars
392 PIATs
38 flame-throwers
23 20mm cannon
27 75mm pack howitzers
84 6-pounder anti-tank guns
16 17-pounder anti-tank guns

Sources: https://assets.publishing.service.gov.uk/government/uploads/system/uploads/attachment_data/file/30056/ww2_market_garden.pdf

Some 20,190 troops were dropped by parachute, 13,781 landed by glider and 905 air-landed on a strip prepared by airborne engineers. A total of 34,876 landed out of 36,228 dispatched from the UK. Altogether 3,520.8 tons of supplies were dropped by parachute plus 278 artillery weapons. Gliders delivered 1,259.1 tons of supplies and equipment, 1,689 vehicles and 290 artillery weapons. Some 451 tons of supplies and 258 vehicles were landed by aircraft. Total deliveries came to 5,230.9 tons of equipment and supplies, 1,927 vehicles and 568 artillery weapons.

[First Allied Airborne Army statistics, NARA RG331/Entry 254/Box20]

Appendix VII

How Much is a Dutch Bridge Worth?

Allied Forces

- 1,485 Allied troops were killed or died from their wounds
- 3,910 were evacuated
- 6,525 Allied troops were taken prisoner of war
- 5,354 Second Army casualties including 1,480 for XXX Corps

Details of the above are as follows:

- 1st Airborne: 322 killed; 240 wounded; 6,424 missing (mainly PoWs); total 6,986
- 1st Polish: 34 killed; 142 wounded; 207 missing; total 383
- 82nd Airborne: 336 killed; 1,912 wounded; 661 missing; total 2,909
- 101st Airborne: 573 killed; 1,987 wounded; 378 missing; total 2,938
- 377 Allied aircraft and gliders were lost, together with 862 crew members.

German Forces

There were 3,300 casualties (admitted by *Feldmarschall* Model) for the entire MARKET GARDEN area of battle including Eindhoven and Nijmegen, although other estimates put the figure as high as 8,000. Model's figure features in a signal, possibly sent by II SS Panzer Corps on 27 September, which listed 1,300 killed and 2,000 injured around Arnhem and Oosterbeek.

Official German casualty figures have never been released. In the 'Roll of Honour: Battle of Arnhem 17–26 September 1944', J.A. Hey of the Society of Friends of the Airborne Museum, Oosterbeek identified 1,725 German dead from the Arnhem area.

Sources: https://assets.publishing.service.gov.uk/government/uploads/system/uploads/attachment_data/file/30056/ww2_market_garden.pdf

Casualty figures, First Allied Airborne Army NARA RG331/Entry 254/Box20.

Woollacott has different figures (p.207), arriving at 17,200 Allied casualties over the nine days, 45 per cent of which occurred in Arnhem. Robert Kershaw (*It Never Rains in September*) gives 13,300 soldiers, while Will Irwin (*Abundance of Valour*, p.viii) has 17,000 killed, wounded or missing. This figure is about 6,000 more than at the D-Day landings three months earlier.

Appendix VIII

German Forces at Arnhem

Army Group B
Generalfeldmarschall Walter Model
Generalleutnant Hans Krebs

II SS *Panzer-Korps*
Obergruppenführer Wilhelm Bittrich
506 *Schwere Panzer Abteilung* (15 *Königstiger*)
Flak Brigade v. Swoboda (623 officers and men; 24 × 88mm, 26 × 20mm)
9th SS Panzer Division Hohenstaufen – *Obersturmbannführer* Walter Harzer
9th SS Panzer Regiment (without tanks, north of Arnhem)
19th SS *Panzergrenadier* Regiment (in Zutphen)
20th SS *Panzergrenadier* Regiment (in Rheden)
9th SS Artillery Regiment (without guns, Dieren)
9th SS Reconnaissance Battalion (in Hoenderloo)
9th SS *Panzerjäger* Battalion (near Apeldoorn)
9th SS Engineer Battalion (*Hauptsturmführer* Möller)
9th SS Flak Battalion (4 × 20mm, Dieren)
9th SS Signals Battalion

In West Arnhem and Oosterbeek area under command of 9th SS Panzer
Kampfgruppe Spindler
Kampfgruppe Krafft (when reinforced, 939 officers and men; 4 × 88mm, 2 × 80mm mortar; 3 × 37mm Pak, 3 × 20mm)
Kampfgruppe Möller (9th SS *Pionier Abteilung*)
Bataillon Köhnken (573 officers and men; 7 × 80mm mortars, 3 × 37mm Pak, 4 × 20mm flak)
Sturmgeschütz Brigade 280 (424 officers & men; 10 × assault guns)
SS *Werfer-Abteilung* 502 (173 officers & men; 12 × mortar, 2 × Pak 38)

Division von Tettau – *Generalleutnant* Hans von Tettau
Kampfgruppe Lippert (SS *Unteroffiziersschule Arnheim*)
Kampfgruppe Helle (*SS-Wach-Bataillon Nordwest*)
Kampfgruppe Eberwein
Kampfgruppe Worrowski (*Ausbildung und Ersatz* Regiment)
Hermann Göring Division – *Oberstleutnant* Fritz Fullriede)
Panzer Kompanie 224 (16 Renault tanks)
Festung M.G.Bataillon 37
Schiffs-Stamm Abteilung 14 (2 × Soviet Pak)
Fliegerhorst Bataillon (from 3 *Fliegerdivision* Deelen)

10th SS Panzer Division Frundsberg
Brigadeführer Heinz Harmel
10th SS Panzer Regiment (3 × Mk V Panther)
21st SS *Panzergrenadier* Regiment
22nd SS *Panzergrenadier* Regiment
10th SS Artillery Regiment
10th SS Reconnaissance Battalion
10th SS Anti-Tank Battalion
10th SS Engineer Battalion
10th SS Flak Battalion
10th SS Signals Battalion

Arnhem Bridge, then north-eastern Betuwe
Kampfgruppe Brinkmann (1,506 officers and men total)
SS *Panzer Aufklärung Abteilung* 10 (3 × 20mm; 1 × 37mm and 1 × 75mm anti-tank guns)
SS *Panzergrenadier* Regiment 21
SS Flak Battery 102 (8 × 20mm, 2 × 37mm flak)
Kampfgruppe Knaust
Kampfgruppe Mielke (8 Panzer Mk III and Mk IV)
Kampfgruppe Gerhard (1,913 officers and men total)
Kampfgruppe Gräbner (remains of 9 SS *Pz Aufklärung Abteilung*)
Bataillon Schoerken (12 × 80mm mortar)
Flak-Kampfgruppe Ladewig (12 × 88mm, 8 × 20mm)
Flak Battery Krüger (5 × 20mm, 4 × 88mm)

Luftwaffe *Werft. Abt.* **119/XI**
SS *Sicherungs Kompanie*
Artl. Regiment.191 (1,363 officers and men; 26 × 105mm, 3 × 150mm)
Feldgendarmerie Kompanie

Source:https://www.antonybeevor.com/order-of-battle-operation-market-garden

See also: https://web.archive.org/web/20090203172116/http://defendingarnhem.com/index.htm

Appendix IX

Some of the PoW Camps Where the Arnhem Captured Were Sent

- Reginald William Emmins served with the 1st Battalion Parachute Regiment, 'T' Company, No. 9 Platoon, service no. 5679008. He served in North Africa, Sicily, Italy and Arnhem, where he was wounded in the head at 6.00 pm on Monday, 18 September while fighting on the way to the bridge. Reg was taken prisoner on 26 September and sent to Stalag XI-B Fallingbostel. Later he was taken to work in a lead mine until liberated by American forces in 1945. Fallingbostel was the site of two PoW camps: Stalag XI-B and Stalag XI-D/357.
- Private Robert Gilbert (7267084) was in the RAMC (16 PFA). He was active in North Africa, Sicily and Italy, and then went to Arnhem where he was captured and he too was taken PoW to Stalag XI-B, Fallingbostel.
- Harry Houghton, 10th Parachute Battalion, Mentioned in Dispatches. Having been badly wounded and captured in Oosterbeek and taken to Stalag VIII-C Żagań in western Poland, he eventually travelled home via Odessa. Soon after invading Poland, the Nazis established a system of PoW camps in what was then Sagan. In total, the Mannschafts-Stammlager Stalag VIII-C and its sub-camps held more than 300,000 prisoners from some 30 different countries; around 120,000 of them died of hunger, disease and maltreatment. Later, in 1942, an additional camp was set up for Allied pilots called *Kriegsgefangenen* Stammlager der Luftwaffe 3 Sagan. This was where the war's most courageous escape took place, resulting in the killing of fifty prisoners. It was the subject of the 1963 film *The Great Escape*, the biggest and the most deadly escape of officer aircrew captured by Nazi Germany during the entire war. The number of prisoners attempting the escape was 200, of whom 76 managed to leave the camp; 73 were caught and 50 executed on Hitler's orders. Just three successfully escaped: one to Gibraltar and

two to Sweden. In 1971 the 'Martyrdom Museum of Allied Prisoners of War' was established on the site of the camp to house mementos and records of both Stalag VIII-C and Stalag Luft III.

- Private Ivor Ronald Hutt (2050592) was at Spangenberg Bei Kassel (Oflag IX-A), Army Air Corps. Spangenberg Castle was used as prisoner-of-war camp Oflag IX-A/H. There was a second camp a few miles to the south: Oflag IX-A-Z.
- Ernest Hamlett, Signaller, 1st Battalion, Border Regiment, 19 Platoon, 'D' Company. He was captured on 26 September and sent to Stalag XI-0-B at Fallingbostel, Germany, travelling in a dark crowded cattle railcar in appalling conditions, the men becoming so thirsty that they resorted to drinking their own urine. Hamlett's family had received no word of his fate until he arrived on the front doorstep one day, carrying a Red Cross parcel and totally emaciated. He had been 'missing in action' for seven and a half months.
- Corporal Cecil 'Bill' Bailey: Captured on 20 September 1944, he was in 156 Battalion the Parachute Regiment, 'B' Company. After he was captured he was sent by train to Stalag XII-A and twelve days later he was transferred to Stalag II-A, Neubrandenburg. In fact two German prisoner-of-war camps were located in Fünfeichen within the city limits: the large Stalag II-A and the adjacent Oflag II-E/67 for officers. The town was also the location of a forced labour camp for Sinti and Romani people. In 1945, a few days before the end of the Second World War, 80 per cent of the old town was burned down by the Red Army and about 600 people committed suicide as a result. From 1945 to 1948, the special NKVD-camp No. 9 was at the site of the former Stalag II-A.
- Albert Bateman: Shot down at Arnhem, although badly wounded he was a PoW (Stalag XI-B, Fallingbostel). It is not certain but possible that he was T/6479011 (formerly Royal Army Service Corps) Private A. Bateman of No. 1 Section, Mortar Platoon, Support Company, 10th Parachute Battalion, PoW no. 118486.
- George Henry Beynon, 1st Parachute Battalion, 1st Airborne Division. He was a PoW in M-Stammlager 357, Hut E4.
- See https://www.paradata.org.uk/media/1485 for Private Neads' account of his journey to hell. Neads was with 2 Para and was sent initially to XII-A Limburg whence he was cattle-trucked on to a work

camp Stalag XI-B outside Braunschweig and set to work in the Hermann Göring Steel Works where, as well as the execrable conditions at work and in the camp, the inmates had to live with the daily threat of Allied bombers missing the steel plant and hitting the camp. Thousands of Eastern workers were brought to the city for forced labour and in the 1943–45 period at least 360 children were taken away from their parents and died in the *Entbindungsheim für Ostarbeiterinnen* ('Maternity Ward for Eastern Workers'). In 1944, a sub-camp of the concentration camp Neuengamme was established in Braunschweig. Hundreds of prisoners, mostly Jews, lived in brutal conditions and hundreds died from hunger, disease and overwork.

- George Durant, 1st Air Landing Light Regiment was first sent to Limburg – 'a sea of constant liquid mud' – and then to Mühlberg (Stalag IV-B). Durant had already been very disappointed (to say the least) when he and his comrades were ordered to stay put just before the evacuation (recounted above); an order that was never countermanded, with the consequence that they missed their chance to cross the river. Ever on the lookout for an opportunity to escape, Durant volunteered for a working party which, unfortunately, proved to be in a coal mine at Stalag IV-C, Bettyschacht: high-security, twelve-hour shifts, six-day weeks and half a mile underground, with sub-zero temperatures and a starvation diet. In the early New Year he was moved to an open-cast mine near Brux in Czechoslovakia which unfortunately was drawing the attention of the RAF due to the proximity of a nearby benzene plant. Sadly, three Airborne men were killed one night when an ack-ack shell exploded on the roof of their hut.

Notes

Acknowledgements
1. Bob Woollacott served in the 1st Air Landing Light Regiment in Italy and at Arnhem; his book is based on a unique collection of personal documents, files and recollections. In the 1990s he met Bob Gerritsen and they became firm friends until Woollacott's death in 1997. His widow Lori bequeathed the Air Landing Regiment papers to Bob Gerritsen who soon discovered that his friend's *Winged Gunners* only featured a portion of the information contained in the files and papers. The result: *Arnhem Bridge: Target Mike One* comprising material published in *Winged Gunners* and the detail that did not make the final cut.
2. In 1994 Martyn Cornellissen met up with another Arnhem aficionado, Ken Greenhough, and another friendship was struck up, sadly short-lived when Ken died in 1997 aged 29. His beneficiaries gave much of his work to Martyn. This and the two strands mentioned in the note above coalesced to produce *Arnhem Bridge: Target Mike One*.

Chapter One
1. I am indebted to Wilkinson, pp.15–17 for much of this.
2. https://www.paradata.org.uk/event/tragino-operation-colossus
3. https://www.paradata.org.uk/event/bruneval-operation-biting

Chapter Two
1. Otway, p.21; Ferguson, p.6.
2. Truesdale, p.9.
3. *458 Independent Light Battery. Para Data. 1st Air Landing Light Regiment Regimental History*, p.5.
4. Hogg, p.91.
5. Truesdale, p.10.
6. Truesdale, p.10.
7. Woollacott, p.2; Bulford: unfit for human habitation by all accounts (Woollacott, p.4). The situation improved after a visit by General Paget, GOC Home Forces. See also Truesdale, pp.11–12.
8. Woollacott, p.2. Nine out of eleven captains; all CPs; half the WOs, all BQMSs; all FMVs were found from the battery: 'better 3 good batteries than 1 very good and 2 struggling', Woollacott, p.4.

9. By WO letter 20/Misc. 2138 (AG6A) dated 2/2/43. Woollacott, pp.3–4; Truesdale, pp.9–10. For FSMO see http://ayearofwar.com/2018/09/20/www-war-diary-1918-field-service-marching-order
10. 1st Air Landing Light Regiment. Para Data; Middlebrook, p.34.
11. Kinard, p.274; Truesdale, p.13. Woollacott, p.5, tells how the original consignment was fitted with cartwheels, causing much mirth. Two weeks' leave was granted, after which the soldiers returned to find pneumatic tyres had been fitted.
12. *Journal of the Royal Artillery* (1963), p.132.
13. Tugwell, p.39.
14. Fowler, p.9.
15. Peters, p.65.
16. Truesdale, p.11.
17. Truesdale, p.13. *By Air to Battle* describes the Dakotas as 'slow, unarmed and unarmoured transports' (p.96).

Chapter Three
1. The General Service Corps was formed in February 1942. From 2 July 1942, army recruits were enlisted in the corps for their first six weeks so that their subsequent posting could take into consideration their particular skills and the army's specific needs. The 38th Training Regiment Royal Artillery (Signallers & Tech Acks) was formed in July 1941. For details see http://british-army-units1945on.co.uk/royal-artillery/38th-regiment-ra.html
2. 14283058 Gunner E. Chrystal, 'Regular Army Certificate of Service' book. Unpublished correspondence with Bob Woollacott, 1992.
3. Ben Hill, Paradata, 1st AB nominal roll for Op Market Garden for Gunner E. Chrystal 14283058. *1st Air Landing Regiment R.A. Regimental History*, p.6.
4. Reported 'Missing believed Wounded and Prisoner of War'. Reported to War Office Casualty Branch 23/10/1944. Casualty List No. 1584. Another record has him on 25/09/1944 'Prisoner of War in German hands, Location Unknown' and on 18/11/1944 Casualty List No. 1607. Previously reported Missing, Casualty List No. 1584.
5. https://www.gedenkstaette-flossenbuerg.de/en/research/archive
6. 31/07/1945: Casualty List No. 1822. Previously reported on Casualty List No. 1607 as 'Prisoner of War, now Not Prisoner of War. Previous Theatre of War, Western Europe'.
7. *1st Air Landing Regiment R.A. Regimental History*, p.6.

Chapter Four:
1. Atkinson, 2007, p.172.
2. Operation MINCEMEAT was an ingenious and successful British deception operation to obfuscate the 1943 Allied invasion of Sicily. Two members of British Intelligence obtained the body of Glyndwr Michael, a vagrant

who died from ingesting strychnine, dressed him up as an officer of the Royal Marines and placed personal items on him identifying him as the fictitious Captain (Acting Major) William Martin. Correspondence between two British generals was planted on the body: this suggested that the Allies were planning to invade Greece and Sardinia, with Sicily not in the plans.

In support of the wider Operation BARCLAY, MINCEMEAT was based on the 1939 Trout memo, a paper that compared the deception of an enemy in wartime to fly fishing, written by Rear Admiral John Godfrey, the Director of the Naval Intelligence Division and his personal assistant, Lieutenant Commander Ian Fleming. With approval at the highest level (Winston Churchill and the military commander in the Mediterranean, General Dwight D. Eisenhower), the plan kicked off by transporting the body from Greenock to the southern coast of Spain by submarine (HMS *Seraph*). On 19 April *Seraph* set sail and arrived off the coast of Huelva on 29 April after having been bombed twice en route. The corpse was released close to shore, where it washed up and was salvaged the following morning by a Spanish fisherman. The supposedly neutral Spanish government shared copies of the documents with the *Abwehr* (German military Intelligence), before returning the originals to the British. Forensic examination revealed that they had been read and Ultra decrypts of subsequent German messages produced by the Government Code and Cypher School (GC&CS) at Bletchley Park proved that the Germans had fallen for the ploy hook, line and sinker. Reinforcements were accordingly diverted to Greece and Sardinia before and during the invasion of Sicily; Sicily received none.

Operation BARCLAY was the wider deception by the Allies intended to convince the Axis powers of the locations of the invasion and to divert the Axis defence plans and resources. Bogus troop movements, radio traffic, recruitment of Greek interpreters and the acquisition of Greek maps all pointed to an invasion through the Balkans. Operation BARCLAY even spawned a fake army in the eastern Mediterranean: the 12th Army consisting of twelve fictitious divisions. Then there was the decoy invasion force assembled in Cyrenaica (an Italian colony in modern eastern Libya): Operation WATERFALL, and the deployment of Special Operations Executive (SOE), working with the Greek *andartes* in Operation ANIMALS, a series of concerted attacks on rail and road networks (between 21 June and 11 July 1943). The deception worked: German forces in the Balkans were reinforced from eight to eighteen divisions, and the Italian fleet was diverted into the Adriatic Sea.

Macintyre (2010) has written that the exact impact of MINCEMEAT is impossible to calculate. Although the British had expected 10,000 killed or wounded in the first week of fighting, fewer than 1,500 became casualties; the Navy expected 300 ships to be sunk in the action, but they lost only 12. The predicted ninety-day campaign was over in thirty-eight days.

3. O'Reilly, 2001, pp.37–38.
4. Molony, 2004, pp.26, 27.
5. Molony, 2004, p.83.
6. Hoyt, 2007, p.12. The units of the 1st Air Landing Brigade were the 1st Battalion, Border Regiment; the 2nd Battalion, South Staffordshire Regiment; the 181st (Air Landing) Field Ambulance; and the 9th Field Company, Royal Engineers.
7. Hoyt, 2007, p.21.
8. Molony, 2004, pp.81–82.
9. Molony, 2004, pp.79–80; National World War II Glider Pilots Association, p.17.
10. Molony, 2004, p.81.
11. Mitcham, p.75.
12. Woollacott, p.8. MV *Staffordshire* was built by Fairfield Shipbuilding & Eng. Co., Govan for the Bibby Line and completed in January 1929. She was requisitioned as a troopship in April 1940. On 28 April she was outbound from Liverpool to Rangoon and bombed 150 miles north-west of the Butte of Lewis, set on fire, beached at Loch Ewe on the 29th, abandoned and re-boarded ten hours later, after which she sailed for the Tyne. Fourteen crew and fourteen passengers were lost. She returned to service in January 1942 after repairs.
13. Woollacott, p.9.
14. Woollacott, p.10. Winston Churchill called the FW 200 the 'Scourge of the Atlantic' during the Battle of the Atlantic due to its contribution to the heavy Allied shipping losses. The Seafire was a naval version of the Supermarine Spitfire adapted to operate from aircraft carriers. The name Seafire is an abbreviation of Sea Spitfire.
15. According to John Widdicombe. Woollacott, p.10; Truesdale, p.16.
16. Woollacott, p.12; Truesdale, p.17.
17. *1st Air Landing Light Regiment RA Regimental History*, p.5; Truesdale, p.18. The word 'mascara' is the Francization of the Arabic word معسكر (*mouaskar*), meaning 'camp'. The airfield at Mascara was used by the United States Army Air Force Twelfth Air Force during the North African campaign against the German Afrika Korps.
18. Woollacott, p.16; Truesdale, p.21. The Battle of Kasserine Pass was fought by the Axis forces led by Rommel and his Afrika Korps Assault Group, the Italian Centauro Armoured Division and two Panzer divisions detached from the 5th Panzer Army (the 10th and 21st Panzer Divisions). The Allied forces consisted of the American 1st Armoured Division and 168 Regimental Combat Team, the British 6th Armoured Division and other parts of the First Army.

The battle was the first major engagement between US and Axis forces in Africa. Although numerically superior, the Americans lacked experience and were poorly led; they suffered many casualties and were pushed back more than 50 miles from their positions west of Faïd Pass. After this, elements of the US II Corps, with British reinforcements, rallied and held the exits through mountain passes in western Tunisia, defeating the Axis offensive.

19. See Truesdale, p.27. Crawfurd can take credit for consolidating the different independent artillery units of the 'new' Airborne Division, all of which had been converted from existing formations and then brought up to strength with volunteers.

    In April 1943 he, along with his HQ, the 1st Air Landing Light Regiment, the 1st and 2nd Air Landing Anti-Tank Batteries, Royal Artillery left for North Africa. Here they trained for and planned the first major airborne operation of Britain's Airborne Forces. He was killed in action during Operation FUSTIAN, the parachute and glider assault on the Primosole Bridge by the 1st Parachute Brigade. He now lies in Catania War Cemetery. See also Woollacott, p.26.

20. Salerno was also the location of the Salerno Mutiny on 16 September where 500 or so men of the British X Corps, which had by this time suffered more than 6,000 casualties, refused to be re-assigned to new units as battle casualty replacements. About 1,500 men from the 50th (Northumbrian) and 51st (Highland) Infantry divisions sailed from Tripoli; their understanding was that they would be returned to their own units from which they had been separated (mainly due to injury) during the North African campaign. When they learned they were going to Salerno, many of the soldiers felt they had been deliberately misled. About 1,000 of the men, who were raw recruits, were taken off to join new units, leaving 500 veterans, 300 of whom were billeted in a nearby field. Of these, 108 elected to follow orders, leaving a hard core of 192. They were all charged with mutiny under the Army Act; the largest number of men accused of mutiny at any one time in all of British military history. The accused were shipped to Algeria, where the courts-martial opened towards the end of October. All were found guilty and three sergeants were sentenced to death. The sentences were subsequently commuted to twelve years' forced labour and eventually suspended.

21. https://ww2db.com/battle_spec.php?battle_id=307; Contributor: C. Peter Chen.

    This is the account on veteransgca.can: Canada – Italy 1943–1945. https://www.veterans.gc.ca/eng/remembrance/history/second-world-war/canada-Italy-1943-to-1945:

    The Eighth British Army (including the 1st Canadian Division, the 5th British Division and the 1st Canadian Army Tank Brigade) would lead the way across the Strait of Messina to the toe of Italy and then advance toward Naples. The Fifth US Army (with two British and two US divisions) would make a seaborne landing in the Gulf of Salerno, seize Naples and advance on Rome. The 1st British Airborne Division would land by sea in the Taranto region and seize the heel of the peninsula.

The assault across the Strait of Messina began on 3 September 1943. The Canadians, directed on Reggio Calabria, met little resistance since the Germans had withdrawn to establish a line of defence across the narrow, mountainous central part of the peninsula. The Canadians captured Reggio Calabria and advanced across the Aspromonte Mountains and along the Gulf of Taranto to Catanzaro. In spite of rain, poor mountain roads and German rearguard actions, they had moved 120 kilometres inland from Reggio by September 10.

22. Blumenson, p.33.
23. Ferguson, pp.9, 11, 13.
24. Blumenson, p.95.
25. Tugwell, p.168.
26. Chant, p.254; Cole, pp.51–52; *1st Air Landing Light Regiment RA Regimental History*, p.5.
27. Cole, p.52; Chant, p.254.
28. Morrison, pp.235–36.
29. Blumenson, p.73.
30. Woollacott, p.30; Truesdale, p.28.
31. Morrison, p.256.
32. Styling, p.25.
33. Woollacott says 120 officers and men of the Airborne Division, p.30, as does Truesdale, p.28. Cole says 130 officers and men including the RAMC CO, Lieutenant Colonel M.J. Kohane, 2 other officers, 15 other ranks and all the unit's medical equipment.
34. Reynolds, p.37.
35. F. Ashe Lincoln QC RNVR, *Secret Naval Investigator*, pp.132–33.
36. Cole, pp.222–23: An airborne field ambulance was commanded by a lieutenant-colonel, with a major as the second-in-command and a regimental sergeant major as the senior non-commissioned rank. Headquarters staff included two specialist surgeons and a specialist anaesthetist, a pharmacist and an Army Dental Corps dentist. To assist in the operating theatre and with post-operative care, there were six operating room assistants, a sergeant nursing orderly and six nursing orderlies. Other medical staff were a sergeant sanitary assistant, a masseur, a dental orderly and five stretcher-bearers, one of whom was trained as a shoemaker. The rest of the headquarters consisted of a quartermaster, clerks, cooks, storemen, an Army Physical Training Corps instructor, a barber and a joiner from the Royal Engineers.

    Cole, p.55: By 22 September the 133rd had taken over, 320 beds in the Rondinella Hospital (the size of a normal army general hospital) and as such was taken over by No. 70 General Hospital when they landed. On 30 September the 133rd moved to Gioia del Colle establishing a 140-bed MDS in a school.

    The 133rd also took over eighty beds in the Ospedale Maritima where casualties from HMS *Abdiel* were treated along with sixty-seven other wounded by the morning of the 15th (Cole, p.53).

For Hopkinson see Woollacott, pp.30–31 and Cole, p.53, n.1.
37. Harclerode, p.262.
38. https://www.paradata.org.uk/unit/1st-airlanding-light-regiment-ra; *1st Air Landing Light Regiment RA Regimental History*, p.5.
39. Woollacott, p.43.
40. See https://nzhistory.govt.nz/media/sound/orsogna-joseph-bacos. For a detailed blow-by-blow account see W.A. Glue, *20 Battalion and Armoured Regiment* (1957). Here is part of the review for Jeffrey Plowman's *Orsogna*, published in *After the Battle* 192:

'In early December 1943, the 2nd New Zealand Division, advancing northwards from the Sangro River in central Italy, came up against Orsogna, a small town perched on the edge of an escarpment overlooking the wide valley of the Moro River. Staunchly defended by German infantry, tanks and paratroops, the position proved a very tough nut to crack. Five times the New Zealanders launched a determined attack on the town – on 2, 7, 15 (twice) and 16 December – but each time they were thrown back, with heavy losses in men and tanks. A final attempt, aimed at outflanking Orsogna from the north, bogged down on Christmas Day without achieving the objective either. For the New Zealand Division it constituted its first defeat after a long series of successes and its most costly battle in the Italian campaign.'

https://www.pegasusarchive.org/arnhem/batt_light_reg.htm.

'During the evening of 2 December 1943, 4 PARA (as part of the 2nd Independent Parachute Brigade) had been put under the command of the 2nd New Zealand Division, with the task of defending the Division's left flank during the advance on Orsogna.'

Di Cintio, *A Mountain to Win.*

Gessopalena was the scene of one of the most disgusting atrocities by the Nazis in Italy. On 21 January 1944 in the district of Sant'Agata, forty-two women, children and elderly were burned alive by Nazi troops. This led to many of the young people of Gessopalena establishing one of the first partisan bands, which later joined the most famous Maiella Brigade.

Mark Zuehlke, *Ortona: Canada's Epic World War II Battle*, p.289.
41. https://www.canadiansoldiers.com/history/battlehonours/italiancampaign/campobasso.htm. Wright (1947) somewhat vaguely says in his description of the 1st Canadian advance to Busso 'set out at 0330 hrs on October 19th with two six-pounder Anti-Tank guns and two three-inch mortars under command. Also in support were two Regiments of Field Artillery and one Regiment Medium Artillery.'
42. Gerald Nicholson, *Official History of the Canadian Army in the Second World War*, Volume II: *The Canadians in Italy, 1943–1945*, 1957, p.251.
43. Woollacott, pp.33–34; Truesdale, p.30.

44. Woollacott, p.48.
45. Woollacott, p.57.
46. Woollacott, pp.65–66. The city was liberated by the West Nova Scotia Regiment of the First Canadian Division which launched a night attack against the hilltop monastery that overlooks the city on 22 November, but had to withdraw after suffering heavy losses from machine-gun positions of the 3rd Battalion of the German 1st Parachute Regiment. The Canadians attacked again on 24 November supported by a heavy artillery bombardment which forced the Germans to withdraw, allowing the regiment to occupy the monastery without losses, bringing Castel di Sangro and the south bank of the Sangro River into Allied hands. Canadiansoldiers.com. and Nicholson (1957), *The Upper Sangro*, pp.284–85.
47. Woollacott, pp.63, 68–69; Truesdale, p.51.
48. The internment camp in Casoli was one of several set up by the fascists when Italy entered the Second World War. It operated from July 1940 to September 1943, with a capacity of eighty to ninety people. Jewish refugees from Germany and Austria were interned first, then 'ex-Yugoslavs'.
49. Woollacott, p.79; Truesdale, p.51.
50. SS *Ranchi* was a P&O Steam Navigation Company R-class steam ocean liner that was built in 1925 and scrapped in 1953. From 1939 to 1943 she was the Royal Navy armed merchant cruiser HMS *Ranchi*. From 1943 to 1947 she served as a troopship for the Ministry of War Transport and post-war Ministry of Transport.
51. Truesdale, p.56.
52. Woollacott, p.87.
53. Peters, p.10; Middlebrook, p.34.
54. Woollacott, p.92.
55. RAF Harwell was 17 miles north-west of Reading. In March 1944, it was reallocated to 30 Group Airborne Forces, where it operated tug aircraft towing Airspeed Horsas. Operations included carrying the first glider-borne troops into Normandy to secure vital strategic positions in advance of the main landings on D-Day, and Arnhem. The airfield was also used briefly for Special Operations Executive (SOE) operations between July and September 1944.

    RAF Down Ampney was 3 miles south-west of RAF Fairford, Gloucestershire and was one of a group of airfields involved in air transportation. No. 48 Squadron and No. 271 Squadron flew Douglas Dakotas: on D-Day they dropped the main elements of the 3rd Parachute Brigade in Normandy as well as towing Airspeed Horsa gliders across the English Channel and were active in Arnhem and the Rhine crossing. The same squadrons also flew Casevac flights to bring home wounded from B landing grounds and airfields after the D-Day landings. These flights took about eighty minutes and included RAF nurses. The local memorial reads:

FROM THIS AIRFIELD IN 1944–5 DOUGLAS DAKOTAS
FROM 48 AND 271 SQUADRONS RAF TRANSPORT
COMMAND CARRIED THE 1ST AND 6TH AIRBORNE
DIVISIONS UNITS OF THE AIR DESPATCH REGIMENT
AND HORSA GLIDERS FLOWN BY THE GLIDER PILOTS
REGIMENT TO NORMANDY – ARNHEM AND ON THE
CROSSING THE RHINE OPERATIONS
WE WILL REMEMBER THEM

RAF Broadwell was 2 miles from RAF Brize Norton: 512 Squadron and 575 Squadron were based here flying Douglas Dakotas. No. 512 arrived in February 1944 as a tactical Dakota squadron and started training glider-towing and parachute-dropping. No. 512 Squadron can claim that they were the first planes over France on D-Day as three Dakotas piloted by Flight Lieutenant Hyde, Warrant Officer James Proctor and a C Flight Flying Officer dropped a specialist team at 00.02 on 6 June to try to disrupt the Merville Battery before the main assault.

On the eve of D-Day, 575 Squadron dropped 5 Para into the invasion drop zone and on 6 June it towed twenty-one Horsa gliders into France, while in the following weeks it started a casualty evacuation service from France back to England. In September 1944 its involvement in Arnhem saw the squadron suffer severe casualties. For full details see Steve Smith's excellent article (10 August 2009) at http://www.aeroresource.co.uk/historic-reports/raf-broadwell

56. Peters, p.21.
57. Peters, p.26.
58. Peters, pp.28, 40–41.
59. Cotterell, pp.59–67.
60. Woollacott, pp.98ff.

Chapter Six
1. For example, Middlebrook (1994); Beevor (2018); Wilkinson (1999), pp.26ff.
2. The RAF was instrumental in this decision, arguing that casualties from flak would be 50 per cent higher if the drops and landings were any nearer the bridge.

    For the issues relating to the radios, see Hall, Leo J., *Signals from Arnhem Bridge*, 1996.
3. Operation VARSITY in 1945 involved more aircraft, gliders, while there were more troops on D-Day in June 1944 than in MARKET, but troops flown in on later days made MARKET GARDEN the larger operation. See MacDonald, 1963, p.132. MARKET would, as stated, be the largest airborne operation in history, delivering more than 34,600 men of the 101st, 82nd and 1st Airborne divisions and the Polish Brigade. Some 14,589

troops were landed by glider and 20,011 by parachute. Gliders also brought in 1,736 vehicles and 263 artillery pieces. Some 3,342 tons of ammunition and other supplies were brought by glider and parachute drop. See Warren, pp.226–27.
4. Wilmot (1997).
5. The ground forces designated to link up with the airborne troops would be headed by XXX Corps (2nd Household Cavalry Regiment, Guards Armoured Division, 43rd (Wessex) Division, 8th Armoured Brigade, 50th (Northumbrian) Division and Royal Netherlands Brigade ('Prinses Irene')) advancing northward up the 'Club Route', with XII Corps (7th Armoured Division, 15th (Scottish) Division and 53rd (Welsh) Division) supporting on the left and VIII Corps (11th Armoured Division, 3rd Division, 4th Armoured Brigade and 1st Belgian Brigade) lending support on the right. The Guards Armoured Division was to head XXX Corps' advance and, as it linked up with each airborne division, it would take control of them and hand off forces further south to VIII Corps. If any of the main bridges were destroyed by the Germans, the Guards would secure the riverbank and the 43rd (Wessex) Division would mount an assault crossing.
6. See Neillands, Chapter 4.
7. Woollacott, p.105.
8. For example, 'Seen by even his most staunch supporters as one of the darkest stains on his military record, the operation has come to overshadow many of Montgomery's European successes.' *Operation Market Garden: Netherlands 17–25 September 1944.* https://assets.publishing.service.gov.uk/government/uploads/system/uploads/attachment_data/file/30056/ww2_market_garden.pdf
9. Bennett (2008), pp.19–21.
10. Pogue (1954), p.281.
11. The Siegfried Line, known by the Germans as the Westwall, was a monumental German defensive line built from 1936 facing the French Maginot Line. It extended more than 390 miles from Kleve on the border with the Netherlands, along Nazi Germany's western border to Weil am Rhein on the border with Switzerland, and comprised more than 18,000 bunkers, tunnels and tank traps. After D-Day on 24 August Hitler ordered renewed construction on the Siegfried Line: 20,000 forced labourers and members of the Reichsarbeitsdienst (Reich Labour Service), mainly 14- to 16-year-old boys and local people, tried to consolidate and refortify the line for defence. It was increasingly clear that the bunkers would not withstand the newly-developed armour-piercing weapons. At the same time small concrete 'Tobruks' were built along the borders of the occupied area; these bunkers were mostly dugouts for single soldiers. See McNab (2014).

The Allies could reasonably expect the Germans to blow the bridges once they cottoned on to the Allied strategy, although Model later refused to do so in order not to compromise a German counterattack. In the event of

bridges being destroyed, XXX Corps planned to rebuild them. To this end, a vast quantity of bridging material was shipped, along with 2,300 vehicles to carry it and 9,000 engineers to assemble it. Also, *Operation Market Garden: Netherlands 17–25 September 1944*.
12. This is when Montgomery 'lost it', to use common parlance. Ryan (1975), pp.85–88, recounts how, with regard to the additional plan of a single thrust to Berlin.

    Angered by Eisenhower's reluctance, Montgomery flew to Brussels that afternoon to meet him. Montgomery demanded that Eisenhower's chief of staff leave the meeting while insisting that his own should remain. He then tore a file of Eisenhower's messages to shreds in front of him, argued for a concentrated northern thrust and demanded priority in supplies. So fierce and unrestrained was Montgomery's language that Eisenhower reached out, patted Montgomery's knee and said: 'Steady, Monty! You can't talk to me like that. I'm your boss.'
13. Hibbert (2003), pp.30–31.
14. MacDonald (1963), p.129.
15. Ellis (2004), pp.21–23.
16. http://www.historyofwar.org/articles/battles_arnhem.html
17. *Operation Market Garden: Netherlands 17–25 September 1944*. See also Baxter, *The Waffen-SS at Arnhem* for details.
18. Beevor, p.74.
19. Beevor, p.74. Buckingham, p.73; see also Middlebrook, p.77.

Chapter Seven
1. Truesdale, pp.65–66.
2. This was a newly-created unit to support the 1st Airborne who would normally expect divisional artillery to provide radio-linked artillery support, but because the 1st Air Landing Light Regiment so far had no combat experience of working with Division, No. 1 Forward was set up in June 1944. It comprised experienced volunteers from other units with parachuting experience. Along with dispatch riders, signallers and jeep drivers, they were attached to every infantry battalion, every brigade, at Divisional HQ, at XXX Corps and at each of the three supporting regiments of the ground forces so that artillery support could be given to every unit in the 1st Airborne as soon as they came within range.

    Other divisional units included:

    21st Independent Parachute Company, Army Air Corps (the Pathfinders for the division).

    1st Airborne Reconnaissance Squadron (the 'eyes' of the division, equipped with unarmoured jeeps with a single Vickers K machine gun) and motorcycles, two 3in mortars and two 20mm Polsten cannons.

    9th (Airborne) Field Company, Royal Engineers; 261st (Airborne) Field Park Company, Royal Engineers; 591st (Antrim) Airborne Squadron,

Royal Engineers (from 1 June 1945); 250th (Airborne) Light Company, Royal Army Service Corps; 93rd Company, Royal Army Service Corps; Detachment, Ordnance Field Park; Detachment, Royal Electrical and Mechanical Engineers Workshop 89th Field Security Section, Intelligence Corps; sixty-one men of the 1st Airborne Division, Provost Company, Royal Military Police.

Medical support came courtesy of the 16th and 133 Parachute Field Ambulance and 181 Air Landing Field Ambulance, totalling 600 medics. See Cole, 1963, pp.109–110.

The 1st Polish Independent Parachute Brigade Group comprised three battalions of infantry, an anti-tank battery, a light artillery battery, medical, engineers, signals and transport companies; just over 1,600 men in total. See Truesdale, p.66.

Signals for the 1st Air Landing Light Regiment were provided by E Section, No. 2 Company, Royal Signals attached to Regimental HQ providing communications with the rest of the division and XXX Corps. Truesdale (p.67) emphasizes the difference between signallers and signalmen: the former were gunners who operated the local wireless network within the regiment, while signalmen were members of the Royal Signals who did everything else relating to communications.

Chapter Eight

1. For Loder-Symonds' distinguished RA career, see Truesdale, pp.61–62.
2. Truesdale, pp.62–63.

The Norfolk Tank Museum (at Forncett St Peter, NR16 1HZ, approximately 10 miles from Diss and 12 miles south of Norwich) tells us all about sabot rounds: http://norfolktankmuseum.co.uk/types-of-ammunition/: *APDS (Armour-Piercing Discarding Sabot)*:

> 'The British army was the first to use APDS rounds, introducing them in 1944 for use in the quick-firing 6-pound and later 17-pound anti-tank gun. Armour-piercing discarding sabot (APDS) is a type of kinetic energy projectile fired from a gun to attack armoured targets.
>
> The need to be able to penetrate the thicker armour that was continually being developed was needed, and one way to achieve this was to increase the impact velocity of the warhead. With the development of materials science and the resulting discovery of much stronger and denser materials (up to twice the density of currently available steels), achieved with the introduction of tungsten, greater hardness and shock resistance were created and when these properties were combined with the higher muzzle velocities provided by the new propellant explosives that were being developed, a significant improvement in penetration properties was achieved.'

See also Truesdale, Appendix C: Guns, Ammunition and Training.

Chapter Nine

1. See https://www.pegasusarchive.org/arnhem/dennis_munford.htm
2. Gunner Bowles was awarded the Military Medal in March 1944, *London Gazette*, 9 March 1944.
3. Middlebrook, pp.70–71.
4. Woollacott, pp.106–107. Jock Lawson was killed on 22 September in E Troop Command Post.
5. Woollacott, p.106; Truesdale, pp.72–73.
6. Woollacott, p.107.
7. Truesdale, pp.70–71.
8. Map reference 7177 or Oosterbeek Railway Station Laag. See Wilkinson, p.31.
9. Truesdale, p.73.

Chapter Eleven

1. Truesdale, p.74.
2. Woollacott, p.110; Wilkinson, p.37.
3. Truesdale, pp.74–75; Woollacott, p.111; Wilkinson, pp.37, 39.
4. For more on Leahy and other evaders who occupied Boxtel 24 October, see Woollacott, Appendix 4.
5. Woollacott, p.111; Truesdale, pp.77–78. The Horsa carrying Sergeant Thain and Lance Sergeant Gibson along with their jeep and trailer carrying sixty rounds of ammunition made a forced landing in England due to a faulty tow-rope; they made it to the Netherlands the following day. See Wilkinson, p.37. For Munford, see Buckingham, p.80 and Ryan, pp.180–81.
6. The irony of war: Martin Middlebrook (p.88) points out how

   'The death of the lieutenant, Ralph Maltby, had an ironic twist. He had become a glider pilot after serving in the Royal Artillery and was an expert on anti-aircraft fire. Earlier in the war he had flown as a passenger on RAF bomber operations to observe the effects of the German defences and had been decorated with the 'Order of the Patriotic War' by the Russians for some raid which had benefited them. He had often lectured glider pilots on flak, stressing that it was "nothing to worry about".'

7. The Rebecca/Eureka transponding radar was a short-range radio navigation system used to facilitate the dropping of airborne forces and their equipment as well as supplies for partisans supported by the SOE. It consisted of two parts: the Rebecca airborne transceiver and antenna system, and the Eureka ground-based transponder. Rebecca calculated the range to the Eureka based on the timing of the return signals, and its relative position using a highly directional antenna. Rebecca comprises a high-power transmitter radiating from the nose of the aircraft and a receiver and display for use by the navigator. The 'Rebecca' name derives from the phrase 'Recognition of

beacons'. The 'Eureka' name comes from the ancient Greek word εὕρηκα meaning 'I have found it!' The Airborne Forces Equipment Committee took over development of the system in 1942, funding low-priority development of a Mark II system intended for use on glider tugs and paratroop aircraft. It was decided that each Eureka should be able to handle interrogation from up to forty aircraft at a time.

8. Bennett (2007), p.42. For the fascinating story of the deployment of carrier pigeons in military history, see Chrystal, *Biological Warfare* (2023). See also *Arnhem 1944 Veteran's Club Newsletter*, June 1990: Roger King, *Pigeons: The Winged Messengers from Arnhem*.
9. Truesdale, p.75.
10. Woollacott, pp.112–14.
11. Woollacott, pp.112, 115.
12. Woollacott, p.115 and Appendix III. Harry's account is lodged with the Airborne Museum in Oosterbeek. See also Truesdale, pp.76–77, 78.
13. Woollacott, pp.115–16.
14. Woollacott, p.116; Truesdale, pp.76, 77, 78. Hall (p.15) refutes Harrison's version (in a transcript of handwritten notes with other officers) of who was in the parachute party: i.e. Harrison, Hall and Gunners Perkins, Morrison and Chubb. Harrison's version was written after the return to Boston, October-November 1944.
15. Truesdale, pp.78–79. Dags were batteries, named after the factory in Dagenham where they were made.
16. Private correspondence, September 1987, Eric Chrystal to Colonel P.R.R. de Burgh (1923–2010), then Badley Library, The Royal School of Artillery, Larkhill but in 1944 at Arnhem Staff Lieutenant, HQ RA, 1st Airborne Division to Lieutenant Colonel R.G. Loder-Symonds. Private correspondence with Bob Woollacott, 1992.
17. Truesdale, pp.75–76.
18. Thompson, *Daily Telegraph*, 18 September 1974.
19. The *Nebelwerfer* (smoke mortar) was initially developed by and assigned to the Wehrmacht's 'smoke troops' (*Nebeltruppen*). It was named thus as a disinformation strategy designed to fool observers from the League of Nations, who were looking for any infractions of the Treaty of Versailles, into thinking that it was merely a device for creating a smokescreen. They were primarily intended to deliver poison gas and smoke shells, although a high-explosive shell was developed for the *Nebelwerfer* from the start.

    See also the F Troop 3 Battery report written by TSM Major Kent (?) for battery records.
20. Woollacott, p.117; Truesdale, p.84.
21. Truesdale, p.80.
22. Ibid.
23. Truesdale, p.81; see http://www.historyofwar.org/articles/battles_arnhem.html

24. Woollacott, pp.118–19.
25. Woollacott, p.118.
26. Woollacott, p.119.
27. Beevor, pp.126–31.
28. See https://www.paradata.org.uk/people/j-leo-hall
29. NA WO219/5137, Part II (note 5), Appendix E.
30. NA WO219/5137 (note 5).
31. Nalder, *Signals*, (note 6), p.205.
32. Beevor (p.129) adds that some sets were issued with the wrong crystals. See Greenacre, pp.283–84.
33. Greenacre, pp.283–284. Greenacre tells us how

> 'This article will examine if it is possible to objectively assess if poor radio equipment alone was responsible for communication failures at Arnhem. If an objective assessment can be made and the equipment is found to have been theoretically capable of the tasks it was set then other possible reasons for failure will be explored. A modern signal communications prediction software model is used to assist this objective assessment. Focus is placed upon communication links between 1st British Airborne Division Headquarters, its subordinate brigades and battalions and between the divisional artillery headquarters and sub-units. All the links studied are high-frequency (HF) band sky wave communications. The purpose of this piece is not to retrospectively lay the blame at any one door but rather to assess how risks taken in communications planning impact on operations during their execution.'

34. Much of this was contributed by Roger King in 1995 and can be found in Ministry No. 49 in the Hartenstein Library.
    Operation JEDBURGH was a clandestine Second World War operation in which three-man teams of soldiers of the British Special Operations Executive (SOE), the US Office of Strategic Services (OSS), the Free French *Bureau Central de Renseignements et d'Action* and the Dutch and Belgian armies in exile were dropped by parachute into occupied France, the Netherlands and Belgium. The name was chosen at random from a Ministry of Defence code book. The idea was that small groups of military personnel would be embedded by parachute inside territory occupied by Nazi Germany to assist local Resistance forces and to carry out military operations. Unlike SOE agents, the JEDBURGH teams would be armed and uniformed military personnel. Fluency in the language of the European country where they would operate was required, although the language requirement was relaxed for radio-operators. The 'Jeds' were all volunteers. As well as their personal weapons which included an M1 carbine and a Colt automatic pistol and sabotage equipment, the teams dropped with the Type B Mark II radio, the B2 or 'Jed Set', critical for communicating with Special

Forces Headquarters in London. They were also issued pieces of silk with 500 phrases that they were likely to use in radio traffic replaced with four-letter codes to save time in transmission and one-time pads to encipher their messages. Each officer wore a money belt containing 100,000 francs (or the equivalent in the country they were dropping into), equivalent to £500 or US $2,500) and $50. Radio-operators carried only 50,000 francs. The money was to distribute to Resistance fighters, many of whom had families to support. Equipment and supplies were air-dropped with the Jeds.

Dennis Munford recalls Harvey Todd: 'He joined me in the OP with his Springfield automatic carbine and let me have a bang. I was green with envy.' (In *Resistance, Civil Affairs and Counter-Intelligence Instructions* held at the Public Record Office in the Divisional RE Diary (WO171/397).)

35. Truesdale, pp.82–83. For the team in the jeep see Fairley, pp.73–74 and the Regimental War Diary: WO166/14933 entry for 23.30, 17/09/44.
36. Hall, *Signals from Arnhem Bridge* (p.16) points out that Golden, *Echoes from Arnhem*, 1984, perpetuates this 'error' on p.154. Hall also cites testimony (unreferenced on p.16) from Lance Bombardier J.W. Crook, Munford's driver: 'Neither Major Munford, Dennis Bowles or myself left the Bridge for Oosterbeek at any time.' Hall says that 'they had suffered some enemy Tiger route damage in the afternoon to jeep and trailer, and possibly to the 22 set. They returned to the Battery for repairs, then set off once more for the Bridge, this time along the Lion route.' Mike Dauncy (then a lieutenant glider pilot in G Squadron), in his Foreword to Peter Wilkinson's *Gunners at Arnhem* (p.10) says that Munford 'returned by jeep to the gun positions and then went back to the bridge a second time – an extremely hazardous journey' to recharge his wireless batteries.
37. Greenacre, p.283.
38. Woollacott, pp.118–19; Truesdale, pp.83–84, 85; Buckingham, p.130.
39. Hall: 'Registration involves the use of one gun to drop one or two HE shells on targets judged to be of importance to the enemy, e.g. a crossroad. Once the range etc. has been adjusted using the single gun, an order would be sent – as was done for the Southern approach to the Bridge – "Record as Target Mike One". This order would ensure that the gun data would be ready to direct the fire of all 24 guns in the Regiment (with adjustments) on the Southern approach to the Bridge with the minimum delay, when the order "Target Mike One, one round gun fire, fire" was given (i.e. one round from each of the 24 guns).... But Mike Targets are expensive on ammunition that had to be dropped from supply aircraft – a single shell weighing 15 pounds, plus the weight of the propellant and brass case. Normally an officer would call for a Troop Target (4 guns) or Battery Target (8 guns). To call for a Mike is a serious matter and must be justified, one round from each of 24 guns using half a ton of a Dakota payload.'
40. Regimental War Diary: WO166/14933 entry for 23.30, 17/09/44 and in Buckingham, p.163.

41. Truesdale, p.84.
42. Middlebrook, pp.55, 57; Bennett (2007), p.41. Bennett tells us 'The Dutch were able to utilize three phone networks: the national Ryks Telefoon system; the Gelderland Provincial Electricity Board (Dutch acronym PGEM) private network with its head office in Nijmegen; and a clandestine network operated by Resistance technicians whereby they could call many places in the Netherlands without going through an operator.' Despite the order not to destroy local telecommunications facilities, on D+3 the British blew up the Post Office Exchange in Oosterbeek and the Germans reoccupied the Arnhem exchanges.
43. Urquhart, *Arnhem*, p.47.
44. NA WO219/5137.
45. Letter, 3 December 2003, sent by Major (Retd) P. Wilkinson MC, Command Post Officer, 3 Battery, Light Regiment RA to Greenacre. Greenacre describes the effect of fierce enemy opposition and problems of resupply on the communications problems:

> 'The most obvious effect of enemy action was the physical loss of valuable, highly trained signallers. By the end of the battle of the 348 men of the Divisional Signals Regiment that flew into Arnhem, 28 were dead and 171 were missing, a casualty rate of more than 50 per cent. These losses could be ill afforded as the order of battle had been scaled down to a minimum so as to save aircraft. In addition "experience showed that reserve detachments must be provided on a lavish scale to allow for initial casualties", reserves that at Arnhem simply were not available. The communication plan was bound to suffer.
>
> The attrition of signallers was not the only consequence of the unexpectedly fierce enemy opposition to impact on signals communication. As well as soldiers, equipment was also bound to suffer. "A mortar bomb had landed in the attic during the day and… it had burst amongst the signaller's wireless sets." Resupply of vital signals equipment was essential. Equipment was dropped by air throughout the battle including 6 No. 76 radio sets, 17 No. 68P sets and 29 No. 22 sets. However, the same enemy attention that was causing the attrition of equipment was also making movement in order to collect dropped stores very difficult, those that is which did not fall directly into enemy hands. In fact the divisional logistic personnel only managed to collect 7.4 per cent of the total 106 tons of stores dropped in and around Arnhem. Again, as radio sets failed or were destroyed communications were eroded.'

46. Berry, *Communications*, p.8.
47. Letter, 2 December 2003, sent by Major General (Retd) A. Deane-Drummond CB DSO MC, second-in-command of the Divisional Signals Regiment to Greenacre.

Chapter Twelve

1. E. Mackay, *Whoa Mahomet. De strijd om de Rijnbrug*, Aalten, 1947, p.12.
2. Ibid, p.14.
3. Ibid, p.15.
4. D.G. van Buggenum, *B Company Arrived: The Story of B Company of the 2nd Parachute Battalion at Arnhem, September 1944*, Renkum, 2003, pp.89–95.
5. Wright, Draft Account 3rd Parachute Battalion, 'C' Company, p.16.
6. Telephone conversation between Frank van Lunteren and Private Sid G. Blackmore, veteran of 'A' Company, 2nd Parachute Battalion, Monday, 7 May 2007.
7. Telephone conversation between Frank van Lunteren and sapper Robert Hepburn, veteran of B Troop, 1st Parachute Squadron, RE, Wednesday, 9 May 2007.
8. Zwarts, *SS-Panzer-Aufklärungs-Abteilung 9 en de Arnhemse verkeersbrug*, p.11.
9. Ibid, p.10.
10. Mackay, *Whoa Mahomet. De strijd om de Rijnbrug*, p.18.
11. Truesdale, pp.85–86.
12. Truesdale, p.86; Woollacott, pp.120–21.
13. Woollacott, p.120; Truesdale, p.86.
14. Woollacott, p.119.
15. Truesdale, p.87; Woollacott, p.120. Watkins, pp.18–19; Beevor, p.137. See also Wilkinson, p.57.
16. *By Air to Battle*, p.103.
17. Beevor, p.137. Dauncy, in Wilkinson, p.10.
18. Beevor, p.147.
19. Truesdale, p.88.
20. Beevor, pp.147–48.
21. Truesdale, p.89; Buckingham, p.183; Wilkinson, p.64.
22. Truesdale, p.89; Woollacott, p.123.
23. Truesdale, p.90.
24. Truesdale, p.90; Woollacott, pp.123–24.
25. Truesdale, pp.90–91.
26. Truesdale, pp.91–92; Woollacott, pp.124–25; Wilkinson, p.65.
27. Truesdale, p.92. Glider pilot Ron Watkinson says it was Gunner Tyson who was shot.
28. Wilkinson, p.64.
29. Ibid.
30. Truesdale, p.93; Woollacott, p.122.
31. Buckingham, pp.185–86.
32. Woollacott, p.125.
33. Woollacott, p.126.

Chapter Thirteen
1. Chrystal, Eric, Unpublished correspondence with Colonel P.R.R. de Burgh, 1987; Bird: Woollacott, p.130.
2. Truesdale, p.93; Woollacott, p.127; F Troop 3 Battery report, TM Kent (?).
3. Beevor, p.172ff. Beevor also writes of a melodramatic scene from hell on the battlefield (p.174) contributed by 'a Parachute regiment lieutenant identifiable only as "David"… while in hiding after the battle.' Beevor offers no reference to his sources.
4. Truesdale, pp.93–94; Woollacott, pp.127–28. The term sangar derives from the days of the North-West Frontier of India and denotes a small temporary fortification from the Hindi and Pashto words for stone.
5. Truesdale, pp.94–95.
6. See Truesdale, p.95 and https://www.pegasusarchive.org/arnhem/Leo_Hall.htm
7. https://www.pegasusarchive.org/arnhem/dennis_munford.htm. Inevitably, Munford had his critics: see Hall, *Signals from Arnhem Bridge*.
8. https://www.pegasusarchive.org/arnhem/Leo_Hall.htm and Truesdale, p.95.
9. Truesdale, p.96; Woollacott, p.129.
10. Truesdale, p.97.
11. Truesdale, p.97; Woollacott, p.130.
12. Truesdale, pp.97–98; Woollacott, p.131.
13. Truesdale, p.98; Woollacott, pp.132–33.
14. Truesdale, p.99; Beevor, pp.233–34; Wilkinson, pp.79–80; Buckingham, pp.255, 257.
15. Truesdale, p.100.
16. Ibid.
17. See Woollacott, pp.134–35 for his incredulity at this diary entry: 'One wonders if they were part of the same battle!' The diary does mention, however, 'Local inhabitants provided a pot of first-rate vegetable mash for dinner' and an old man who was 'worried about damage to plants by soldiers'.
18. Truesdale, p.100; Wilkinson, p.77. The Tigers would have been stationed at what later became Barker Barracks in Paderborn. Gunner Eric Chrystal was stationed there between 1964 and 1969 with 24 Missile Regiment RA. See Chrystal, *BAOR* (2018).

Chapter Fourteen
1. Truesdale, p.101.
2. Truesdale, pp.104–105; Woollacott, p.136.
3. Truesdale, p.105; Woollacott repeats this inaccuracy, pp.136–37.
4. Truesdale, p.105.
5. Truesdale, p.106.
6. Truesdale, p.107.
7. Truesdale, pp.107–108; Woollacott, p.138.

8. Hall, *Signals from Arnhem Bridge*; Truesdale, p.109.
9. Hall, *Signals from Arnhem Bridge*; Woollacott, p.138.
10. Not recorded in *Signals from Arnhem Bridge*.
11. Truesdale, pp.108–109; see also https://www.paradata.org.uk/people/j-leo-hall
12. Truesdale, p.108.
13. Truesdale, p.109.
14. Ibid.
15. Unpublished correspondence between Gunner Eric Chrystal and Colonel P.R.R. de Burgh, 1987.
16. Truesdale, pp.109–10.
17. *By Air to Battle*, pp.116–17.
18. Middlebrook, pp.310–311. Middlebrook points out that the Germans were intent on blowing the archway over the road nearest the river (easily bridgeable later), and *not* the bridge itself.
19. Truesdale, p.110. An account by Jack Briggs (Woollacott, pp.139–40) says that all three were killed.
20. Truesdale, p.110.
21. Cole, pp.117–24.
22. Middlebrook, pp.318–20.
23. Middlebrook, p.321.
24. Middlebrook, p.325.
25. See Middlebrook, pp.325ff for details.

Chapter Fifteen
1. Beevor, p.274; Wilkinson, pp.96–97.
2. Horst house Truesdale, p.111.
3. Woollacott, p.146.
4. Truesdale, pp.111–12; Woollacott, p.146; Wilkinson, p.106.
5. Woollacott, p.145; Wilkinson, p.102.
6. Beevor, p.270.
7. Truesdale, pp.114–16; Woollacott, pp.152–53; Hibbert, *Battle of Arnhem*, p.171; Buckingham, pp.373–74; Wilkinson, pp.103–104. See also Chris van Roekel, *Mini Story II*: 'German Tank on the Beneden-Weverstraat' for details. Major Cain, in a post-war account now in the Airborne Forces Museum (File No. 54), says of the incident 'and I was blind. I was shouting like a hooligan…I blubbered and yelled…they dragged me off to the Aid Post.'
8. Wilkinson, p.131.
9. Truesdale, pp.116–17; Wilkinson, p.105.
10. Buckingham, p.74.
11. See Wilkinson, p.104 for Barrett's citation.
12. Truesdale, pp.117–18.
13. Wilkinson, p.102.

Chapter Sixteen
1. Wilkinson, p.109.
2. Truesdale, p.120; Woollacott, p.155.
3. Woollacott, p.155; Wilkinson, p.110.
4. Woollacott (p.158) writes that it was Pepys Moore's testimony. Wilkinson (p.111) writes that Lieutenant Pearson accompanied Moore.

Chapter Seventeen
1. Quoted in Wilkinson, pp.119–20. Kate ter Horst, *Cloud over Arnhem*, p.54.
2. Truesdale, p.126; Woollacott, pp.165–66.

Chapter Eighteen
1. Ryan, p.491.
2. Private correspondence September 1987, Eric Chrystal to Colonel P.R.R. de Burgh (1923–2010), then Badley Library, The Royal School of Artillery, Larkhill but in 1944 at Arnhem Staff Lieutenant, HQ RA, 1st Airborne Division to Lieutenant Colonel R.G. Loder-Symonds. Christie: Wilkinson, pp.120–21. Woollacott, pp.172, 177.
3. Woollacott, p.171; Truesdale, pp.128–29; Wilkinson, p.121.
4. Woollacott, pp.171–72.
5. Truesdale, pp.130–31.
6. Truesdale, p.130; Woollacott, p.173.
7. Ryan, p.506.
8. Truesdale, p.131.
9. Truesdale, p.133.
10. Truesdale, pp.141–43.
11. Truesdale, p.133.

Chapter Nineteen
1. Truesdale, p.137.
2. Ibid; Wilkinson, pp.137–38.
3. Truesdale, p.50: the testimony of TSM Tom Kent, F Troop; Woollacott, p.191.

Chapter Twenty
1. Woollacott, p.192.
2. Truesdale, p.144.
3. Lance Bombardier Parkes served with the 1st Air Landing Light Regiment in North Africa and during their action in Italy. At Arnhem, he was assistant to the Gun Position Officer of 'C' Troop, Lieutenant Adrian Donaldson. This is taken from his account of Operation MARKET GARDEN. [https://www.pegasusarchive.org/arnhem/percy_parkes.htm] An ambulance gave him a lift to Nijmegen where he crossed the bridge, under shellfire, before going on to a hospital where he spent the next two days asleep on a floor. An

ambulance then moved him to Borg Leopold, then to Diest, Brussels, and via an ambulance train to Amiens. He left Amiens of his own volition and hitch-hiked his way to the Mulberry Harbour at Arromanches, Normandy. He got aboard a ship bound for Southampton, where he caught a train back to Regimental Headquarters at Boston, Lincolnshire; here he was given sixteen days' leave, a new uniform and £20 in cash. Lance Bombardier Parkes later joined the Derbyshire Constabulary.
4. *Arnhem Assault: A Story of the First Airborne Division by a Member of the Derbyshire Constabulary who took part.*
5. Truesdale, p.146; Woollacott, p.193; Wilkinson, pp.141–42.
6. Wilkinson, p.143.
7. Truesdale, p.151; Woollacott, pp.199–200.
8. Woollacott, p.195.
9. Truesdale, pp.152–53.
10. Wilkinson, pp.143–44.
11. http://www.historyofwar.org/articles/battles_arnhem.html

Chapter Twenty-One
1. See https://www.veterans.gc.ca/eng/remembrance/wars-and-conflicts/second-world-war/battle-of-the-scheldt; Major Michael Paul Williams, The Rough Road To Antwerp https://apps.dtic.mil/sti/pdfs/ADA612127.pdf; https://definingmomentscanada.ca/veday75/historical-articles/battle-scheldt/ and others.

Chapter Twenty-Two
1. Limburg, Germany. District: Wehrkreis XII – Wiesbaden. East of Koblenz and north-west of Frankfurt.
2. In his letter of 2 September 1989 to Eric Chrystal. The Forces War Records [https://www.forces-war-records.co.uk/european-camps-british-common wealth-prisoners-of-war-1939-45] listing for Limburg unintelligibly reads 'Stalag XII-A to IX-B Limburg An Der Lahn Hessen-Nassau, Prussia Location N/E 50–08. Housed 42202 PoWs with 27 officers, 271 British.' Pegasus Archive posits 'upwards of 20,000 would be a likely figure'.
3. Megargee, p.1953. Wolfgang Vogt; trans. Kathleen Luft. Wetzlar is to the north-east of Limburg.
4. https://www.pegasusarchive.org/PoWPoW/cSt_12A_History1.htm
5. Pegasus Archive records the memories of a number of Arnhem survivors who passed through Limburg on their way to other Stalags. They are as follows:

- Lance Corporal John James Bird, No. 1 Medium Machine-Gun Platoon, 2nd South Staffordshires; 1st Air Landing Brigade. Camps: Stalag XII-A, Stalag VIII-C, Stalag IX-B https://www.pegasusarchive.org/PoWPoW/jack_bird.htm

Notes   255

- Sergeant Ron A.D. Garnham, 'A' Squadron, No. 1 Wing, The Glider Pilot Regiment. Camps: Stalag XII-A, IV-B https://www.pegasusarchive.org/PoWPoW/ron_garnham.htm
- Private William George Gibbard, Mortar Platoon, Support Company, 2nd Parachute Battalion, 1st Airborne Division. Camps: Stalag IV-?, XII-A https://www.pegasusarchive.org/PoWPoW/bill_gibbard.htm
- Lance Sergeant Harold Padfield, B Troop, 1st Parachute Squadron, RE; 1st Airborne Division. Camps: Stalag XII-A, XVIII-C https://www.pegasusarchive.org/PoWPoW/harold_padfield.htm
- Sergeant Douglas Smithson, No. 10 Flight, G Squadron, No. 1 Wing, The Glider Pilot Regiment. Camps: Stalag XII-A, Stalag Luft VII, Stalag III-A. https://www.pegasusarchive.org/PoWPoW/douglas_smithson.htm

6. https://en.wikipedia.org/wiki/Flossenb%C3%BCrg_concentration_camp#Subcamps; Fritz, Ulrich (2009). 'Flossenbürg Subcamp System' in Megargee, Geoffrey P. (ed.), *Encyclopedia of Camps and Ghettos: 1933–1945*, Vol. 1, translated by Pallavicini, Stephen. Bloomington, pp.567–69. Fritz, Ulrich (2009). Flossenbürg Concentration Camp 1938–1945: Catalogue of the Permanent Exhibition. Göttingen: Wallstein; https://encyclopedia.ushmm.org/content/en/article/flossenbuerg

Chapter Twenty-Three
1. Post-traumatic stress disorder was finally officially recognized as a real disorder in 1980 when it was listed in the third edition of the *Diagnostic and Statistical Manual of Mental Disorders (DSM-lll)*.
2. Indeed, some authors, including those with some celebrity, interpolate within their texts events that clearly did not take place, or that happened but in a different place at a different time. This sensationalism is often recognizable by the absence of references in what is otherwise a text heavy-booted with references and evidence. The same disingenuous writing and editing is even more apparent in recent best-selling books on the Holocaust.
3. Patients can experience memory loss, especially in regard to the traumatic event. More seriously, hopelessness about themselves and their future, difficulty in maintaining relationships and a struggle in experiencing positive emotions can recur.
4. https://www.nationalww2museum.org/war/articles/wwii-post-traumatic-stress
5. Crocq, M.A. and Crocq, L. (2000), 'From shell shock and war neurosis to post-traumatic stress disorder: a history of psychotraumatology', *Dialogues in Clinical Neuroscience*, 2 (1): pp.47–55.
6. Friedman, Matthew J. et al, *Psychiatric Clinics of North America: Post-Traumatic Stress Disorder*, 17 (2): pp.265–77.
7. https://www.bbc.co.uk/news/stories-48528841 Engelbrecht, A., Burdett, H., Silva, M.J., Bhui, K., Jones, E. (2018): 'The symptomatology of psychological

trauma in the aftermath of war (1945–1980): UK army veterans, civilians and emergency responders', *Psychological Medicine*, 1–8.
8. Symptoms of avoidance behaviour include avoiding thoughts and conversations relating to the event, as well as people, places or other things that recall memories of what happened. A government spokeswoman said: 'We take the wellbeing of our personnel extremely seriously and we fund research so we can continue to improve the way we support them. Military personnel receive stress management training before, during and after operational deployments, and consultant psychiatrists are available by phone 24/7 should individuals require support. We encourage anyone struggling to come forward and seek help, including through our two 24-hour help lines, and veterans can access specialist medical care through the NHS.' See Foa, E.B. et al., 'The expert consensus guideline series: Treatment of post-traumatic stress disorder', *Journal of Clinical Psychiatry*, 60, 3–76, 1999.
9. Charities devoted to helping patients include Combat Stress https://combatstress.org.uk/#:~:text=Combat%20Stress%20provides%20a%20range,and%20via%20phone%20and%20online
10. See Kenneth Lesley-Dixon, *Northern Ireland: The Troubles From The Provos to The Det, 1968–1998*, Barnsley, 2018.
11. 'Mental health outcomes at the end of the British involvement in the Iraq and Afghanistan conflicts: a cohort study' Stevelink et al, *British Journal of Psychiatry*, DOI: 10.1192/bjp.2018.175.
12. Michael Fass, *The Railway Man: Next Stop PTSD*, 'A Review of The Railway Man' (2013) by Jonathan Teplinzky (Director), *PsycCRITIQUES* 2 February 2015, Vol. 60, No. 5, Article 10 © 2015 American Psychological Association; https://www.apa.org/pubs/highlights/psyccritiques-spotlight/PSQ_a0038592.pdf
13. In his valuable *Beyond a Bridge Too Far* which relies not just on Ryan, *A Bridge Too Far* and the Arnhem discussion in Lou de Jong's *The Kingdom of the Netherlands During World War II*, Amsterdam, 1969–1991 Vol. 10A-1, 1980, but also on 'a range of contemporary eye witness reports'. He adds: 'We have an important source for Arnhem's deconstruction and rebuilding in the findings of local historians.' What follows here owes much to Salverda's article. He gives numerous references in German and Dutch (mainly first-hand eye-witness accounts) which have provided the basis for his article. I have not included them here, but they are of course available at https://www.jstor.org/stable/pdf/j.ctt1g69z77.10.pdf?refreqid=excelsior%3A3c041f0225afcd8ce26dbc16e90f2385&ab_segments=&origin=&acceptTC=1, and https://www.jstor.org/stable/j.ctt1g69z77.15?seq=3
14. Rauter had been active, with his troops, in Arnhem during the battle. Earlier in the year he had moved from Wassenaar, with his family, to a villa in Arnhem. When his new address was published in June 1944 by the underground newspaper *Trouw*, Rauter retaliated with the summary trial

and execution, on 9 and 19 August 1944, of twenty-three men who were in prison for distributing *Trouw* (see *Trouw*, 9 August 2014).
15. Compare with the German fire-bombing of Rotterdam in May 1940 when 900 civilians and 185 Dutch soldiers were killed and 80,000 people were displaced and lost everything.
16. Wilkinson, p.154.
17. Ter Horst, Kate, *Cloud over Arnhem*, p.15.
18. See Wilkinson, pp.151–54, 155–57.
19. Kamphuis, *Operation Market Garden*, 176. 'In Arnhem today, German participation in the airborne commemorations, although accepted, is still a sensitive issue.' In 1989, at an Anglo-Dutch University College London conference only two 'good' Germans were allowed to take part, namely London-based diplomat Count Von Stauffenberg and Dr Gerhard Hirschfeld, a German historian then working in Britain. Cf. Gerhard Hirschfeld, Nazi Rule and Dutch Collaboration: *The Netherlands under German Occupation, 1940–1945* (Oxford, Berg, 1988) and Foot, *Holland at War against Hitler*. In Arnhem in 1990, great commotion ensued when Mayor Scholten wanted to allow Germans to take part in the airborne commemorations. Unlike in Coventry, the people of Arnhem were not prepared to accept even a 'good' German like President Richard von Weizsäcker, and it was not until September 2009 that the ambassadors of Austria and Germany were allowed, for the first time, to lay a wreath at the airborne monument in Arnhem.
20. Henri A. Van der Zee, *The Hunger Winter: Occupied Holland, 1944–1945*, Lincoln, NE: Bison Books, 1982, p.305.

Bibliography

Primary Sources

The 1st Air Landing Light Regiment: Regimental History 1941–1945 (Aldershot, no date)

'Bridging and rafting to Arnhem', *Military Review*, Vol. 25, No. 7, October 1945, pp.123–27.

'Market Garden airlift and resupply: 25 years since Arnhem', *Air Clues*, Vol. 24, No. 3, December 1969, pp.98–99.

'Pegasus and the Wyvern: the evacuation of the 1st Airborne Division from Arnhem', *Royal Engineers Journal*, March 1946, pp.22–25.

Aalders, Gerard, *Nazi Looting: The Plunder of Dutch Jewry During the Second World War* (Utrecht, 2004)

Allen, Simon, *The Effect of Communications on the Battle of Arnhem* (Unpublished paper, circa 1978)

Altes, A. Korthals, *September 1944: Operation Market Garden* (Weesp, Fibula-Van Dishoeck, 1984)

American Psychiatric Association, *Diagnostic and statistical manual of mental disorders: DSM-5* (Washington, DC, 2013)

Andidora, Ronald, *Home by Christmas: The Illusion of Victory in 1944* (Westport, CT, Greenwood Press, 2002)

Angus, Tom (alias of Geoffrey Powell), *Men at Arnhem* (London, Leo Cooper, 1976)

Antill, Peter, *Operation Market Garden: 17–27 September 1944* http://www.historyofwar.org/articles/battles_arnhem.html (2001)

Arnhem 1944 Veterans' Club Newsletter, November 1996. Obituary: Captain Anthony Harrison MC, p.10.

Arthur, Max, *Men of the Red Beret: Airborne Forces 1940–1990* (London, Hutchinson, 1990)

Ashe Lincoln, F., *Secret Naval Investigator* (London, 2017)

Atkinson, Rick, *The Day of Battle: The War in Sicily and Italy 1943–1944* (London, 2007)

Bacon, Donald J., *Second World War Deception: Lessons Learned for Today's Joint Planner* (pdf) (Montgomery, Alabama, Air University Press, 1998), pp.3–4.

Badsey, Stephen, *Arnhem 1944* in Guard, Julie (ed.), *Airborne: World War II Paratroopers in Combat* (Botley, Osprey, 2007)

Bauer, Cornelis and Boeree, Lt. Col. Theodoor A., *The Battle of Arnhem: The Betrayal Myth Refuted* (London, Hodder & Stoughton, 1966)

Baxter, Ian, *The Waffen-SS at Arnhem* (Barnsley, 2022)

Baynes, John, *Urquhart of Arnhem: The Life of Major General R.E. Urquhart, CB, DSO* (London, Brassey's, 1993)

Beevor, Antony, *Arnhem: The Battle for the Bridges 1944* (London, 2018)

Bennett, David, 'Airborne Communications in Operation Market Garden', *Canadian Military History* 16, Issue 1, 2007.

Bennett, David, *A Magnificent Disaster: The Failure of Market Garden, the Arnhem Operation, September 1944* (Newbury, Casemate, 2008)

Berry, John, *Communications at the Battle of Arnhem: A Modern-Day Technical Analysis*, Unpublished Report: ATDI, 2003.

Bidwell, Shelford, *Gunners at War: A Tactical Study of the Royal Artillery in the Twentieth Century* (London, 1970)

Bjorge, Dr Gary J., 'Operation Market Garden, September 1944' in Spiller, Roger J. (ed.), *Combined Arms in Battle since 1939* (Fort Leavenworth, KS, US Army Command and General Staff College Press, 1992)

Blair, Clay, *Ridgway's Paratroopers: The American Airborne in World War II* (Annapolis, MD, Naval Institute Press, 1985)

Blandford, Edmund L., *Green Devils, Red Devils: Untold Tales of the Airborne Forces in the Second World War* (London, Leo Cooper, 1993)

Blockwell, Albert, *Diary of a Red Devil: By Glider to Arnhem with the 7th King's Own Scottish Borderers* (Solihull, Helion, 2005)

Bookman, John T., *The March to Victory: A Guide to World War II Battles and Battlefields from London to the Rhine* (New York, Harper & Row, 1986)

Bradbeer, Thomas G., 'Gunners at Arnhem', *World War II Magazine*, October 2007 https://www.historynet.com/gunners-at-arnhem.htm

Bradley, Lt. Col. Philip G., *Market Garden: Was Intelligence Responsible for the Failure?* (Maxwell Air Force Base, AL, USAF Air War College, 2001), 16p.

Buckingham, William F., *Arnhem 1944: A Reappraisal* (Stroud, Tempus, 2002)

Buckingham, William F., *Arnhem: The Complete Story of Operation Market Garden 17–25 September 1944* (Stroud, 2019)

Budani, Donna Martha, *Women, war, and text: Orsognese women's experience in a sector of the Italian front in World War II* (PhD Diss., American University, 1997)

Butler, J.R.M., *The Mediterranean and Middle East*, Vol. 5, *The campaign in Sicily 1943, and the campaign in Italy 3rd September 1943 to 31st March 1944.*

By Air to Battle: The Official Account of the British Airborne Divisions (London, 1945)

Carver, Michael, *The Imperial War Museum Book of the War in Italy 1943–1945* (London)

Chant, Christopher, *The Encyclopaedia of Codenames of World War II* (London, 1986)

Chatterton, George, *The Wings of Pegasus: The Story of the Glider Pilot Regiment* (London, Macdonald, 1962)

Cherry, Niall, *With Nothing Bigger Than a Bren Gun: The Defence of the Schoolhouse at the Road Bridge at Arnhem, September 1944* (Brendon Publishing, 2008)

Cherry, Niall, *Striking Back: Britain's Airborne and Commando Raids 1940 to 1942* (Helion & Co. Ltd, 2009)
Cherry, Niall, *Arnhem Surgeon: The Story of Captain Michael James of 181 Air Landing Field Ambulance RAMC 1944* (Brendon Publishing, 2010)
Cholewczynski, George F., *Poles Apart: The Polish Airborne at the Battle of Arnhem* (London, Greenhill Books, 1993)
Chrystal, Eric, Unpublished correspondence with Colonel P.R.R. de Burgh, 1987.
Chrystal, Eric, Unpublished correspondence with Bob Woollacott, 1992.
Chrystal, Eric, Unpublished correspondence with Bob Gerritsen, 1996.
Chrystal, Paul, *The British Army of the Rhine* (Barnsley, 2018)
Chrystal, Paul, *The Troubles* (Barnsley, 2018)
Chrystal, Paul, *Biological Warfare and Bioterrorism: Weaponising Nature* (Barnsley, 2023)
Clark, Lloyd, 'Operation Market Garden 1944: the bridge at Arnhem' in Badsey, Stephen (ed.), *The Hutchinson Atlas of World War II Battle Plans* (Oxford, Helicon Publishing, 2000)
Clark, Lloyd, *Arnhem: Operation Market Garden, September 1944* (Stroud, Sutton Publishing, 2002)
Clark, Lloyd, *Arnhem: Jumping the Rhine 1944 and 1945: The Greatest Airborne Battle in History* (London, Headline Publishing, 2008)
Clarke, Carter W., 'Signal Corps Pigeons' in *The Military Engineer* 25.140 (1933), pp.133–38.
Cochran, Major D.J.S., *What were the principal lessons learnt from Operation Market Garden and are they still relevant today?*, Watchfield: Joint Services Command & Staff College, 2004, 37p. ACSC 7 Defence Research Paper.
Cole, Howard N., *On Wings of Healing: The Story of the Airborne Medical Services 1940–1960* (Edinburgh, 1963)
Comfort, Charles Fraser, *Artist at War* (1956)
Copp, Terry, 'Pushing To Campobasso: Army', Part 65, *Legion*, 1 July 2006.
Cotterell, Anthony, 'Waiting to be Scrubbed' in Watkins, *Arnhem*, pp.59–67.
Cummings, Colin, *Arnhem Sacrifice: A Miscellany of Information about Personnel and Units Involved in the Battle of Arnhem 17th to 26th September 1944* (Yelvertoft, Nimbus Publishing, 1998)
Daily Telegraph, p.19, Thursday, 7 September 1995, Obituary: Captain Anthony Harrison.
Dank, Milton, *The Glider Gang: An Eyewitness History of World War II Glider Combat* (London, Cassell, 1978)
David, Saul, *Military Blunders: The How and Why of Military Failure* (London, Robinson Publishing, 1997)
Deane-Drummond, A., *Return Ticket* (London, 1953)
de Jong, Lou, *The Kingdom of the Netherlands During World War II* (Amsterdam, 1969–1991), Vol. 10A-1, 1980. The series comprises 14 volumes published in 29 parts.

Devlin, Gerard M., *Silent Wings: The Story of the Glider Pilots of World War II* (London, W.H. Allen, 1985)

Di Cintio, Francesco, *A Mountain to Win – Battlefield Study of the 4th Battalion The Parachute Regiment along the Gustav Line*. http://www.historyandgeotours.com/blog/second-world-war-109/a-mountain-to-win--battlefield-study-of-the-4th-battalion-the-parachute-regiment-along-the-gustav-line.html

Dixon, Norman, *On the Psychology of Military Incompetence* (London, 1994)

Duxford Radio Society, *A Brief History of Rebecca & Eureka*.

Ellis, L.F. et al (eds), 'Victory in the West: The Defeat of Germany', *History of the Second World War United Kingdom Military Series*, Vol. II (paperback reprint, Naval & Military Press, Uckfield, 2004)

Esler Smith, Allan, *Revisiting 'Theirs Is the Glory'* (Robert Sigmond Publishing, Renkum, NL, 2012)

Esler Smith, Allan, 'Theirs Is the Glory', Part 3: Arnhem, the greatest drama ever told and the section 'a script honed by experts', *Pegasus, Journal of the Parachute Regiment and Airborne Forces*, Summer 2013.

Fairley, John, *Remember Arnhem: The Story of the First Airborne Reconnaissance Squadron at Arnhem*, second edition (Bearsden, Peaton Press, 1990)

Farrar-Hockley, Anthony, *Airborne Carpet: Operation Market Garden* (London, Macdonald, 1970)

Fass, Michael, *The Railway Man: Next Stop PTSD*, 'A Review of The Railway Man' (2013) by Jonathan Teplinzky (Director), *PsycCRITIQUES* 2 February 2015, Vol. 60, No. 5, Article 10 © 2015 American Psychological Association; https://www.apa.org/pubs/highlights/psyccritiques-spotlight/PSQ_a0038592.pdf

Ferguson, Gregor, *The Paras 1940–84*, Volume 1 of Elite Series (Oxford, 1984)

Flanagan, R., *The Narrow Road to the Deep North* (New York, NY, Knopf, 2014)

Flint, Keith, *Airborne Armour: Tetrarch, Locust, Hamilcar and the 6th Airborne Armoured Reconnaissance Regiment 1938–50* (Solihull, Helion, 2004)

Foa, E.B. et al, 'The expert consensus guideline series: Treatment of post-traumatic stress disorder', *Journal of Clinical Psychiatry*, 60, 3–76, 1999.

Foxall, R., *The Guinea Pigs* (London, 1983)

Frost, John, *A Drop Too Many* (Barnsley, 1980)

Frost, John, *Nearly There* (London, Leo Cooper, 1991)

Fuller, Les, film clip of Les's experiences at the bridge where he lost an arm with 3 Para: https://www.youtube.com/watch?v=76s3Xnh6KqA&ab_channel=RoyalDutchMint

Gallagher, Mike, *With Recce at Arnhem: The Recollections of Trooper Des Evans – A 1st Airborne Division Veteran* (Barnsley, 2015)

Gavin, James M., *Airborne Warfare* (Washington DC, Infantry Journal Press, 1947)

Gavin, James M., *On to Berlin: Battles of an Airborne Commander 1943–1946* (London, Leo Cooper, 1978)

Glover, Michael, *Battlefields of Northern France and the Low Countries* (London, Michael Joseph, 1987)

Golden, Lewis, *Echoes from Arnhem* (London, 1984)
Gray, Jennie, *Major Cotterell at Arnhem: A War Crime and a Mystery* (Stroud, 2012)
Green, Alan T., *1st Battalion the Border Regiment: Arnhem 17th September–26th September 1944* (Carlisle, Museum of the Border Regiment, 1991)
Gregory, Barry, *British Airborne Troops 1940–45* (London, Macdonald and Janes, 1974)
Greenacre, John W., 'Assessing the Reasons for Failure: 1st British Airborne Division Signal Communications during Operation "Market Garden"', *Defence Studies*, 2004, Vol. 4 (3), pp.283–308.
Hackett, General Sir John, *I Was a Stranger* (London, Chatto and Windus, 1977)
Hagen, Louis, *Arnhem Lift: A German Jew in the Glider Pilot Regiment* (reprint, Stroud, 2013)
Hall, J. Leo, *Signals from Arnhem Bridge*, 1996. Unpublished manuscript available at https://www.pegasusarchive.org/arnhem/Leo_Hall.htm
Hanbury Brown, Robert, *Boffin: A Personal Story of the Early Days of Radar, Radio Astronomy and Quantum Optics* (Boca Raton FLA, CRC Press, 1991)
Harclerode, Peter, *Para! Fifty Years of the Parachute Regiment* (London, Arms and Armour Press, 1992)
Harclerode, Peter, *Arnhem: A Tragedy of Errors* (London, Arms and Armour Press, 1994)
Harclerode, Peter, *Wings of War – Airborne Warfare 1918–1945* (London, 2005)
Harvey, A.D., *Arnhem* (London, Cassell, 2001)
Heaps, Leo, *The Grey Goose of Arnhem* (London, Weidenfeld and Nicolson, 1976, 245p. Republished as *The Evaders*, Annapolis, MD, Naval Institute Press, 2004)
Hibbert, Christopher, *The Battle of Arnhem* (London, B.T. Batsford, 1962)
Hibbert, Christopher, *Arnhem* (London, 2003)
Hogan, David W., *U.S. Army Special Operations in World War II* (pdf) (Washington D.C., Center of Military History, Department of the Army, 1992)
Hogg, I.V., *Artillery Weapons & Ammunition 1914–1918* (London, 1972)
Holland, James, *Italy's Sorrow: A Year of War 1944–45* (London, 2009)
Holt, Tony & Holt, Valmai, *Major and Mrs Holt's Battlefield Guide to Operation Market Garden* (Barnsley, Leo Cooper, 2001)
Hooiveld, Jelle, *Dutch Courage: Special Forces in the Netherlands 1944–45* (Stroud, Amberley Publishing, 2016)
Horlings, A., *Arnhem Ghost Town. Eyewitness accounts of the Battle and Evacuation*.
Horrocks, Lt. Gen. Sir Brian, *A Full Life* (London, Collins, 1960)
Horrocks, Lt. Gen. Sir Brian, *Corps Commander* (London, Sidgwick and Jackson, 1977)
Hoyt, Edwin P., *Backwater War: The Allied Campaign in Italy, 1943–45* (Mechanicsburg, PA, 2007)
Irwin, Will, *The Jedburghs: The Secret History of the Allied Special Forces, France 1944* (Public Affairs, 2005)

Irwin, Will, *Abundance of Valor: Resistance, Liberation and Survival 1944–1945* (New York, Random House, 2010)
Jackson, Mike, 'A brave, bold failure', *The Spectator*, 19 May 2018.
Jackson, Robert, *Arnhem: The Battle Remembered* (Shrewsbury, Airlife, 1994)
Jeffson, Joel J., *Operation Market Garden: Ultra Intelligence Ignored* (Diss. Fort Leavenworth KS, US Army Command and General Staff College, 2001)
Jones, Major Lee M., 'Operation Market Garden and significant logistical deficiencies contributing to its partial failure' in *Combat Studies Institute: Military History Anthology* (Fort Leavenworth, KS, Combat Studies Institute, 1984)
Kamphuis, Piet, 'Operation Market Garden' in Foot, M.R.D. (ed.), *Holland at War Against Hitler: Anglo-Dutch Relations 1944–1945* (London, Frank Cass)
Kent, Ron, *First in! Parachute Pathfinder Company: A History of the 21st Independent Parachute Company, the original pathfinders of British airborne forces 1942–1946* (London, B.T. Batsford, 1979)
Kershaw, Robert J., 'Kampfgruppe Spindler in Arnhem September 1944' in *World War II Investigator*, Vol.1, No. 8, November 1988, pp.21–24.
Kershaw, Robert J., *It Never Snows in September: The German View of Market Garden and the Battle of Arnhem, September 1944* (Hersham, 2004)
Kessell, Lipmann, *Surgeon at Arms: Parachuting into Arnhem with the First Airbornes* (Barnsley, 2011)
Kiln, Major Robert, *D-Day to Arnhem with Hertfordshire's Gunners: A Personal Account* (Welwyn Garden City, Castlemead Publications, 1993)
Kinard, Jeff, *Artillery: An Illustrated History of its Impact* (Weapons and Warfare, Zurich, 2007)
Kist, J., 'Disaster at Arnhem: the role of information during the Operation "Market Garden" in September 1944' in Horton, Forest, *Great Information Disasters* (London, ASLIB, 1991)
Konstam, Angus, *Salerno 1943: The Allied Invasion of Italy* (Barnsley, 2007)
Konstam, Angus, *Salerno 1943: The Allies Invade Southern Italy* (Oxford, 2013)
Koskimaki, George E., *Hell's Highway: Chronicle of the 101st Airborne Division in the Holland campaign September-November 1944* (Havertown, PA, Casemate, 2003)
Koskodan, Kenneth K., *No Greater Ally: The Untold Story of Poland's Forces in World War II* (Botley, Osprey, 2009)
Kosnet, Phil & Patrick, Stephen B., 'Highway to the Reich: Operation Market Garden, 17–26 September 1944' in Nofi, Albert A. (ed.), *The War Against Hitler: Military Strategy in the West* (New York, Hippocrene Books, 1982)
Latimer, John, *Deception in War* (London, 2001)
Laurens, Anne, *Lindemans Affair: Betrayal of the Arnhem Drop* (Allan Wingate, 1971)
Lesley-Dixon, Kenneth, *Northern Ireland: The Troubles From The Provos to The Det, 1968–1998* (Barnsley, 2018)
Linklater, Eric, *The Campaign in Italy* (1977)

Lloyd, Alan, *The Gliders* (London, Leo Cooper, 1982)

Lomax, Eric, *The Railway Man* (London, 1996)

Longson, Jim, *An Arnhem Odyssey: 'Market Garden' to Stalag IV-B* (London, Leo Cooper, 1991), 184p.

Lowden, John L., *Silent Wings at War: Combat Gliders in World War II* (Washington, DC, Smithsonian Institution Press, 1992)

Lynch, Tim, *Silent Skies: Gliders At War 1939–1945* (Barnsley, 2008)

MacDonald, C.B., '19 The Decision to Launch Operation Market Garden' in *Command Decisions* (2000 edition), CMH, OCLC 1518217, 1960.

MacDonald, C.B., *The Siegfried Line Campaign* (pdf) (Washington, DC, Office of the Chief of Military History, Department of the Army, OCLC 494234368, 1963)

Macintyre, Ben, *Operation Mincemeat* (Crown Publishing Group, 2010)

Mackay, E.M., 'The Battle of Arnhem Bridge', *Royal Engineers Journal*, December 1954, pp.305ff.

Mackenzie, C.B., *It was Like This! Zo was Het!: A Short Factual Account of the Battle of Arnhem and Oosterbeek* (13th edition, Stichting Airborne Museum, Oosterbeek, 1981)

Macksey, Kenneth, *Military Errors of World War Two* (Poole, Arms & Armour Press, 1987)

Margry, Karel, *Operation Market Garden – Then and Now*, Volume 1, *After the Battle*, 2002

Margry, Karel, *Operation Market Garden – Then and Now*, Volume 2, *After the Battle*, 2002

Martens, Allard, *The Silent War: Glimpses of the Dutch Underground and Views on the Battle of Arnhem* (London, Hodder and Stoughton, 1961)

Mawson, Stuart, *Arnhem Doctor* (London, Orbis Publishing, 1981)

McKee, Alexander, *The Race for the Rhine Bridges 1940, 1944, 1945* (London, Souvenir Press, 1971)

McNab, Chris, *Hitler's Fortresses: German Fortifications and Defences 1939–45* (London, 2014)

Megargee, Geoffrey P., *The United States Holocaust Memorial Museum Encyclopedia of Camps and Ghettos, 1933–1945*, Volume IV, *Camps and Other Detention Facilities Under the Germans* (Bloomington, IN, 2022)

Merglen, Albert, *Surprise Warfare: Subversive, Airborne and Amphibious Operations* (London, George Allen & Unwin, 1968)

Middlebrook, Martin, *Arnhem 1944: The Airborne Battle, 17–26 September* (New York, 1994)

Military Library Research Service, *Operation Market Garden and the Battle of Arnhem* (Buxton, 2007)

Mitcham, Samuel W., *The Battle of Sicily: How the Allies Lost Their Chance for Total Victory* (Mechanicsburg, PA, 2007)

Molony, C.J.C., *The Mediterranean and Middle East: The Campaign in Sicily 1943 and the Campaign in Italy 3 September 1943 to 31 March 1944* (History of the Second World War, United Kingdom Military Series, Vol. V (paperback reprint, Naval & Military Press edition), Uckfield, 2004)

Morison, Samuel Eliot, *History of United States Naval Operations in World War II: Sicily, Salerno, Anzio, January 1943–June 1944*, Volume 9 of *History of United States Naval Operations in World War II* (Champaign, IL, 2001)

Mrazek, James E., *The glider war* (London, Robert Hale, 1975)

Mrazek, James, *Airborne Combat: Axis and Allied Glider Operations in World War II* (Military History Series, Mechanicsburg, PA, 2011)

Nalder, R.F.H., *The History of British Army Signals in the Second World War* (London, Royal Signals Institution, 1953), p.144.

The National Archives (TNA) WO219/5137, Report on Operation Market Garden: 17 Sep 1944–26 Sep 1944 (1944) (Public Record Office), Part III, Index E.

National World War II Glider Pilots Association, *World War II Glider Pilots* (Kentucky, 1991)

Neillands, Robin, *The Battle for the Rhine 1944: Arnhem and the Ardennes, the Campaign in Europe* (Lume Books, 2015)

Nicholson, G.W.L., *Official History of the Canadian Army in the Second World War*, Volume II: *The Canadians in Italy, 1943–1945* (Ottawa, ON, 1957)

Nicholson, G.W.L., *The Gunners of Canada*, Vol. II (Beauceville, Imprimerie L'Éclaireur, 1972)

Norton, G.G., *Red Devils: The Story of the British Airborne Forces* (London, Leo Cooper, 1971), subsequently republished as *The Red Devils: from Bruneval to the Falklands* (London, Arrow Books, 1988)

O'Reilly, Charles, *Forgotten Battles: Italy's War of Liberation, 1943–1945* (Lexington Books, 2001)

Otway, T.B.H., *The Second World War 1939–1945: Army – Airborne Forces* (Imperial War Museum, 1990)

Pack, S.W.C., *Operation HUSKY: The Allied Invasion of Sicily* (Hippocrene Books, 1977)

Paradata, *Theirs Is The Glory (1946)*; https://www.paradata.org.uk/article/theirs-glory-1946

Pauli, Kurt, 'The Arnhem victory: a German account', *Military Review*, Vol. 24, No. 11, February 1945, pp.111–112.

Peatling, Robert, *Without Tradition: 2 Para, 1941–45* (Barnsley, Pen & Sword, 2004), 254.

Perrett, Bryan, *Last Stand! Famous Battles Against the Odds* (London, Arms & Armour Press, 1991)

Peters, Mike, *Glider Pilots at Arnhem* (Barnsley, Pen & Sword, 2009)

Piekalkiewicz, Janusz, *Arnhem 1944* (London, Ian Allan, 1977)

Piper, Major Arnold C., *Intelligence planning for airborne operations: a perspective from Operation Market Garden* (Fort Leavenworth, KS, Army Command & General Staff College, 1997), 75p.

Plowman, Jeffrey, *Orsogna: New Zealand's First Italian Battle* (Willsonscott, Christchurch)

Pogue, Forrest C., *The Supreme Command* (pdf) (Washington DC, Office of the Chief of Military History, Department of the Army, OCLC 318368731, 1954)

Powell, Geoffrey, *The Devil's Birthday: The Bridges to Arnhem* (London, Buchan & Enright, 1984)

Prodger, Lt. M.J., 'Nothing heard? Communication problems in Operation Market Garden 1944', *Journal of the Royal Signals Institution*, Vol. 19, No. 4, 1990, pp.241–246.

Reinders, Philip, *Officers of the 1st Air Landing Light Regiment Royal Artillery during the Battle of Arnhem, 17th-26th September 1944* (Elburg, Arnhem Battle Research Group, 2016)

Reynolds, David, *Paras: An Illustrated History of Britain's Airborne Forces* (Stroud, 1998)

Roberts, Captain Harry, *Capture at Arnhem* (Moreton-in-Marsh, Windrush Press, 1999)

Rossiter, Mike, *We Fought at Arnhem* (London, 2011)

Rosson, Steven D., 'An Examination of the Intelligence Preparation for Operation MARKET GARDEN, September, 1944; (1997), Master's Thesis. 1824. https://thekeep.eiu.edu/theses/1824

Ryan, Cornelius, *A Bridge Too Far* (London, 1974)

Rydell, Anders, *The Book Thieves: The Nazi Looting of Europe's Libraries and the Race to Return a Literary Inheritance* (London, 2018)

Salverda, Reinier, '"Beyond A Bridge Too Far": The Aftermath of the Battle of Arnhem (1944) and Its Impact on Civilian Life' in *Discord and Consensus in the Low Countries, 1700–2000*, edited by Jane Fenoulhet et al., 1st edition, Vol. 1, London, 2016.

Sarkar, Dilip, *Arnhem 1944: The Human Tragedy of the Bridge Too Far* (Frontline Books, 2019)

Saunders, Anne Leslie, *A Travel Guide to World War II Sites in Italy: Museums, Monuments and Battlegrounds* (2016)

Saunders, Hilary St George, *The Red Beret: The Story of The Parachute Regiment at War 1940–1945* (London, Michael Joseph, 1950)

Saunders, Tim, *The Island: Nijmegen to Arnhem* (Barnsley, Leo Cooper, 2002)

Seager Thomas, Mike, 'The WW2 Foggia Airfield Complex in the Bradford Archive of Aerial Photographs', *Artefact Services Research Papers* 10 (Lewes, Artefact Services, 2020), pp.42 & Appendix 5.

Shears, Philip J., *The Story of the Border Regiment 1939–1945* (London, Nisbet, 1948)

Sims, James, *Arnhem Spearhead: A Private Soldier's Story* (London, Imperial War Museum, 1978)

Skeat, Major C.N.R., 'A study of the Wehrmacht's ability to improvise effective ad-hoc battle groups during Operation Market Garden, with emphasis on battlegroup composition, leadership, organisation, training, experience and the associated staff processes in order to draw lessons for force improvisation in modern high intensity combat' (Camberley, Army Staff College, 1994), 24p. ACSC 28 Commandant's Research Paper.

Smith, Claude, *History of the Glider Pilot Regiment* (Barnsley, 2007)

Society of Friends of the Airborne Museum, Oosterbeek, *The Tommies are Coming! – Diary of an Oosterbeek Girl, September 1944* (1998)

Sosabowski, Major General Stanislaw, *Freely I Served* (London, William Kimber, 1960)

Spence, Wing Commander Fraser, *European airborne operations in the Second World War prior to Arnhem* (Watchfield, Joint Services Command & Staff College, 2005)

Stainforth, Peter, *Wings of the Wind* (London, Arms and Armour Press, 1985)

Steer, Frank, *Arnhem: The fight to sustain: The untold story of the airborne logisticians* (Barnsley, Leo Cooper, 2000)

Steer, Frank, *Arnhem: The Landing Grounds and Oosterbeek* (Barnsley, Leo Cooper, 2002)

Steer, Frank, *Arnhem: The Bridge* (Barnsley, Leo Cooper, 2003)

Styling, Mark, *B-26 Marauder Units of the MTO* (Oxford, 2008)

Tanner, John (ed.), *RAF Airborne Forces Manual: the official Air Publications for RAF paratroop aircraft and gliders, 1942–1946*, RAF Museum Series, Volume 8 (London, Arms & Armour Press, 1979)

Ter Horst-Arriëns, Kate A., *Cloud over Arnhem: Oosterbeek – September 1944* (Uitgeverij Kontrast, Oosterbeek, 2009)

Thompson, Julian, *Ready for anything: The Parachute Regiment at War, 1940–1982* (London, Weidenfeld and Nicolson, 1989)

Thompson, Sheriff, 'Some Airborne and Mountain Artillery Techniques and Tactics Developed by 1 Air Landing Light Regiment, R.A.', *Royal Artillery Journal*, 1947.

Truesdale, David, *Arnhem Bridge: Target Mike One, An Illustrated History of the 1st Air Landing Regiment RA 1942–1945*, R.N. Sigmond, Renkum, NL, 17 September 2015.

Truesdale, David, 'Theirs Is the Glory', *Arnhem, Hurst and Conflict on Film*, 2016.

Tucker-Jones, Anthony, *The Devil's Bridge: The German Victory at Arnhem, 1944* (London, 2020)

Tugwell, Maurice, *Arnhem: A Case Study* (London, Thornton Cox, 1975)

Urquhart, R.R., *Arnhem: Britain's Infamous Airborne Assault of WWII* (1958)

Urquhart, Robert, *Arnhem* (Barnsley, 2007, reprint)

Van der Zee, Henri A., *The Hunger Winter: Occupied Holland, 1944–1945* (Lincoln, NE, Bison Books, 1982), 305.

Van Hees, Arie-Jan, *Tugs and gliders to Arnhem: a detailed survey of the British glider towing operations during Operation Market Garden 17, 18 and 19 September 1944* (Eijsden, A.J. van Hees, 2000)

Van Hees, Arie-Jan, *Green on! A detailed survey of the British parachute sorties during Operation Market Garden* (Eijsden, A.J. van Hees, 2004)

Van Roekel, Chris, *Mini Story II: 'German Tank on the Beneden-Weverstraat'*.

Vredenberg, J., *Reconstruction: Urban planning and architecture in Arnhem 1945–1965* (Utrecht, Matrix Publishers, 2004)
Waddy, John, *A tour of the Arnhem battlefields* (Barnsley, Leo Cooper, 1999)
Wallace, Robert, *The Italian Campaign* (New York, 1981)
Warden, Bernard, *The Forgotten Army, Italy 1943–1945*, https://www.italystarassociation.org.uk/history/the-forgotten-army-italy-1943-1945/comment-page-15
Warrack, Graeme, *Travel by Dark: After Arnhem* (London, Harvill Press, 1963)
Warren, John C., *Airborne Operations in World War II* (USAF Historical Studies, no. 97, 1956)
Watkins, Ernest, *Arnhem: 1 Airborne Division* (Ulster, 2016)
Whately-Smith, Peter, *The 94th (Dorset & Hants) Field Regiment, Royal Artillery, 1939–1945* (Dorchester, G.H. Rose, 1948)
Whiting, Charles, *A Bridge at Arnhem* (London, Futura, 1974)
Wilkinson, Peter, *The Gunners at Arnhem* (East Haddon, Spurwing Publishing, 1999)
Williams, Dennis, *Stirlings in action with the airborne forces: air support for SAS and Resistance operations during WWII* (Barnsley, Pen & Sword, 2008)
Winchester, Clarence, ed., 'RMMV *Stirling Castle*', *Shipping Wonders of the World*, pp.1306–1310, 1937.
Winstanley, Wing Commander D., *How critical was air power in the failure of 'Operation Market Garden'?* (Watchfield, Joint Services Command & Staff College, 2003), 34p. ACSC 6 Defence Research Paper.
Winterbotham, F.W., *The Ultra Secret* (London, Weidenfeld and Nicolson, 1974)
Wood, Alan, *The Glider Soldiers: A History of British Military Glider Forces* (Wellingborough, 1990)
Wood, Alan, *History of the world's glider forces* (Tunbridge Wells, Spellmount, 1992)
Woollacott, Robert, *Winged Gunners* (Quote Publishers, Harare, Zimbabwe, 1994)
Wright, G.K., *The Road to Campobasso and Beyond: October 11 to November 2, 1943* (1947) http://www.regimentalrogue.com/rcr_history/1939-1945/campobasso_wright.htm
Zabecki, David T., 'Operation Mincemeat', *World War II Magazine*, History Net (November 1995)
Zuehlke, Mark, *Ortona: Canada's Epic World War II Battle* (Stoddart Press, 1999)
Zuehlke, Mark, *Operation Husky: the Canadian invasion of Sicily, July 10–August 7, 1943* (Douglas & McIntyre, 2010)
Zwarts, Marcel, *German Armoured Units at Arnhem – September 1944* (Concord Publications Co., 2001)

Archives
1 Airborne Division report on Operation Market Parts I-V, 1st Airborne Division, 1945, CONF 4074

1 Airborne Division Signals Operation Market, Diary of events at Div HQ 1944, CONF 4074E

Toler, Major T.I., Diary of events leading up to Arnhem, with covering letter to the Staff College dated 2 April 1987, CONF 22

Online

https://combatstress.org.uk/

https://www.veterans.gc.ca/eng/remembrance/history/second-world-war/canada-Italy-1943-to-1945

https://ww2db.com/battle_spec.php?battle_id=307: Operation Baytown; Operation Slapstick

https://military-history.fandom.com/wiki/133rd_(Parachute)_Field_Ambulance

https://nzhistory.govt.nz/media/sound/orsogna-joseph-bacos

https://nzetc.victoria.ac.nz/tm/scholarly/tei-WH2-20Ba-c14.html

https://marketgardenveterans.nl/download/MarketGarden75thfootsteps.pdf

https://warfarehistorynetwork.com/2016/11/30/arnhem-bridge-why-it-was-britains-alamo-in-wwii

https://vriendenairbornemuseum.nl/wp-content/uploads/2020/10/A-week-in-Oosterbeek-by-George-Nattrass.pdf

https://web.archive.org/web/20090203172116/http://defendingarnhem.com/index.htm

Audio Visual Media

Baskeyfield VC, Heritage Video, 2004. VHS Video

Battlefield: Arnhem Operation Market Garden, Cromwell Productions, 2001. DVD

A Bridge Too Far, United Artists, 1977. DVD

Escape from…a bridge too far, Channel 5, 2004. VHS Video

Great Battles of World War 2: Arnhem, Channel 5, 2000. VHS Video

Great military blunders: a bridge too far?, History Channel, 2001. VHS Video

Line of Fire: Arnhem, Cromwell Productions, 2000. DVD

Return to Arnhem, Ministry of Defence, 1990. Five-part series. VHS Video

Theirs Is The Glory, Rank Film, 1985. DVD

The true glory: from D-Day to the fall of Berlin, DD Video, 2004. VHS Video

https://www.youtube.com/watch?v=76s3Xnh6KqA&ab_channel=RoyalDutchMint Les Fuller, 3 Para

Websites

Combat Stress: https://combatstress.org.uk/#:~:text=Combat%20Stress%20provides%20a%20range,and%20via%20phone%20and%20online

The Airborne Soldier.com http://www.theairbornesoldier.com

BBC website: World War Two http://www.bbc.co.uk/history/worldwars/wwtwo/battle_arnhem_01.shtml 22

Defending Arnhem http://www.defendingarnhem.com

https://www.qsl.net/g4bxd Bernard Nock's Military Wireless Museum, Kidderminster

Market Garden.com: the digital monument http://www.marketgarden.com

Operation Market Garden, 17–27 September 1944 (History of War website) http://www.historyofwar.org/articles/battles_arnhem.html

Paul Reed's battlefields of WW2 http://battlefieldsww2.50megs.com/index.html

The Pegasus Archive: the Battle of Arnhem archive http://www.pegasusarchive.org/arnhem/frames.htm

Remember September '44 http://www.rememberseptember44.com/rs44.htm

https://assets.publishing.service.gov.uk/government/uploads/system/uploads/attachment_data/file/30056/ww2_market_garden.pdf

https://www.bbc.co.uk/history/worldwars/wwtwo/battle_arnhem_01.shtml

Author's website: www.paulchrystal.com

https://www.pegasusarchive.org/arnhem/batt_light_reg.htm

https://www.pegasusarchive.org/arnhem/batt_1st_air.htm

https://web.archive.org/web/20110616044810/http://www.pegasusarchive.org/arnhem/frames.htm

https://marketgarden.com/2010/UK/statistics/statis1.html

https://vassallohistory.wordpress.com/military-hospitals-in-malta

https://www.qaranc.co.uk/bmhmalta.php

https://www.maltaramc.com/articles/contents/reghosp.html

https://en.wikipedia.org/wiki/RNH_Mtarfa

https://www.independent.com.mt/articles/2014-08-26/newspaper-lifestyleculture/Second-World-War-Malta:-The-Advance-Dressing-Station-in-Wardija,-1942-%E2%80%93-RAMC-6346866689

Index

22 radio set, 77, 95, 100, 102, 137, 155
68 radio set, 57, 77, 94–5, 100, 102–103, 139, 145, 154
75mm pack howitzer, 7–8

Abdiel, HMS, 23, 25–6, 53
A Bridge Too Far film, critique of, 96
Airborne troops at Arnhem, Appendix II
American airborne forces, 7
Arnhem, Battle of,
  1st Air Landing Light Regiment, 164
    misinformation at 1st Air Landing Light Regiment pre-battle briefing, 58
    role of the regiment, 7
  1st Seaborne Echelon, 40–1
  2nd Lift, 127
  3rd Lift, 127
  16th (Parachute) Field Ambulance, 87, 156
  30 Coy, Royal Army Medical Corps, 43
    see also Royal Army Medical Corps
  131st (Parachute) Field Ambulance, 74
  133rd (Parachute) Field Ambulance, 26, 165
  181st (Air Landing) Field Ambulance, 87
  'A' Echelon, 34
  After the Battle, 199ff
  Allied Firepower at Arnhem, Appendix VI

Ammunition, 59, 169; Appendix VI
Arnhem battle plan, 60–1; Appendix III
Arnhem casualties, 74
Arnhem dead, evacuated, missing (PoWs mainly), 191
Arnhem Order of Battle, Appendix III
Arnhem town, Appendix IV
assessments of the battle, final, 52, 193
Atrocities, German, 126, 149–50, 158, 168, 210ff
Atrocity, British, 126, 158
bridge at Arnhem, Appendix IV
Bridge, British force reach the, 89, 97–8
British troops evacuated, 191
British burials, 81, 120, 124, 167, 173, 175, 183, 215
British fatalities, 69, 108, 110, 112–13, 120, 123–4, 126, 130, 132, 134, 136, 139–41, 144–6, 148–9, 152, 154, 156, 158, 161–2, 167, 170–3, 175–6, 178, 181, 183–4, 191, Appendix VII
British acts of surrender, 113–14, 139, 149–50, 153, 158–9, 165, 167, 184, 186
British wounded, 80–1, 90, 100, 110–11, 113, 128, 130–1, 134, 144–5, 147–50, 154, 159–60, 162, 164–5, 167, 170, 173, 178–9, 181–2, 184
Compassion and decency shown by Germans, 157–8, 165, 186

fake news, 134, 145
fear and terror during the battle, 69–70, 177–8, 201–202
friendly fire, 139, 190
German fatalities, 108, 114, 123–4, 126, 153, 187, Appendix VII
German forces, of variable quality, 168
German perspective at the bridge, 151ff
German preparations for Arnhem, 50
German reprisals during and after the battle, 5, 81, 168, 193ff, 210ff
German wounded, 164
glider crashes and fatalities, 67–70, 73–6, 85, 127–31, 140
Hotel Taffelberg, 163–4
'How Much is a Dutch Bridge Worth?' Appendix VII
intelligence issues and controversy pre-battle, 44–5, 97
landing procedure, 61, 67, 70–1
landing zone (LZ) issues, 47, 67, 73
landings, by individual regiment, 73
'Lion', 'Leopard' and 'Tiger' routes into Arnhem, 77, 79, 86
Medical care and facilities, 64, 75, 87, 88, 139–40, 145, 162–5, 173, 177ff, 179, 182f
Old Vicarage (Kate ter Horst), 120, 139–40, 173, 177ff, 182f
padres at, 103, 161, 163, 179, 183, 201
plan on the ground, the, 79–80
PoWs, 58, 91, 114, 128–31, 134, 137, 140, 150, 159, 165, 182, 184, 190, Appendix IX
PoWs, German, 143
Queen Wilhelmina's, Het Loo, Apeldoorn, 134
radio sets, issues with, 77, 84, 92–7, 100, 102, 104–107, 121, 130, 168

railway bridge at Oosterbeek blown up, 79–80, 83, 90, 121
reservations about MARKET GARDEN, 58–9, 61
reservations by Dempsey, 49
reservations by Urquhart, 46
statistics for the battle, 191–3
St Elisabeth Hospital, 87–8, 134, 140, 157, 165
supply drop issues, 139, 142, 145, 160–1, 167, 169–71, 176, 181
Target Mike One, 103, 117–18, 122, 138, 145
unbearable and unrelenting noise of battle, 133, 144, 156, 177, 179–80, 183, 186, 189, 202–205
Victoria Crosses awarded, 133, 144, 160, 171, 192
weather, 67, 133, 144, 167
'White House' (Hotel Schoonhord), 64, 88, 145, 162, 182
Artist at War, Comfort (1956), 35

Bari, German air raid on, 36–7
Benzedrine tablets, 113, 151
Bernhard, Prince of the Netherlands, 52
Bittrich, SS *Obergruppenführer* Wilhelm, 44–5, 46, 50–1, 78, 97, 125, 167
Boston, 199ff
Boston, Lincolnshire, 10–11, 37–8, 40, 199–215
Brereton, Lieutenant General Lewis Hyde, USAF, 50, 66, 118
Brindisi, 24
British Army forces,
1st Allied Airborne Army (the US Army's 82nd and 101st Airborne divisions, the British 1st Airborne and the 1st Polish Parachute Brigade), 45, 47–8, 50
1st Airborne Corps, 38, 129

Index 273

1st Airborne Division, 2–5, 11, 14, 16, 22–3, 27–8, 34, 37, 53ff, 106, 167
1st Air Landing Anti-Tank Battery, 5, 55–6, 81, 89, 119, 133, 170
1st Air Landing Brigade, 2–3, 5, 14–16, 19, 22, 25, 27–8, 53, 78, 132
1st Air Landing Light Battery, 6
1st Air Landing Light Regiment, 3, 10, 16, 22–3, 28, 34, 37, 44, 47, 53, 56–7, 66, 70, 74, 106, 139, 140–1, 144, 160–1, 166–7, 169, 175, 179, 188, 190, 200
   Fatalities, evacuated, PoWs, 200
   Secrecy surrounding movements, 16–17
1 Battery, 16, 23, 28, 33–4, 36–7, 39, 47–8, 58, 69, 74–5, 85, 88, 103, 117–18, 121, 124, 129, 131, 139, 141, 145–6, 161, 169, 172, 178, 184, 186
   Fatalities, evacuated, PoWs, 200
2 Battery, 16, 31–4, 38–9, 47, 58, 74, 118, 126–31, 139–40, 145–6, 170, 172, 175, 178, 180–1, 183–4, 186
3 Battery, 16, 23, 29, 31–5, 37–9, 44, 47–8, 58, 74–5, 85–6, 88–9, 103, 117–23, 134–5, 139, 141, 145, 157, 161, 169, 175, 185–6
   at Campobasso, 30–4
   D-Day, Normandy landings, 10, 39, 40–1
   disbanded 1945, 4, 11
E Troop, 6, 19, 57, 60, 76, 106–107, 119, 121, 131, 161, 173, 188–9, Appendix I
   essential items taken to the battle, 60
   evacuation from Arnhem, 58
   see also Operation BERLIN
   fatalities, Italy, 31–2, 34–5
F Troop, 31, 37, 69, 76, 118–19, 121, 125, 134, 169, 170, 176, 178, 181, 190

   Fatalities, evacuated, PoWs, 200
   formation of, 4, 7
   Forward Observation Officer (OP) party, 4, 10, 58, 76–7, 83–4, 88–9, 95, 98, 101, 120–3, 134–8, 146, 200
   HQ Battery, 16, 33–4, 36, 39, 75, 103, 106, 119, 124, 139, 161, 181, 185
   Italian campaign, 16, 25, 28–9, 36–7
   Medals awarded, 32
   Norway, 1945, 4
   Signallers (RA), 93–4
   at Taranto, 21, 28
   training, 6–7, 38
   weapons, 60
   withdrawn from Italy, 37
   Z Troop, 60, 69–70, 129, 189
1st Battalion, Border Regiment, 53, 69, 78, 103, 141, 145, 174–5
1 Forward Observation Unit RA (FOURA), 55
1st Mountain Regiment with 451, 452, 453 and 454 Mountain Batteries, 4–5
1st Parachute Battalion, 53, 79, 105, 134, 140, 144
1st Parachute Brigade, 2, 4, 14, 16, 22–3, 27, 53, 79, 106, 131, 134, 135
1st Parachute Squadron, Royal Engineers, 109, 114
2nd Air Landing Anti-Tank Battery, 55–6, 131
2nd (Oban) Air Landing Anti-Tank Battery, 6, 127
2nd Battalion, South Staffordshire Regiment, 15, 19, 52–3, 70, 78, 105, 133–4, 141, 144, 171
2nd Battalion, South Staffordshire Regiment, 15, 19, 52, 53, 70, 78, 105, 133, 134, 141, 144, 171
2nd Independent Parachute Brigade, 36–7

2nd Parachute Battalion, 53, 76–7, 79, 84, 95, 105, 124, 135–6, 142, 165
2nd Parachute Brigade, 2, 22, 25–6, 28–9, 34, 71
3rd Parachute Battalion 53, 58–9, 72–3, 79, 82, 105, 134, 144, 147
4th Parachute Brigade, 22–3, 27–8, 53, 118, 128, 130, 139
5th Infantry Division, 14–15, 28, 34
6th Airborne Division, 3, 71
6th (Royal Welch) Parachute Battalion, 25
7th Battalion Cameron Highlanders, 2
7th Galloway Battalion, King's Own Scottish Borderers, 53, 59, 62ff, 141, 145, 165
7 Medium Regiment, 184
8th Army, 4, 14, 28, 30
9th Field Company, Royal Engineers, 23, 142
X Corps, 21
10th Battalion Royal Welch Fusiliers, 2
10th Parachute Battalion, 25–6, 53, 139
11th Parachute Battalion, 105, 131, 133, 141, 144
11th Special Air Service Battalion, 2
XIII Corps, 20
XXX Corps, 47, 54, 87, 122, 125, 133, 138, 144, 148, 157, 165, 174, 188
21st Army Group, 45–6, 193
21st Independent Parachute Company, 14
31st Independent Infantry Brigade, 5
43rd (Wessex) Division, 174–5, 188
53rd Air Landing Light Regiment, 39
64 Medium Regiment, 168, 172, 175, 184
78th Infantry Division, 23, 29
92 Field Regiment, 34
129th Infantry Brigade, 174
132nd Field Regiment, 37
156th Parachute Battalion, 53
165th Field Regiment RA, 37
181 Air Landing Ambulance, 20, 87–8, 162–3
204 (Oban) Air Landing Anti-Tank Battery, 25
283 (City of London Yeomanry) Anti-Aircraft Battery, 5–6
458th Independent Light Battery, 4–6
Airborne Reconnaissance Squadron, 19
Glider Pilot Regiment, 2, 7, 25, 57, 66–7, 166, 178, 190
C Squadron, 71
F Squadron, 88
G Squadron, 70, 75, 129
Grenadier Guards, 164
Irish Guards, 169
JEDBURGH Team, 98
Reconnaissance Squadron, 55, 166
Royal Army Medical Corps (RAMC), 87–8, 159, 166
Royal Army Ordnance Corps (RAOC), 148
Royal Artillery, 30, 55ff, 105–106, 126
Royal Engineers, 147, 149, 160
Royal Signals, 148
Brown, Gunner F.V., 3 Battery E Troop, 69
Browning, General F.A.M., 2, 38, 46–7, 104–105, 118, 175
Bruneval Raid, 2–3
Bulford Camp, 5–6, 16, 39

Campobasso, Italy, 10, 28–30, 32–3, 35
Canadian forces, 30–1

Index 275

1st Canadian Armoured Brigade, 29
1st Canadian Infantry Division, 28–30, 33
2 Canadian Infantry Brigade, 34
3rd Brigade, 31
3 Field Company, 33
XIII Corps, 24
48th Highlanders, 34
Carlton and York Regiment (2nd Canadian Infantry Brigade), 33
Hastings and Prince Edward Regiment, 32, 34
Casoli, Italy, 10, 29, 37
Children, mutilated, 32
Christiansen, General Friedrich, 50, 86
Chrystal, Gunner Eric, x, 6, 9
   3 Battery E Troop Forward Observation Party, 76–7, 83–4, 121, 135–6
   71st (Forth) Heavy Anti-Aircraft Regiment, RA, Canal Zone, Egypt 1950–52, 11
   Aden, 1960–61, 11
   Arnhem, 10–11 and *passim*
   At the bridge, 96, 99, 101 (part of the Jeep journey?), 121–3, 137–8, 146, 147, 152
   BAOR, 24 Missile Regt, RA, 1964–68, 11
   Cyprus, 1956–57 (where he was Mentioned in Dispatches), 11
   Death, 215
   Evacuated to Malta, 10, 31, 43
   Fear, 83, 85, 202
   Glider flight over to Arnhem, 83
   Italy Campaign, 9ff
   Joins 1st Air Landing Light Regiment, 9
   Noise of battle, unrelenting, 84–5, 133, 180, 202
   Pilgrimages to Arnhem, 215
   Reaches the bridge, 84, 89
   Repatriated, 11, 199ff
   School of Artillery, Larkhill, 9
   Stalag XII-A, Limburg, 194
   Stalag IV-B, Mühlberg, 196
   Surrender, humiliation and interrogation, 143, 158–9
   Taken PoW, 11, 194ff
   Vacating the shelled-out building, 158–9
   With 38th Signal Training Regiment RA, 9
   With 240th Light Anti-Aircraft Training Regiment, Tonfanau, Gwynedd, 1946, 11
   Wireless problems, 84, 92–3, 94–7, 100, 102–107, 121
   Wounded, 10, 31–2
   Zwickau, satellite (Flossenbürg concentration camp) labour camp, 196–8
Churchill, Winston, 4
Cloud over Arnhem, Kate ter Horst, 88, 120, 212
Command Post Officer (CPO), 56
Crawfurd, Lieutenant Colonel C.H.P., 6, 19

Dempsey, General Sir Miles Christopher GBE, KCB, DSO, MC, DL, 49
De Tafelberg Hotel, 88, 120
Deventer, 46, 77, 80
Doetinchem, 45–6, 87
Dutch civilians, 51, 63, 73–4, 79–81, 83, 88, 90, 103–104, 108, 117–18, 128–30, 139–40, 143, 154, 165, 168, 179, 193, 202, 210ff
   deaths/murders of, 214
Dutch government in exile, 51
   calls national rail strike, 51, 193, 215
Dutch resistance, 44–6, 96, 98, 104–105, 112, 131, 138, 143
Dutch telephone system, 98–104

Dutch, starvation of, and famine 193, 210ff
DZs, 67, 71, 118, 127

Egos, battle of the Allied Commanders', 46, 48, 193
Eindhoven, 47, 48
Eisenhower, Dwight D., 45, 48–50
Eusebiusbinnensingel, Arnhem, 102, 108–10, 125
Eusebiusbuitensingel, 109–10, 116
Eusebiusplein, Arnhem, 66, 81, 125, 138, 152
  Battle of, 109ff, 108–12

Famine in the Netherlands, winter 1944–45, 51, 193
Fleurus transit camp, Algeria, 17
Flossenbürg Concentration Camp, 11
Foggia, Italy, 24–5, 27, 30
  allied atrocity, 27
Forward Observation Officers (FOOs), 55
Franklin, Benjamin, 1, 103
Frost, Major General J.D. CB, DSO, MC, DL, 2, 76, 79, 88, 89, 90, 94, 97, 103, 110, 111, 114, 116, 117, 118, 125, 134, 147, 152, 159, 165

Gambatesa, Italy, 31
German army units, Appendix VII, VIII
  1st *Fallschirmjäger* Army, 44
  1st Parachute Army (1 *Fallschirmjäger* Army), 26, 28–9, 50
  2 *Kompanie* SS *Panzer-Grenadier-Ausbildungs und Ersatz-Bataillon* 16, 86, 88
  II Parachute Corps, 87
  II SS Panzer Corps, 44–6, 50, 86, 167
  7th *Fliegerdivision*, 1
  9th SS *Hohenstaufen*, 45, 78

9th SS Panzer Division, 45, 78, 114f, 166, 167, 174
10th SS, 77
10th SS *Frundsberg*, 45, 78
10th SS Panzer Division, 45, 78, 165, 174
10th SS Panzer Division 21st *Panzergrenadier* Regiment, 151
13 SS Division *Handschar Regiment Götz Berens von Rautenfeld*, 73
15th Army, 50
21 *Panzergrenadier* Regiment, 152
67 *Panzergrenadier* Regiment, 28
LXXVI Panzer Corps, 21, 36
107th Panzer Brigade, 87
208th Assault Brigade, 135
280th Assault Gun Brigade, 86
Army Group B, 44, 46, 50
Dutch SS *Wachbattalion* III (the 3rd SS Guard Battalion), 78
Flak Brigade *von Swoboda*, 135
Herman Göring Division, 174–5
Panzergrenadier Training and Replacement Bocholt, 117
Panzer Kompanie 224, 171
Schwere Panzerabteilung 506, 142
Schwere Panzer-Kompanie Hummel, 174
Sperrverband Harzer, 167
SS *Kampfgruppe Brinkmann*, 91, 117, 142
SS *Kampfgruppe Chill*, 86
SS *Kampfgruppe Frundsberg*, 46, 51, 79, 87
SS *Kampfguppe Harder*, 87
SS *Kampfgruppe Heilmann*, 28
SS *Kampfgruppe Hohenstaufen*, 46, 51, 87, 90, 104, 111, 125
SS *Kampfgruppe Knaust*, 111, 117, 124, 152, 169, 174
SS *Kampfgruppe Spindler* (part of SS *Kampfgruppe Hohenstaufen* under *Oberstturmbannführer* Harzer), 79

Index   277

SS *Kampfgruppe Weber* (Luftwaffe troops), 78, 86
SS NCO Training School 'Arnheim', Wolfheze (SS *Unterführerschule Arnheim*), 132
SS *Panzergrenadier* Depot and Reserve Battalion 16, 82
SS Training and Replacement Battalion, 78
Training Battalion 1/6, 78
German PoWs, 76, 78–9, 90
German weapons, 86
Gildone, Italy, 32
Glider transport, 7, 59, 66, 70
    Airspeed Horsa, 7–8, 14, 38, 57, 59, 70, 100, 127, 132
    Hamilcar, 67, 127–8
    Routes, 70
Gräbner, *Hauptsturmführer* Viktor Eberhard, 114f, 122–3, 125, 151
Grave Bridge, 47
Greenock, 38
Gun Position Officer (GPO), 56, 93, 161, 169, 185–6

Hackett, General Sir John Winthrop GCB, CBE, DSO & Bar, MC, 53, 170
Hall, Bombardier Leo, 38, 57–8, 60, 76–7, 83, 92–4, 98–100, 102, 125–6, 137–8, 147, 154–5, 157–8
Harrison, Captain 'Tony', 6, 19, 32, 57, 60, 76, 88–9, 94–5, 98–102, 120, 125, 131, 155, 161
Hartenstein Hotel, Oosterbeek, 46, 133, 144
Heidrich, *Generalleutnant* Richard, 29
Heveadorp, 79
Hibbert, Major Tony, 80, 98, 100, 135, 150, 164, 165
Hopkinson, Major General George Frederick OBE, MC, 5, 14–15, 25–7

Indian Army units, 29, 30
    8th Indian Infantry Division, 23
    50th Indian Parachute Brigade, 2
Isernia, Italy, 28–9, 34
Italian Fascist government, 13–14, 24
Italy Campaign, 5, 13ff, 16
Italian surrender, 23–5

Kaserne Wilhelm III, 88
Kasserine Pass, 18–19
Kesselring, Albert, 20–1, 24, 30
Krafft, SS *Hauptsturmführer* Sepp, 78–9, 82, 86
Kussin, *Generalmajor* Friedrich, 82–3, 128

Larkhill ranges, 7
Lathbury, General Sir Gerald William GCB, DSO, MBE, 53, 79, 89, 95, 97, 99
Limburg, Stalag XIIA, 11
Lincoln, Commander F. Ashe QC RNVR, *Secret Naval Investigator*, 25–6
'Lonsdale' Force, 144
Lord Haw-Haw, 17, 159
Luftwaffe, 25, 86, 124, 133, 167
LZs, 67, 71, 73, 100, 118, 127–8, 132

Malaria, 18, 35
Malta, 24, 31–2, 42–3
Marriott, Sergeant 'Lofty', 75
McLeod, Lieutenant Colonel R.W. 'Roddy', 6, 19
Model, *Generalfeldmarschall* Walther, 44, 46, 50, 86, 87, 211
Montgomery, Field Marshal Bernard Law, 45–7, 49–50, 52
Moore, Lieutenant Frank 'Pepys', 19, 119, 175
Morrison, Gunner Jock, 57, 94, 137
Morse, 155
Mühlberg, PoW camp, 11
Mules, 7

Munford, Captain Dennis S., 6, 10, 32–3, 35, 68–9, 86, 88–9, 93–4, 100–101, 103, 106, 117–20, 122, 125, 135–8, 146–7, 154–5
Mustard gas, 36

Nattrass, Sergeant George, 62ff
Nazi atrocities, 35
New Zealand forces, 30, 36
   2nd New Zealand Division, 29, 35, 37
   28th (Maori) Battalion, 36
Nijmegen, 47, 48
Northwest Frontier, 5

Ogle, Bombardier Mike, 10, 76–7, 89–90, 94–5, 99, 120, 137, 158
Old Vicarage, The, 88, 120, 170
Oosterbeek, 4, 46, 79, 103, 165
   1st Air Landing Light Regt at, 10–11, 117ff, 125, 134, 144–6, 155, 168–9, 185
Operation AVALANCHE (Salerno), 19–20, 27
Operation BAYTOWN, 20–1
Operation BERLIN (Arnhem evacuation), 187ff
Operation COLOSSUS, 2
Operation COMET (an earlier MARKET GARDEN plan), 48–9
Operation DIADEM (Monte Cassino), 30
Operation DOOMSDAY, 4
Operation FUSTIAN, 22
Operation GARDEN (Eindhoven and Nijmegen), 47
Operation HUSKY (Sicily), 13–14, 27
Operation LADBROKE, 16
Operation LINNET (Normandy), 40–1, 49
Operation MARKET (Arnhem), 10–11, 43ff, 61, 97–8 and *passim*

Operation MARKET GARDEN (Arnhem, Eindhoven and Nijmegen), 46, 48ff, 51, 58, 66, 118, 186
Operation MERCURY (Crete), 46
Operation MINCEMEAT, 13
Operation OVERLORD, 28
Operation SEARAY, 19
Operation SLAPSTICK (Taranto and Brindisi), 10, 14–15, 20–1, 23–4, 27
Operation TORSO, 36
Operation WASTAGE (Normandy contingency), 39
Oran, Algeria, 16
Ortona, Battle of, 29

Paderborn, 142
Panther tanks, 152
Pathfinders, 67, 71
Pescopennataro, Italy, Nazi atrocity, 35
Pigeons at Arnhem, 71–2
1st Polish Parachute Brigade, 47, 54, 127, 133, 139, 144, 167, 184, Appendix VII
Pre-Arnhem cancellations and operations, summer 1944, 39–40, 49
PTSD, 40, 46, 59–60, 63, 65, 85, 145–6, 157, 171, 177, 180–3, 190, 200–10
Putten reprisal, 168

Radar, 2–3
Redford Barracks, Edinburgh, 9
Reggio Calabria, 20, 22
Royal Air Force, 27, 51, 66, 68, 74, 118, 133, 171, 176, 184
   16 Squadron, 45
   RAF Blakehill Farm, 57
   RAF Broadwell, 39
   RAF Down Ampney, 39, 57, 83
   RAF Fairford, 57
   RAF Harwell, 39
   RAF Keevil, 57

RAF Manston, 52, 57
Royal Navy, 22–3
  12th Cruiser Squadron, 22–3, 25

Salerno, 19–21
Sangro River War Cemetery, Italy, 29–30
SHAEF, 45
Sicily, 13–15
SLIDEX, 72
Sosabowski, Major General S., 167
Sousse, Tunisia, 18
Stalag IV-B, Mühlberg, 196
Stalag XI-B, Fallingbostel, 182
Stalag XII-A, Limburg, 11, 124, 194
Student, General Kurt, 1, 44, 7, 867

Taranto, 23–4
Ter Horst, Kate, 88, 120, 139–40, 173–4, 177–8, 182, 212, 214
Theirs is the Glory, Appendix V
Thomas of Celano's *Dies Irae* (*The Day of Wrath*), 34–5, 170
Thompson, Lieutenant Colonel W.F.K. 'Sheriff', 6, 19, 28, 33, 35, 118–19, 129, 168
'Thompson's Force', 141, 144
Thompson, Lieutenant 'Teddy' FOO 3 Battery, F Troop, 31
Tiger and other German tanks, 56, 102, 108, 113, 117, 142, 151–2, 173–4, 177–8, 184
The Tommies are Coming!, 202, 205, 212

Ultra (Bletchley Park), 44–5
Urquhart, Major General Robert Elliot 'Roy' Urquhart, CB, DSO & Bar, 44–6, 61, 96–7, 100, 106–107, 133, 168, 175
US forces, Appendix VII
  1st Allied Airborne Army, 45, 50
  2nd Tactical Air Force, 51, 133
  5th Army, 14, 21

VI Corps, 21
8th Air Force, 51
XIII Corps, 28
21st Army Group, 50
82nd Airborne, 21
82nd Airborne Division, 14, 47, 70, 87, 105, 129, 146
101st Airborne Division, 47, 107, 105
325th Glider Infantry (82nd Airborne), 133
504th Parachute Infantry Regiment, 164
505th Parachute Infantry Regiment, 14–15
USAF, 46, 68
  9th Bombardment Group, 24–5
  17th Bombardment Group, 24
  310 Bombardment Group, 24
Utrechtseweg, 77, 82, 100, 129, 166, 171

V2 rocket sites, 47–9, 91
Van Kuijk, Sergeant, 66, 81, 112, 138, 143
Van Limburg Stirum School, 91–2, 108ff, 123, 147–8
Veghel Bridge, 47
von Rundstedt, Karl Rudolf Gerd, 46

'Waho Mohammed', 84, 124, 138
Widdicombe, John, 31, 33, 35
Wolfheze Hotel, 88
Wolfheze Mental Hospital, bombed, 51, 74, 85
  escapees, 83, 88
Woollacott, Robert, 37, 74, 83, 97, 120
WVS, 61

Yellow fever, 35

Zwickau, satellite PoW labour camp, 11, 196–7